Enigmas of Sacrifice

Studies in Violence, Mimesis, and Culture

SERIES EDITOR

William A. Johnsen

The Studies in Violence, Mimesis, and Culture Series examines issues related to the nexus of violence and religion in the genesis and maintenance of culture. It furthers the agenda of the Colloquium on Violence and Religion, an international association that draws inspiration from René Girard's mimetic hypothesis on the relationship between violence and religion, elaborated in a stunning series of books he has written over the last forty years. Readers interested in this area of research can also look to the association's journal, *Contagion: Journal of Violence, Mimesis, and Culture.*

Enigmas of Sacrifice

A CRITIQUE OF JOSEPH M. PLUNKETT AND THE DUBLIN INSURRECTION OF 1916

W. J. Mc Cormack

Michigan State University Press · *East Lansing*

♾ The paper used in this publication meets the minimum requirements of ANSI/NISO Z39.48-1992 (R 1997) (Permanence of Paper).

Michigan State University Press
East Lansing, Michigan 48823-5245

Printed and bound in the United States of America.

22 21 20 19 18 17 16 1 2 3 4 5 6 7 8 9 10

LIBRARY OF CONGRESS CATALOGING-IN-PUBLICATION DATA
McCormack, W. J., author.
Enigmas of sacrifice : a critique of Joseph M. Plunkett and the Dublin Insurrection of 1916 / W. J. McCormack.
pages cm.—(Studies in violence, mimesis, and culture)
Includes bibliographical references and index.
ISBN 978-1-61186-191-4 (pbk. : alk. paper)—ISBN 978-1-60917-478-1 (pdf)—ISBN 978-1-62895-251-3 (epub)—ISBN 978-1-62896-251-2 (kindle) 1. Ireland—History—Easter Rising, 1916. 2. Plunkett, Joseph Mary, 1887–1916. I. Title.
DA962.M243 2016
941.5082'1—dc23
2015017727

Book design by Charlie Sharp, Sharp Des!gns, Lansing, Michigan
Cover design by David Drummond, Salamander Design, www.salamanderhill.com
Cover artwork is *An Allegory* (Oil on Canvas, 102cm × 130cm, 1924), © Estate of Seán Keating (1889–1977), IVARO/ Artists Rights Society (ARS), New York / 2015. Used with permission. All rights reserved. Photo © National Gallery of Ireland (NGI.1236).

green press INITIATIVE Michigan State University Press is a member of the Green Press Initiative and is committed to developing and encouraging ecologically responsible publishing practices. For more information about the Green Press Initiative and the use of recycled paper in book publishing, please visit *www.greenpressinitiative.org*.

Visit Michigan State University Press at *www.msupress.org*

Remembering Padraic Colum

The reason why any dirty trick is permissible in politics, where the crucial test is clever or stupid, not good or bad, seems to be as follows: The public body does not die and so does not have to answer for itself before any God.

—Cesare Pavese, *Diaries*

"Mental illness" and rebellion, like the sacrificial crisis they resemble, commit the individual to falsehoods and to forms of violence that are certainly more damaging *to him* than the disguised violence channeled through sacrificial rites but that bring him closer to the heart of the enigma.

—René Girard, *Violence and the Sacred*

Contents

Acknowledgments

Many individuals contributed to the making of this book, none to be held responsible for its shortcomings. Charles Benson (The Library, Trinity College, Dublin); Ciaran Brady, Liam Breatnach; Tom Desmond (National Library of Ireland); Eoin Dillon, Denis Donoghue, Jeff Dudgeon, Tony Farmar, Brian Farrell, Garret Fitzgerald, Tom Garvin, Patrick Gillan, Patrick Healy, Aidan Heavey, Barbara Hussey, Bill Johnsen, John Horne, Justin Keating, Carla King, David Knight (Stonyhurst College); Michael Laffan, Commandant Victor Laing (Military Archives, Dublin); Muiris Mac Conghaill, James McGuill, Robert Mills (Royal College of Physicians in Ireland); Beatrice Moloney, Oliver Murphy (Belvedere College); Michael Neal (Paris), Gearóid O Brien (Longford-Westmeath County Library), Paul O'Brien, Cormac O Cuilleanáin, Eamon O'Flaherty, Felicity O'Mahoney (Manuscripts, Trinity College, Dublin), Jean-Paul Pittion, Seoirse Plunkett, Zuleika Rodgers, Robert Schmuhl, Richard Synge, Veronica Watts, Harriet Wheelock (Royal College of Physicians, Ireland), Larry White (*Dictionary of Irish Biography*), Christopher Woods.

Above all others, Honor O Brolchain has made this book possible by the generosity of mind with which she has given me access to Plunkett papers in her possession. While recognizing how different our assessments of her kinsman are, she opened her files and her personal memory with equal courtesy, allowing me to copy material, to question her, and to draw on accumulated traditions of interpretation and family commemoration. To her is owed a greater debt than professional acknowledgment can accomplish.

Unpublished material by Joseph Plunkett is quoted with the kind permission of the National Library of Ireland and Ms. Honor O Brolchain, as appropriate.

Abbreviations

BL	British Library
BMH	Bureau of Military History (Dublin)
ICA	Irish Citizen Army
IRA	Irish Republican Army
IRB	Irish Republican Brotherhood
NAA	National Army Archives (Cathal Brugha Barracks, Dublin)
NLI	National Library of Ireland
TCD	Trinity College Dublin
UCD	University College Dublin

A LONG PROLOGUE

Crisis and Criticism

A rat or small animal, eats of the consecrated wafer.
1) Does he ingest the Real Body, or does it not?
2) If he does not, what has become of it?
3) If he does, what is to be done with him?

—Samuel Beckett, *Watt*

Multiplex

It is unlikely that the Victorian crisis of belief, loosely associated with the impact of scientific and philosophical discoveries (e.g., those of Charles Darwin, Charles Lyell, and John Tyndall), has been seriously proposed as a relevant context-background for reconsiderations of the insurrection that broke out in Dublin on Easter Monday 1916. Less unlikely, yet still remote, would be an examination of the impact of more specifically Christian-focused and critical works, most notably David Strauss's *Das Leben Jesu* (1835–1836) or Ernest Renan's *Vie de Jésus* (1863). None of these momentous developments occurred in Ireland, though the physicist Tyndall (1820–1893) was born in Carlow and delivered his most renowned public address in Belfast. W. B.

Yeats (1865–1939), whose "Easter 1916" contributed much to the insurrectionists' memorializing, claimed in *The Trembling of the Veil*, book 1, "Four Years 1887–1891" (1921) to have lost his faith under the influence of Tyndall and T. H. Huxley, and consequently hated them.[1] Writing of the 1880s and 1890s, recalling the midcentury assaults on fundamental Christian beliefs, the poet invoked a biblical passage, which was already used by Mallarmé in connection with radical changes in style. At the close of Jesus's time on the cross, "the veil of the temple was rent in twain from the top to the bottom . . . and the graves were opened; and many bodies of the saints which slept arose, and came out of the graves after his resurrection" (Matthew 27:51–53). Later in *The Trembling*, Yeats recounts incidents of 1898, condemning John Dillon (1851–1927) by way of biblical allusion (1 Kings 16:8–20) and recalling James Connolly (1868–1916) as a young man, dejected by his failure to recruit Maud Gonne (1866–1953) as a public speaker—he who "is to make the Insurrection of 1916 and to be executed."[2]

Certain ambiguities are buried here. "Is to make" looks like a present-tense phrase, but implies a future action ("shall make," "will make," or some such). Within this implied future there exists an implication of nonhuman agency, for "is to make" can also be expanded to read "is fated to make" or, more cheerfully, "is destined to make." By such localized verbal details, Yeats evolves a notion of time in which past and future are present in time present. By allusion, retrospective (to Mallarmé) and prophetic (to 1916) vis-à-vis the 1890s, he implicitly reconstructs the beliefs that Tyndall and Huxley had taken from him, though in drastically altered form. The Insurrection is a group resurrection, albeit of the odd kind noted by Matthew, alone among the New Testament writers.

If the events of Easter Week 1916, as conventionally and perpetually commemorated, approximate to a profane representation of Christ's sacrifice, they are further distinguished by their emergence from a society that had not intensely experienced the Victorian crisis of belief—that is to say, Irish society. Of course, it would be possible to argue that those events emerged from British society as a whole—or, more accurately—from the social multiplex formally known as the United Kingdom of Great Britain and Ireland. Within the Victorian United Kingdom, religious argument took place on several avenues, some of which never interconnected. For example, in Ulster political unionism energized itself around the notion of "the whole Protestant community," blithely ignoring fundamental differences of theology, liturgy, church government, and private practice Anglicans and dissenters, the latter a rich motley of traditions. Elsewhere in Ireland, Catholicism built upon a "revolution" in devotional activities, the influence of foreign (mainly French) teaching and nursing orders, and the political emancipation of 1829, which brought members of the Roman church into Parliament and, ten or so years later, into borough corporative life.

Max Weber, Briefly

Generally speaking, we regard the Tractarian, or Oxford, Movement of the 1830s and 1840s as a distinctly English phenomenon. Verdicts on it vary sharply. An American theologian in 1961 thought it the equivalent of Joseph de Maistre's French traditionalism. John Morley, twice chief secretary for Ireland and biographer of W. E. Gladstone (1809–1898), felt its workings were "inward, in the sphere of the mind . . . in idealised associations of historical grandeur."[3] Yet it was the Irish Church Temporalities Act (1833) that, by trimming the numbers of prelates and slimming the established Church of Ireland's worldly substance, provoked John Keble (1792–1866) to deliver an Oxford sermon on National Apostasy. What was at stake was the unity of church and state through establishment; the Church of Ireland would indeed be disestablished in 1871. There does not appear to have been a Dublin edition of Keble's best-known best seller, *The Christian Year* (1827 and many subsequent editions), though this omission reflects the preoccupations of Ireland with the muscular side of ecclesiastical affairs, the campaign for and vigorous opposition to Catholic Emancipation (1829). Similarly, when the Tractarians in the mid-1840s displayed a growing affinity with Rome, Ireland was entering its grimmest years of the century. When John Henry Newman (1801–1890) entered the Catholic Church in 1845, the country was on the brink of starvation. Newman, a quintessential Englishman (if quintessentialism is tolerated these days), reached Dublin in 1854 as head of the newly founded Catholic University of Ireland. Out of this experience he wrote *The Idea of a University*, in which a via media between unhindered research and moral (that is, theological) authority was approved. Newman's institution evolved indirectly into University College Dublin, where Patrick

Pearse (1879–1916), Thomas MacDonagh (1878–1916), and numerous lesser figures of Easter 1916 were educated.

It is neither assumed nor proposed here that religion is a causal force in the making of Easter 1916. These remarks are intended to do no more than sketch one background to the high rhetoric employed to commend and vindicate the insurrection, the language of religiously approved sacrifice. They are necessarily selective, reductive, and designed to set a scene rather than inaugurate a five-act drama. They pay no attention to important gender (or sexual) issues, for example in the notion that clerical celibacy involves sacrificing a human function elsewhere tolerably commended by the churches. Yet they address a question almost posed in a topical book by Ivan Strenski—*Why Politics Can't Be Freed from Religion* (2010).

Though discussion of the Anglican tradition could focus initially on the Cambridge Platonist Ralph Cudworth (1617–1688) and his *Discourse Concerning the True Nature of the Lord's Supper* (1642) or Simon Patrick's much reissued *Christian Sacrifice* (1671), the early starting point would be in danger of concealing the impact of censorship by state and church. It can economically commence with the Tractarians' concern with the significance of Holy Communion (or the Eucharist) in the life of the church. By the 1820s, freedom to publish dissenting and nonestablishment doctrinal views was relatively unchallenged. Protestant bodies tended to regard the sacrament as commemorative or memorial—some indeed scarcely treated it as a sacrament at all. (An exception in Ireland was Alexander Knox [1757–1831], whose *Inquiry, on the Grounds of Scripture and Reason, into the Use and Import of the Eucharistic Symbols* [1824] commended a High Church interpretation for the Church of Ireland. Knox's *Grace of Sacraments* was republished in 1905.) Rome's doctrine of the Real Presence had convinced a number of the Tractarians, and a lively pamphlet war of well over one hundred items raged for decades. By the turn of the century, the notion of sacrifice had attracted the attention of two contrasting professions—anthropologists, of whom J. G. Frazer (1854–1941) is the best known, and France's new nationalists, for whom literature was a strategic field of encounter. In both cases, a central Christian doctrine was translated into profane terms, either through broad comparative studies that denied the uniqueness of sacrament, or through a process of secularization that paradoxically elevates a commitment to race, class, or nation to quasi-religious levels. It is no mere coincidence that, in

1904–1905, Max Weber (1854–1920) explored a similar paradox of transferred valuations in *The Protestant Ethic and the Spirit of Capitalism.*

Weber's central thesis was that the breakup of the medieval monastic system facilitated the growth of capitalism. While this might be read simplistically as the replacement of a religiously-driven system by a secular and worldly one, he shows that Calvinist "incorporation into the body of Christ" replaced monastic communality but did so by requiring a commitment to success in the world as evidence of God's grace to the elect. This worldly commitment on their part acquires and demands the status of a vocation, religious in its absolutes though empty of manifest religious content. Fredric Jameson, in a lucid if inelegant formulation, states the matter as follows: "the rationalization of ends is to the religiousization of means as the rationalization of means is to the 'non-finalization' of religion." Or, in Weber's terms, all "the active energies of the elect, liberated by the doctrine of predestination, thus flowed into the struggle to rationalize the world." In the revealing idiom of paradox, John Calvin (1509–1564) turned the entire world into a business monastery.[4]

Enigmas and its author have more limited ambitions. Fascinated by the challenge to write the biography of a man who died violently at the age of twenty-nine in the service of a highly-secretive organization, he finds that the conventional need to "contextualize" the individual life went far beyond domestic boundaries and the stated political opinions of the young man and his associates. Joseph Mary Plunkett (1887–1916) passed his adult years in a strange pattern of wandering and fixity, traveling in Algeria, Egypt, England, France, Germany, Italy, Spain, Switzerland, and the United States, yet increasingly bound to a conspiracy designed to establish a republic in his native Ireland. His commitment came relatively late in his life and was cut short by the firing squad. Its character may have been best caught by Thomas MacDonagh when he remarked that, until he joined the Irish Volunteers in the autumn of 1913, he had no purpose in life and, thereafter, his purpose was to find a purpose.[5]

Jameson, in a profound essay, began by addressing Weber's recommendation of *Wertfreiheit* (or value-free-ness) in research and intellectual debate. This concept, Jameson argued, was a passionate value judgment called forth in the hectic climate of Wilhelmine Germany, especially to confront the racism and militant imperialism of Heinrich Gotthard von Treitschke

(1834–1896) and his ideological children whether in uniform, academic gown, or civvies. When two London publishers issued translations of substantial works by von Treitschke in 1915, they may have done so with a whiff of wartime British fair play, but the underlying motive was to display the true nature of the Hun's *Kultur* rather than any shared *Wertfreiheit*.[6] Reviewing one of these, a Dublin-based Jesuit monthly observed, "with Treitschke . . . Political Philosophy is not, as with us, a dispassionate search into the kind of constitution which will suit each country's needs and circumstances."[7] J. H. Newman might not have been so positive on dispassionate searching without church guidance.

In miniscule, a not dissimilar ideology is inscribed throughout Irish public debate on select historical topics, finding louder echoes in ill-informed commentary abroad. The aggressively anti-British strain is relatively muted, yet manifests itself discreetly but insistently in the treatment of 1916 on television and in the marshaling of handbook biographies for the centenary in 2016. Professional historians take second place to what in Britain and Ireland are sometimes called "anoraks," dedicated folk with a strong, perhaps obsessive, interest in "niche" subjects. Comparative analysis is avoided; close examination of accidents, the merits of opponents, awkward parallel developments, contradictions, and personal faults rarely occurs. Revisionism, the anorak turned inside out, is scorned as sleeping with the enemy or—worse—dreaming with him/her. The results come onstream in happy endorsement of the fundamental proposition—Ireland's innate and eternal right to national independence, immaculately if belatedly achieved.

The World and Its Parts

Taking courage, also fright, from Jameson on Weber and from Lucian Goldmann's treatment of Pascal in *Le Dieu caché* (1959), I embark trepidatiously to write a short life of Joseph Mary Plunkett inside a series of dispersed studies in contextualization. The first of these, already sketched, deals with the concept of sacrifice liberally applied by leading figures in the insurrectionary cabal during the months before April 1916. Others closely examine Plunkett's unpublished and published writings on poetry and philosophy, and offer comparative accounts of several Irish contemporaries. Finally, the writings of René Girard and Onora O'Neill are applied lightly, in the hope that some coherence might be elicited from the meager evidence of Plunkett's recorded thought and action.

A feature of Blaise Pascal's *Pensées*, which Goldmann (1913–1970) explored to unexpected advantage, was its fragmentary character, further complicated by noncongruent decisions made by various editors. Plunkett was no Pascal (1623–1662), nor do I claim any comparability with the author of *Le Dieu caché*. Goldmann's opening chapter, dealing with the relationship between "the whole and the parts," offers suggestive models for undertakings of the present kind, despite obvious differences of scale and implication. What he sought was an understanding of a "world vision," in the case of both Pascal and Racine (1639–1699), a "tragic vision." Within Irish nationalism, the former might seem unlikely, though both Yeats and J. M. Synge (1871–1909) attempted modern tragedy in the uncongenial circumstances of Edwardian Ireland within the Edwardian United Kingdom. Of the two dramatists, Synge (unquestionably further from nationalism than Yeats) made some effort to acknowledge religious conflict, through satiric buffoonery in *The Tinkers' Wedding* (completed 1907). His defensive annotation declared that "in all Roman Catholic countries the cleric has been made fun of with good humour from the early ages down and there is no reason why the same thing should not be done in Ireland where the clerics with all their fine qualities are humorous and genial also beyond any that I have met in Europe."[8] Other authorial notes on drafts of the play reveal that he had Henrik Ibsen (1828–1906) and even Arthur Pinero (1855–1934) in mind as he wrote, though the Englishman's name is crossed out and replaced with "the Germans and their power." These vestigial references to fellow dramatists constitute Synge's only acknowledgment that Ireland in November 1907 is a part of literary Europe, as are Norway, England, and Germany. What is more obviously central to *The Tinkers' Wedding* is the social institution of marriage sought by a couple who to all intents and purposes live outside Irish society. Though Synge had worked on the script four years earlier, its revision and completion in the autumn of 1907 deserves close attention. In August of that year, the Vatican had issued a decree, *Ne Temere*, requiring the non-Catholic partner in a mixed marriage to ensure the children were raised and education as Catholics. Here again, the issues are best understood within a Pascalian dialectic of the whole and the parts. Are tinkers (itinerants, knackers, members of the traveling community) part of an entirety that can be named properly as Irish society? Are nonpracticing Catholics non-Catholics? It is not irrelevant to add that Rome found it advisable to modify its ruling by another decree, *Provida*, relating to Germany alone. Were Ireland and Germany similar or dissimilar parts of Catholic Europe?

The concrete reality of sectarian conflict in western Christendom was plainly obvious in the Ireland of Synge and Plunkett's day. I have argued elsewhere that early drafts of *The Playboy of the Western World* (also 1907) allowed for some admission of this explosive theme, with evidence traceable even in the final version. Marriage is a theme raised in the opening lines, as Pegeen Mike goes through a list of requirements for her wedding. If, as I suggest, Christy Mahon at one stage of composition was tentatively developed as a Protestant or a refugee from the bitter sectarian clashes of Ulster, to what extent had that ur-script anticipated the problems addressed in and exacerbated by *Ne Temere*?[9] In what complex sense are Christy and his father not parts of the rural society depicted in the play. And why is the (necessarily celibate) priest wholly absent? Marriage, a sacrament in Catholicism but not in the reformed churches, caused difficulties for both the Synge and Plunkett families. But we might achieve more by concentrating on a different point of difference.

Breaking the Sacrament

The Roman, the Eastern, the Anglican, and the reformed churches share two sacraments, the first being baptism. Generally speaking, little serious conflict has arisen on this topic. The churches recognize each other's baptized persons and, in the event of conversion to a different church, no rebaptism is required. However the second of these shared sacraments has given rise to a high degree of disputation. Various names are used—Eucharist, Holy Communion, the Lord's Supper, the Mass. From the sixteenth-century Reformation onward, theological distinctions between the Real Presence through transubstantiation and various reformed/Protestant formulas (e.g., consubstantiation) raged. In nineteenth-century Britain, some Anglicans sought a revivified apprehension of that sacrament's place in parochial worship and national life. For the Tractarians, the Roman theological position was both attractive and defensible, especially when compared to the status of commemorative or memorial act to which nonevangelical nonconformists had relegated the taking of bread and wine, which remained bread and wine. Debates on these points flourished in a long pamphlet war, beginning no later than the ninety tracts issued from 1833 by what became known as the Oxford Movement. Three of these (nos. 26–28) dealt with Anglican Holy Communion and "popish transubstantiation," using material taken from authors of the distant past. For economy within my long prologue, the contentious issue of this sacrament alone will be taken as representative of a much wider controversy involving rival versions of Christianity and, separately, the rivalry between Christian belief and acceptance of modern science, and that between belief and agnosticism. In the Eucharist, dogmatic "objective supernaturalism" was made perfectly plain.[10]

The Victorian era was the high point of pamphlet controversy, on topics ranging from agriculture to zoology, moral exhortation and popular science. It would be futile to estimate the number of items devoted to the efficacy, liturgy, and theology of the Eucharistic sacrament, the varieties of its presentation or interpretation. But one bald statistic does readily emerge; these discussions only rarely involved Irish contributors. While the contents will certainly be of interest, the proportions of difference deserve attention too, and the concentrations of Irish engagement at specific dates.

On All Saints' Day 1845, Edward A. Stopford (1810–1874) preached a sermon titled "The Bread of Life" at Kingscourt, county Cavan. His audience consisted mainly of "Irish Teachers," that is, members of the Irish Society for the Education of the Native Irish through the Medium of their Own Language (1818), active on the bilingual frontier between Ulster and north Leinster. Contesting the Catholic view of Holy Communion, Stopford climaxed by declaring his own church's interpretation a scriptural doctrine "witnessed in the flames by the martyrs of Christ" for which "it becomes us to be zealous, even unto death."[11] This was no time or place to raise the ghost of religious martyrdom: reports of potato blight had begun to appear in September, and the omens were under anxious public scrutiny. Kingscourt had been a center for Protestant missionizing from the 1820s onward, with schooling through Gaelic a favored means of propaganda.[12] A moderate evangelical, and an opponent of the Oxford (or Anglo-Catholic) Movement, he foresaw church disestablishment as inevitable and strove to devise ways of adapting to the change. Alone among Church of Ireland clergy, he met with Gladstone in advance of the 1868 disestablishment act to discuss its implications; he is also said to have devised an Irish affairs reading list for the new prime minister. His daughter, Alice Stopford Green (1847–1929), became a distinguished historian and a supporter of the Irish Volunteers.

Stopford returned to the theme in 1866 and 1870. On the former occasion, he replied to A. A. Dawson's "The Christian Sacrifice," an "admirable sermon" in the opinion of a reviewer in *The Ecclesiastic*, who also noted that Dawson had withdrawn it as a peace offering, under pressure from his archbishop, Richard Chenevix Trench (1807–1886), who in turn was reacting to vigorous condemnation by the plain Protestants of Dublin. Dawson came from a landed Ulster family, the Dawsons of Castledawson, county Londonderry: his grandfather had been an MP. Bishop Trench is now best remembered as a philologist, whose advocacy resulted in the *New English Dictionary*, later the *Oxford English Dictionary* (OED). Though the incident reveals both discretion and aggression within the Church of Ireland, when dealing with the Real Presence issue and the associated idea (or ideology) of sacrifice, it also involved substantial minds capable of assessing the risks, theological and social. "The Church is now disturbed about such words," Stopford wrote, and proceeded to quote (without identifying) Dawson's pamphlet.[13] Dawson, incumbent of the new High Church Saint Bartholemew's, Dublin, went on to publish *Sacrifice, Patriarchal, Jewish, Christian* (1873).

These bouts of *odium theologicum* were interrupted by the Fenian outrages of the mid-1860s, in Ireland, Britain, and Canada. Militarily of little significance, they illustrated what might lie behind the "Proclamation the Irish People of the World" issued by the movement. In addition to proclaiming a republic, its authors ("the provisional government") declared that it would be "based on universal suffrage" and would "secure to all the intrinsic value of their labour." Absolute liberty of conscience was assured, together with a complete separation of church and state. There was, however, no specific promise of elections, elective assemblies, or any form of representation.[14]

The Irish twins, nationalism and religious prejudice, did have an impact within a few years. By the time Stopford published *The Keystone of the Sacerdotal System* (1870), Gladstone's Irish Church Act had passed into law, though not yet fully implemented, and resisted almost unanimously by the church in question. In substance, it is largely a compendium of extracts from the writings of others, beginning with the Tractarian E. B. Pusey (1800–1882), but developing a long string of quotations to refute Anglo-Catholicism. These authorities were for the most part English, but included John Bramhall (1594–1663), who became archbishop of Armagh, and Charles Leslie (1650–1722), a nonjuror—that is, a member of the established church who refused to acknowledge William III as its head—whom Stopford describes as a "Catholic Protestant." As in *The Altar which We Have* (1866), he is responding to another publication that he identifies simply as *Short Prayers*—that is, *Short Prayers etc. for Those Who Have but Little Time to Pray* (1867), published in London and printed in Derby. This then pervasive now elusive compendium stirred up colossal agitation in Dublin, including (1) *The Protest of the Three United Dioceses, Comprising the Archdiocese of Dublin, against the Manual Short Prayers . . . with a List of the Names of Those Who Have Signed it*; (2) *Protestantism v Ritualism; the Maberly Correspondence Containing Protests with Signatures of Eighty-two Clergymen*; and (3) Stopford's pamphlet, already mentioned.

Unlike the pamphlet exchanges in which Stopford had been previously involved, the affair of 1870 had a traceable popular outlet, through newspapers, especially the *Irish Times*. In the wake of the disestablishing act, many ordinary members of the church felt disorientated or insecure, anxious about the manner in which the act would be implemented (in 1871). Parish meetings were organized to discuss *Short Prayers*, the efficient distribution of which remains something of a mystery. Archbishop Trench was seen as weak in defense of true Protestant principles, indulgent of ritualism, and out of touch with the congregations. In resolutions passed throughout the archdiocese of Dublin, Glendalough, and Kildare, little if any reference was made to the Real Presence, or to the wider theme of sacrifice in the Old and New Testaments, and in church liturgy, which underpinned it. Ritualism was the bogeyman, a vague enough notion but useful in bringing the malcontents together. Several parishes went out of their way to record sympathy with their "dissenting brethren"; these included Saint John's in Sandymount, where the Yeats family dwelt and sometimes worshipped. Outside the city of Dublin, county Wicklow accounted for a significant number of protests and resolutions. Beyond the archdiocese, the bishop of Cork was vocal, for the county was home to a substantial non-Catholic population. And beyond that, protests were also recorded for parishes in what we would today call the border counties, notably Monaghan (Clones and Enniskeen).

In *The Keystone*, Stopford tried to defend the archbishop against his Low Church critics. As to the challenge posed by *Short Prayers*, he particularly warned against its insinuations and things that it "does not distinctly say." As to the occasion, "the Church of England has suffered deeply, and is now in great peril from such teachings. The Church of Ireland cannot be too careful to guard against it."[15] He then proceeds to cite the martyrs of old and to quote from Anglicanism's great seventeenth-century thinkers. Trench was not the only Dublin cleric to come under pressure. The Reverend William Maturin (1806–1887), perpetual curate in the north-city parish of Grangegorman, leaned toward Puseyism, and had decorated his church in a style associated with ritualism. A parish meeting in May 1870 heard a Captain Brinkley loudly say, "I protest," and matters became disorderly. At a further meeting, reference was made to bands of young men who had disrupted morning services conducted by Maturin; such behavior was reprobated, but the right to conduct services was pointedly linked to their according with "the principles of the Prayer Book and the Reformation."[16]

On the same day that the *Irish Times* carried this account of the Grangegorman meetings, it published a similar account of matters in the fashionable center-city parish of Saint Anne, Dawson Street. A very large and respectable audience turned up for a discussion of Portal's *Short Prayers*, but the vicar was not among them. This led to unkind remarks, which included an accusation that the archbishop was a Puseyite; "otherwise he would not go to Grangegorman church." As for the absent vicar, he was "a second Maturin." There was much hissing. Later in the year when Maturin lectured on what a High Churchman was, a member of the public interrupted to answer on behalf of Protestant workingmen. Maturin specifically defended the sacrament of Holy Communion, but avoided any detailed discussion of High Church views on the topic.[17]

A contemporary pamphleteer noted that "the newspapers teem with leaders and letters, rarely conciliatory, usually vying with each other in virulence . . . many have avowed their determination to withhold all aid from their Church in this her hour of direst need."[18] Irish affairs, however, were about to take on a different coloration through the Home Rule movement, established in September 1870 and fated to acquire a central place in

Anglo-Irish relations through the leadership of C. S. Parnell (1846–1891). Excitements within the now disestablished church died down as new administrative structures were quickly put in place. In 1879, the Land League was founded by Michael Davitt (1846–1906), and, with it, the focus of political action shifted decisively toward the conditions in which tenants lived, worked, and held their homesteads. The language of sacrifice had little to contribute, least of all the language used by rival parties inside the Church of Ireland. The Catholic Church, gaining in influence and authority, knew no internal differences of opinion on the Real Presence, especially in Ireland. Much of its public energy was committed to negotiations over the control of education. Protestant agitators occasionally inveighed against the doctrine as held by their Catholic neighbors, but the consequences were now minimal. Some Catholic priests involved themselves in Land League activities, partly at least as a pastoral duty to those in need. A now familiar political narrative unfolds—Home Rule as a parliamentary goal, the New Departure bringing physical force nationalism into cooperation with the politicians, Gladstone's conversion to Home Rule, and Ulster Unionism's popular resistance to it—and so on until the fall of Parnell in 1890 brings the giddy tale to a conclusion later to be classified as tragic.

Parnell's entanglement in divorce proceedings, his party's divided responses, Catholic opinion in Ireland and nonconformist opinion in Britain, the bitterness of elections, and the sudden "death of the hero" all contributed to the perception of a crisis. Nothing remotely comparable had occurred in Ireland since 1843, when Daniel O'Connell (1775–1847), the Liberator, canceled a mass meeting of his followers at Clontarf. And the comparison is very imperfect. By the late 1880s, the interplay of external and internal forces, the political and the intimately personal, had become a force field in itself, probed by newspapers and a new journalism and then reconstructed by them. The case of the radical Charles Dilke, in 1886, illustrated the explosive results when political interests, exotic sex, and Victorian moralism came together. Other scandals were financial at heart but, as Oscar Wilde (1854–1900) indicated in *An Ideal Husband* (1895), personality was not immune to manipulation on the international markets. On a broader canvas, Freud was already at work. In France, combinations of military, clerical, and literary ultranationalists sought to undermine the Third Republic: the most celebrated or notorious episode of the era was the Dreyfus Affair, commencing in 1894 and running into the new century. For years, crisis was the norm, and August 1914 was its apogee.

I have written at length on the ideology of this French new nationalism and its affinities (to say the very least) to the mind-set of the 1916 insurrectionists, especially the shared rhetoric of violent sacrifice, veneration of the dead, and "religionized" politics (to echo Jameson on Weber).[19] Other enquiries into the influences and affinities going to make the far-from-native-purebred nationalism of Patrick Pearse and Joseph Mary Plunkett are urgently needed, both to activate comparative attention to the topic and to challenge the monolinear "tradition" of native insurrection running from Wolfe Tone to the latest republican dissident. *Enigmas* is only a step in that direction, for it is also centrally concerned with a related problem: the deconstruction of a hagiographical tradition of nationalist biography.

Social Salvation

Plunkett will turn out to be an exceptional figure among the insurrectionist leaders, at once voluble and secretive, energetic and frail, public-school educated yet unfocused in his intellectual interests. He also had money, or access to his family's immense resources. He was not an extensively published writer, though after his death his poetry was gathered in a collective volume. This latter factor makes a study of his rhetoric (in the proper sense) difficult. For contrast, we could look at one or two articles by Patrick Pearse, while still attending to the question of religionized politics. "The Coming Revolution," written in November 1915, declares its concern with "men and movements that have sprung from the Gaelic League or have received from the Gaelic League a new baptism and a new life of grace." The sacramental idiom cannot be denied and, indeed, transcends itself almost beyond restraint.

> [The League] was no reed shaken by the wind, no mere vox clamantis: it was a prophet and more than a prophet. But it was not the Messiah. I do not know if the Messiah has yet come, and I am not sure that there will be any visible and personal Messiah in this redemption: the people itself will perhaps be its own Messiah, the people labouring, scourged, crowned with thorns, agonising and dying, to rise again immortal and impassible [*sic*].

Yeats occasionally deployed imagery of this kind—for example, in "The Crucifixion of the Outcast" in *The Secret Rose* (1897) but thoroughly without any populist implication. A late trial-poem under the title "A Crowded Cross" (1934) sardonically considered that prospect, but turned in other directions during completion. James Connolly, in many ways the antithesis of Pearse, occasionally used language of a not dissimilar kind, more sparingly. While still in Edinburgh, he met refugees from the Paris Commune. One of these, Leo Meillet, addressed an 1889 commemoration of the 1871 events, declaring that "without the shedding of blood there is no social salvation."[20] More than a quarter of a century later, Connolly declared in the *Workers Republic* (5 February 1916):

> Without the slightest trace of irreverence but in all due humility and awe we recognise that of us as of mankind before Calvary it may truly be said: *Without the Shedding of Blood there is no Redemption.*

A careful writer, Connolly goes to some trouble to indicate a biblical source (Paul's Epistle to the Hebrews, 9:22) for his quotation. He does not worry that the first thirteen verses of the chapter's twenty-eight attend to the role of sacrifices in Old Testament times, which Christians claim has been absolutely transcended on Calvary. Verses 19–23 constitute a summary of how things had been under the Mosaic Law when "almost all things are by the law purged with blood; and without shedding of blood is no remission." Pearse would cast the Gaelic League in language taken, consciously or otherwise, from Jesus's characterization of John the Baptist (Matthew 11:9)—and then lose the run of himself. Connolly, opting for "redemption" where Leo Meillet had "social salvation," commits the lesser offense against accuracy and responsible interpretation.

One further instance of Connolly's use of a religious vocabulary is peculiarly relevant. Writing in mid-1913 about repressive and divisive eighteenth-century Irish conditions, he instanced the Presbyterians who paid "tithes for the upkeep of the Episcopalian ministers, were fined for not going to the Episcopalian Church, and had to pay Church cess for buying sacramental bread, ringing the bell, and washing the surplices of the Episcopalian clergymen."[21] Strictly speaking, we cannot charge him with any *use* of religious language, related to the Eucharist or not, simply with writing historically about discriminatory taxation on religious grounds. It is different matter seven months later where he concludes an account of the Lockout:

> And so we Irish workers must go down into Hell, bow our backs to the lash of the slave driver, let our hearts be seared by the iron of his hatred, and instead of the sacramental wafer of brotherhood and common sacrifice, eat the dust of defeat and betrayal.[22]

Here, direct reference to historic conditions has been replaced by mobilization of the sacramental bread/wafer as an emotive metaphor to valorize the communion of workingmen in their shared labor and the sacrifices involved in labor militancy. Connolly's application of Hebrews 9:22 follows two months later, after his compact with the Irish Republican Brotherhood (IRB) and within its seven-man cabal within the Volunteers. In an opinion attributed to Eoin MacNeill, Connolly "was a bit of a mystic, and believed that an insurrection would electrify the people. He believed in insurrection for the sake of insurrection."[23]

In the terms of I. A. Richards's *Philosophy of Rhetoric* (1936), the structure of a metaphor consists of two parts: the "tenor" relates to the concept, object, or person meant, the "vehicle" being the image that carries the weight of the comparison. In Connolly's first use of "sacramental" no metaphoric dimension exists: it is a historic datum. In the second, the word/phrase is applied metaphorically to suggest a high degree of ironic comparability between the sacramental wafer and the diet of exhausted and humiliated workers. The wafer signifies brotherhood and sacrifice but now in circumstances of utter defeat, itself perhaps comparable to consignment to hell.

The uses of Hebrews 9:22 in 1889 (with Connolly in the audience) and in 1916 (with Connolly the author) vary more radically. Meillet had modified his biblical source to employ "salvation" rather than "remission," but, more significantly, the noun was qualified (in the grammarian's sense) by the adjective "social." There was no ambiguity about the concept or object meant. Connolly's variation on the text does far more. A part, but only a part, relates to his substitution of "redemption" for remission (used in both the Douay and the King James translations). Remission relates to sins, in keeping with the Old Testament covenant under discussion. Redemption, of course, goes much further, and is habitually associated with the Christian era. Beyond this, however, his whole sentence demands analysis phrase by phrase:

1. "Without the slightest trace of irreverence but in all due humility and awe"—these three nouns work successively to minimize any distinction between the human voice and his audience or readers (*we* and *us*), on the one hand and the subject of the phrase to follow.
2. "we recognize that of us as of mankind before Calvary it may truly be said": the collective indicated in the preceding phrase is rendered highly comparable to "mankind" or least "mankind before Calvary." An ambiguity in "before" needs clarification; what is intended is, I think, clearly "in front of" or "confronted by" (not "at an earlier time").
3. "*Without the Shedding of Blood there is no Redemption.*" This is a grammatically independent statement, prefaced by the impersonal phrase "it may be said." By implication it may be said by "us" or "mankind." Pearse's spectral messiah in "The Coming Revolution"—"the people itself will perhaps be its own Messiah, the people labouring, scourged, crowned with thorns"—may fit the ideological requirements.

An Age of Looming Crisis

Having taken some measure of the extent to which Pearse's thought, and to a lesser degree Connolly's, was suffused with religious imagery, we might return to the issue that characterized the pamphlet skirmishes of Archdeacon Stopford in 1845, 1866, and 1870. Whether in response to Tractarianism or to disestablishment, the arguments then advanced touch on the Roman Catholic doctrine of the Real Presence. On the Catholic side, it was held that the Real Presence had been accepted by some church fathers, yet its importance as a point of contention can hardly be dated to any earlier than the Council of Trent (1545–1563). Both Tractarianism and Irish disestablishment act as occasions of contention, with a consequent renewed focus on the doctrine.

There were other unrelated intellectual developments contributing to the nineteenth-century renewal of interest. The religious side of existentialism, beginning with Søren Kierkegaard (1813–1855), emphasized commitment to the ever-present existence of the divine, beyond creeds or formulas. In *Fear and Trembling* (1843) he scrutinized the biblical account of Abraham and Isaac, the moment at which God intervenes in the rites of human sacrifice to provide a substitute or a sublimating alternative.[24] Ernest Renan (1823–1882) moved in quite different directions; recounting the life of Jesus as if no question of divinity were involved; presenting a sympathetic race-picture of the Celts; and advancing a definition of nationhood suitable for the times and the times to come. Gladstone's copy of *Vie de Jésus* is richly annotated with scathing comment by a lay theologian influenced by the Oxford Movement in his early manhood. Later, in 1874, he published *The Vatican Decrees in their Bearing on Civil Allegiance*, an equally scathing response to what he deemed Roman interference in sovereign states. Toward the end of century the novelist Leo Tolstoy (1828–1910) wrote essays in support of an anarchist Christianity, scorning all churches and organizations, and commending simplicity in life. His personal allegiance to an ethical faith may scarcely touch on rival interpretations of the Mass or Holy Communion, yet demonstrates the extent to which the institutional churches had become remote from ordinary life. The absolute supernaturalism of Real Presence doctrine at once consolidated and isolated Roman Christianity at a time of accelerated scientific, cultural, and philosophical advance. And, meanwhile, the scandals and seismic controversies—the Dilke business in Britain, the fall of Parnell, the Panama Scandal and Dreyfus Affair in France, with the Marconi Scandal (1912)—reached almost to the eve of war.

In politics, the advances were more often reactionary. The inauguration of the German Reich in 1871 inevitably bred nervous resentment among neighbor and near-neighbor alike. French nationalism fed off the loss of Alsace and Lorraine. Britain feared for its dominance of the seas. Bismarck's *Kulturkampf* through the 1870s alarmed Catholics across the continent, yet had no lasting effect on Irish separatist nationalism. The "advanced party," quietly contemptuous of Home Rule possibilities, learned much from France's new blend of religion and politics, only to ally itself with the Kaiserreich in 1914. Pearse's essay "The Coming Revolution" unveiled presuppositions of a strictly religious character in their migration to the rhetoric of politics. The people may be its own Messiah and, as such must suffer, indeed sacrifice itself. Cesare Pavese observed in his diary for 14 June 1940, "The political body does not die and so does not have to answer for itself before any God."[25] If political body becomes identical with "the people" and establishes itself as its own savior—an eternal business in Pearse's view—then its Real Presence is always and everywhere active as the sacramental alternator in the national engine, destructive and re-creative at once. The insurrection of April 1916 led to no such regime, just a very pale imitation tempered with durable residues of democracy. But the inversion of Richards's tenor and vehicle, according to which the vehicle (image) leads rather than illuminates the tenor (topic), certainly informed a few of the principal insurrectionists' published thoughts.

On Myth and Sociology

The power politics of late nineteenth-century Europe is so vast a topic, and so pervasive in its implications, that these remarks must seem no more than marginalia. Yet the growth of a religiously charged nationalism within that period involves terms central to the declared values and objectives of the 1916 insurrectionists. Of these, sacrifice has principally featured here, through observations on Irish sectarian or theological disputes. In turn, the nature of a sacrament is considered, though the latter term is infrequently used by Pearse, Connolly, and other publishing leaders of the April insurrection. Elsewhere, anthropological research was steadily transforming the context in which previously restricted terms were employed. A Scotsman, James George Frazer (1854–1941), was to become the best known of these pioneers through *The Golden Bough*, a gradually expanding multivolume work dealing both with ancient mythology (Egyptian, Greek, Roman) and contemporary folk practice in Europe, Africa, Asia, and the Americas. T. S. Eliot, in notes to *The Waste Land* (1922), acknowledged a debt to Frazer's book, "one which has influenced our generation profoundly."[26]

Though Frazer is nowadays regarded more as precursor than a founder of professional anthropology, his findings certainly shifted the frames in which religious terminology was understood. Commencing publication in 1890, *The Golden Bough* challenged any privileged use of the term "sacrament" and demonstrated the many ways in which sacrifice had been—and still was—practiced in society. Its perspective was cultural rather than theological, its materials surprisingly ordinary. Chapter 50, entitled "Eating the God," began:

> We have now seen that the corn-spirit is represented sometimes in human, sometimes in animal form, and that in both cases he is killed in the person of his representative and eaten sacramentally. To find examples of actually killing the human representative of the corn-spirit we had naturally to go to savage races; but the harvest-suppers of our European peasants have furnished unmistakable examples of the sacramental eating of animals as representatives of the corn-spirit. But further, as might have been anticipated, the new corn is itself eaten sacramentally, that is, as the body of the corn-spirit.

Frazer then proceeded to give examples from rural Sweden, Scotland, and France. Instead of an ecclesiastical setting, the occasion is low-civic: "the mayor breaks the dough-man in pieces and gives the pieces to the people to eat." At the beginning of the twentieth century, overlaps between formal religion and folk practice persisted even in England. "In one part of Yorkshire it is still customary for the clergyman to cut the first corn; and my informant believes that the corn so cut is used to make the communion bread." Of a related practice involving potatoes, Frazer comments that "it shows how the Christian communion has absorbed within itself a sacrament which is doubtless far older than Christianity." Far from modern Yorkshire, he avers, "The custom of eating bread sacramentally as the body of a god was practised by the Aztecs before the discovery and conquest of Mexico by the Spaniards."[27]

Instead of treating these observations as proven evidence of a widespread human practice of ritual eating as propitiation, we should note Frazer's application of "sacrament." Some might argue that his task is made easier by repetition of the familiar word, and that the theological meaning of an institutional Christian term defined in catechisms and accepted as a precise denotation, cannot be assumed in these widely diverse practices. The significance of his usage may lie elsewhere. As employed in *The Golden Bough*, "sacrament" is treated as if it were no longer exclusively a reserved term meaning "an outward and visible sign of an inward and spiritual grace." Its fixed and rooted position in the language and what is more loosely called the culture has become less firm, more connotational, less definition-bound. James Connolly's "sacramental wafer of brotherhood" is not so far off the new map. Whether Pearse's more effusive usage of such terminology earns a similar endorsement remains to be seen.

The Golden Bough found a wide appreciative literate readership in the English-speaking world and beyond. In Ireland, the learned response was concentrated within the discipline of Celtic studies. At a more popular level the *Irish Times* briefly ran a column named after the book, describing the midwinter ritual of mistletoe, "selected as the outward sign that was once fraught with some deep meaning."[28] The *All Ireland Review* in September 1901 directed readers to the National Gallery on Dublin's Merrion Square to see J. M. W. Turner's *The Golden Bough*, depicting a scene in Virgil from which Frazer had taken his title. The principal Celticists deploying Frazer were Julius Pokorny (*The Celtic Review* July 1908) and Josef Baudis (*Eriu* 1914). The latter referred to *The Golden Bough* in connection with notions of "the external soul," while Pokorny on at least five occasions referenced it in writing on the origin of druidism. Other distinguished commentators in passing included George Coffey, R. A. S. MacAlister, and Goddard H. Orpen.

In the present context, the attention given by the *Irish Church Quarterly* is remarkable. The Church of Ireland's one serious (or high-brow) publication had no confessional reason to flatter *The Golden Bough*. Nevertheless, a writer on "The Laying on of Hands" noted courteously that "There is no allusion to such a practice in Frazer's book . . . notwithstanding the wonderful extent of the field of magical practices which it surveys."[29] The same issue published a sympathetic review of *Taboos and the Peril of the Soul* (a component part of *The Golden Bough*). On the Catholic side, it was only in 1923 that the Jesuit *Studies* got round to assessing Frazer, devoting a mere page to the abridged edition of more than seven hundred pages—"serious students have never taken *The Golden Bough* too seriously."[30]

Irish readers with specialist interests were not limited to native publications; the far greater volume of books and journals emanating from Britain was readily accessible. Middle-class Catholics looked to *The Dublin Review* (founded 1836 by, among others, Daniel O'Connell), a London-based monthly. An immediately prewar issue carried a review of Frazer's ever expanding *Bough* in which the reviewer found pleasing indications of modesty, even uncertainty, on the author's part. He was less impressed by Emile Durkheim's *Elementary Forms of the Religious Life* (published in French 1912), which dealt principally with Australian aboriginal practices. Two authors are cited to rebut Durkheim's association of these with sacrifice—one of them a Lutheran who protested that violence is done to words when "communion" is applied to the eating of a slain kangaroo. For the other, a sentence by Durkheim is dismissible because "every single word, save that perhaps of animal, is to be regarded as pure metaphor."[31] Irish authorities had less to say about Henri Hubert and Marcel Mauss, whose *Essai sur la nature et le fonction du sacrifice* first appeared in 1898, the year of commemoration for the United Irishmen's rebellion.

Aside from the hostility of Catholic reviewers toward a more professionalized anthropology than Frazer's, the last complaint identifies a major shift in the usage and understanding of "sacrifice" in the early twentieth century. Never exclusively a Christian, or even a religious, term, it acquired a breadth of connotation beyond its use in relation to ritual: the Great War would add to that with extreme prejudice. It is within this expanding circumference of meaning that Pearse's rhetoric should be read, its effusions neither denounced as blasphemy nor accepted as moral patriotism.

Durkheim's book also caught the attention of *The Irish Church Quarterly* in a terse review by William Townley Beckerson (1890–1974). He is willing at first to give a benefit of doubt to the implication of the author's researches for "the highest forms of religious thought." He is however shocked by Durkheim's remark that "the Christian communion is inseparable from the myth [*sic*] of the Last Supper," and chides him for failing to know that the Anglicans claim to be part of the wider "Catholic church."[32] Beckerson went to become a wartime padre, later retiring to a parish in county Kerry.

Leaving the Prologue

It is surely time to welcome or confront *Enigmas*'s principal subject, Joseph Mary Plunkett, whose brief life should follow without delay. The preceding efforts to contextualize the period in which he grew up and the cause to which he committed himself have perhaps been most successful in demonstrating how elusive context is, how it spills outward or draws into itself as if at will. A central presupposition is that the years 1880–1920 were dominated in Europe by successive crises, culminating in world war. A second would have it that semantic change is crucial within these crises and crucial in our efforts to understand them. Given the terms employed by Plunkett and his colleagues of April 1916 to articulate their objectives, the idiom of religious ritual plays a crucial role. Consequently, a minihistory of some debates taking place in Victorian Ireland constitutes part of that protean context. To get a purchase on the linguistic problem, we turned very briefly to I. A. Richards's account of metaphor. To move on, we should now look a little further at one of his successors, Paul Ricoeur. In *The Rule of Metaphor* (1975), the French philosopher opens by observing that the study of rhetoric as a discipline "died towards the middle of the nineteenth century."[33] The historical datum relates to France's lycée system, and finds only awkward analogues in British and Irish education of the same period. Plunkett, however, was educated by Jesuits, both in Ireland and in England, and had ambitions to study at the Jesuit-influenced University College of his native Dublin. In these institutions, protected from state regulation, Rhetoric endured in the classification of subjects and courses, as James Joyce learnedly could testify. Plunkett was not a diligent pupil, and never became an undergraduate. Can we read his experience as something other than a personal, idiosyncratic case? Does he become exemplary rather than exceptional, in some critical perspective yet to be demonstrated?

Ricoeur acknowledges his debt to Richards. Metaphor is their common field of enquiry and, I suggest, crises in the use and understanding of metaphor in the late nineteenth century form a background—generally quite distant, but not always so—to Plunkett's experience and his political milieu. What Ricoeur said on the question of tenor/vehicle was positive: "the advantage of this esoteric terminology is precisely that it combats every allusion to a proper meaning, every return to a non-contextual theory." By proper, he means privileged or substantial, on the one part, as distinct from the notion of ornament, on the other. Accordingly, metaphor cannot be subdivided into parts, distinct from the whole. Similarly, metaphor "does not represent some additional power, but [is] the constitutive form of language."[34] More expansively:

> metaphor holds together within one simple meaning two different missing parts of different contexts of this meaning. Thus, we are not dealing any longer with a simple transfer of words but a commerce between thoughts, that is, a transaction between contexts.[35]

If we were to take Plunkett's best-known composition, it poses a cluster of valuable questions:

I see his blood upon the rose
And in the stars the glory of his eyes,
His body gleams amid eternal snows,
His tears fall from the skies.

I see his face in every flower;
The thunder and the singing of the birds
Are but his voice—and carven by his power
Rocks are his written words.

All pathways by his feet are worn,
His strong heart stirs the ever-beating sea,
His crown of thorns is twined with every thorn,
His cross is every tree.[36]

If metaphor is our first concern, then a quick response might be to treat the poem of twelve lines as twelve consecutive metaphors constituting one. Each of the three stanzas is made up of a single sentence. The word "his" appears twelve times, though not with a once-per-line regularity. But what noun does "his" stand for? Conventionally, the answer is Christ, signifying the omnipresence of God. To accept this, one has to concede that Christ is also excluded from the poem, at least formally or nominally. He is, in Ricoeur's terms, a missing part. This feature of the poem can readily be accounted for through absolute Judaic prohibitions on the writing of God's name, or by more recent theological ideas of negativity. The poem evidently works on the basic of its pervasive metaphoricity.

Can anything similar be offered in explication of Pearse's rhetorical practice? Writing about the men (not, it seems, the women also) who joined the Gaelic League, he referred to some who had gained "a new baptism and a new grace of life." This allusion to the one sacrament that virtually all Christian churches mutually recognize has its puzzling features, notably in referring to a *new* baptism. The League, it must seem, has gone further than any church would. Of course, one can read the passage as a metaphor that suggests that what League membership conferred was (in some respects like a) new baptism. The metaphor, Ricoeur might be willing to say, "holds together within one simple meaning two different missing parts of different contexts of this meaning." However, as with Plunkett's poem, the characteristic missing part is crucial. Who instituted this new baptism and conferred grace? Hardly a god-equivalent within the metaphor, because the passage continues by expressing doubts about any new messiah except the people as a whole. A collateral missing part haunts "The Spiritual Nation," a later essay (February 1916) where the only reference to denominational difference (and, hence, to sectarian conflict) comes in a benign quotation from Theobald Wolfe Tone (1763–1798). Writing before the insurrection, Pearse omits any reference to the divisions that posed such a threat to any general welcome for his efforts. This omission of February 1916 we might regard as political folly or culpable imperception. The earlier celebration of the Gaelic League is better classified, not as metaphor, but as catachresis, that is, in the words of the *Oxford English Dictionary*, "improper use of words, application of a term to a thing which it does not properly denote; abuse or perversion of a trope or metaphor."

Terminology Terminating What?

Learned apologists for Pearse's rhetoric could argue that, in this instance, he was guilty of nothing worse than a category mistake.[37] A league cannot baptize, they could murmur apologetically and reasonably. By the same token, though with less hope of success, German apologists twenty years later could have argued that human beings cannot be vermin and, consequently, to say that Jews are vermin is a category mistake, that's all. Rhetoric, in a sense consolidating itself in the later nineteenth century, employs catachresis deliberately for its emotive power. In doing so, it unquestionably initiates "a commerce between thoughts, that is, a transaction between contexts." The major contexts between which Pearse works his transactions are Christian theology (more exactly, Christology) and nationalist politics; one may assume these to be categorically distinct, but historians of a dozen regions in Europe (the Balkans, the Celtic periphery, the Low Countries, etc.) could instance exceptional cases even to the point of implying interdependence.

Irish nationalism had not always featured in such a transaction with theological idiom; to Wolfe Tone and Thomas Davis (1814–1845), whom Pearse quoted at length in "The Spiritual Nation," it would have made little sense. Its practicality in the 1890s and after was historically conditioned. Its constituent parts likewise depended on changing circumstances. By definition, Irish nationalism aimed to end British control of Ireland. But was it control, domination, or occupation that was opposed? What word generated the optimum emotive power? Certainly *slave* and *slavery* worked with thumping insistence. For example, the passage about the Gaelic League from Pearse's "The Coming Revolution" was quickly followed by another almost as remarkable:

> I am glad that the Orangemen have armed, for it is a goodly thing to see arms in Irish hands. I should like to see the [Ancient Order of Hibernians] armed. I should like to see the Transport Workers armed. I should like to see any and every body of Irish citizens armed. We must accustom ourselves to the thought of arms, to the sight of arms, to the use of arms. We may make mistakes in the beginning and shoot the wrong people; but bloodshed is a cleansing and a sanctifying thing, and the nation which regards it as the final horror has lost its manhood. There are many things more horrible than bloodshed; and slavery is one of them.[38]

Pearse's wish to see opposed bodies of Irishmen armed has its childish side, but it discloses his preference for violence over amity. Strictly speaking, there were no Irish citizens at the time he wrote, but that is a minor transgression. His admission that the Irish Volunteers might shoot the wrong people also has its charm, but the sentence following interprets even this as "a sanctifying thing." Who, we might ask even now, is sanctified? Issues of large-scale bloodshed, whether of fellow Irishmen or presumably of an external enemy, are admitted to be horrible. But *slavery* is worse. Sean MacDermott (1883–1916), the purest of "physical force" republicans among the signatories on Easter Monday 1916, condemned Irish parliamentarians as "place-hunters . . . dastards, cowards and slaves." The first allegation has some truth behind it, for place-hunters thrived; the second and third are difficult to judge; but the fourth is ludicrous exaggeration or a category mistake. Yet it exercises colossal emotive power. Its immediate origins lie in the first instalment of John Mitchel's *Jail Journal*, in *The Citizen* (New York) on 27 May 1848. Leaving Dublin, he described it as a "city of bellowing slaves [and] villas of genteel dastards." When he eventually reached the United States after imprisonment in Australia, he became a vigorous supporter of the Confederates and their "peculiar institution" of slavery.[39]

In 1911 *Irish Freedom*, a separatist paper edited by Thomas Clarke (1858–1916), the oldest signatory and a veteran of British imprisonment, condemned King George's visit. Under the headline "The English King and Irish Serfs," he came "guarded by spies and mercenaries and welcomed by helots [i.e., slaves]." What is implied is not a legal fact, though slavery had and has its legal definition as an international crime; what is implied is the psychological condition of having placed oneself into mental or spiritual slavery by thinking or behaving in a certain manner that, in other people, might be unremarkable. This, then, was the thing to be terminated, an Irish condition of allegedly self-induced slavery under the British, the consciousness of which had been inculcated by the would-be terminators themselves—a political version of hellfire preaching, with redemption for afters.[40]

As in much else, Connolly differs from his April 1916 associates in employing these terms. In January 1903, he stood in the labor interest for the Dublin municipal elections; his address linked the rhetoric of slavery to the specific historic instance of the American South: "This is what I call wage-slavery, because under it the worker is a slave who sells himself for a wage with which to buy his rations, which is the only difference between this system and negro slavery where the master bought the rations and fed the slave himself." The idea of wage slavery may have originated at the end of the American Civil War, but it was taken up by Marx and Engels in their critique of capitalism. Application of the broader terms, slave and slavery, ran the risk of losing contact with practical realities. In the climactic last word of its title, Connolly's "Some Irish Slaves and Slavishness" (*Workers' Republic* 25 September 1915) indicates the powerful role of mental attitude as distinct from any objective condition, legal or otherwise. The article lays out his account of the means used by the war machine to corrupt Irish workers into regarding their self-interest best served by serving the machine. A lot of this could be assigned to the Marxism for which he is celebrated by some admirers. However, the argument is not conducted essentially on economic or class grounds; the war machine is British, and Britain is characterized as the invader of Ireland. Nationalism works more fundamentally, even to the point where Connolly alludes to "the invader in his murderous conspiracy against a free nation," where the free nation cannot by any reasonable definition be Ireland but—imperial Germany.

In the sixth chapter of *The Re-conquest of Ireland* (1915), devoted to women in the workplace, the argument is far less cross-grained:

> The worker is the slave of capitalist society, the female worker is the slave of that slave. In Ireland that female worker has hitherto exhibited, in her martyrdom, an almost damnable patience. She has toiled on the farms from her earliest childhood, attaining usually to the age of ripe womanhood without ever being vouchsafed the right to claim as her own a single penny of the money earned by her labour, and knowing that all her toil and privation would not earn her that right to the farm which would go without question to the most worthless member of the family, if that member chanced to be the eldest son.
>
> The daughters of the Irish peasantry have been the cheapest slaves in existence—slaves to their own family, who were, in turn, slaves to all social parasites of a landlord and gombeen-ridden community.[41]

The subject of the passage is the female worker, characterized as slave by way of a verbal practice running back to antiquity. That outstanding classical scholar Moses Finley (1912–1986) posits "slave" as the most commonly perceived instance of bondsmen of whatever kind, "hence the metaphorical use of 'slave,' 'slavery,' 'slavish,' in non-labour contexts in western languages ever since the ancient Greek."[42] Connolly for the most part recognizes this metaphorical use as such, and avoids rhetorical inflation of the kind indulged in by Mitchel. A man in leg irons, bound for many years imprisonment, might be allowed some indulgence in his literary style, but the same man when confronted with the leg irons and sweatboxes of South Carolina might have been expected to oppose, not justify, the system.

We need perspective. MacDermott cannot be taken as the original diagnostician of slavery as a general complaint, nor even Mitchel, whose *Jail Journal* was republished in 1913 by Gills of Dublin. Surely the source lies a century and a half earlier, in the opening sentences of Rousseau's *Social Contract* (1762)—"Man is born free; and everywhere he is in chains. One thinks himself the master of others, and still remains a greater slave than they."[43] The idea is further investigated in book 1, chapter 4, which cites Hugo Grotius

(1583–1645) as a precursor. Rousseau's originality lies in his attending equally to the political and the psychological. The origins of the rebels' preoccupation with their condition as slaves lie in early French romanticism, just as their concern with sacrifice indicates a close, if unconscious, engagement with contemporary French ideology. Rousseau, however, is relevant for more than his perception of a tyranny underling formal protections or rights. His concept of the general will has long been recognized as informing democratic theories of sovereignty. Rousseau, crucially, predated the era of nationalism; notions of the general will inevitably alter in conditions generated by ethnic, regional, economic, and ideological factors as themselves molded and intensified by nationalism. The hypothesis that Pearse's idea of the people as its own messiah owes a debt to Rousseau would be obliged to explain how the attendant rhetoric of crucifixion, degeneration, redemption, sacrifice, and sin got into the mix. Other mixes can be safely assumed. G. D. H. Cole (1889–1959), writing in 1913, pointed out certain overlaps in the thought of Rousseau and Immanuel Kant, the latter a philosopher whose name will arise in the pages that follow. The comparison, of course, is directed toward areas of strong contrast within Rousseau's work.[44]

Ireland could predate Rousseau on the issue, though not to everyone's satisfaction. In the fourth of the *Drapier's Letters* (1724), written in opposition to the English government's imposition of a debased coinage in Ireland, Jonathan Swift declared, "all government without the consent of the governed is the very definition of slavery."[45] But when he addresses "the whole people of Ireland" he does not have in mind the electorate of 1868 or 1906. The general will never crossed his mind. A "mass Catholic democracy" would have sent that mind reeling. Yet his emphasis on consent recurs in twentieth-century debates on sovereignty, democracy, and the Kantian contribution to political philosophy. An early issue of *The Irish Review*, of which Joseph Plunkett became editor and proprietor, carried an article on "Swift as an Irishman," a point contemptuously dismissed by the Irish-Ireland zealots of the time.

Many words are employed at multiple levels: specialist, technical, casual, metaphorical. *Sacrifice* and *slavery* have been two of interest in the present enquiry. Indeed the Ireland we are about to investigate was suffused or permeated with sacrifice and debates about sacrifice in the highest sense. *Sacrament* is almost exclusively reserved for clearly defined theological or liturgical

Christian contexts and, on extremely rare occasions, for blasphemous oaths. *Sacrifice* is conserved in its historical context in chapter 2, while *slavery* has fully made its contribution in the present prologue. *Sacrament* occupies a different position in the argument. Historically, contentious differences among the Irish denominations in the nineteenth century had centered on the name, meaning, and substance of one sacrament, the Eucharist or Lord's Supper. Throughout that prolonged exchange, the use of *sacrifice* to characterize what occurs in the sacrament was critically examined or dogmatically defended. When, from circa 1890 onward, a looser, more rhetorically charged use of *sacrifice* grew apace, it carried into the context of political violence, civil commotion, and warfare something of the aura of the Eucharist, of communal sacrifice drastically laicized or secularized.

That idiom can be cited in the Irish insurrectionist context through quotations from essays by Connolly and Pearse. Joseph Plunkett does not appear to share that taste in rhetoric though his father, a feebler poet, was a veritable gourmet. It features centrally and dispassionately in the fiction of one contemporary who shared Plunkett's education in Dublin, from "the distant speck of red light which was suspended before the high altar" in *Dubliners* (1914) at least to *Ulysses* (1922). Here, if nowhere else, the distant presence of the Real Presence is scandalously noted by the heresiarch. "Eveline," the fourth of James Joyce's short stories, arranges enigmatic "promises made to Blessed Mary Alacoque" on a wall in the heroine/victim's home: Marguerite-Marie Alacoque (1647–1890) was a French nun whose spiritual experiences led to a cult of the Sacred Heart, an authorized visual emblem of the Real Presence. Her name features, with stylistic mortifications, on several occasions in *Finnegans Wake* (1939). In *A Portrait of the Artist as a Young Man* (1916), the stages of Dedalus's advancement toward his vocation as writer are charted. They include episodes in which "the Blessed sacrament" can be physically moved aside to provide for athletics, or it constitutes the absolute focus of theological meditation, manipulative or devout.

In *Ulysses*, most references relate to the professional life of Father Conmee in "The Wandering Rocks," though it is also noted as an odd liberality that Mrs. Purefoy's fifty-year-old husband is "a methodist but takes the sacrament." The first and last appearances of *sacrament* mark relations of a primary kind for Stephen. He remembers with undecorated poignancy his late mother and "her glass of water from the kitchen tap when she had approached the sacrament." The final reference comes in degraded circumstances, though with delicate implication. In the verbally fantastic knockabout scene at Barney Kiernan's pub, Leopold Bloom is offered bottles of stout for his unfaithful wife. His response inflates the moment by a metaphoric drift from shop counter to altar:

> BLOOM: (*Solemnly*) You call it a festivity. I call it a sacrament.

The internal ironies of this hyperbole—Bloom is Jewish, the wine bottled stout—recall the early-teenage Dedalus's most searching thought in *A Portrait*:

> Why was the sacrament of the eucharist instituted under the two species of bread and wine if Jesus Christ be present body and blood, soul and divinity, in the bread alone and in the wine alone?[46]

The challenge has, appropriately enough, its school-boy cleverness. Later, confronted by missionaries for the new Irish nationalism, Dedalus repels them in words applied equally to their politics and to the "Roman Catholic religion"; he scorns the "attitude of a dullwitted loyal serf."[47] Later still, almost conclusively, he characterizes himself as "a priest of the eternal imagination, transmuting the daily bread of experience into the radiant body of everliving life." Metaphor of course, though the clanging emptiness of "everliving life" gives it away before it is accomplished. This high vocation is to withstand the pressures on his soul exercised by three masters detailed in *Ulysses* as the imperial British state, the Roman Catholic Church, "and a third, Stephen said, there is who wants me for odd jobs."[48] The third had been represented in *A Portrait* by Davin and other fellow students, keen to recruit Stephen to the cause of Sinn Féin and the juvenile marching Fianna. He would see them damned first.

If Stephen experiments cerebrally with the dream of embodied imagination (say, a novel) as the Real Presence in a religion of art, it would be vain ambition to attempt a parallel religion of politics or to pursue a nationalist Holy Grail in which the Real Presence (Beckett's Real Body) had lain and might lie again. Pearse toys with the notion when he suggests the people as their own messiah, but the metaphors trip over each other in his argument. He is clearer, if no more reassuring, when he writes, "like a divine religion, national freedom bears the marks of unity, of sanctity, of catholicity, of apostolic succession." In the same essay, he concedes that he could not think of any writer or activist "who has left behind him a *body of teaching* that requires to be examined."[49] Briefly, the beloved past is vacant of guidance.

Plunkett remains a minor figure in everybody's history of Western civilization. However, the period during which his short life impinged on public events in Ireland contributed mightily to modern literature. Bernard Shaw (1856–1950), W. B. Yeats (1865–1939), and James Joyce (1882–1941) continue to attract serious attention in the theater and seminar room, and among general readers. He is not on a par with any of these, nor even with lesser figures in the Irish Literary Movement—Augusta Gregory (1852–1932), Sean O'Casey (1880–1964), or J. M. Synge (1871–1909). Nevertheless Plunkett can be located in a European movement of politico-literary reaction, nurtured on Catholicism and a mystical sense of *La patrie* or, across the channel, of pre-Reformation merrie Englande. G. K. Chesterton (1874–1936) was a favorite author of Joe's even as he journeyed toward Berlin in the spring of 1915, hoping for military support.

The relationship between Britain and Ireland or, more sharply, the desire to modify it drastically was pervasive in the cultural milieu Plunkett grew up in. In a late dialogue-poem, one side of Yeats asks

> Did that play of mine send out
> Certain men the English shot?[50]

Certainly, Plunkett died by firing squad after a British army court martial in May 1916. Yet it would be precipitous to conclude that Cathleen ni Houlihan (1902) pushed the young man into armed revolt, for he was never an admirer of Yeats. The play turns on a demand that, if anyone would help the (unstatable) cause of Ireland, "he must give me himself, he must give me all."[51] The appropriation of Christ's injunction (in Mark 8:34) to a nation allegorized as female messiah does not set up the latter as a rival to the church but as a coming, reciprocating adjunct. The conjunction is achieved with the 1916 insurrection, of which Plunkett was an acknowledged leader.

Is *insurrection* the right term to describe or classify the events of April

1916 in Dublin? Others have been used—most frequently *rising*, or *rebellion*, or less frequently *revolt*. Traditionally, a rebellion was collective action against God and his created world, beginning with Satan. Milton, in *Paradise Lost* book 5, line 715, observes "rebellion rising" and, a few lines later, the Son addressing the Father calls Satan and Company "thy rebels." *Rebellion* condemned and did not merely classify. Of course, the emotive charge diminished with the onset of modernity. In the present-day Irish context, the term *rising* remains popular in official circles, partly at least because it appears to have a Gaelic equivalent or even a Gaelic origin in *erigh amach* (literally, rising-out). However, here is a case to answer: is not *erigh amach'* a *calque* to match English terms notably used for the various active oppositions to Henry VIII—the Pilgrimage of Grace (1536) and others known to authority as risings or risings-out in Lincolnshire, Yorkshire, and the northwestern English counties at that time?

No strict taxonomy can be attempted here, with a view to the more accurate description of what happened under the leadership of Patrick Pearse, James Connolly, Joseph Plunkett, and the others in April 1916. *Rising* implies a large popular movement—fewer than two thousand men bore arms during the fighting. *Rebellion* and *revolt* suggest an action based on some kind of institutional authority—of, for example, the colonies in North America, or the Dutch provinces. For present purposes, I have settled on *insurrection* partly at least relying on one of several definitions provided in the OED—"an incipient or limited rebellion."

We already have two areas of constructive uncertainty—the ideological contours of nationalism (twentieth-century Irish nationalism, for example), and the social character of small-scale military actions (Dublin, five days in April 1916, to be exact). In the first case, contour is important because the ideological problem is that of excluded content. That is, nationalism denies the reality of, or at the very least, minimizes the value-significance of, forces operating upon it and simultaneously within it. The spatial metaphors bewitch—within and without, upon and from, internal and external, intrinsic and extrinsic—and can be exaggerated in either direction. Irish-American opinion, we are to believe, is purely the nationalism of Ireland forcibly extruded, uncontaminated by pragmatism, Tammany Hall or transcendentalism; French nationalism is inoperable because it had been denied.

The second case, that of nomenclature, reproduces the first, with an additional twisting of the contour. Events in Ireland at successive dates—1641, 1689, 1798, 1803, 1848, 1867, 1916—are variously described as insurrections, rebellions, revolts, risings, as if these terms were interchangeable. They are all English-language terms used, though with different frequencies, by both sides to the conflict. Someone should look at Gaelic terminology on a comparative basis. Or consider a remoter alternative. The late Mary King generated much trouble for herself when, at a seminar in Halle (German Democratic Republic), she proposed that the events of Dublin 1916 should be treated as an attempted putsch.

To these two areas of constructive uncertainty may be added a third—biography as it relates to individual agency. Arguments for and against the writing of "lives" are too well known to bear repetition. Nor is it necessary to list the celebrated argufiers who discourage any reliance on biography as a source of understanding—Schopenhauer, Darwin, Freud, and the monstrous platoon of latter-day theorists from Althusser to de Man and beyond. Biography is not just the history of an individual human being; it can be an approach to history through an individual career however private or domestic. Joseph Plunkett is not to be set up as a person of large achievement or influence—the German military project was already Roger Casement's affair, and the poetry scarcely reached the level of Pearse's or MacDonagh's. Through him, however, one gains access to areas of nationalist thought more often assumed or repressed than publicly formulated. Things that are assumed are, at a conceptual level, repressed.

Attempting to overcome this hiatus, I have written this study of Plunkett in three chapters, each complementing the others. In order of appearance, they deal first with some materials of biography, then with the public framework in which the subject emerged, and finally with the evidences and assessments of his intellection. This last proceeds by two complementary methods, analysis of significant texts by Plunkett, and exposition of critical perspectives on his milieu, notably those of René Girard and Onora O'Neill. With the exception of Sean Moran's *Patrick Pearse and the Politics of Redemption* (1994), the present book is, I believe, the only sustained attempt to understand a major figure of Irish nationalism of the early twentieth century in terms other than pervasively those of Irish nationalism.

The completion of *Enigmas* coincided with preparation of another book, *Northman: John Hewitt (1907–1987); an Irish Writer, His World, and*

His Times (Oxford University Press, 2015). Both deal with Irish poets who adopted distinctive political positions. However, their backgrounds differ in so many interlocking ways that quite different approaches are required in assessing their lives and their writings. The comparison may illuminate both; it would indicate that the approach adopted in *Enigmas* cannot be transferred at will to other cases. Personally, I have been brought to realize that the bulk of my literary historical work since 1980 has concentrated not on any linear narrative nor on the towering monuments, but on the awkward corners and unexpected turns occurring in Irish cultural history. Perhaps, because one has to slow down to negotiate these hairpin bends and dangerous intersections, one sees more closely and thinks more deliberately into the terrain. Readers are not passive passengers, but may be required to consult the atlas and other traveling aids from time to time.

CHAPTER 1

Naming the Parts of a Life

Rich and Unhappy

Joseph Mary Plunkett was born on 21 November 1887 at No. 26 Upper Fitzwilliam Street, Dublin, a Georgian house standing four stories high above basement and area. It was the home of his parents, bought for them when they married in June 1884 at the Church of the Sacred Heart, Donnybrook. "A Baby Sonnet" appeared in *The Irish Monthly* (a devout Catholic periodical) of January 1889 that ended on the conceit that the "year-old babe" was himself a sonnet. The poet-father, George Noble Plunkett (1851–1948), was a prosperous speculative builder—Noble had not appeared in the baptismal details, but added later for effect. The mother, Josephine Mary (1858–1944, née Cranny), was the daughter of a Carlow-born businessman and property developer. Bride and groom were second cousins. At the time of G. N. Plunkett's death, he was said to possess ninety-three items of substantial Dublin When the future papal count was a student of seventeen or eighteen years in Dublin, he helped to found a lighthearted club called Gelasmuthos (supposedly taken from the Greek and roughly meaning a laughing tale). The club's preoccupations included mesmerism (none too seriously) and cricket as a science. There were also experiments in verse-writing, highly conservative experiments.[2] These were post-Fenian days, when '67's brief alarms were gradually replaced by mollifying terms like amnesty and Home Rule. Young G. N. Plunkett would associate himself with this reformist version of Irish nationalism. Despite his ardent or, at least, diligent Catholicism, he is said to have supported Parnell when the bitter divisions of 1891 occurred. Evidence of this Parnellism is elusive or ambiguous.[3] And meanwhile, he and his household were gliding upward on warm currents of middle-class prosperity.

The infant's second (feminine) Christian name, taken as a baptismal name and derived also from his mother, represents a variant on declining traditional practices in certain parts of rural Ireland. There is one recorded instance of the future martyr signing himself in Gaelic as Ioseph Oilbherius Máire ó Pluingéid, that is, incorporating the Christian name (Oliver) of a Catholic archbishop of Armagh, executed for treason in 1681, with whom the family claimed kinship without ever documenting it.[4] Joe (as he became known) was the second child and eldest son in a growing household, his elder sister Philomena having been born the previous year. "Our Child Angel," another poem by George Noble Plunkett, published in April 1876, may suggest an early death somewhere in the family.[5] Delicate from birth, Joe received his earliest education at a primary school (Catholic University School) attached to the Catholic University in Lower Leeson Street, a short distance from the family home. According to a sister, writing as late as 1950, by the age of two the boy had contracted "bovine T. B.," affecting his glands; this condition became increasingly serious from age twelve onward.[6] Though his mother took him to France for his health, she herself fell ill, leaving Joe at a Marist school in Passy, on the edge of Paris.[7] A winter spent in the city, with inadequate warm clothing, did nothing for his condition. A number of surgical operations were required in Dublin between 1899 and 1905, while he was still a child of the household. These were not the last. What information is available about his early upbringing suggest that Plunkett's mother was a high-spirited, negligent woman.

Her husband had also spent time in southern France in his youth, arising from poor health—tuberculosis ran in the family, as it did in so many. Here, the classic language of Boileau, Pascal, and the philosophes had not quite vanquished powerful dialects and distinctive cultural regions. Later, George Noble Plunkett, the son of Patrick Joseph Plunkett (c. 1821–1918) from

Meath, acquired a Jesuit education at Clongowes Wood (shortly to be James Joyce's alma mater also) before proceeding to a law degree at Trinity College Dublin (TCD). He was declared a papal count by Leo XIII for assistance rendered to the Little Company of Mary, or the Blue Nuns; the assistance involved property in Rome.[8] The "Noble" of George Plunkett's flourished cognomen derived from his mother's Italian family: it and the papal title encouraged a legend that Joe Plunkett's ancestry lay close to the Norman aristocracy.[9]

Patrick Plunkett may have come in from rural Ireland at a time of agricultural disaster, but the opportunities for personal advancement soon opened up for enterprising migrants in the city. Protestant Ireland still disdained the manual professions; if civil engineering could be dignified through a university degree, building as such remained a greenfield opportunity for entrepreneurs of the other religious persuasion. Surviving to the age of ninety-seven (at least), and working his way on to the Rathmines Urban District Council in the classic transmutation of interest into patronage, old Plunkett may have benefited from the occasional politico-sectarian boycott, while his son moved gracefully into the lower strata of commercial plutocracy.[10] By 1913, when Ireland's leader of capital, William Martin Murphy (1844–1919), confronted the Dublin workers in a manner that outraged even the occultic Yeats, young Joe Plunkett could rage with other poets, as if his own inheritance really was of aristocratic origin. He raged discreetly.

Living first on Upper Fitzwilliam Street, a dignified thoroughfare in the southeastern residential-becoming-professional part of Dublin, and later also at remoter Kilternan Abbey, Joe Plunkett's family thus exemplified the success of some Irish Catholics after famine devastated the country in 1845–1850. (Joyce's short story "The Dead," completed in September 1907, provides an oblique perspective into a more modest household of similar experience and background.) Both family lines of the future poet and republican "martyr" came from rural Leinster.

At the time of the Plunkett-Cranny marriage in 1884, the reception had been held in Muckross Park, the bride's parental home on Marlborough Road, Donnybrook. The honeymoon was spent touring in the United States. As part of her dowry, Josephine received the title to several houses nearby, all built by her father—as indeed Muckross had been.[11] Later she owned property in Hardwicke Street, on Sandymount Green, and at Larkfield just beyond the city's southwestern boundary. In each of these three instances, Countess Plunkett's new landed wealth was put at the disposal of cultural, political, and military activities in which her eldest son became engaged. Nevertheless, the family's ownership of, and income from, slum housing (off Upper Abbey Street) did not go unnoticed.[12]

Two younger sons—George Oliver Michael (1894–1944, or Seoirse) and John Patrick Joseph (1897–1960, known as Jack)—and four younger daughters brought the Plunkett offspring to a total of eight. Of the girls, Geraldine Mary Germaine (1891–1986) and Josephine Mary (1896–1976, known as Fiona) were to play significant roles in looking after the eldest brother through years when gaps and digressions were more noticeable than solid milestones. Joe got back from France in 1900, but he was not enrolled in Belvedere College until October 1901.[13]

The *pater familias* had left commerce and building well behind, and turned to the humanities. His town house lay close to the universities and museums of Dublin, in which milieu he felt increasingly at home. In addition to poems in anthologies, he began to research Irish history, collect books, and write on the visual arts. In 1894, G. N. Plunkett edited an account called *The Jacobite War in Ireland* with Father Edmund Hogan, SJ. Six years later, before his eldest son was enrolled under the Jesuits at Belvedere, he issued a short study of the Renaissance Italian painter Sandro Botticelli (1445–1510), through a well-known series published by George Bell in London.

He also took a serious interest in the history of printing on the European continent, noted the earlier Chinese inventions, lectured on incunables (books before 1501) and the elegance of the Aldine Press's productions, the value of the private press movement, and so forth. Around 1902, he lectured on bibliographical topics in Dublin and further afield. Though he was not a scholar, he clearly assembled a serviceable reference library on the topic, and was keen also to raise aesthetic questions—"What Constitutes Good Printing?" The aspirant poet Joe Plunkett would in time operate his own handpress, edit a literary magazine, and engage in diverse printing escapades, including forgery. His father's zeal for the history of print provided a source of reference as the apprentice work was under way.[14]

G. N. Plunkett's favorite themes included the printing of Bibles. His exposition was not lacking in good-humored partiality:

> Protestant printers naturally looked for business from Catholics, so we need not be surprised that they found an expedient for preserving their good name for orthodoxy and yet [gap on line] For example, Daniel Elzevier copied accurately the fine Vitré edition of the Vulgate, in 8 volumes 8vo in 1666. But Daniel did not choose to come to judgment: so the titles [i.e., title pages] of the vols substituted Cologne for Amsterdam [as the place of publication], and the name of one Balthazar ab Egmondt for his own. In this pious fraud he only followed his father's[.] As not a few of his Dutch neighbours were doing the same thing the public conscience was satisfied. However, we who have to deal with these things must remember not to judge the book by the titlepage.[15]

It has been said that Plunkett, by now a dignified patrician with full beard and high forehead, lobbied to become undersecretary for Ireland, but lost out in 1902 to Sir Anthony McDonnell (1844–1925), a reforming administrator to whom the 1903 Land Act is a fitting monument. These maneuvers occurred while George Wyndham (1863–1913) was chief secretary. In 1907, the count was appointed director of the National Museum of Science and Art, under an enlightened new chief secretary, Augustine Birrell. January of the same year had seen Dubliners riot at the first performances of J. M. Synge's *Playboy of the Western World*. During the summer, a trial involving forgery and intimidation brought a London-based family friend, Tom Gurrin, to Dublin as an expert witness. A suspect document, addressed to "a true Catholic and Irishman with the welfare of your religion and country at heart and a faithful member of our Land League," proposed to blow up Lord Ashdown "while he is praying to his friend the devil in church next Sunday, and send him home to hell."[16] The Ireland into which the Plunketts had established themselves was shifting under their feet, shifting both backward and forward.

Even while future energies were still gathering pace, stalwarts of the ancién regime Union caused minor difficulties for G. N. Plunkett. Notable among these was his near-namesake, George Tindall Plunkett (1842–1922), who, like the count, was a museums administrator publishing on artistic matters. He also had traveled in the Near East, compiled a phrase book in English and Arabic, and written a guide titled *Walks in Cairo* that Joe would use on location in the summer of 1908. This second and older George Plunkett possessed the distracting ability to duplicate Joe's father and contradict him, doppelgänger effects not unlike some we will find in Joe's early experimental writings.

In addition to CUS Leeson Street and the Marist school in France, the boy had received casual instruction from a governess and also lessons in mathematics from a teacher, Mr. Greenan, attached to a national or primary school at Sandyford, county Dublin, close to Kilternan Abbey.[17] On the eve of the Second World War, the count published a very brief "Personal Note" about his late son, recalling how "at Kilteran Abbey he planned and 'staged' an extravaganza that nearly set the old house on fire." A pyrotechnical figure dances through the brief note, for, we also learn, "as soon as verse became his natural expression he burned all his trial pieces" while "*afflamé de justice* he staked everything."[18] Of Plunkett's early training in life, his sister could later admit that "he had no formal education at this time."[19] At Belvedere, then going through a slack managerial phase, the frail latecomer developed a precocious intellectuality in defense of his corner. The precocious intellectuality does not appear to have produced academic results. A few enigmatic examination marks survive from April 1903, indicating reports ranging from "unsatisfactory" to "good" (in English). A seven in French was a commendable result, indebted perhaps to the year spent in Passy. Mathematics undistinguished, Latin marks largely undistinguishable. That the college buildings in shabby north Dublin incorporated the former town house of the lords Fingall (family name, Plunkett) did not damage his standing. Joyce, the most infamous recent product, would later publish a compelling fictionalized account of spiritual life at Belvedere. The original "hell-fire" sermon, recounted at length in *A Portrait of the Artist as a Young Man* (1916), was preached in 1896 by Father James Cullen; his "trace of sadism" was noted by another contemporary, the art critic Thomas Bodkin (1887–1961), who noted also a questionable tone of address—"My dear little brothers in Jesus Christ."[20]

Characteristically, not much personal material survives from the schoolboy period. In what was then known as a "copy" or school exercise book, dated April 1904, there are a few leaves of very short stories, the most amusing of which concerns a ghost called Shady and a bullfrog. Another (which may hold some minor biographical reference) tells of Fanny Lecksonbridge and her father, a chemist researching radium, and a more fully sketched "Confession of a Murderer":

> Though still a young man I have committed more murders than any man living or executed by law. In fact, there is, or rather was, only one man who came any near me in the number of killing, and he, poor fellow, (strange that *I* should feel pity for any one!) met an ignominious end in the electric chair.[21]

Plunkett was sixteen when these drafts were committed to paper, an age of adolescent fantasy and virtual exploration of the unknown; or, for others, religious fervor and anxiety. If there is a common theme across the mere five surviving leaves of fiction, it is the relationship between science—hypnotism, radium, electricity, and so on—and trumpery spiritualism, by means of planchette and clairvoyance. There is little evidence of a decisive Jesuit influence.

If Joyce is the most renowned Belvedere boy of the period, the Plunketts were not surrounded by rebellious aesthetes. In any case, the future novelist had left in 1898. Other pupils with whom the boys would work closely in the ranks of Irish republicanism were Charles William St John Burgess (1874–1922, or Cathal Brugha), who had to leave prematurely on the collapse of the family business, and the academically gifted future novelist Eimar O'Duffy (1893–1935).

Belvedere's response to the events of 1916 was cautious. An obituary for its better-known casualty—the other was shot by the rebels—did not appear until 1917 when a two-part article by two different old-boys appeared in *The Belvederian*. First, Norman Reddin recalled how

> His companions classed him with those whom they called "queer fellows." He puzzled them. They joked at his expense and treated him sometimes with school-boy harshness. Cold, haughty and independent towards strangers, he grew into early manhood with these characteristics more emphasised than they were in his boyhood. . . . Many a time I have heard him, in some heated argument, first prove conclusively that he was right, and then turn round and prove that he was absolutely wrong![22]

There was no mention of Joe Plunkett's brothers, also Belvederians, and no mention of Plunkett's marriage to Grace Gifford, despite the prominence given it and its pathetic brevity in the public press. In a companion piece devoted to the poet as distinct from the man, Austin Clarke (1896–1974) detected Plunkett's reading of Saint John of the Cross, Saint Theresa of Avila, and "the high poet Francis Thompson." In his own literary career, Clarke was to wrestle more successfully and evenhandedly with the leading protagonists in Plunkett's. In attempting to understand either poet, one finds much that is guarded in the tribute of 1917:

> Mysticism would seem vision, that is, a mode of being; in its transcendence, logical, disciplined. All must indeed, at some time or always, wrestle like Jacob with the stranger, seeking to know his name.[23]

Plunkett's Belvederian career was interrupted by more than one serious bout of illness, requiring surgery. In ways more misleading than illuminating, his upbringing resembles that of J. M. Synge a quarter-century earlier—irregular education, poor health of at least a superficially similar kind, a shifting home-base involving both the city of Dublin and the hilly southern outskirts of the county. But the Plunketts were upwardly mobile Catholic bourgeois, whereas the Synges were Protestant former landowners in decline.

Well-to-do Dublin middle-class families could afford to send their sons—occasionally their daughters—to English schools. If it took three generations to make a gentleman, the process was rendered smoother through genteel education. Saint George's College, Weybridge, took in sufficient Irish boys to justify a member of staff escorting them back to Dublin at Christmas. Two weeks before the break in 1904, Joe wrote home on his own behalf and that of his brothers—"Georgie & Jack are quite well"—but the big news was his success in Chemistry (85 percent), in ping-pong (probably second in the school), and even in a fight (Quin shook Joe's hand afterward).[24]

Though Weybridge features in one of his brother's flowcharts of education, it is dropped from Joe's, whether for reasons of ill health or poor academic performance. His sister Geraldine's memoir provides an unflattering account of the school, intertwined with a vigorous critique of the countess's stewardship of the boys' education. She had heard some unspeakable rumor of an expulsion from Clongowes, the Jesuit boarding school in county Kildare, and so opted on impulse for Saint George's, even sending young Jack when he was only six. During home leave occasioned by an outbreak of scarlatina, Joe managed to convey how very unsuitable was the school, "because of what went on there"—Clongowes was not alone in its vice. Two years later, the school closed down (according to *All in the Blood*), though hardly as a result of the countess's protests. Besides this confusion on the formal side of Joe Plunkett's education, there was a domestic equivalent. When the boys returned in quarantine, they were hidden away in a bungalow at Kilternan, their whereabouts unknown even to their sisters in Mount Anville convent, while the count had taken up temporary residence in distant Cork.[25] Family cohesion was not a major influence on Joe's development.

At the prompting of Tom Gurrin, whose sons were doing well, Joe entered Stonyhurst, in rural Lancashire, the Jesuit answer to Eton, on 1 October 1906. A few weeks short of his nineteenth birthday on admission, the college logged him "educated chiefly at home." On this basis of fragile truth, he was assigned to Philosophy, a class or course designed for youths above school age, entitling members to be termed Gentlemen Philosophers and to be addressed as Mister.[26] There were eleven recruits in the year, with a further nine seniors in second year.[27] Among them were four Belgians, three Irish, two Hungarians. Englishmen, though constituting the largest element, were not a majority. Franz Karl, a grandson of the Austrian emperor, did not arrive until 1912.[28]

Nonetheless, "at the opposite side of the table at meals . . . sit two Philosophers. One is an Italian prince, Colonna by name who is about twice as English as any Rajah. He speaks English with an English accent . . . rides a Hawss, wears Puttee leggin's don cha knaow . . . The other is the ideal hero of all 'Chums' serial stories, the 'tall, broadshouldered, genial (but not to [*sic*] genial) Englishman'! Taciturn except when familiar, not too intelligent, handsome. No sense of humour, except English humour."[29] Joe's initial difficulties in finding his bearings in this international mix where Catholicism was a mark of distinction, not opprobrium, were not aided by a distaste expressed by some for Irish coreligionists, an attitude that went back to the time of Daniel O'Connell. Inevitably, Father Gibb had a joke about the Irish farmer and his pig; for streaky bacon, feed it every second day.

In mid-November, he received bad news from home: a friend, Eddie MacCormack, had died. Joe dutifully wrote to the mother, reporting his prayers for the deceased while adding confidently that Eddie was already in heaven. He prayed for the entire family, especially the girls.[30] Ending a letter to his sister Philomena, Joe reported another indulgence in less than high literature. He had just finished R. L. Stevenson's macabre tale of the split personality—"Dr Jekyll & Mr Hyde & it was not at all what I thought. Must stop now. Love from both to all. Rameses II Rex Aegypt." The curious "both" may be a nod toward his fellow consumptive's novel of 1886, the year before Plunkett's birth, that is, a nod toward the split personality. Such is further inscribed in the double mock-regal signature, which foreshadows Plunkett's use of Egyptian motifs in his later efforts at drama. There were more demanding exercises in composition to require his attention.

Three handwritten sheets, dated 19 November 1906 and bearing a school essay on "People I would Like to Have Seen," constitute the sole surviving example of work done at Stonyhurst. It was virtually a debut submission to unknown judges. Plunkett's nominations were The Mad Hatter from Lewis Carroll's *Alice in Wonderland*; Shakespeare; a music-hall comedian named Dan Leno (1860–1904), of genuine historical significance but irredeemably vulgar to Jesuit eyes; and the title character from *Lady Baltimore* (1906), a novel of South Carolinian "aristocrats" by Owen Wister (1860–1938), inventor of cowboy fiction. The enthusiasm for Wister was prompted by an American copupil, named Avery, who understood Joe's problem with English attitudes. However, the English master termed the essay "studied nonsense" and threatened a fine if Plunkett's punctuation did not improve.[31]

As he won second prize in Mental and Moral Philosophy at the end of this first year, we may conclude that the red ink had some effect. At the end of his second and final year at Stonyhurst, Plunkett was given a Certificate of Proficiency, plus an award of £5 to buy books. The prize essay topic was "The Truths, alleged as the Basis of Pantheism and Deism, Find the Only Full and Complete Expression in Theism." The notes that survive in the National Library of Ireland as evidence of Plunkett's application to scholastic philosophy suggest a reasonably diligent student occasionally distracted into recreative doodling and alien thoughts. The right-hand (or recto) side of the notebook records lectures or readings in metaphysics on a day-to-day basis, commencing on 21 January and running through to Monday, 6 April. From a short series of internal datings, one can attribute these studies to the year 1908, when Plunkett was twenty. At least some of the entries are the result of dictation, rather than the scrutiny and criticism instilled through Jesuit discipline. Nevertheless, Joe learned about the many arguments for the existence of God, Dominican, Thomist, and Molinist. More abstractly, when contemplating the possible existence of things not now extant, he instanced a lady prime minister.[32]

Given his undistinguished school career at Belvedere and Stonyhurst, one cannot seriously consider the possibility that Joseph Plunkett's study of philosophy was a prelude to training for the priesthood, at least not as a Jesuit. The left-hand (or verso) sides of the Stonyhurst notebook indicate a variety of digressions. The first leaf alludes to a need or desire to "Rise above Sc [Space] & Tm [Time] By means of Transcendental introspection." On the next, one finds a half-canceled flippant riposte to scholastic method, in which the first line is crossed through.[33]

{I ask for proof}
I've got it,

Thereafter, drawings emerge; for example, a head of Dante in relief against a night sky with mountains (13v) or ornamental lettering with heavy shadow effects (36v–37r). There are, however, semiverbal inscriptions of greater inscrutability. Three major terms of ethical or moral discussion are represented in the following schema:

Goodness = Bm
Good = gd.
Love =

The third equation was completed with four heart-shapes in a row with the word "or" between each pair.

In some manner, these are three abbreviations; in the first English "goodness" is represented by a Latin contraction (of *bonum*). In the second, Latin does not feature, and English "good" (the adjective, presumably) is itself contracted into "gd," which hardly will save space and may look like a contraction also for "God." But the final line, seeking a contractive representation of "love," requires both the emphatic repetition of the symbol chosen and, at the same time, the near-avoidance of words (whether English or Latin) in preference of the conventional heart-symbol, qualified by the nervous alternative-seeking "or."

Two pages later, the exercise book shows a child at table or desk with a faint apparition appearing behind. In this drawing, the furniture is more solidly drawn than the figures. Four pages later again, there is a rough sketch of an ancient Greek-style vase, with the word "Priceful" attached—presumably as a sardonic comment on the notion of priceless antiques. A vague Beardsley influence might be discerned in the malevolent figure on 25v, but gradually these verso inscriptions are increasingly verbal and explicit. There is a reference to John Henry Newman's *Grammar of Assent* (1870), very proper for a Catholic Dubliner, but toward the close of the book there are lengthier notes on Buddhism (51v, 74v–75v) and Hinduism (73v). Clearly Plunkett was not taking dictation at all times during his Stonyhurst days.

The jottings on Eastern religions do not amount to much more than the registering of an intellectual fashion of the late nineteenth century to which Yeats and other Irish writers were responding in greater depth. From Buddhism, Plunkett takes the snippet that "Not to exist is the highest good" (51v), though the idea also echoes the Chorus in Sophocles's *Oedipus at Colonnus*. One or two drawings accompany these notes, now geometrical as well as figurative. There is an eye, the pupil of an eye, and geometrical lines within a parallelogram. With these is the injunction, "see 'Anti-Theistic Theories' Prof. Flint" (70v), a book that Plunkett bought.

His mental investment in the £5 award has clearly begun. As a possible mentor, Robert Flint (1838–1910) is an unexpected name. A dominant figure in Scottish academic philosophy, and an ordained Presbyterian minister, he had held chairs in moral philosophy, political economy, and divinity at Saint Andrews and Edinburgh. His prolific writings included books on socialism (1894), Hindu pantheism (1897), and agnosticism (1903). In 1903, at the age of sixty-five, Flint had defined philosophy as *scientia scientarum*, or the theoretical basis for the rational discussion of relations among different individual sciences, biological, physical, mathematical, and so on. It was, of course, an intellectual edifice on the point of collapse.[34]

The *Anti-theistic Theories* had begun life as a series of lectures in 1877 and frequently republished. In 1904, a new edition had been issued by Blackwood in Edinburgh, and it was thus that Plunkett came in touch with Flint's approach to the philosophy of religion. Flint was not an unbeliever but, in Stonyhurst circa 1904, he was close to being a pariah. Plunkett's investigations cannot be traced further than the journal entry transcribed above, but its existence scarcely supports any notion that the short-term student was following a vocation.

Dutiful Stonyhurst Philosophers read a set of textbooks deliberately prepared for them. A powerful influence toward this course of education had been *Aeterni Patris*, a papal encyclical letter of 1879, devoted to the restoration of Christian philosophy (and Thomism, in particular). Infrequent allusions to "Rick" with a page reference in Plunkett's one surviving journal refer to works in the series either by the Reverend John or Joseph Rickaby, SJ—both were contributors. The former's *First Principles of Knowledge* (1888) and *General Metaphysics* (1898) were solid expositions of their topic, if always orthodox in their relationship to Catholicism. Joseph Rickaby's *Moral Philosophy* (1889), on the other hand, had been found wanting by a recent alumnus, especially in its treatment of social theory, applying merely pragmatic arguments against socialism and too lightly passing over the grossness of the dominant system. C. S. Devas's *Political Economy* (1892) was quite a different matter. Devas (1848–1906) was one of the originators of the Catholic Social Doctrine that came to be so influential in England during and after the Great War, albeit through the propaganda of Hilaire Belloc and G. K. Chesterton.[35] Though Devas died the year Plunkett transferred to Stonyhurst, and the author of *Political Economy* had not been a member of the teaching staff, it is reasonable to trace one source of Plunkett's enthusiasm for Chesterton to the influence of Devas's writings, with an additional motivation lying in the old man's earlier attachment to the Catholic University of Ireland.

In the life of a young man who will be hailed as the military strategist of the 1916 Dublin insurrection, enquiry into membership of the Stonyhurst officers' cadet corps is unavoidable. Contrary to statements repeatedly made over three-quarters of a century, Joseph Plunkett did not join up—though his younger brother George was a very active and successful member of the corps.[36] There was a feature of the Cadet Corps routine that may have recurred to Plunkett seven or eight years after he had left Stonyhurst. Annual maneuvers were held at Easter. In 1908, agile and valiant Red Force was totally annihilated by Blue Force, an entrenched enemy armed with modern weapons.[37] *Defensive Warfare, a Handbook for Irish Nationalists*, published by the Belfast branch of Sinn Féin in 1909, expounded an economic-cultural version of much the same strategy.

The older Plunkett's hobby was photography. Philosophers also staged an annual play for the entire school community. It seems reasonable to assume that his fondness for acting was not wasted before a captive audience. Only one of his contemporaries has been recognized among the names that crop up in subsequent diaries and letters—a Maltese named Alfred Asphar or "Taffy." The July 1908 *Stonyhurst Magazine* carries a group photograph of the Philosophers. From the middle row, two of the seated figures will die violently during the Great War—Aidan Liddell of the Royal Flying Corps, and Joseph Plunkett of the Irish Volunteers. By the time this issue was distributed, Plunkett was in Egypt for his health, where he met a future Reuters chief, W. J. Moloney (1882–1952) of Limerick. Both young men were briefly convalescing, though Moloney worked locally as a journalist on the *Egyptian Standard*, an anti-imperialist newspaper founded by the radical English landlord Wilfred Scawen Blunt (1840–1922). What little can be added to this meager record for 1908 is summarized in Joe's signature on a copy of *Steps to the Temple* being the collected poems in Latin and English of Richard Crashaw (1613?–1649).[38]

In old age, Plunkett's sister Geraldine blamed everything on the confused state of Irish affairs before 1916:

> The family atmosphere was full of hair-splitting argument, it got worse when he came home [from Stonyhurst]. He took a violent interest in everything intellectual, from physics and chemistry, colour photography and wireless to mysticism, and was too logical for ordinary life. Nothing, on the other hand, could have been too logical for the years before the Rising; nothing was more lacking than logic from the politics of the Irish Party. He then spent a year in Springfield, Kilternan, with our friends, the Raffertys, and seemed to be a bit stronger.[39]

It is a strictly professional recollection, moving from the family to the atmosphere to the pursuit of politics as rapidly as decency allowed. "Witless," a surviving and unpublished poem by Joe Plunkett, offers a different perspective on the process of growing up:

> When I was but a child
> Too innocent and small

To know of aught but Love
I knew not Love at all.

But when I put away
The things I had outgrown
I learnt at last of Love
And found that Love had flown.

Now I can never find
A feather from his wings
Though every day I search
Among my childish things.[40]

The neighborly exile to Springfield had probably occasioned by the countess's absence from home—she was fond of travel and disinclined toward domestic routine. For one reason or another, at the age of eighteen Joseph had been dispatched to the vast buildings of Stonyhurst with fees to match. Family pride apart, the reasons must include an unreadiness on his side to matriculate for the Royal University, and an unwillingness (on the family side) to send him to TCD.

For University College Dublin (UCD), the Royal University's successor in Dublin, he would eventually need a qualification in Gaelic—later sought through the instruction of Thomas MacDonagh. At TCD, he would have encountered a predominantly Unionist and Protestant college community where his father had studied law decades earlier. In fact, Irish higher education was under the heated microscope of government enquiry, leading in a few years to the establishment of the National University. An Elizabethan and Protestant foundation, TCD was itself to be the subject of a Royal Commission enquiry in 1906, when issues such as the status of the Gaelic language, the confessional needs of Catholics, and the place of women in higher education were to be teased out. It has been said that Joe passed matriculation examinations for the Royal College of Surgeons in Ireland in June 1911, but there is no evidence of how this was achieved and less of any practical steps taken toward a medical education.[41]

There were wider horizons than the Irish educational scene, some with clouds, other balmy. For Catholics throughout Europe, the papal encyclical of 1891, *Rerum Novarum*, held out the prospect of a compromise between the stridency of labor demands and the necessity of maintaining social order. It would be cited by more than one participant in the Irish Troubles of 1916–1923 as the justification of his actions. Colm Ó Lochlainn (1892–1972), who with George Plunkett would print the alleged "secret orders to military officers" (actually forged by Joe Plunkett), took strength from Leo XIII's social credo.

January 1906 had brought a Liberal landslide in the general election. In May, Arthur Griffith (1872–1922) published the first number of *Sinn Féin*; later in the month, the veteran Land Leaguer and human rights campaigner Michael Davitt died in the same nursing home where Synge would die three years later. It was the best of times, it was the worst of times.

The Wander Year

In December 1907, a middle-aged man of modest means returned to Ireland, one of the Irish Republican Brotherhood, by name Thomas James Clarke (1857–1916). He had been born on the Isle of Wight, a decade after the Great Famine, and later lived in South Africa and the United States of America. A succession of calamitous events had sent generation after generation of Irishmen and women abroad—the Flight of the Earls (1607), "Aughrim's Great Disaster" (1691), the migration of surviving United Irishmen (1798–1803), the Great Famine (1845–1847), and then a steady annual loss through emigration that would continue until the close of the twentieth century. Then, with the death of the Celtic Tiger, it resumed, carrying off many talented as well as many desperate citizens.

Over the longer period, it was increasingly a movement of the poor or, at least, of the able-bodied and enterprising among the poor. To make recent experience consistent with the past, it became necessary to recast Irish history, to blend selfish princelings with landless potato-pickers in a mythic tradition. Song and story followed. By 1907, however, the traffic was not entirely one-way. People could return, with a practical intention of removing "the cause of all our woes"—the link between Ireland and Britain. To be effective, the tradition spoke of failure in the past, defeat, and overwhelming odds. It found little use in statistics of wealth among middle-class

Irish Catholics. It spoke little of their Pacific and Orient travels. Geraldine Plunkett summarized the rationale adopted by one family in this complex and anxious society—"we were rich and unhappy, so those who were poor must be happy."[42]

Plunkett's summer of 1908 in North Africa was almost certainly his first excursion so far from home, probably suggested, if not indeed assisted, by friends at Stonyhurst. Geraldine oddly omits any reference to it in her memoir, as published. Having finished at the school, he followed Horace Greeley's advice and went west—to Achill Island, off the coast of Mayo for three months, a place of cultural resort for a few progressives among the Dublin middle classes. In the summer and autumn of 1909, this produced a good quantity of verse, and some less determined efforts to learn Gaelic from the Gaelic League. The idea had been the countess's; she packed off the three boys and two of their sisters, with an aunt returned from America as chaperon. Accommodation was obtained from the local evangelical mission, probably chosen for its cheapness. Other holidaying guests included a police inspector and his ill-mannered wife. The young Plunketts recoiled from the proselytizing behavior of the mission people, enjoyed the island's natural charm, and began to notice the evidence of extreme rural poverty around them. On the annual pilgrimage to Croagh Patrick, Joe collapsed during the arduous climb to the summit and was bedridden for some days.

Of time spent abroad we know most about his trips to Italy and Algeria in 1911, through a diary that survives where others clearly were lost or deliberately destroyed. It is not a travel journal, but simply a pocket diary recording day-to-day meetings with people, events attended, books read, and very occasional inner reflections upon this external cavalcade of incidents. Only portions of the year were passed outside Dublin, and the initial impression is of a well-to-do, intelligent, and cultivated young man staying well within the confines of middle-class taste and behavior.

At this period Joe read a lot of Rudyard Kipling (1865–1936) and Chesterton, and also Arnold Bennett's novel *Clayhanger* (1910) and its sequel, *Hilda Lessness*, which he reread on his way to Germany in 1915. Again the influence of the Lancashire Jesuits may be detected, undercut by his tendency to mix the solemn and the flippant, Shakespeare with Dan Leno. To judge from his own account, he ignored Irish writers of fiction, including active contemporaries such as George Birmingham (1865–1950), Shan F. Bullock

(1865–1935), George Moore (1852–1933), Gerald O'Donovan (1871–1942), Patrick Sheehan (1852–1913), Somerville and Ross (1858–1949; 1862–1915), or Bram Stoker (1847–1912). Of these, the most striking absence is the prolific Moore, whose themes—Irish society, opera, the Holy Land, religion, the self, theater—were close to Plunkett's own interests. Though Plunkett encountered Moore's work in bookshops abroad, he does not appear to have read them. His fellow Belvederean James Joyce, of course, had begun to publish the stories that eventually cohere as *Dubliners* (1914), but these apparently incidental pieces in newspapers or magazines were not the kind of thing one noted in a diary. Stonyhurst was not yet up to speed with Dedalus.

The year began with some nonliterary, decidedly Irish initiatives. Confined to bed in mid-January with flu, he read John Mitchel's *Jail Journal* (1854) and found it "Great!" Perhaps this choice of hardcore nationalist complaint had been suggested at the O'Connell household on New Year's Day, if—that is—the family in question was that of J. J. "Ginger" O'Connell (1887–1944), who later played a distinguished military role in the insurrection and the War of Independence. *Jail Journal* was the work of a man resembling Joe Plunkett in one important regard—both committed themselves to a political and military project quite incompatible with the social background they came from, Mitchel having been the son of a liberal Presbyterian minister of the New Light tendency. More important, however, was the strong and explicit ego at the root of Mitchel's excoriating damnations of British rule in Ireland.[43]

The broader social context which the young man was observing is indicated in a diary entry for 18 January 1911: in almost Jeevesian fashion, it is recorded that "Bertie got his Little Go," that is, passed a significant examination at TCD.[44] (Bertie was one of Moya Plunkett's admirers.) Before the month was out, Joe had begun to read Henri Bergson's *Time and Free Will* (1889), a difficult philosophical text translated from French the previous year. He also typed up his poems, practiced on the cello, and went skating.

Having wintered in Dublin, Plunkett left for Malta at the end of February, with the family of "Taffy" Asphar playing the role of hosts and guides to the little island fortress. These precautions were based on medical and domestic assessments of Plunkett's health, and the 1911 diary somberly recorded his weight from time to time—on 1 April in Naples, he was just eight stone and eleven pounds (about 123 pounds), "ridiculous for my height and age." Italy in spring did not prove sufficient to restore his strength, and so by October he was en route, through London and Paris, for Algiers. He was rarely unaccompanied by relatives; his mother traveled to Italy, his father escorted him as far as the South of France in the autumn, and a sister (with a seventy-year-old companion) joined him in Algiers.

Viewed from the perspective of Irish politics, the year was significant for Plunkett's attendance at meetings of the Irish Self-Government Alliance, and his election into the Young Ireland Branch of William O'Brien's United Irish League (both in late January). This was where a tough-minded bunch of young people, with liberal-radical views, tried to build a political base, independent of Sinn Féin. William Moloney had been of this company, together with Frank Skeffington, who was murdered by a British officer in April 1916. James Joyce was very close to Skeffington as polemico-literary pamphleteers; Moloney knew them both through Mrs. Sheehy's Second Sundays—all this a liberal, even socialist milieu in which Plunkett is not to be traced.[45] Joe's decision to join the Young Ireland Branch was taken against the advice of his future brother-in-law, Thomas P. Dillon (1884–1971), and Dillon's friend Rory O'Connor (1883–1922); he attended a few meetings before deciding that the Irish Party's hostility to the Branch made it useless as a springboard for new thinking.[46]

In literary terms, 1911 matters because Joe wrote his two best-known poems, "The Stars Sang in God's Garden" (19 February) and "I See His Blood upon the Rose" (28 September) at a relatively early point in his adult career. On the other side of the account, *The Eye Witness* returned a poem in mid-August, unpublished. Founded by Hilaire Belloc (1870–1953) in 1911, the magazine was the first in a series reaching into the 1920s that supported distributism, an economic theory compatible with papal teaching and nostalgic for traditionalist, premodern society. Closer to home, his friendship with Thomas MacDonagh was crucial for developments both literary and political, for when Plunkett was confined to bed through illness or otherwise prevented from going about his business, MacDonagh calls to the house.

The two had met when the countess-mother sought a tutor in Gaelic. Their friendship was maintained through Saint Enda's, a Gaelic-speaking school founded by Patrick Pearse in September 1908, just when Plunkett finished at Stonyhurst. Tipperary-born, MacDonagh was a member of the school staff, with university qualifications and a burgeoning literary reputation. A book of MacDonagh's poems, unfortunately called *The Golden Joy*, had appeared in 1907, the third from his hand and inexpertly published.[47] In the drama, he was faring better, with a play, *When the Dawn Is Come*, performed at the Abbey Theatre in October 1908, having been accepted on the company's behalf by Synge. The title oddly echoes that of a piece written by Synge (but never staged)—*When the Moon Has Set*—and in the two awkward prentice plays are to be found divergent perspectives of the transformation of Ireland. The action of MacDonagh's is set in the future and explores the conditions, and the conflicts, pertaining to Irish independence.

Since the 1970s, Karl Marx's "Eighteenth Brumaire of Louis Bonaparte" had slipped from the international academic hit-parade. Oddly, it never had much success in Irish seminars of revolutionary change, perhaps because its dominant trope—theatrical representation—had in Ireland as much appeal to the conservative imagination as it had for radical politicians of the Left. Marx's sardonic reference to "world historical necromancy" mocked the French bourgeoisie of the 1850s, but it also identified a specific form of irrationalism that will prove potent for the later history of Irish nationalism in both its cultural and military wings, the staging of the past and the conjuring of dead heroes.[48]

In all of this, the Abbey Theatre was and remains foremost. As a modern mystery-play, Yeats's *Countess Cathleen* (1892) yoked national "salvation" to spiritual self-denial, at once echoing the Faust legend of the German lands and Jeanne d'Arc of France.[49] It was condemned by leading Catholics and nationalists alike, neither party willing at the time to grant the other full partnership in the bargain. Indirectly, Yeats's mature drama, serviceable plays by Augusta Gregory, and, by consummate irony, the oeuvre of J. M. Synge followed.

The Theater of Ireland, commencing in 1906, deliberately marked itself off from the Abbey, promoting plays by Padraic Colum, Rutherford Mayne, and MacDonagh himself. Its premises were in Hardwicke Street, a property owned by Josephine Plunkett, a real-life countess. Her son was very keen on drama, sat on the Theater of Ireland committee, and acted on stage. In February, he played the part of Kuligin in *The Storm* by Russian dramatist Alexander Ostrowsky, at the Molesworth Hall.

This was an essentially amateur world, in which individuals participated in overlapping activities—creative, administrative, social, and ideological—and in which people mixed easily. An early notebook in the National Library of Ireland is annotated as containing "a lock of hair" though this is in fact a stage moustache. In the same place, Plunkett experimented with verbal disguises: for example the word "anagrams" is proven to be an anagram of "a ram sang." These devices provided a screen or mask or just a moustache behind which emotional possibility might be safely investigated. Sylvia Sheridan may have been the object of real interest; what he demonstrated was that her name could generate nineteen anagrams, including "Heavy lard is sin."[50]

The personality is opaque, even at moments of revelation. Humor, even private humor, is deployed like the ventriloquist's free hand, attracting attention *away*. Gradually, over the next four years, Plunkett would become focused on a very tightly defined objective, moving from the casual interaction of theater and politics into a sphere more univocally political, and from there to an inner core clandestine in its politics and ultimately militarist in its modus operandi. The ventriloquist waves a sword.

For the moment, aged twenty-three in the spring of 1911, Plunkett was evidently happy with the plurality of life, despite his illness and the emotional battleground of home. He conducted a long, entirely one-sided affair with a successful doctor's daughter, Columba Mary Dolores O'Carroll (1893–1955), mixing easily with her family. From county Donegal he had written the previous autumn, "the people I get most letters from are the O'Carrolls."[51] Back in Dublin he attends dances and ceilidh, on one occasion spending (by his own estimate) six hours talking to Miss Kathleen Cruise O'Brien at an event in Rutland Square. The diary somewhat insistently recorded meetings with young women or, rather, simply records their names—"Met Columba, Nuala & the rest. Walked back with Frank" (31 August) and "Met Columba and Nuala" (5 September). Visiting London or Florence, he attended the opera, goes to art galleries, and generally observes the cultural protocols. But the 1911 diary does not suggest anything deeper. When an exhibition of postimpressionist painting reached Dublin, he had duly gone along, suggesting in notes scribbled on his catalog that some of the exhibitors should be shot.

In Florence during April, he "saw Botticelli's 'Prima Vera' & thousands of others," then later the same day went to the Uffizi for "more Botticellis & millions of others." Count Plunkett had published a monograph on Botticelli in 1900, who then overstayed his welcome in young Plunkett's mind.

The day following, and still in Florence, he bought two books by Chesterton, and promptly "read *The Man Who Was Thursday* for the fourth time."

The pages for 11 April to 4 May 1911 have been torn out of Plunkett's diary, and when the record resumed he was back in Dublin. MacDonagh informed him that *The Irish Review* had accepted his poem "The White Dove of the Wild Dark Eyes." Plunkett was ill in bed, though by 31 May he was able to attend the Theater of Ireland's Annual General Meeting, at which the poet James Stephens (1882–1950) and Countess Markiewicz were present. The diary for June and July is scantily maintained, with a few statistics of weight and height recorded. He attended the Gaelic cultural festival, An t-Oireachtas, on 1 August, but the diary simply lists notable people whom he met—Mrs. Salkeld, MacDonagh, Stephens and his wife, Joseph Campbell (1879–1944), and the great Celtic scholar Douglas Hyde (1860–1949). Added is a subparagraph noting other people whom he merely saw—Eoin MacNeill (1867–1945) and the fiction writer Padraig Ó Conaire (1882–1928).

In practical terms, however, the effect renewed his interest in learning Gaelic. The Belfast-born poet Joseph Campbell (1879–1944) took up from where MacDonagh had left off, for whatever reason. But, by early September, the doctor was insisting that Plunkett get away early for a winter abroad. "I don't want to," he complained feebly to his diary. Several matters demanded his attention before he left Dublin. A Smith and Wesson revolver required attention, and an evolving manuscript of poems was delivered to printers. Columba O'Carroll's birthday fell on 20 September: Joe bought her a cake and gave her Chesterton's *Ballad of the White Horse*—he particularly memorized the poem "King's Cross Station"—and bought *The Innocence of Father Brown* for himself. His own poems returned from the printers, unprinted.

MacDonagh applied himself to the business of getting his friend's work properly published. A manuscript was sent to George Roberts, the notoriously sloppy manager of Maunsel & Co., which had published J. M. Synge's *Collected Works* in 1910. Plunkett signed an agreement on 29 September, on which day he also noted that "Italy has declared War with Turkey on account of Tripoli." This apprehension of a minor prelude to the Great War of 1914 is just one of several details in the diary indicative of Plunkett's concern with global, or at least, European affairs, political and military. At home, he stood among the "tremendous crowd" at the unveiling of the Parnell monument on 1 October. It is an ominous monument, with the commemorated figure placed beneath a towering obelisk.

Two days later, Joe had reached London with his father. At an old masters exhibition in the Grafton Gallery, he was sufficiently impressed by Lord Curzon (till recently viceroy of India) and the Duke and Duchess of Connaught to record their presence in his diary, without any details about pictures. Later father and son dined at Gianello's in the Strand, then saw Sarah Bernhardt at the Coliseum. By Wednesday 4 October, Joe had sized up the greatest city on earth, "there is no authentic news in London re. Italo-Turkish War."

France had been an object of admiration for Irish nationalists since the 1790s; the recession of Jacobinism, defeat of the Commune, and the growth of a bourgeois French Catholic culture made this relationship all the more palatable to Irish families of the Plunketts' social and financial standing. In Lyons, while heading south to embark for North Africa, Joe bought *Revelation de l'amour de Dieu* by Julian of Norwich—that is, a work of late medieval English devotion, in modern French translation. The next day, he wrote to Wilfrid Ward, editor of the misleadingly named *Dublin Review*. A confessional apologist and biographer of cardinals, Ward played a major role in the literary campaigns of the Catholic Revival in England—with Hilaire Belloc in loud support. In the middle of France, while traveling toward the world of Arabic Islam, Plunkett tentatively asserted his inherited Catholicism, albeit through indirect means. His business with Ward involved the submission of poems for the *Dublin Review*, an essentially English publication. These were not accepted.

On his first day in Algiers, Saturday, 14 October 1911, he "walked around and watched things in church," a phrase that mixes curiosity and distance. At Mass on Sunday, he heard Mgr. Bollon preach "extremely well on Faith and Reasonable Certitude." One cannot suppress the suspicion that this entry was less concerned with doctrinal precision and more with the diarist's ability to absorb a complex oral discourse in French. In Dublin, his sister Moya became concerned at their parents' casual dumping of Joe in an unknown and difficult city. Contrary to the impressions recorded in the diary, he was very unwell from the outset and "very unwelcome in the hotel as no money had been sent" to meet his ongoing expenses.[52]

Algiers was a divided city, the bulk of the population being Muslim in religion and Arabic-speaking. Two or three days were devoted to "watching the people, who are extremely dignified (except the young ones!) and fascinatingly artistic." Though he quickly took steps to learn some Arabic (three lessons a week), and visited two Arab households with his instructor (a French officer), Plunkett's attitude toward the population remained cautiously watchful. In addition to Arabic, he took lessons in Italian with Father Luigi Attard, a Maltese priest attached to the cathedral.

In a foreword to the immediately posthumous *Poems* (1916), Plunkett's sister offers unsought commentary on the Algerian interlude. She thought it possible "the queer, flamboyant and melodramatic happenings which there came his way may have coloured that part of his verse which is more unrestrained and violent than the rest, for instance some of the sonnets in 'Occulta.'"[53] As the earliest of these poems was written in November 1911, it is not clear what relationship between Algerian experience and Irish verse is posited. Other comments on Plunkett's time in North Africa will embroider on his sister's account for which there was, by implication, the tacit approval of a sister who had been with Joe in Algiers. At the outset, and in a dutiful letter home, he had mentioned exploring the city at night by tram.[54]

To a degree that the diary does not authenticate for the months spent in Dublin, Plunkett in Algiers led a life of diligent religious routine. He not only attended Mass but went to confession. He read part at least of Saint Thomas's *Summa Theologica* (16 November), and spent a great deal of time with Father Attard. By now he had been joined by Moya, and her chaperone, Mrs. Carbery, who arrived in time to celebrate his twenty-fourth birthday. An early morning duty involved his writing to MacDonagh, congratulating him on the lectureship in English at UCD, to which the older man had just been appointed. Then,

> Fr Attard came & brought us to see apartments where we took three rooms. Also out to Villa des Orangers [a clinic] at the Colonne Voirol kept by secularised nuns. Then back & arranged meals at a gambling club! A sort of private hell! But used as a restaurant !!! V. G. Wedding party in Hotel & piano all night.

The private hell may have been just a noisy establishment in which to sleep; in Victorian Dublin, however, "the hells" were disreputable clubs, places of vice and related diseases. Plunkett's letter to MacDonagh crossed in the post with one from him: the news now was of MacDonagh's imminent marriage to Muriel Gifford (1885–1917), older sister of the woman whom Plunkett will marry in Kilmainham Gaol less than five years later. The absence of reference to Grace Gifford at this moment in the diary—or anywhere in 1911—underlines the lateness of their meeting and the consequent pressure of military plotting on their relationship. Plunkett's choice of reading, on that day in Algiers when he learned of MacDonagh's intention to marry, was Bennett's *Clayhanger*, a novel of dispirited English industrial life infused with a dilute of French naturalism.

He tried smoking kif a few times—"absolutely no effect." The discovery of a local skating rink brought greater pleasure. One legend suggests that he was offered the post of manager, attractive for its uniform, but not practical for a tubercular Irishman. Odd copies of the *Irish Times* arrived, prompting a diary entry followed by a penciled challenge to the veracity of newspapers: "Seventeen Italians crucified by the Turks (or Arabs).—P. S. Perhaps." It was at this point in early December that his teacher of Arabic, Albert Stackler, brought him on tour in the Arab Quarter, the account of which is interrupted by minimal notes of confession at St Augustine's and benediction at the cathedral. The more exploratory narrative then continues, "Arab quarter very gay. Fine clothes. Curious women unveiled. Negro music (Save the mark!)"

The cramped and staccato language of pocket diaries allows for depths of ambiguity that the writer may never have intended. Were the unveiled women curious about Plunkett, or was he curious about them? Three days later, on 5 December, the venture into Arab life was pressed home:

> At 4pm Stackler came and brought us to the house of an Arab friend of his. The friend's mother was making a blanket on a hand loom. Then to friend's cousin's house where he gave us coffee, sitting on cushions on the floor. His wife also came in and had coffee and was very shy. Her silver anklets were in pawn. Fr. Attard came to see us. Benediction.

Friday of that week was the feast of the Immaculate Conception of the Blessed Virgin. The Arabic lesson went ahead as usual. After a procession at the cathedral, and benediction, Plunkett brought Father Attard back to the rooms where he and his female relatives were staying. A furious row broke out between the two men, one an Irish English speaker and the other an Italian- and Maltese-speaking priest of the French church. The topic?—"The Empire of Death (The 'British')."

The argument is no further reported in the diary. A European season of festivities is unfolding. A production of Giacomo Puccini's *La Bohème* may have gratified Father Attard's dual or triple loyalties, while Plunkett bought a three-volume *Anthologie des poètes français contemporains*, and began translating a few pieces. On the Thursday before Christmas, the Irish party visited the archbishop's house—one occasionally detects the influence of Papal Count Plunkett. His son thought it "beautiful—indeed perfect." But the absolute approval of religious arrangements is promptly undercut when a servant's injury at the dentist's hands is smothered in condescending largesse—"we gave him six relics of Martyrs." And so on, with the relentless truthfulness of diaries. "The Dec[ember] no. of the *Irish Review* came. I wrote 8 lines against Yeats."

In the course of his sojourn in Algeria, Plunkett had received (19 October) and corrected the proofs of his first book of poems. He continued to write during this period abroad. Indeed, the title piece of *The Circle and the Sword* appears to have been written on 5 December, immediately after the poet's visit to the Arab household where the shy wife's anklets were in pawn. The proofs required a lot of work.[55] MacDonagh, who was diligent in getting his friend's book into print, favored *Signs and Wonders* as a title. Joe, however, had got the notion of an image that, however, he could not draw on paper. "I don't even remember what a crusader sword is like—though indeed I think it ought to be an ancient Irish sword . . . and the circle and hilt form an Irish cross." Ideally, the design would be reproduced on the cover in gold—mother to pay.[56]

On delivery of advance copies in Algiers, Plunkett promptly posted off (20 December) a copy to Chesterton, whose address features in a list at the end of the diary. Later that day, Stackler lent him a book about Kabyle, the language of some Berber peoples in remote interior North Africa. This was probably Adolphe Hanoteau's *Essai de grammaire kabyle*, a tome of four hundred pages published locally in 1906. On Christmas Day, the Plunkett party "dressed for dinner and astounded the natives."

There is little evidence of a postcolonial sensibility in the future republican martyr. He commissioned a local Arab silversmith to make a brooch combining the ancient Egyptian crown of Osiris on the cross-pin and Celtic motifs elsewhere. The ostensible purpose was to puzzle archaeologists through a practice of cultural or ideological fabrication that will recur in his career.[57] The year ended with more precise information about MacDonagh's marriage at the University Church on Saint Stephen's Green. The diary ends with Dr. de Szendeffy's recipe for the treatment of tuberculosis—"1 cc to be injected daily for 30 days."

If the year 1911 was a strange one for Plunkett, as the final pages of the diary declare, then the diary too has its strangeness. All diaries do, when read by outsiders a century after their inscription. Although it is a far from universal rule, one is advised to pay attention to what is *not* recorded as well as what is. Of course, a vast amount of what happened in Dublin, and what happened to Plunkett, went unnoted, either because it was trivial (the weather) or because it did not interest the diarist—the census of April 1911, for example, which showed a continuing decline in the population. As a near unique item among Plunkett's papers, the 1911 diary calls for attention in this negative light. Two absences raise questions about his political awareness at this juncture. In July, George V paid a six-day visit to Dublin and its environs. According to Grace Gifford's advocate, she participated in a successful protest outside the City Hall against any granting of a Loyal Address to the new king on his arrival in Dublin.[58] Plunkett makes no reference to these, despite the protests against royalty in Ireland and the jailing of at least two protesters. It is true that, in July, he was making fewer entries in his diary than was usual, for which there may be perfectly banal explanations.

Later that summer, a long and bitter industrial dispute erupted in Wexford the resolution of which constituted a major success for James Connolly and trade unionism generally. Neither the king, against whom Plunkett will commit treason, nor Connolly, a fellow insurgent in 1916, finds a place in Plunkett's 1911 diary. The king's uncle—the Duke of Connaught—was admitted to the record of Plunkett's social life when the two of them visited the Grafton Gallery—Count Plunkett's role in gaining the invitation may be assumed. With reference to neither royal personage does the future insurrectionary mastermind display any animus five years before the Easter Rising. But neither does he record any interest in the labor side of his fellow rebel's political activities.[59] When Connolly addressed a large public meeting to greet the two protestors—members of the Socialist Party of Ireland—on their release from prison, Plunkett does not indicate any interest. Little more than a month later, he attends with evident approval the unveiling of Parnell's monument, at which the Irish parliamentary leader, John Redmond (1856–1918), spoke.

At the close of the Algiers sojourn, Joe was brought back home by his mother, in a characteristic intervention. Geraldine Plunkett Dillon's brief account of her brother's movements after Algiers records how "he had a house of his own in Donnybrook" where she looked after him for two and a half years. The cause of this segregation from the family was the persistence of tuberculosis. In a later memoir, she complained that the big house on Upper Fitzwilliam Street had comparatively few bedrooms, thus necessitating the bachelor establishment in one of the inherited properties on Marlborough Road.

Sometime early in 1912, G. N. Plunkett decided to regularize his standing as a papal count in the eyes of the secular authorities. The use of foreign titles was a delicate matter, and, while relations between the United Kingdom and the papacy had improved in the previous half century, the matter required careful application and the approval of sundry political and protocolic senior figures. Lord Aberdeen, and his even more popular wife, had presided benignly in the Vice-Regal Lodge since 1905. In April a Home Rule bill was placed before parliament by the Liberal prime minister Herbert Asquith (1852–1928) and, while we do not know the date of Plunkett's application for royal approval, the move toward a solution to the constitutional issue seems likely to have encouraged his ambition. The viceroy thought it necessary to consult cabinet members in London about the count's request, and to enquire how these matters were treated in the Indian empire. The advice that Aberdeen received, and which in turn was placed before the king, turned out to be negative—not only in Plunkett's case but in one other parallel application. By July George V had formally approved the home secretary's recommendation that "the Humble Petition of George Noble Plunkett of Upper Fitzwilliam Street" be rejected.[60]

It was a year of omens. The *Titanic*—pièce de résistance of the Belfast shipyards and, hence, of the Protestant working class in that city—had sunk in April. In June, a Sunday school outing was attacked by the Ancient Order of Hibernians. Before James Stephens published his delightful novel *The Crock of Gold*, Unionists in their many thousands signed a Solemn League and Covenant—not in ink, for the most fervent, but in their own blood—against Home Rule. Blood symbolism had made its twentieth-century debut in Irish politics, while the Plunketts reflected on an unexpected rebuff.

On their return to Fitzwilliam Street, Joe and Moya were in turn rebuffed by the countess, who chose to blame them for travel difficulties caused by her own parsimony. Their coming-home presents were simply thrown away. The impact was to be cumulative. With damaged eyesight, and a personality "all too biddable" (in Geraldine's words), Moya chose within a year or so of her Algerian adventure to enter an order of nursing sisters. Her experiences with the Saint Vincent de Paul Society during the bitter industrial disputes of 1913 reinforced her sense of vocation. Authorities of church and family took control; a Jesuit confessor redirected her to a Sacred Heart convent near London, while the countess practically embezzled her daughter's property—two large houses in Elgin Road, Dublin, and considerable additional real estate.

Behind Moya's decision to adopt the religious life lurked unpleasant experiences of family. These were not uniquely female experiences, though the girls suffered more traceably than Joe or the younger boys. In the autumn after their Algerian sojourn, Moya and Joe were involved in a violent incident arising from their mother's refusal to buy a coat for their sister Fiona:

> As she screamed and worked herself into hysterics she started hitting Moya, who was standing on the stairs, with her walking stick. Pa, hearing the racket, came out of his study, saw Moya with her hands over her head and thought that she was attacking Ma so he also began to hit Moya with his walking stick. Joe arrived in the hall to this appalling scene, took the stick from Pa and broke it over his knee. Ma took this as a personal insult and redoubled her screaming.[61]

These revelations of a profoundly dysfunctional household go a long way toward explaining why *All in the Blood* was published posthumously ninety years after Joe Plunkett's execution. They may also cast an oblique light on certain silences, notably concerning Joe's visit to Egypt, for which we have some independent testimony of W. J. Moloney. Plunkett family commemorations of its most famous son were not only obliged to conform to the protocols of republican orthodoxy, they also had to steer clear of personal contextualizing, whether of Joe himself or the household in which he had been reared.

It was only in 1912 that Geraldine succeeded in bringing her mother's aggression under control. The struggle occurred when the girl—she was twenty-one—went in search of a book. "I knocked on her bedroom door and she came out, dressed in her curious underwear." The countess began to strike out, but her daughter was now too strong and held her at arm's length until she subsided. "That was the last physical violence on any of us."[62] Causes and effects are difficult to pin down, though Geraldine's occasional remarks are acute, if awkwardly phrased.

On two occasions, she used the obscure colloquialism "brass rags" to convey her mother's temper. About the countess's outrage at her children's concern for the welfare of working people in 1913, she wrote that "she [the countess] always got an immoral excitement from fictitious vices." Before George went to Stonyhurst, he was "a funny combination of great innocence and bad temper." Explaining how she got rid of a guest who overstayed his welcome, Fiona Plunkett reportedly told the man that "he did not really exist, that she invented him and she had a bad mind."[63]

These observations could not be analyzed to produce a scientific diagnosis, though they tend to indicate severe frustrations of development (retarded maturation) in several members of the family, and at least two generations. At the age of twelve, the eldest daughter complained how terrible it was to be in the care of a forty-year-old child; before she was thirty, she crossed the Atlantic with secret messages and money for the IRB. Such an acceleration of responsibility was not universal in the family. Moya's career as a nun was frustrated by her order's shameless manipulation, and she died in Port Said, Egypt, aged thirty-nine. Fiona, whose coat prompted the final incident of maternal violence, suffered in adult life from prolonged mental illness. The innocent and bad-tempered George Plunkett was strongly (but wrongly) suspected of assassinating Kevin O'Higgins in 1927. Joe, who devised spurious jewelry uniting ancient Egypt with the Celts, was shot in 1916 for his part in events to some degree provoked by a document he forged.[64]

The wander half-year in Algeria was not the occasion of his growing up, but merely a remission from the pressures of a family life marked by intensities of neglect and demand, expectation and contempt. Mother oscillated between physical intimidation and sudden prolonged absences. After one particularly rough surgical operation on Joe's glands, she took a three-month cruise to the Canaries; he went to convalesce on semirural Firhouse Road, just southwest of Dublin. There were other remissions—notably a period (amounting almost to a year) spent with the Rafferty family when Joe's intellectual interests were taken seriously and his social existence nurtured. There were, however, other and less benign absences from home, sometimes in the care of this sister or that, sometimes with little furniture, and always with inadequate funds for a respectable growing-up.

Concerning Matisse and Other Painters "To Be Shot"

Trying to characterize the mid-Victorian Edinburgh into which James Connolly was born, one biographer had recourse to fiction, even science fiction. The nobility of Old Town lived in obvious elevation, while artisans almost like Morlocks were condemned to dwell below. Elsewhere in the United Kingdom the class system was less openly stratified. Indeed, by the 1880s its complexities required more than a picturesque approximation at feudal or geological analogies. The middle class worked subtly at a moral *embourgeoisement* of all who differed, taming raffish earls and restless proles with equal hypocrisy. To facilitate these accommodations, the early growth of mass culture propagated myths of individual promotion through, for example, Oscar Wilde's "purple of commerce." Refinement was the poisonous mercury that turned plate glass into looking glass. Behind the looking glass, as Lewis Carroll had presciently noted, the very playing cards took up arms.

Popular literacy, machine-generated images, penny dreadfuls—the late-Victorian United Kingdom never rested in its vast production of print material. While individual magazines were aimed at niche markets, a broad incorporativist drive impelled rivals and dissidents toward the same goal. The Dublin household where Count Plunkett strove to hitch his papal title to the imperial cause subscribed to the *Illustrated London News* and similar periodicals. Irish nationalism of a certain social class aimed at maintaining the class element, the epitome of which was the "the Party" at Westminster, with

Home Rule as its objective. The literary movement led by Yeats despised this hare-and-hound maneuver, while maintaining its own duplicitous rhetoric of Celtic revivalism. By the early years of the twentieth century, an emergent generation was tiring of slogans that promised even less than their authors had achieved.

A young man, still unsure what a different world would be like, what a different life would be like, what something quite different from unsteady life would be—Joe began independent experiments in printing which, exceedingly small in scale, offered a possible alternative to the commercial outlets used for *The Circle and the Sword*. A remote influence was William Morris (1834–1896), for whom the private press offered a reconciliation of design with technology. More locally, Yeats had founded the Cuala Press in 1908, with the additional objective of controlling limited publication of his own work.

The evidence for Plunkett's experiment is slight, poignantly so. Two single small sheets of printed matter, dating from 1912 and early 1913, indicate divergent tendencies in his thought at this time—the political and the literary. Neither carries matter of any consequence and, to be fair to Plunkett, it cannot be shown conclusively that he set the type for one or both, though the Columba Press imprint is present in each case. The earlier of the two, simply dated 1912, is a flyer advertising a proposed poetry magazine or series of discretely printed poems by Joseph Campbell (1879–1944), Nancy Maude (Mrs. Campbell), An Claideam [*sic*] beo, Caitria [*sic*] Nic Cormaic, Thomas MacDonagh, W. E. Grady, Dionysius [*sic*] O ffłahertie [*sic*], Lucas Mor, Joseph Plunkett, and others unnamed. The publication, to be called *The Rann*, never came to fruition, and its original source of energy may have been Campbell rather than Joe Plunkett, or may have been Plunkett aspiring to impress Campbell. Yet whoever set the type for this modest exercise in advance publicity had only a smattering of the black art.[65] Some of these authorial names are bogus, in keeping with Plunkett's commitment to writing nonsense verse, anagrams, and other spoofs.

"The Donnybrook News" (Monday, 3 March 1913) is riddled with typographical error, and amateurishly designed. Its seven paragraphs amount to less than a hundred words, on topics ranging from Mexican disturbances to an abandoned cheetah in the quiet suburb of Rathmines. These trial pieces should probably be recognized as practice work for a typesetter, who may by this date have been Joe Plunkett (owner of the press) or some associate (Colm Ó Lochlainn, for example) with an interest in printing. Nevertheless, the content is not devoid of interest. If the release from prison of a man named (Patrick) Arkins is noted without further comment, a longer paragraph, headed boldly "THE WAR," proceeds to interpret "a Constantinople canard" in a slyly pro-German fashion. The local events implied were two Balkan wars that, in retrospect, are acknowledged preludes to the four-year carnage of 1914–1918. John Buchan's espionage novels, most notably *Greenmantle* of 1915, arise from this exotic *embroglio* on the crumbing edge of the Ottoman Empire. Perhaps the "canard" referred to by Plunkett might be traced back to an earlier and Irish-born Reuters man other than Buchan. William Moloney had worked in Cairo on Blunt's anti-imperialist *Egyptian Standard.* The notion that Plunkett too had been in Cairo has some currency in amateur websites but features also in Charles Townshend's authoritative military history of the insurrection: which came first is difficult to tell.[66] The Limerick man was now practicing a more conventional journalism in the Near East. Predictions of war, anonymous settling of a personal score, and whimsical humor all suggest Plunkett as the onlie begetter. "The Donnybrook News" doubles up as a mini-tabloid middle-class parish bulletin for noncirculation and as insurgent news from a monstrous Donnybrook Fair soon to burst on Europe.[67]

Joe Plunkett embarked on numerous critical essays and reviews, principally relating to contemporary Irish writing, Bernard Shaw (1856–1950) to G. W. Russell (1867–1935). Little of this reached completion. His approach to paper was often incisive; equally often it was indecisive. He read a good deal of fiction, non-Irish for the greater part, but preferred to discuss poetry. If his personal collection of books ever came to light, it's likely that pithy marginalia might be recovered. Of the nonliterary arts he took little recorded notice. Music seems to have left him cold. The great debate in Dublin about Sir Hugh Lane's collection of French paintings did not impinge. His father's activities as an art historian inevitably gave the youth a vocabulary and a checklist of great masters, all dead. Trekking round the galleries of Italy in 1911 did not prove inspiring. Plunkett found classicism as unrewarding as the revolution in culture getting under way in Paris.

The United Arts Club is now located a hundred yards from No. 26 Upper Fitzwilliam Street, but in 1911 its premises were at No. 44 St Stephens

Green. Mimi Plunkett enrolled for classes, only to have her mother sabotage yet another effort toward self-expression and independence.[68] With the count now directing affairs in a section of the museum, an exhibition of post-impressionist painting could not be totally ignored. Things were happening in France. Sometime during its three-week showing, in January-February 1911, Joe inspected the work, writing his name neatly at the top of the catalog. Inside, he recorded his reactions tersely. There was some conventional approval of drawing technique, and occasionally the generous bourgeois added "not bad" against a work of the heart. Harsher criticism was applied in certain cases. Maurice de Vlaminck (1876–1958) was an idiot, but Pablo Picasso (1881–1973) was an idiot who "can't do anything." Coming to Jules Flandin (1871–1947), the criticism became more practical—"to be shot." The same verdict dispatched Matisse (1869–1954) and Van Gogh (1853–1890), better-known victims.[69]

None of this is to be taken seriously, or is it? Joe was a social member of the club, and the exhibition was its first serious undertaking on behalf of the arts. The local organizer was Mrs. Ellie Duncan (1850–1939), aided almost certainly by Roger Fry from London. She had taken an independent, not uncritical view of Synge's *Playboy* in 1909. The Arts Club exhibition certainly went far beyond what limited tolerance of modernism Joe Plunkett could muster. The view of *Irish Freedom*, a decidedly "advanced" journal of nationalist opinion, was comparatively approving.[70] Nevertheless, Mrs. Duncan took the precaution of sending a defense of the exhibition to *The Irish Review*, "aware that many people in Dublin, especially the painter-critics, regard these men as charlatans and poseurs; and look upon critics like [her] self as timid souls, afraid to condemn what they do not understand."[71]

Two years later, Dublin witnessed another contest of public opinion when Lane offered to give his collection of paintings to the city on condition that a suitable gallery was built to house them. Yeats, in his battle with the philistines, detected the hostility of an elder Plunkett but could never decide whether George Noble or George Tindall was the more likely antagonist. Certainly, the count disliked Yeats, whom he had met on various occasions. The first Hugh Lane controversy, in which Dublin opinion thought poorly of French impressionists like Renoir, does not appear to have excited a response among the younger Plunketts. By then, Joe was absorbed in the finer implications of labor militancy.

The Little Wars of Chesterton and Wells

If one were to imagine a force field in which Plunkett could find stability and motion, its pole stars might be Georges Sorel (1847–1922) and H. G. Wells (1866–1946); or, French radical politics and English literary fantasy. These are not figures with whom he can be shown to have had any direct contact or even extended indirect contact. What the two share, and in doing so cast a spotlight on Plunkett's emerging idées fixes, is a preoccupation with self-canceling transition. For the theoretician of syndicalism, the most important transition will lead from Left to Right, while denying the distinction; for the novelist, it will take the form of repeated narrative devices—time machines, centuries-long sleep, etc.—in which the future (very occasionally the past) enters into the apprehended and apprehensive present, without transitional arrangements. Objects, which are usually held at a safe and respectable distance from each other, vie each for total domination in what yet remains total congruence.

The French poet Charles Péguy (1873–1914) provided an example of this mode of thought in terms peculiarly suggestive of Easter 1916, when he declared (in April 1913)—"La République, une et indivisible, c'est notre royaume de France."[72] At a banal level of resemblance, some of the Irish republicans three years later will debate the advisability of inviting a German prince to head up the new state they well know cannot emerge from their endeavors. The Republic does not exclude hereditary or aristocratic innovations, but neither does it exist. At a more philosophical and yet subjective level, Péguy suggests a transition-between (by declaring an identity of) the third-personal ethical realm of guaranteed rights for all and a possessed protective "our kingdom" in which the universality, remoteness, and impersonality of Enlightenment republicanism has become a named and gendered subject, La France.

The Plunketts did not reason abstractly, nor did they intuit sensitively. Péguy, whom no party could claim as its own, was a cut above their buttermilk. They were at heart straightforward, even blunt, in practicing comfortable reasonableness. A reason given in retrospect for taking *The Illustrated London News* was its weekly article by Chesterton. The middle-brow often defined their horizons, while at the same time giving rein to prancing fantasy. According to Geraldine Plunkett Dillon, "Joe frequently used Chesterton's and [Hilaire] Belloc's novels to illustrate the mistakes people made in interpreting political news."[73] At the time, Irish fiction may not have been the distinguished thing achieved by Joyce, but it could boast George Moore, Patrick Sheehan, and a few shrewd others. Sheehan was a canon of the Catholic Church, whose literary interests related to German rather than English or French authors.

Plunkett's fondness for Chesterton's novels is the best authenticated detail of his taste in literature, Irish or otherwise. By mid-1911, he had read *The Man Who Was Thursday* (1908) at least four times, a circumstance prompting closer attention than perhaps the book deserves. The plot revolves round a council of anarchists who aim to destroy organized civilization: seven in number, they use the days of the week as a name code for their identities. One of them (Friday, or the decrepit and near-senile Professor de Worms) displays extraordinary talents in following Gabriel Syme, a police agent who has infiltrated the council disguised as Thursday. This accomplishment is so against the evidence that the narrative deliberately observes—"unless the philosophical entities called time and space have no vestige even of a practical existence," then the "infernal cripple" has chased an omnibus and climbed on board.[74] The philosophical idiom is maintained in a breathless dialogue between Thursday and Friday, when Syme denies that he is a police detective and de Worms suddenly claims to be one. Petrified in his dilemma, Syme expostulates:

> Perhaps I misunderstood the delicacies of your German philosophy. Perhaps policeman is a relative term. In an evolutionary sense, sir, the ape fades so gradually into the policeman, that I myself can never detect the shade. The monkey is only the policeman that may be. Perhaps a maiden lady on Clapham Common is only the policeman that might have been. I don't mind being anything in German thought.[75]

These are amusing passages in Chesterton's novel, but they are insufficient to establish it as a philosophic work. On the contrary, they merely reveal its preoccupation with debates—about evolution, notably—which have effectively been won and lost a decade or more earlier. Similarly, the political threat with which the novel is obsessed is that of international anarchism, distinctly a phenomenon of the 1880s and 1890s, though popular discussion maintained the currency of anarchism in the next century when newer forces were at work. A deeper fictional study of these prewar anxieties occurs in novels by Joseph Conrad (1857–1924), especially *The Secret Agent* (1907) and *Under Western Eyes* (1911), whom Plunkett ignored.

Repeatedly, Chesterton specifies dynamite as the weapon of anarchism, a new material invented by Alfred Nobel in 1866, and exploited by a wave of Irish nationalist would-be assassins in the 1880s, including Thomas Clarke. A regular police constable in *The Man Who Was Thursday* advises that the anarchy of the Seven should not be confused with "those chance dynamite outbreaks from Russia or from Ireland, which are really the outbreaks of oppressed, if mistaken men. This is a vast philosophic movement [whose object is] to abolish God."[76] Between the local or ludicrous and the ponderously universal, Chesterton flicks the shuttlecock of paradox, in a manner highly flattering to spectators. Foreigners are generally suspect, Jews more specifically so. But pious subjects of the czar and good Irish Catholics may be trusted to save God from abolition. Five years after his fourth reading of the novel, Plunkett will sit in another Council of Seven, committed to the abolition of British rule in Ireland. The philosophical auspices under which the Easter Rising takes place are no more exact than those animating *The Man Who Was Thursday*. They will draw, however, on debates about the transition from nineteenth-century anxieties, about Bergson and the once accepted "entities of time and space," and about German *Kultur*.

According to his sister Geraldine, "Joe always used books to illustrate his arguments and in Mick's [i.e., Michael Collins's] case he used *The Man Who Was Thursday* to broaden his views of the use of the IRB and conspiracy in general." This is a—presumably unintentional—equation of the IRB with an anarchist plot to abolish God. More convincing is Mrs. Plunkett Dillon's noting that, when her brother was young, he "liked the fantastic side of the story but as time went on there was no longer any need for fantasy; the reality was fantastic enough."[77] There was a strong, and certainly much reiterated, sense that life in Ireland persisted under a species of constitutional fantasy after August 1914, even after the Unionist importation of arms in April 1914. It served the cause of dedicated separatists to stress this nightmarish quality, blaming London for a breach of faith on the issue of Home Rule. But a profound, if for the moment pacified, social unrest had been in place ever since the autumn of 1913, especially in Dublin. Measured from the earlier date, unrest was not exclusively nationalist or anti-British. Indeed, at the time of the Lockout, workers' families had received—gratefully—much support from the other side of the Irish Sea. Larkinism, as the labor cause was branded in the press, was often equated with godless international socialism. As time passed, and the national animus grew under provocation from Ulster, southern Irish discontent changed in degree, if not fundamentally in character. The covertly emergent Military Council (of which Plunkett would become a member) was less and less vulnerable to any accusation of a desire to abolish God, despite the hostility of the Catholic hierarchy toward republicanism. In the end, the insurgent proclamation began, "In the Name of God."

Chesterton's categories become blurred as the Irish reality is more and more taken as near-fantasy. Or, to put it in a different idiom, the apparently irreconcilable divisions gradually pervade each other, like water permeating concrete, and concrete leaching into water. The fictional police and anarchists always had one thing in common, a determination to defeat the enemy. The Irish conspiracy mimics the hermetic secrecy of Privy Council, Cabinet, and Unionist collusion with the army. The much-celebrated consciousness of inevitable defeat, associated with Pearse and his coconspirators, might be read as an inadmissible identification with the foe—a complex, never-to-be-voiced anxiety arising from the English or otherwise alien origins and associations of the leading conspirators—the Pearse brothers' English father, MacDonagh's Unitarian mother, Plunkett's Stonyhurst education, De Valera's Spanish-American father, Connolly's Scottish birth, even the old Fenian Tom Clarke's birth on the Isle of Wight. Or, in less ad hominem terms, their determined hopelessness arose from conflictual desire for the enemy-brother. The Fenian hero John O'Leary (1830–1907) is attributed with observing, against his own "race," that the English are better than we are, but we can't be English. For later Fenian would-be heroes, the underlying fear whispered that "we" might by one process or another become fully English.

Plunkett cannot have been unaware of the coincidence of number in the Military Council of 1916 and the anarchist council of *The Man Who Was Thursday*, and indeed another septemvirate in MacDonagh's play. A characteristic of Chesterton's villains was a defect in the physiognomy or gestural repertoire of each man. Among the IRB conspirators, a curious similarity underscored the coincidence: Pearse had a squint, MacDermott was lame, Plunkett himself tubercular, and Clarke (who had spent eighteen harsh years in jail) was prematurely frail (like the soi-disant Friday). In a practical sense, this meant nothing, but it informed Plunkett's awareness of his enterprise. Though he turned to it less often, Chesterton's other novel of the period was equally suggestive. *The Napoleon of Notting Hill* (1904) combines an interest in aggressive individualism with a canny knowledge of urban guerrilla warfare. Had Plunkett read it four or more times, Chesterton's influence on the military tactics of the IRB might have been better. An editor in the 1990s reflected that the novel could "still be admired by today's Irish rebels."[78]

Chesterton was no empire loyalist or champion of an English mission to civilize the world. At a time when it was a deeply unpopular position, he supported the Boers (as Michael Davitt and many Irish leaders did also). He believed in small nations, but most ardently he believed in Little England, its traditions and folkways (however bogus). The neomedievalism underpinning this political credo demanded not only religious belief but religious uniformity, together with a class system in which everyone was content with his place, whether he knew it or not. *She* did not count. "The brute powers of modernity" are fatal to all distinction, and only a magnificent contempt for rational explanation offers any hope of survival. Early in *The Napoleon*, Chesterton summarized this view in a parable:

> In a hollow in the grey-green rainy hills of Ireland, lives an old, old woman, whose uncle was always at Cambridge at the Boat Race. But in her grey-green hollows, she knew nothing of this: she didn't know that there was a Boat Race. Also she didn't know that she had an uncle. She had heard of nobody at all, except of George the First, of whom she had heard (I know not why), and in whose historical memory she put her simple trust. And by and by, in God's good time, it was discovered that this uncle of hers was not really her uncle, and they came and told her so. She smiled through her tears, and said only, "Virtue is its own reward."[79]

Plunkett's appetite for such fantasy might be read as a discreetly suppressed revulsion against anti-Irish prejudice, a willed tolerance of the half-recognized enemy, a sweet-and-sour enemy. By good fortune, in the Chestertonian futuristic world of 1984, a hero arises who will assault the "horrible silence of modernity" more thoroughly than any sub-Yeatsian little old woman or Field Day philosopher. The task is to be accomplished with a painted shield and "the purchase of a doubtful sixteenth-century sword for an exaggerated price." (Plunkett bought two swords in New York.) The description of Adam Wayne, a sword-waving prophet of this past, rewrites the anti-Irish parable, for it anticipates the Cuchulain of Pearse's *Claidheamh Soluis*—"the red raiment of his office flapping round him like the red wings of an archangel."[80]

Despite all this harrumphing medievalism, Chestertonian ideas had immediate aims and enemies. Though the novelist is the more familiar bearer of the name, his brother was busy as a political journalist, having joined *The Eye Witness* as assistant editor. Nationalistic, aggressive, given to hyperbole, Cecil (1879–1918) became embroiled in the Marconi Scandal of 1912 when he was sued for libel by Godfrey Isaacs.[81] In the words of Belloc's biographer, the younger Chesterton was "spittingly, uncontrollably anti-semitic."[82] The Chester-Belloc, a Shavian invention, had collaborated on *The Party System* (1911), denouncing the corruption prevalent under the Westminster model. Similar concerns about the morality of the Irish Party were expressed in more "advanced" nationalist circles; disillusion with parliaments, and democracy in general, formed a backcloth against which the rhetoric of Belloc, Carson, the Chestertons, Connolly, and Pearse boomed loudly. The European post-war crisis provided an ideal platform for renewal of the diagnosis, especially in Carl Schmitt's *Die geistesgeschichtliche Lage des heutigen Parlamentarismus* (Berlin, 1923).

Plunkett's skittish humor and piety reflect something of the elder Chesterton's influence. His concern was not just literary. On 15 January 1915, he wrote to his hero's wife:

> Dear Mrs Chesterton,
>
> I was very sorry indeed to hear that Mr Chesterton is ill. I hope he will soon be well again.
>
> There are many people in Dublin who love Mr Chesterton's work, and some of them I know are praying for him.
>
> All the members of our family desire me to send their best wishes to you and to Mr Chesterton.
>
> I am, dear Mrs Chesterton,

Yours very sincerely,

Joseph Plunkett[83]

With five Chestertons in as many sentences, the letter sustained deference to a fault, though its twenty-seven-year-old author was a senior officer in the Irish Volunteers and the director of a theater company. Like his submission to *The Eye Witness* four years earlier, it was a once-off approach. Indeed there is no evidence that Plunkett had any contact whatever with G. K. C., the author of those much-read novels. His confidence did not adopt an outward-going pose; he flourished in hide-and-seek conditions, whether behind an editor's desk or in clandestine military planning.

When the MacDonaghs' first child was born in December 1912, Joe Plunkett suffered a diminution in his small circle of visitable friends. Their house on Oakley Road, Ranelagh, faced Pearse's former school premises in Cullenswood House, but the arrival of baby Donagh MacDonagh gave an additional focus to Thomas's life. On the far side of Ranelagh, Joe often found that his illness confined him to the always-temporary home he shared with his sister Geraldine. During the next few months, a giant of contemporary English letters, H. G. Wells published a short book called *Little Wars* to explain the rules of an elaborate game designed by the author himself. Joe acquired this latest fad and laid out a room in No. 17 Marlborough Road, covering the floor with toy soldiers and other paraphernalia of pretense. For comrades in arms, he recruited his brother George, the future printer Colm Ó Lochlainn, Theo McWeeney (son of a polyglot microbiologist), and anyone else willing to play.

Thousands of spare bedrooms across the United Kingdom were dedicated to the same pursuit, such was Wells's popularity as the author of *The Time Machine* (1895) and *The War of the Worlds* (1898)—Winston Churchill was an avid fan. *Little Wars* not only upgraded children's play to the level of instruction, it applied literary gymnastics to the concealment of adult suffering—"Occasionally men came into contact, with remarkable results." Its author nevertheless prided himself on facing unpalatable facts: "I see no inconsistency in deploring the practice [of war] while perfecting the method."[84] Though it paid no great attention to defense as a tactic or strategy, *Little Wars* listed the Defensive Game among major variants of the enterprise, even when the defenders had only two-thirds of the manpower available to the aggressor.

But Wells was not only a writer of science fiction; *Tono-Bungay* (1909) described the moral dissolution of English society in a way comparable (said the author) to Balzac's brilliant treatment of postrevolutionary France. Baden-Powell's Boy Scout movement in Britain, followed in Ireland by Bulmer Hobson's Fianna (1903), represented outdoor equivalents in field training. Hobson's success in translating play into reality came years after the foundation of his first youth movement: the Howth gunrunning (July 1914) was organized by him, with the boat commanded by Erskine Childers using skills displayed in his derring-do novel *The Riddle of the Sands* (1903). Plunkett's war games were confined to indoors, though his sister held that he learned much about tactics and strategy from Wells's book. "It led him to look at historical battles and so on, all of which he used when he made the plans for the Rising."[85] Joe's game-play began shortly after the Third Home Rule Bill had been passed by the House of Commons and defeated in the Lords (January 1913). His articles on Irish battles of the past appeared anonymously in the Irish Volunteers' newspaper.

Little Wars made no allusion to Ireland, and its utility for training would-be insurgents was severely limited, being based on presumptions of equal power and resources on each side of the game. Wells did however acknowledge the advice of a professional soldier, Mark Sykes, who had served as parliamentary secretary to George Wyndham (1863–1913), man of letters and chief secretary for Ireland from late 1900 to 1905. Sykes, though a full-blooded imperialist, later encouraged both Arab nationalism and Zionism as forces to replace the crumbling Ottoman Empire in its buffer role between greater powers. Plunkett's fascination with the game compensated for his noninvolvement (on medical grounds) in Stonyhurst's Officers' Cadet Corps, while also serving to introduce Thomas MacDonagh to thoughts of modern warfare.

Joe Plunkett's mixture of dogged conservatism in critical judgement and neoconservative brio in literary composition owes much to Chesterton's example. Perhaps the most striking implementation of this debt to the English author occurred in September 1914. The occasion was a Dublin recruiting rally at which Herbert Asquith was due to speak. Connolly's Irish Citizen Army had vowed to prevent the meeting, and the authorities had moved in reinforcements. To break the blockade, Joe Plunkett gave his brother George an envelope addressed to the prime minister. "Letter for Mr Asquith, letter for Mr Asquith," the youngster cried out as he moved among the sentries on Dawson Street, before finally reaching the Mansion House with his message. "What was in it was a quotation from G. K. Chesterton, 'Your beauty has not left me untouched' and it was signed 'Little Snowdrop.'"[86]

For Geraldine Plunkett Dillon, writing from the safety of an independent Ireland, the incident vividly encapsulated her brother's impish humor. The quotation has its exact source, even if someone (Joe or Geraldine) got the phrase somewhat wrong. In a late chapter of *The Man Who Was Thursday*, the president of the anarchists is escaping from his pursuers in London, first by elephant, then by balloon. The third of three teasing notes, which he deliberately drops, reads, "Your beauty has not left me indifferent [*sic*]," and is signed in the manner borne by George Plunkett to Herbert Asquith.[87] Die-hard Freudians might linger over the tactile substitution of *untouched* for *indifferent*, wondering what if anything it might contribute to an analysis of Joe Plunkett's puzzling evidences of sexuality—gorgeous rings, undelivered love-letters, unconsummatable marriage on the eve of execution. But Chesterton's conspiracy of bomb-makers does not require psychologizing as a prelude to its Irish reading in 1914. Early in February, a visitor to No. 17 Marlborough Road delivered to Joe and Geraldine Plunkett two Gladstone bags filled with gelignite and rifle ammunition. The bullets were subsequently moved by Jack Plunkett and Eamon de Valera, while the low-strength explosive was stored first with Joe's motorbike, and buried much later in the garden of another Plunkett house on Belgrave Square.[88] Geraldine's future husband, the chemist Thomas Dillon, manufactured better stuff for the Rising.

The Industrial Peace Committee

Quite when Plunkett achieved the name of action is a question open on two sides—Do we know enough of his life to provide a biographical answer, and How should action be defined? Conventionally, the Lockout of autumn 1913 is considered the moment when he entered the world of politics and conflict. The Dublin workers' cause in late 1913 exposed the raw violence upon which the amenities of civil society were built. The city's tramlines served the better outlying suburbs, not the congested working-class districts. Choosing to organize a transport union, Larkin and Connolly were not only intervening in crucial industrial sectors like the docks, but also into the daily routine of Pa Plunkett, his fellow professionals, and their lesser types in business and commerce.

Support for the Union came from Yeats, G. W. Russell, the painter William Orpen (1878–1931), and dozens of others with little or no commitment to a social philosophy of the kind voiced by Larkin and Connolly. The workers' cause attracted the practical sympathy of young Giffords and Plunketts partly at least because it provided an alibi in their uneasy examination of inheritance, status, and morality. In this wider sense, the suggestion that Joe Plunkett rebounded from an unresponsive Columba to a needy good cause is no merely crass juxtaposing of the personal and the political. His engagement in an Industrial Peace Committee organized by Thomas Kettle deserves credit, though Geraldine Plunkett Dillon's memoir has surprising little to add. Here, the classification of Joe's feelings as "quite unreal" deserves closer attention than it can now attract, a hundred years after his death. For, if his love for Columba was more a matter of conscious, deliberate commitment rather than passion, then the dynamics of his rebound would be less than massive.

The conflict between the Transport Union and the Employers' Federation had persuaded a sizable number of Dublin citizens to constitute themselves as a mediating body, the Industrial Peace Committee. Through the Young Ireland branch of the United Irish League, which in turn was an organizational network for the Irish Parliamentary Party at Westminster, Plunkett was invited by his future brother-in-law Thomas Dillon to act as assistant secretary to the Peace Committee.[89] Dillon was, or became, a sworn member of the secret IRB, effective sponsors of the 1916 insurrection.

Information about the short-lived Peace Committee is scarce. Its principal convener was Thomas Kettle (1880–1916), professor of national economics at UCD, and sometime member of Parliament (MP) for East Tyrone. A series of articles that he published in the *Freeman's Journal* during September concluded by proposing a peace committee.[90] In the November issue of *The Irish Review*, he published a lengthy article describing "The Agony of Dublin," but, by then, the struggle was turning decisively against the workers. The correspondents' column of the *Irish Times* from 6 October onward provides a better guide to who was acting as press officer for the committee. On that date, Dillon published a letter announcing the postponement of a public meeting and its substitution by a private meeting of members. Who were the members? Given the brevity of its existence, and the urgency with which it belatedly recognized the need for action, it is unlikely that formal membership was a factor. Letters to the newspapers were signed variously by Dillon (6 October); Kettle, Dillon, and Plunkett (9 October); Conal O'Riordan (23 October); and R. M. Gwynn, B. J. Collingwood, and Conal O'Riordan (15 November).[91]

The last three deserve some identification. Robin Gwynn (1877–1962) was a TCD lecturer in divinity who, in 1912, had been active in a college mission to working-class Belfast, and so was recently familiar with social conditions in the two main cities of Ireland. English born and Oxford educated, Benjamin Collingwood (1871–1936) had arrived at UCD in 1912 and held chairs in physiology and mathematics; he was a talented soccer player. O'Riordan (1874–1948) was a novelist, playwright, and a friend of Wilfred Owen. However, reports of public meetings held in October give a wider perspective on the Peace Committee's following. In the first, employers and workingmen were present, together with public figures including Padraic Colum (poet), William Crawford (briefly principal of Wesley College), David Houston (founder of *The Irish Review*), Thomas MacDonagh (poet), Sir Thomas Myles (retired surgeon), J. C. Meredith (barrister), and W. A. Sinclair (art dealer). Dillon's and Plunkett's names were also listed. With Dillon, Houston, and MacDonagh nearby, Plunkett was by no means isolated though he is not reported as contributing to the meeting. His position was shortly compromised by his mother's obstruction of efforts to move children out of the crisis zone to families who could feed them.

At the later meeting, speakers included the dean of Saint Patrick's Anglican cathedral, Father Aloysius of the Carmelite order, W. B. Yeats, Kettle, William Field MP, Miss Cunningham (warden of Trinity Hall), Rev. Abraham Gudanski (a Dublin rabbi), and Meredith.[92] Despite the breadth of clerical representation at these meetings, the Lockout occasionally disclosed a sectarian subplot. The Catholic publisher and vender of liturgical objects M. H. Gill dismissed George Harry Walton, an employee of nearly forty years standing, for helping to distribute breakfasts to the poor at an evangelical center in Abbey Street. Gills protested that proselytism lay behind

Walton's charity, but failed to acknowledge that an employer's might did not confer automatic rights.[93]

On the whole, the committee laid the weight of responsibility for distress in the city on the employers' shoulders. It nominated a deputation to visit the lord mayor, including Mahaffy of TCD and Kettle of UCD. However, as its powers effectively to mediate were proven to be limited, it dissolved in late November, to be replaced by a Civic Committee in which Joseph Plunkett evidently took no part. From this development the Irish Citizen Army (ICA) emerged, with Houston and Gwynn assisting in the early stages. Certainly Plunkett had no place in a working-class militia.

Viewed from within the Plunkett household, things looked different. Early in the Lockout, Joseph had brought up the topic of social hardship at the dinner table, only to be rebuked furiously by his mother. Unknown to him, and he appears to have gone to his death still ignorant of the fact, she had recently acquired slum or tenement property near the Abbey Theatre. When, through Dillon's agency, he found himself sitting at public meetings among dignitaries such as the lord mayor, high-ranking clergy, artists, and even some conscientious businessmen, domestic opinion swung round to compliment him. At the age of twenty-five, he was perhaps an apprentice to public service, but scarcely more. The countess's property transactions cut across his best efforts. In October, the *Freeman's Journal* published a photo of Sandymount Castle (former home of Yeats's Corbet ancestors), noting that she had acquired it to house 150 children in distress. To the best of her daughter's recollection "not a single striking worker's child" ever entered the Castle.[94] There was, however, one condition that Young Plunkett (as some called him) shared with working-class housing—tuberculosis.

Mild Love

Dat veniam corvis, vexat censura columbas.

—Juvenal, *Satires*, Book 2

If documentation is sparse, it does not follow that a thin linear narrative results. Given ideally sufficient material, a biographer could perhaps move instant to instant in his or her subject's life, rather like Yeats's horse, rider, and birds in "Easter 1916"—"From cloud to tumbling cloud / Minute by minute they change." But, in practice, no such full richness is possible; all lives are left bereft of this page or that illumination. And biography is not by definition a narrating of life, rather an understanding of it through literary composition, with all its overlapping experiences and its vacancies. *Enigmas* offers rather less, allowing more room for telling detail among the relics.

Take, for example, an empty brown envelope with a latter-day unsigned inscription in Biro, preserved in the National Library of Ireland. The inscription reads, "This is a letter to Columba O'Carroll from Joe Plunkett. It {wa} is obviously never intended to be sent to her."[95] Manifestly, it is not a letter, it is at best an envelope. Strictly speaking, we have no documentation of Joe's relationship with Columba, beyond a few diary entries. The envelope is empty, and even if it contained what, before accession to the library, it apparently had contained, the letter in question had apparently not been sent.

Literary love stories are rarely so paper starved as this. Keats and Fanny Brawne, Robert Browning and Elizabeth Barrett, John Synge and Molly Allgood had their obstacles to overcome, and each couple experienced some difficulty with which Plunkett became familiar. Keats, in 1819, wrote to assure his beloved that "I have two luxuries to brood over in my walks, your Loveliness and the hour of my death. O that I could have possession of them in the same minute."[96] If the sentiment of this feels grossly romantic in the wrong sense, there was nothing imaginary or misdiagnosed about the Cockney poet's tuberculosis, and nothing unrequited about his love of Fanny. Those letters remain, in all their intellectual hodgepodge of brilliance and pathos.

Plunkett's private reflective writings, as distinct from critical essays, do not amount to more than a few aphorisms. On a stray leaf almost certainly dating from late 1915, one finds the dictum, "Undoubtedly it is a grievous heresy and worthy of condemnation to hold that Woman is the origin of all evil—Man is the origin of Woman."[97] Anxious biblical scholars might trace this to Cranmer's Book of Common Prayer (1549), where, in the Prayer of Humble Access, sixteenth-century communicants read or heard, "This is a true saying, and woorthie of all men to bee received, that Jesus Christe came into thys worlde to save sinners." Echoes of the Catholic Confiteor can also be heard. More to the carnal point, the woman in question was Columba O'Carroll, daughter of an eminent Dublin physician, Catholic by denomination.

Joseph Francis O'Carroll (1856/7–1942) reached the top of his profession. A graduate of the old Royal University who had also studied briefly in Vienna, he became professor of medicine in UCD in 1912. His remit extended beyond the traditional Catholic social precincts; he also acted as consultant to Dr Steevens' Hospital, a teaching school affiliated to TCD. A nationalist in politics, a supporter of Home Rule, he would be appointed consulting physician to the British forces in Ireland at the outbreak of the Great War, retaining the position until 1918. His political investments quickly began to fall. Sinn Féin triumphed in the general election of November 1918, and the War of Independence began in January. In 1920, he was awarded a CBE by the British crown for his medico-military services, but thought it wise to refuse it.[98]

Apart from his daughters' interests, Dr. O'Carroll's world outlook had been expressed by his son Frank's decision to join up.[99] Posted to Gallipoli, he survived four days. Another son, Charles, wounded in France, was evacuated to a hospital in England, but died in action on his return. Not all disaster was actively violent. The eldest son, Joseph Berchmans Ely O'Carroll (born 1888), had departed for Canada in 1907, possibly in reaction to the accidental drowning of a younger brother, Murrogh (1899–1904); indeed, murmurs had arisen about the elder brother's responsibility for the death. Reaching New York, Joe quickly became involved in hard left-wing politics, meeting Emma Goldman, John Reed, and other red stars. The New York Police Department heavily favored the Irish in its recruitment, who loathed Italians, Jews, and anarchists without further discrimination. Another in this circle of anarcho-socialists was Charles Plunkett (1892–1981), born in New York to Catholic parents from Cork—his grandfather was a builder and property developer, like G. N. Plunkett.[100] In 1915, Dr. O'Carroll had mentioned to a colleague "a boy in America whose lungs I fear are in a bad way."[101] This was a manifest euphemism, though it is not clear whether politics or sexuality was the topic to be euphemized—Plunkett family tradition has it that Joe O'Carroll's row with his father arose from the young man's homosexuality.[102] Wild Joe O'Carroll was severely beaten by the police on several occasions, eventually withdrew to Los Angeles, where he worked on the *Times*, but maintained a fiery opposition to capitalism down to the end.[103] Since his New York days, he had been active in literary circles, published poetry (some of it supporting the Industrial Workers of the World), and mixed with Ambrose Bierce, Jack

London, and Upton Sinclair. In the mid-1920s, Wild Joe was still in touch with home, at least through his youngest sister, Blanaid Mary (born 1902).[104] He attended his father's funeral in 1942.

We know from Joe Plunkett's diaries something of his meetings with Columba O'Carroll, the whens and wheres of theater performance or trip to the countryside. The two behave in accordance with Edwardian notions of group activity, modified by the particular Irish interest in language. In September 1909, having boasted of frequent correspondence with the O'Carrolls, he wrote to his mother from a Gaelic summer school in Donegal giving an account of his progress:

> I never heard of anyone learning to speak it or understand it properly in less than two years and I've only been a few months altogether (counting Achill). Also Northern Irish is different in pronunciation and often in idiom to Munster or Connaught Irish but still I have learnt a good deal . . . I could give elementary lessons in the modh direac[h] (direct method).[105]

This, and later evidence, suggests that Plunkett had difficulty in acquiring a language the Gaelic League declared essential for de-anglicizing Ireland. Letters to his family, or to MacDonagh, might commence with a formal greeting or salutation in Gaelic, before moving into the shared tongue of the conqueror—like the standard bureaucrat of today's Dublin government. Even when he came to know the Pearse brothers, and to become acquainted with southern Connemara (and its Connacht dialect), Plunkett never adopted the ruralizing vision so prevalent in the overlap of the Irish Volunteers on to the Gaelic League. His nationalism had its roots in the soils of other and more exotic regions, not excluding the France of Rousseau and Paul Bourget.

Commencing no later than the summer of 1909, and lasting into the autumn of 1915, Plunkett's emotional commitment to Miss O'Carroll was one of the essential ingredients of his poetry. As he wrote virtually nothing in the last six months of his life, the collapse of the "affair" more or less coincides with the closure of his literary career. Poetry, especially lyric or "love" poetry, is notoriously difficult to read as documentation. Some interpretations of his work will follow in due course while, in more strictly biographical mode, one can only lament the absence of any surviving correspondence between the two young people. For external comment, there is little beyond the Plunkett family's polite observation that Joe's feelings were not reciprocated.

All in the Blood discloses that close relations with the O'Carrolls dated back to the countess's teenage years. Once she had turned sixteen, three young men seemingly proposed marriage to wealthy Patrick Cranny's youngest daughter. That would have occurred about 1874 or 1875. One of the suitors, Joseph Francis O'Carroll (1855–1942), will recur in young Plunkett's life story as Columba's stern father. In the event, Josephine married G. N. Plunkett in June 1884, though he had been in love with his second cousin for more than ten years. Through all this, the Crannys, O'Carrolls, and Plunketts remained on excellent terms as they advanced steadily upward in their chosen professions. Dr. O'Carroll was part of the increasingly Catholic social establishment, with a residence on Merrion Square (four servants) and a country house in Donegal. Behind the Georgian facade, grander than its narrow-chested Upper Fitzwilliam Street neighbor, the O'Carrolls suffered their own occasional bout of domestic turmoil even after Wild Joe had been expelled. When young Columba brought home Dudley Heathcote, her father took so deep a dislike to the suitor that he later beat her round the room with his stick. At least, that is the recollection of Geraldine Plunkett Dillon, who had some experience of parental walking aids. When Dr. O'Carroll died in 1942, F. Heathcote (grandson) stood among the mourners.

Geraldine's account of Columba is entirely sympathetic, to the point where Plunkett's conduct is exposed to serious questioning. "Joe's love for her was quite unreal . . . she needed an adult type to give her freedom from her father."[106] In August 1913, the two were in Donegal, Joe having traveled from Dublin on his motorbike for Gaelic classes at Cloughaneely. As Geraldine narrates the events of late summer, the Lockout of 1913 provided her brother with an alternative focus for his emotions, after fruitless courtship of Columba in the northwest. Sydney Gifford, sister of MacDonagh's wife and of Joe's future wife also, was one of Jim Larkin's few middle-class supporters.[107] Another sister, Nellie, became an ardent supporter of the Citizen Army. Though the trade union cause had little appeal to people of their class generally, the events of September 1913 stirred the emotions of individuals who, from different causes, rejected the ordained official view. Yeats's poem, with its mordant chorus—"Romantic Ireland's dead and gone"—represented more than its author's aesthetic distress at present vulgarities.

The Gifford family was a sadly fractured one, Catholic on one side, Protestant on the other, not an unheard-of situation. However, the twelve children were early separated both from their parents (or at least one of them) and from each other.[108] In domestic experience, the Giffords matched the Plunketts for unhappiness if not, perhaps, wealth. Circa 1910, the (elder) Giffords were Unionist, the Plunketts constitutional nationalist. Fitful commitments to an education in art classes gave access to an "alternative," mildly Bohemian, lifestyle: this was the case for Grace Gifford and her brother Gabriel, also for Philomena (Mimi) Plunkett. Emotional resources, strength as well as vulnerability, sought an adequate locus to compensate for the loss of domestic security, while the loss of this security was precisely the channel through which new emotional bonds were made possible.

Joseph Plunkett's feelings for Columba, whatever they are called, endured. The Columba Press, using a machine acquired from Thomas MacDonagh, was named in her honor, and its only quasi-book-size publication was *Sonnets for Columba* (1913), published in an edition of thirteen on the last day of '13. There were growing commitments in other areas. His mother's purchase of a complicated property at Larkfield led into the establishment of a veritable armed camp of Irish Volunteers. On at least one occasion, Miss O'Carroll traveled out to Larkfield to make it clear that Joe's attentions to her, or his expectations of her, must come to "a complete end."[109]

In September 1915, Joe Plunkett was in New York on political or military business of the same kind that brought him to Germany. Any IRB plot to bypass the Irish Volunteers' leadership would require practical support from overseas. The United States was home to the great mass of Irish emigrants, especially those who harbored active resentment against Britain. Germany was the assertive rival to Britain in Europe and on the high seas. Coordination of these potential allies with the plotters inside the Volunteer movement was essential to success at home. Earlier in the year he made his way to Berlin, heart of the *Kaiserreich*; now he was on the banks of the Manhattan.

During the same period, the countess was also in America, though on a different mission. Her concern was the beatification of Oliver Plunkett (1625–1681), an archbishop of Armagh executed for treason in connection with the "Popish Plot" of Titus Oates. Whatever degree of kinship existed between her husband's ancestors and the archbishop's was slight, and remains to be documented. The countess, however, was able to assimilate the beatification to Ireland's cause: though not a member of Cumann na mBan, she acquired a uniform to take on tour—a striking platform device to identify nationalism, a kind of feminism, and the Counter-Reformation. Mother and son took separate routes; "Joe if he saw her at all in America had no contacts with her, and told her none of his business. In any case he would not have trusted her. Her conduct was incalculable [*sic*] and she had a fatal habit of making friends with spies."[110]

At some point in the difficult and exhausting pursuit of one Irish-American chief after another, Joe Plunkett turned aside from politics to consider at length and in depth his relations with Columba O'Carroll. There is no reason to believe that she or her family was aware of his activities or sympathetic with his "advanced" position in politics. Everything we can say about her household—including Wild Joe—denies any such sympathy. Hence, the turning aside constituted a drastic, if short-lived abandonment of the official covert agenda for a private one.

When documents are described by their author as "unwritten letters," then documentation has become not just scarce but scary. The drafts of three letters survive, one dated Tuesday, 7 September 1915. A second is bylined "New York USA a week before your 22nd Birthday": Columba's birthday was 20 September (in 1893), so we can assign it to 13 September or thereabouts. A third, numbered Letter III, is undated. All are written in pencil, on paper of standard size. Together, they constitute an undelivered proclamation, the manifest subject of which changes from poetry to God, or from beauty to conventional living, while the latent theme is always Plunkett himself or, to be more abstract, the ego. Reading the letters, one has to bear constantly in mind that they were deliberately written not to be read.[111]

The first opens boldly with the remark that "In his essay on the Poet, Emerson has said: 'The man is only half himself; the other half is his expression.' The dichotomy expresses half a truth." In its mental shape, Plunkett's commentary on the text chosen to head up a letter to the Beloved retains much of the strategy employed in the early Stonyhurst days in his own defense against disciplined Jesuit instructors and very high-born fellow students. Having decided to begin a tripartite letter of courtship, he sticks to the terms of his chosen text because they conform to preoccupations that predate his first meeting with Columba.[112] His progress toward addressing the woman rather than the topic is tortuously slow and indirect, reaching something like the point with a declaration, "This is the miracle, that man expressing himself through art should mould the divine substance, and I can speak within the truth and say that Man is God's expression and poetry, life, is man's expression and you are my expression."

Were it not for the thousand or so human lives that (through common purpose) Plunkett would terminate within eight months of committing them to paper, these words might be dismissed as postjuvenile philosophizing, ignorant of real emotional experience, actual people. The equation of poetry with life as man's expression is rhetorical and slipshod, providing the writer with a skater's flourish—"you are my expression." But if this last statement is to be taken at all seriously, its recipient (or, rather, grammatical object) is reduced to the status of a product or attribute, dependent on the writer as subject. And so he moves to close down his first instalment with a neat question and answer, "Does this to you savour of blasphemy? Believe me I would not speak it profanely."[113]

In one regard, he accurately summarizes his position on art, for he rejects the familiar Romantic doctrine of creativity in favor of a theory by which the artist is the shaper, the giver of form, not the creator of art. Leaving Columba aside, one could read the first letter as an early and very brief attempt at an aesthetic theory that is fundamentally religious, and by no means original. Psychologically, however, the letter is a digression away from its purpose. The second, written some six days later, promptly remedies the defect by dating itself from "your 22nd Birthday" and by commencing with a summary of relations between the young couple. "I am not writing this letter for you to read, that would be impossible because I know we cannot go back to before the irrevocable happened." Even though the account of this crisis will never be dispatched to a reader, Plunkett never specifies (even to himself) what the irrevocable had involved. Nevertheless, "the hopelessness seems to make it easier to be clear and anyway my failure this time wont make tragedy." The first half of the sentence is refreshingly sensible or, at least, it is a plausible utterance by one situated as Joe is in New York writing to a woman with whom he has gone through a profound difference. The second half, however, assumes that the present endeavor at understanding will fail also, though not on the same hyperbolic scale.

There follows on the third sheet of the nine-sheet letter the conventional rebuke of the Beloved intended to win a concession in the amorous exchange: "Is it not six months since I left my country, home, friends and you for your sake?" Though Columba can have known nothing of it, there was an entirely different reason for Joe's leaving Ireland—the German mission to secure arms for rebellion. There had been nothing spectral or merely intentional about the roundabout journey to meet Casement in Berlin, however Chestertonian the diary record of disguises and japes and false names will seem. Was there, however, a duplicity on Plunkett's part in bringing to a head in the spring of 1915 the state of affairs between himself and Columba? Was the crisis required less to clarify relations between them but more to provide a motive or rationale for his departure from home and the Irish political scene? A tubercular poet, rejected by his light-of-love, would be a pitiable tourist in foreign parts, beyond suspicion in the eyes of Dublin Castle.

Nothing of this double life appears in the New York letter drafts, though at the moment of their composition Plunkett is enacting doubleness in his conversations with Irish-American advanced opinion, while also working up an emotional crisis on undelivered paper. To travesty Emerson, the man is half self, and the other half is his repression. "Do you think this is foolishness," he asks the Columba who will never receive the nine sheets of paper. "Perhaps it is but it is not far from divine wisdom, for I find that I am closely paraphrasing and saying in commonplace words what has already been said in poetry." A draft that had begun realistically enough has now veered round to calibrate the emotional lives of two Dubliners with divine wisdom itself. Yet the phrases that bear this awesome task are not even Plunkett's own, for he admits that he is mentally tracing the thought of another, earlier poet—Coventry Patmore (1823–1896).

The prompter of Plunkett's interest in the unctuous Victorian may have been a contemporary American writer, Joyce Kilmer, whom he met at this time. (Kilmer signed a copy of *Trees and Other Poems* for Joe on 5 October 1915.)[114] In the letter, Plunkett transcribes twenty-two lines from *The Angel in the House* (1856), a work of considerable technical accomplishment and insipid domesticity.[115] In theory, not practice, Columba is supposed to accept Joe's proposals of a closer (maybe even married) relationship on the basis of his ideas' coinciding with the laureate of sentimental, desexualized connubiality, not forgetting his earlier announcement that she was a work or product; *she was his expression*. That at least is the clearest gloss on his words. The O'Carroll household on Merrion Square was no bohemian den, where convention was trampled nightly underfoot. But its commitment to holidays in the Gaelic-speaking northwest—Mrs. O'Carroll had been born in Donegal—and on the rugged island of Achill suggests that it had at least questioned the vision of female submissiveness and emasculated language that Patmore had served up for mid-Victorian consumption.

The resemblances and contrasts in domestic style might act as metaphors in external affairs. In September 1914, the Irish Volunteers had split on the issue of John Redmond's call for Irishmen to enlist in the British forces; accordingly the Plunketts and O'Carrolls exemplified rival factions within the broad nationalist spectrum. The month before Joe Plunkett launched his hopeless attack on Columba's unmarried (or, at least, unattached) state, while conniving with John Devoy and Joseph McGarrity to import German arms, Columba's brother, Captain Frank O'Carroll (1895–1915), was killed at Gallipoli. During this week of Plunkett's renewed campaign for/against Columba, Dr. O'Carroll was citing his son Wild Joe's lungs as the cause of concern. This was not a household to be swayed by mid-Victorian English pieties repeated by a covert Irish hardliner.

Yet the argument in Plunkett's New York letters has not totally veered away from divine wisdom. His commended model, Coventry Patmore, in addition to commending marriage even for the third time, had progressed from a freethinking background through the Church of England into Catholicism. A minor literary figure in the age of Tennyson and Browning, he had his respectable popular readership. His best-known work recites how Felix courts and weds Honoria, a dean's daughter, in the course of which the progress of a deep pure love is traced through incidents of commonplace life, all leading to a mystical conclusion. *The Unknown Eros* (1877), which Plunkett also read, was a collection of odes treating the pressure of former love for a now dead woman upon present love. The treatment was discreet, even when the theme was exploratory.

After a long quotation from his admired poet, Plunkett approached these exploratory themes with a sudden directness. Fairy stories provided an initial code. The situation he and the addressee are in contains the seeds of tragedy, "the true tragedy of Beauty and the Beast, not the ancient comedy with the happy ending." Given that her brother had been killed a few weeks earlier, this realism was uncalled for. Nevertheless, responsibility in emotional matters rested with her, for

> you did not know that in order to love you had to throw yourself to the wolves—christiani ad leones—and the enchantment would be broken, or would begin. The Beast would be made a man and lovable by the power of your {will} love.

The twenty-one-year-old daughter of a successful physician was unlikely to throw herself under this definition of connubial union. The passivity of the writer's role is carefully modified when the power to transform the Beast is (after correction) specified not as the addressee's will, but her love. Despite this adjustment, he confesses that "only in my poems is there anything worthy of your love, and even the celestial glories of which I have written I seem to have obscured with my murky personality."[116]

The final letter attempts to deal with this unhelpful personality, beginning with the jaunty announcement that "I would like to incur [*sic*] your approval." It is syntactically possible to use the verb with a positively charged object, but more often what is incurred is *dis*-approval, wrath, or even punishment. While presenting himself ready to follow advice or even obey instructions, the writer has already skewed the intended process by coloring it with the verb "to incur." A joke, no doubt, but susceptible to Freud's insights (1905) on the relationship between wit and the unconscious.

More exactly, the letter begins, "He said something like this: I would like to incur your approval." In the transition from one letter in the series to the next, the first-personal pronoun is delayed, and its related subjectivity distanced, by the introduction of an otherwise unaccounted-for "he," a pro-person for whom a pro-noun must serve. Once this gatekeeper is outwitted, the reader or addressee is in touch again with the writer, Plunkett. He has asked Columba what he should do or become. Now he states plainly, "there is one thing I can't do if you refuse to specify. I cannot just 'be myself.' Nobody can be themselves. They dont. There is only one way to be oneself and that is to be nobody." Had psychotherapy reached Ireland, an average practitioner might well have diagnosed on this evidence a personality disorder.

In fact, he and she had met frequently in a social forum where one was required to be somebody else—theater. And they had ventured into another—the speaking of Gaelic—which held out the possibility of translating one's experience into a different set of terms, naturalizing it there, and creating new communities of mutual comprehension. But the final New

York letter raises neither of these issues, explores nothing like the psychology of the self. Instead, Plunkett lists a dozen or so hypothetical roles or occupations, playful substitutes for any central concerns with the ego, with expression, mutual love, and divine truth. Why not

> Soldier, Sailor, Tinker, Tailor, Playboy, Gentleman, Apothecary Theory but more wide . . . Bad Man Adventurer Softy Greenhorn Sleuth Napoleon Toots George Washington The Thin Woman's Husband Micawber Romeo Saint Francis Don Juan Robert Emmet Boss Croker Cuchullin Kaiser Bill Don Quixote The Virginian Dante Danton Tomás Sir Roger Casement Father Brown Fool.[117]

The writer lolls on his casting couch and is reviewing the options.

Deaf and highly suspicious, John Devoy, head of Clan na Gael in America, was at first outraged at the folly of sending a twenty-something, visibly tubercular secret envoy to New York. His anger was gradually assuaged, though there remained the problem of what to do with Plunkett in the weeks before his voyage home. The answer took an unexpected form—directing him toward the circle of the poet Joyce Kilmer (1886–1918) author of "Trees." Despite obvious differences—the American was fat and self-satisfied—Plunkett and Kilmer shared an admiration for Patmore; indeed Joe's inclusion of lines from *The Angel in the House* in the Unwritten Letter may have been prompted by conversation with Kilmer, who (like Patmore) had converted to Catholicism and (unlike Patmore) was busy finding his Irish ancestry. A further attraction for Joe was Kilmer's personal acquaintance with Belloc, the Chesterton brothers (Cyril and Gilbert), and the Meynell family, all of whom the American had met in 1914 during an early-wartime visit to England. What other American writers Plunkett met is difficult to establish. Devoy would have prohibited any contact with Joe O'Carroll, whose comrades attracted too much police attention. After the 1916 executions, a group of poets led by Enniskillen-born but New York–based Eleanor Rogers Cox (1865–1936) organized a commemorative event in Central Park. In September 1915, Plunkett was not yet a martyr, just the author of some letters to oblivion.[118]

These baffling, bumptious, and strangely pathetic documents are valuable for whatever light they shed on Joe Plunkett's relationship with Columba

O'Carroll. What survives is draft material, written in pencil, with occasional crossings-out and alterations. Whether it advanced further in composition cannot be stated. If later versions were dispatched to Merrion Square, no account of their reception can now be expected to emerge. Psychologically, the documentation constitutes a self-conscious avoidance of relation, even as it also rolls back into place the protective constructs that conceal the self from itself.

What happened to Columba after 1915 is another unhappy story. Nevertheless, several additional contexts frame the constantly frustrated outgoings of the New York drafts: these most obviously include Plunkett's mission to the Irish Americans and more specifically the IRB; and his relationship with a different woman, Grace Gifford. A third, less assessable, would be Joe's relationship with the Countess Plunkett.

That mother and son should travel at the same time to America, and yet pursue their separate goals by separate routes, sharply underlined a new stage in their relationship. The winter of 1911 in Algiers had been cushioned by the presence of a sister and her chaperon. Mums, always unpredictable in small things, and likely to opt for the economic priority, had nevertheless been a constant, archetypal figure in the background. Now she abandoned him again, as she had done in France during his childhood, while conducting her public campaign in misappropriated clothes. As Cumann na mBan was the (subordinate) women's wing of the Irish Volunteers, she had stolen his clothes.

Clan na Gael in America represented the purely military tradition in Irish republicanism, reaching back to the Fenians of the 1860s. Plunkett, as an emissary of the IRB element inside the Irish Volunteers, was following up the effective American contribution to the acquiring of German arms in August 1914. Clandestine, and thus in a sense doubly theatrical, the mission suited him down to the ground, despite delays and the elusiveness of coconspirators. He had a solitary role, in the long prelude and coda to which he must not "be himself." It is highly unlikely he contacted Columba's brother, Wild Joe, whose direct-action heyday had come and gone in July 1914 when his comrades plotted to assassinate one of the Rockefellers. Charles Plunkett, made of sterner stuff than Wild Joe, was writing a PhD in Columbia University and on his way to an appreciation of Joseph Stalin. He too nowhere surfaces. Arriving in Liverpool from New York on 17

October 1915, Plunkett was granted an import license under the Defence of the Realm Act permitting him to retain two swords each marked "US 1865." Beside the certificate authorizing the importation of stage props for the 1916 insurrection one finds sheets of flimsy paper mainly devoted to aphorisms, including some exonerating Woman from the charge of being the origin of evil. A more striking instance reads, "Damn the populace. There is no such thing. 29th Nov. [1915.]"[119]

Grace Gifford brought out another side to his chameleon self. In relation to the letters of September 1915, and the author's return in mid-October, one should note that Grace accepted Plunkett's proposal of marriage on 2 December, about ten weeks after the third letter to Columba had been written. Toward the end of his American mission, and certainly in the early days of his return to Dublin, his health was visibly poor, with renewed glandular swelling. According to Geraldine, Joe had to spend a good deal of time in bed, before and after Christmas 1915. For Grace's comment on a crucial moment in his and her emotional life, one has to wait till 1949—"I did not know him intimately until late in 1915."[120] Her encounter with and enchantment by Plunkett may have acted as a release from unfocused discontents. Later still, she retrospectively proclaimed herself to have been ignorant of politics. One wonders how much she knew of her precursor in his affections.

It is impossible to write Columba O'Carroll's biography inside the brief and contorted life of Plunkett. Had she accepted his overtures of early- or mid-1915, the history of Ireland—or, at least, the history of 1916—might have been very different. Against that hypothesis, the roles that Joe might have considered at her behest find little room for the uxorious paragon dear to Coventry Patmore's heart. (The inclusion of "gentleman" in a list that runs on to Bad Man, Adventurer, Softy, Greenhorn, Sleuth, does not bespeak confidence in his own position.) Columba evidently did not contemplate passing the rest of her life in the company of a Casement- or Cuchulain-clone. If the Plunkett family's summary is accepted—and it is totally plausible, as far as it goes—she simply did not reciprocate his feelings. Going further, of course, one might enquire more deeply what those feelings had been, which their direction, and what their underlying drive. An Irish John Galsworthy could have made epic fiction from the O'Carrolls and Plunkett.

Columba followed a moderately successful career as a part-time actress with the Abbey and the Dublin Drama League. For the Irish Theater in

December 1917, she played in a lesser-known play by Chekhov, *The Jubilee*, and one critic noted that she "rushed her lines a little—a pardonable fault in a beginner." Kenneth Reddin, brother of Joe Plunkett's Belvederian obituarist, thought her "too self-conscious and affected ever to be a good actress." Nevertheless, by January 1920 she and George Plunkett appeared in the same company's production of *The Cherry Orchard*, both winning the approval of newspaper critics.[121] A decade later, with the pain of two Irish wars still palpable, she had left her home country to acquire more durable qualifications. Having abandoned medical studies at UCD, she took up professional life late-ish, in the early 1930s, when she qualified in England as a doctor. In 1935, she married the botanist Evan Rhuvon Guest (1902–1992), and migrated to Malaya and Iraq.[122] Their marriage ended in divorce in 1952, through no fault of hers, it would seem. William Feeney alludes to her "later, unhappy life." In 1942, she had returned to Dublin during its "Emergency" to attend her father's funeral. Joe Plunkett's brothers were still waiting for German arms. As Juvenal's translator put it, "Censure acquits the raven, but pursues the dove."

Notebook and Friend

The inevitable incompleteness of biography is represented by the documents upon which it is based. The same tension—it is not a contradiction—is at work in representational politics also, affecting the democratic processes. In the case of Joseph Plunkett, the two areas overlap vacantly. That is to say, the absence of surviving documentation in the personal sphere is replicated very exactly in the suppression, post hoc or a priori, of verifiable evidence that might illuminate the military and political engagements leading to his death. Padraic Colum observed that Plunkett's joining the Irish Volunteers provided him with the first human community in which he could be himself. But, while the benefits of day-to-day enjoyment of life through possessing a sense of purpose should not be discounted, the achievement was also its own cancellation. Or, to be more exact, the code of dedication to a project based on a sacrificial logic required the subordination of that potential self. No doubt, scores of other young Irishmen found membership of the Volunteers fulfilling at a profound level, but their prior experience had been less devastating that Joe's. And their dedication was not part-possessed by an ideology of martyrdom, even if they (or a high proportion of them) were prepared to fight to the death, if necessary.

There survives among papers preserved by Honor O Brolchain a notebook internally datable to early 1912, and associated with Algiers. On first inspection, it appears to be a straightforward chronological record of literary compositions, beginning with an amusing six-page satirical poem about Yeats, "Weary Willie." However, folios 16 and 19 are explicitly dated "Jan 27th 1912" and "22nd Jan 1912" respectively, indicating that the notebook is a near-fair copy of poems composed or at least commenced earlier and now annotated with dates and other details drawn either from memory or from other documents. A list on folio 36 includes a poem occurring on a later folio. Finally, and most intriguingly the last folio is elegantly inscribed in Gaelic uncial, "REMFOCUL," that is, foreword.

Thus the notebook itself is more a considered than spontaneous work, being a composition in itself. For example, we know from Plunkett's diary for the previous year that the December issue of *The Irish Review* provoked him to write "8 lines against Yeats." The offense was apparently given by a short poem, then called "On those who Dislike the Playboy." In the notebook, the response includes seventy-five lines of exceedingly free, but witty verse. However slight or superficial in its literary context, "Weary Willie" provides access to Plunkett's attitude toward two of Ireland's literary giants, one poignantly dead, the other formidably active. In the modern phrase, Plunkett is "not best pleased." Yeats is his official target, but to assess whether or not Synge is also a foe or antagonist, one has to examine the remainder of the notebook and to take into account its being apparently composed in Algiers. That the retrospective writing up of the material took place before he left Africa for home can be assumed with a high degree of confidence—brief Arabic inscriptions occur here and there, on the covers and on individual pages. Synge too had his orientalist side, nurtured in part by his reading in French literature and his endeavor to cast the inhabitants of Aran and the West of Ireland into a late-primitivist frame deriving from anthropological research outside Europe.

"Weary Willie" is followed by two sonnets and a poem presented as a translation from Arabic. Other sonnets are found later in the notebook, but the material up to folio 18 is initially unified by the theme of unrequited or unfortunate love, sometimes mediated through an Arabic "original" and, on one occasion, even incorporating the Gaelic word *críoc* (finish) to indicate the end of the poem. There follows a prose fable decidedly limp in its moral conclusion, another poem, and a list of characters for a play (21) either projected or playfully toyed with for the moment.

Three original names of characters, from the play or some other project—Michael, Raphael, and Gabriel—have been crossed out, and replaced by nonangelic ones, Baron, Glaswen(?), and Ross. Other participants include Surgeon Toady, Laird Skirlpipes of Gaberdine, and Sir Careless Crammerin, who seems to have been Past Great Fetich and President of the Fatti-Dejeunerats. The only females mentioned are Lady Darnit and Lady Shadow. The first half of the 1912 notebook emerges as a further exercise in Plunkett's characteristic oscillation between high and low registers, the vatic and the vulgar.

The next folio resembles a basic exercise in Gaelic, being a list of the names of the days—*Dia Luain* (Monday), and so on—in their adverbial form. The first word in these names (*Dia*) appears above the list of seven, perhaps to show that, on its own, it is the Gaelic noun meaning God (though it is also a derivative of Latin *dies*). The notebook continues to bear some inscriptions suggesting that these entries were made in Algiers. The verso of folio 22 carries very little—a few words in what appears to be a compound linguistic or orthographic system of Plunkett's own, with some transliterated Arabic terms (e.g., Zaonia) several of which are place-names. The word *mrabh*, in such close proximity to the Gaelic list of day names, could be taken as the Gaelic word for dead (*marbh*) rearranged, except that the convention of using the letter *h* as substitute for a superior dot was scarcely in use in 1912. A pencil sketch on the facing page shows a motor vehicle, apparently traveling at right angles to its own official trajectory or, possessing wheels allowing it to move either forward or laterally.

In a notebook used intermittently, data of contrasting types can often be found side by side, though perhaps separated in time of inscription by many days. Here, a list of the Scandinavian alphabetical letters is immediately followed by a page of Arabic vocabulary. Among the eleven terms glossed are "perf[ect] accord," "intensive," "ardent passion," "exclusive," "blind," "madness," and "possession." None of this looks like a general-knowledge or touristic approach to acquiring a language. However, the greater problem facing the reader is the choice of deciding whether Plunkett composed or transcribed these "eleven stages of love," as they are termed.[123] Only the first item in the list is sufficiently complex to encourage speculation: does it relate to a saucy painting by Jean-Antoine Watteau (1684–1721), *L'Accord parfait*, in which two seated figures are diverted by a rough-looking musician, while a gentleman leads away the lady who might be their mother or sister? The oil painting remained available through plentiful engraved prints by Bernard Baron, generally bearing a tag from Juvenal's *Satires* (book 2, line 47). *Magna inter molles concordia* can be translated "There is great harmony among the dissolute," though the English slang "mollies" (for homosexuals, cross-dressers, and other male offenders against decency) comes from the Latin. The rapid juxtapositions of Arabic, English, French, Gaelic, and Scandinavian elements do not suggest a disciplined approach to comparative linguistics. Plunkett's method as a note-taker has yet to be deciphered in full, a task that presupposes a willingness to scrutinize poems superficially of doubtful value.

The sonnet inscribed on folio 27 begins, "Though our lips can only stammer we yet chant / High things of God" and ends, "Thy fruit is Love's most holy birth." While this poem does not prompt suspicions of a concealed romantic passion, it shares much of the vocabulary and archness of style that occur in the frankly personal poems. On folio 24, however, Plunkett had already written, "Though our lips can only stammer, we chant the high things of God," and noted it as a quotation from Gregory—that is, from the *Moralia* of Pope Gregory the Great (A.D. 540–604). While the sonnet may not be redeemed for literature, it has at least been clarified as an allusive text. The effect is not pervasively beneficial in reading the notebook. The iambic pentameter question, "what thrones and crowns await His militant[?]" might indeed be traced to some religious source, but the sentence marked off from it by a stroke of the pencil—"The yellow winds were calling to the pools of Poison"—remains in need of assistance.

The earliest entry in the 1912 notebook had been "Weary Willie," prompted by Yeats's response to those who hated Synge's *Playboy of the Western World*. On folio 28 there appears some echo of that theatrical controversy or at least of Yeats's poem. Subsequently dated "Wed 6th March 1912," the lines read:

When Satan laughs the stars
Shudder. Hell's portal jars
Clanging its iron throat
While the demons gloat.

When Satan smiles the sun
Shivers for day is done
To death. Hell's deadly murk
Unweaves his work.

The concluding lines are thoroughly confused, and the reiterative references to Satan and hell stand in marked contrast to Yeats's powerful economy, likewise in contrast to Yeats's taunting portrayal of Don Juan. These were very likely the eight lines Plunkett wrote in December 1911. A poem entitled "When Satan Laughs" was set up on the Columba Press and printed off in March 1912, a timetable suggesting that the added date in the notebook marked Plunkett's limited harvesting of his Algiers notebook. By contrast, "Weary Willie" dwelt at length on the subject's foppish appearance, reaching into more dangerous sexual territory:

Yes, he's queer
With that silly
Love-lock over his eye,
But he wouldn't be Willy
Without it, never fear.
We'd miss it too
Its [*sic*] nearly all that remains
Of the Blue-Mouldy Young Man
With the Devil's chains
And the Turn of the Screw,
He was a weed,
The Blue Mouldy Young Man
And slightly knock-kneed
(That is, in his early days)
His tie was floppy,
Till he took the craze

Of being artistic
His whole appearance was rather sloppy
You couldn't blame him he had'nt [*sic*] a son.[124]

This last line (line 34 of 74) might be justified by Yeats's own bleak statement of childlessness in the prefatory lines to *Responsibilities* (1914) but for the awkward fact of Plunkett's sudden remark coming two years earlier. Of course, "Weary Willie" was a private composition, never pretending to any kind of finish or polish. The other poems recorded in the notebook vary between experiments taken no further and items duly listed for collection between hard covers. The folios 7–13 aspire to the latter status, but there is little to appease the critic. A sonnet dated 19 January, Algiers, opens with addresses—"O Covenant! O Temple!"—and urges these parties to set their snowy feet on the Red Mountain, "while the pinions beat / Of proximate apocalypse." In a moment, Gabriel, Raphael, and Michael are recalled walking the mountain tops. The high falutin' diction and archaic references make no literary sense, even in the age of fauvism and proto-postmodernism. A few leaves further on, the archangelic names are reinscribed but then crossed out in favor of pastiche eighteenth-century dramatic stereotypes, while "proximate apocalypse" will be echoed much later in a list Plunkett will draw up, identifying the significant preludes or portents required for successful revolution. "Proximate famine" sounds almost plausible, except that (in the light of the January 1912 sonnet) it is disclosed as a secularized apocalypse.

The Arabic, or arabesque, tinctures attaching to some of these poems are finally overtaken by Plunkett's deflationary playfulness. On folios 14–18 one finds material largely ascribed to an Arab by name Achmed Bey Chawky, but, as this progresses from page to page, the author is simply reduced to the initial letters A. B. C., the initial letters of the alphabet as it might be childishly written with chalk.[125] However, a distinguished Egyptian poet, Ahmed Chawki or, better, Shawki (1868–1932), may be intended. Like much else in the notebook, these pieces treat of unrequited love, employing some of the basic devices of *amour courtois* (a term coined as recently as 1883) as practiced especially by medieval troubadours in the regions where cultural France and cultural Italy overlapped virtually until August 1914. The first-, second-, and third-person singular (I, you, she) constantly displace each other. The poet as such is a central figure. Prose poems relieve the drone of sonnets not very nimbly constructed. In this last detail, Plunkett follows the example of fin de siècle decadents exploiting Dante's alternation of prose and verse in the *Vita Nuova*. As Alec Davis has convincingly argued, the problem for these neomedievalists was their inability to find a workable linguistic medium. A. B. C. Plunkett urged his Arab Beatrice to "appear in the firmament of your felicity!"

The third and final page of A. B. C.'s (or Shawki's) "Mystical Poem" raises a theme that could have no analogue in the poetic tradition being pastiched. "I have returned to my country which for you I had deserted; I have returned there now endeavoring to break away from you." Though the prose poem was written more than three years before Plunkett's "unwritten" letters to Columba, here we find the same motif; from New York he uttered (but never posted) the deceiving protest—"Is it not six months since I left my country, home, friends and you for your sake?" And, in the same unsent letter, "I find that I am closely paraphrasing and saying in commonplace words what has already been said in poetry." The boundaries between fiction and actuality, poetic convention and personal relation, politics and emotion, apocalypse and famine were, in Plunkett's case, permeable or fluid, shifting, unstable, radically undefined.

In January 1912, he was detained in Algiers longer than originally intended. The weather had been foul; his health now required care at home. A systematic analysis of the surviving notebook must seem a cold response to his predicament. Yet it speaks of the real man as well as the prentice poet. On 27 January, when he wrote both the first page of A. B. C.'s mystical poem and the prose "Fable," time hung on his hands: the fable deals prosaically with the problem of measuring work against drink, and the Mystical Poem shifts into its proleptic return home. The Fable is followed by "The Maid" (dated, however, 22nd January) which applies planetary and military images, grammatical inversions, and Gabriel's trumpet in such a fashion as to identify the subject as Joan of Arc. From this, Plunkett as his own scribe turns to the dramatis personae of an unwritten satire and the Gaelic days of the week. The multidirectional motor vehicle is followed by a Muslim prayer in transliterated Arabic and (on the same page, 23) two quotations from Pope Gregory. The prayer, in pencil, is made up of seven very short numbered parts, and may (in one of these) echo the language of the first surah of the Koran with its emphasis on God Alone to be worshipped.

One minor feature of the notebook deserves attention; with the exception of "Weary Willie" and (perhaps) the mystical poem by Ahmed Bey Chawky / Shawki, no entry exceeds a small page in length. Plunkett's breadth of interest is remarkable, his tenacity less so. The Scandinavian letters, the Arabic vocabulary all remain contained within that field. The eight-line poem "When Satan Laughs" is writ large to fill the space, and is followed on folio 29 with a drawing of Plunkett's personal symbol, the merged cross and sword. A distinct section of the 1912 notebook is brought to an end, with the riposte to Yeats and the design intended for his own book of poems.

The final section (as I read it) consists of folios 29v–40, containing four sonnets in more or less fair copy, a poem in French (two near-identical versions), a verse-prayer to the Blessed Virgin in parallel Gaelic and French texts, a page with some thirty words of Arabic, and miscellaneous technical aids toward the composition of verse. It concludes with an elegant frontispiece-like page in Gaelic. The text of this announces a foreword by Dallán Forgaill (fl. A.D. 600) to a eulogy of Saint Colm Cille (died A.D. 597). Though it has apparently nothing to do with any of Plunkett's other literary interests, he may have read the full text in Whitley Stokes's edition in the *Revue celtique* of 1899–1900, published while he was in France.

The technical aids to composition include a short list of rhyme words—for example, meek, cheek, eke—as well as obscure evaluation of the vowels (with strong and weak markings) in a table that relates them to nine consonants (plus the letter *A*). The succeeding table introduces numerical notation, in which the digits from 1 to 4 are raised to the power x, y, z in a quatrain arrangement. The following illustrates the example:

And you have still your regal pride
And you have sighed that I should see
Your gifts to me beside the gate
Your pride—your great humility:

These are analyzed by the poet as

A twó a síx two thrée a fíve
A twó a fíve a fíve two thrée

Two síx two thrée three fíve an eíght
Two fíve—two eíght two twó sixty-thrée[126]

These lines contain, he notes, 111 letters, thirty-two syllables, twenty-seven words, four lines, and six vowel sounds. (Totals are also provided for audible and inaudible consonants and vowels.) This material is dated 11 March 1912, and incorporates the list of poem titles.

Impressive evidence of his fastidious compositional methods, these tables and examples only serve to underline the antique furniture—or reproduction antique—of Plunkett's poetical kit. Which is to say, also, that they point up the constricted if intensive emotional range upon which he works. The poem in French (16 March) is a farewell to youthful love—"o bouche odorante"—which remains entangled in the clichés of that happy condition. And we, for whom the notebook was never intended, finally arrive at its *remfhocul* or foreword or the announcement of such.

As a piece of calligraphy the word is elegant but asymmetrically placed on the page. Several letters of Gaelic script are practiced—*g* in the margin, *a* six times across the middle of the page. The phrase *amra Chuluim chilli* is repeated. One can only speculate as to its occult significance for Plunkett, unattached as it is to the other contents of the notebook. Dallán Forgaill was the earliest name-identified poet in Gaelic, his theme praise of the virtues of Colm Cille. The saint's Latin name was Columba (meaning dove). Does the last page of the 1912 notebook presage a collection of praise-poems offering to a modern Columba—Miss O'Carroll who rejects him?

Joe Plunkett's personal relationships did not extend far. Before his meeting with MacDonagh, they were of a juvenile kind. During the latter stages of Plunkett's Algiers residence, MacDonagh married Muriel Gifford, effectively curtailing the fellowship Joe could expect on his return home. His emotional life had been powerfully shaped, indeed distorted, by years of domestic knockabout over which the countess presided, inefficiently. His enthusiasms—for gadgets (including radio), for languages, for anagrams, for amateur theatricals, for diverse reading—are easily seen as escapes from Upper Fitzwilliam Street and Kilternan. His behavior at dances was, from what little we know, both excitable and evasive. The poems are laboriously constructed from the materials of ecstasy and rejection, sometimes with a religious, sometimes with a romantic-sexual register.

Psychological bipolarity is a common explanation nowadays of conditions resembling what we know of Plunkett's. Yet differences should be noted with care. The depressive (or melancholic) aspect was concentrated in the literary domain, where it had no monopoly. Melancholy has a distinguished pedigree from Elizabethan drama onward, associated with themes of thwarted love, alienation from nature, ennui, and other social phenomena. Depression, in contrast, should be taken as a nonthematic, nonliterary (hence nonsimulated) state: there is little or no evidence of his having been mauled by Churchill's black dog, despite the familial influences working on him since infancy. At the other end of the scale, it would seem an exaggeration to diagnose mania. Most accounts of his behavior emphasize a degree of calculation, certainly of deliberateness, even in his outbursts.

Earlier attempts to classify behavior in this area identified elation as a psychic state not to be confused with mania. It might serve as a defense against troubles that cannot be admitted to the conscious mind. Psychological discourse lacks a convenient term for "false emotion" (where *delusion* means false idea, or *hallucination* false perception). Hippocrates's *paracrousis* (in music, a false note or discord) might have served, had not the Greek term become obsolete and the musical interest in discord suddenly become positively intense in the twentieth century. The comparison of Plunkett's upbringing with J. M. Synge's naturally has its limitations. But, in measuring the latter's aesthetic and social evolution as a writer, we might pay close attention to the role of music as private recreation. Plunkett's philistine attitude to the visual arts was not matched by any recorded interest in music, though he appears to have played a cello on occasion.

In the 1950s, "morbid elation" was proposed by Bertram Lewin without much enthusiasm.[127] Reverting to a more classic Freudian vocabulary, itself a product of the Great War to which Plunkett contributed, we might see him as a complicated victim of melancholia. War neurosis fed into Freud's account of melancholia, a prolonged state in which loss (notably bereavement) is dealt with through various processes of sublimation and nonconfrontation. Plunkett cannot be classed as a victim of war neurosis, for obvious reasons. But his persistent elation deserves consideration as *negative melancholia*. False emotions are elaborately projected to screen and to repress traumatic experience, without even the consolation that conventional melancholy might offer. If anxiety or fear is sometimes imaged in the phrase "whistling past the graveyard," then Plunkett's behavior related to an inner site of trauma, requiring a whole set of behavioral gestures and ideas—"whistling past the nursery" when the nursery is a thing of the past. This elaborate set is here called the ego, as distinct from the self, which is its antagonist and goal.

Fortunately, a small dossier of letters addressed to a friend who lived beyond the pale offers some opportunity of testing these airy theories. Between August 1913 and February 1916, Plunkett conducted an intermittent correspondence with Aidan MacCabe of Cavan, amounting to eleven surviving letters in all. Aidan's father was clerk of petty sessions in the town of Cavan by 1894. The MacCabes lived on Farnham Street, a broad elegant thoroughfare, ringing one side of the commercial district with a large Catholic cathedral at the northern end, the Church of Ireland at a respectable distance, and the Presbyterians and Freemasons further down toward the junction for Killishandra. County Cavan was religiously diverse, hence politically divided. The MacCabe children's Christian names suggested a cultured awareness of Gaelic traditions: a younger brother and sister were Eamonn and Maire. The household included three servants or other dependents in 1901. The MacCabes and Plunketts were related but not closely. Cavan was a considerable distance from Dublin. In some ways, this successful, provincial, professional family lived a thousand miles from the Plunketts in their Hardwicke Street theater and their short-lease abbey at Kilternan. Joe's *Dance of Osiris*, which had its short premier run in June, was unlikely to appeal in rural Ireland. More attractive, however, was *The Irish Review*, which came under Joe's control in the same month.

Plunkett's motorbike had broken down while he was passing through Cavan in late summer 1913, having been in Donegal once again. He traveled by rail back to Dublin on Monday, 18 August, leaving the bike in Aidan's charge, with instructions for it to be sent on by goods train. The problem was a back tire or tube. If, however, the back tire would stay up for a short trip, then MacCabe might take it to Mass—"Early Mass would be the best."[128] The tone is confident, very mildly satirical. The following night, Plunkett has got himself northwest-wards again, and is staying at the Royal Arms Hotel, Omagh. By a letter that he admits may not reach MacCabe in time, he proposes that they meet in Ballyshannon (in Donegal) at or after eleven o'clock Mass. Plunkett has brought a spare tube, and so can take the machine on the long journey back to Dublin. Though this sounds like a ruse intended to bring him once more into Columba O'Carroll's company, he certainly was "home" in Marlborough Road by 27 August.

Plunkett's report on the week's events, and explanation for his mode of writing, adopts a very different tone. Whereas his second letter had been signed off semiformally, "Joseph Plunkett" (as between friends, not relatives), the third conveys "love to Aunt Fanny." There is a great deal of facetious humor—"grinning, contrary to the popular superstition is not so much done with the face as with the feet." In the final brief paragraph, he mentions the industrial troubles of Dublin in much the same tone—"There is a tram strike on and a Horse Show and a general migration of the Babylonians so that the Promised City appears not only sated but slightly seasick. That's all."[129]

There followed a gap of six weeks before the correspondence resumed, during which the labor troubles reached their climax and Kettle set up his Industrial Peace Committee. Plunkett claimed to have worked himself blue "as one of the Hon. Secretaries" but provided no details of what his activities involved. On the contrary. "There is only one piece of news from hereabouts and I am sure you know that already—about Charley O'Carroll coming home." The letter was addressed "To Our Right Trusty and Wellbeloved Cousin Aidanus Maccabeaus Cavananiensis," and signed off "Your Affectionate cousin."[130]

As MacCabe was now in Dublin, he and his brother were invited to Fitzwilliam Street for Halloween. ("The O'Carrolls are coming as well. Court dress not compulsory.") Another gap in the correspondence occurs, perhaps explained by MacCabe's continuing to be close at hand in Dublin. Plunkett's letter of 4 April 1914 hints at crises of various kinds. His illness was an unavoidable topic, though oddly phrased—"it has been (physiologically) bronchitis etc." Some unspecified dispute had led him to adopt a position he was determined to maintain, a factor contributing to the isolation he had experienced. Charley O'Carroll had visited while Joe was bedridden, but "the rest I have not heard of." All of this adversely affected *The Irish Review*, "which only just wriggled out in March and was a fortnight late and of which the April appearance is quite problematic. I must get rid of it or let it die." The excess of verse by the editor was in practice a desperate remedy to fill otherwise blank pages. While MacCabe pursued the golf ball, his cousin read with his long-established panache—Plato, Plotinus, Henry James, St. Teresa,

Wordsworth, and the thriller-writer E. Philips Oppenheim. And *London Opinion*. The signing-off was now touchingly downbeat, "Yours what's left, if any O Pluingcead."

◆ ◆ ◆

Distance lends clarity where proximate intimacy blurs. In 1942, the English poet Henry Reed was in training as an infantry man, specifically with rifles. His best-known poem balances the implied future with contrasting presents:

> To-day we have naming of parts. Yesterday,
> We had daily cleaning. And to-morrow morning,
> We shall have what to do after firing. But to-day,
> To-day we have naming of parts. Japonica
> Glistens like coral in all of the neighbouring gardens.
> And to-day we have naming of parts.

Plunkett faced an earlier war, preferring to brandish a sword, and little intending to ask where all the flowers would go. But the distinction between the act and the observation, between action and reflection, is more marked still. The incidents of childhood, domestic conflict, haphazard education, emotional impulse, and obsession could never be more than parts. Parts of what—fantasy or action?

Antithetical Comrades

Jean-Jacques Rousseau's *Social Contract* (1762) has been mentioned as a long-distance influence on some of the political ideas preoccupying the Irish insurrectionists. Rousseau's name does not appear in either of the book lists that survive among Joseph Plunkett's papers. Immanuel Kant's does feature, though there is no evidence of any close engagement with the *Critique of Pure Reason* on Plunkett's part. These notable continental philosophers are sometimes presented as, in turn, an early exponent of romanticism and a late disciple of the enlightenment. Yet G. D. H. Cole could point to areas of congruence in 1913. Allowing for a proper assessment of reception as itself a component of philosophical understanding, we should take note of

Rousseau's absence from Irish discourse of the early twentieth century and Kant's presence in a secluded corner of it.

Among the committees set up by the Irish Volunteers after their establishment in November 1913, two men were singled out by the Plunkett family for their nonpartisan manner of conducting of business.[131] One was pretty well known, William Redmond (1861–1917), the more radical brother of the Irish parliamentary leader: Major Redmond was killed in the Battle of Messines Ridge. Despite wearing a British army uniform, he had been a believer in Pearse's doctrine of blood sacrifice for Ireland, and took as his mission the fusing of Unionist and Nationalist differences in the seething pot of trench warfare.[132] The other remains little known, despite unbroken sales of a publication for more than a century.

The Redmonds were middle-class Catholics. James Creed Meredith (1875–1942) came from an involuted Church of Ireland family with clergymen scattered liberally through the generations. His namesake-father was a high-ranking Freemason and lawyer. The son too studied law and became a barrister. However, he also devoted himself to philosophy, later acknowledging debts to Henry Stewart Macran and John Henry Bernard, both of TCD. These mentors make as striking a pair as Willie Redmond and J. C. Meredith. Bernard, who became archbishop of Dublin in 1915, lost a son on the western front, and his attitudes toward contemporary Irish affairs were embittered by his loss. Macran, a Hegelian on holiday, managed to get himself interned for the duration of the war in a German prisoner-of-war camp, visited by Joseph Plunkett in 1915.

Before the war, the great white hope of Irish nationalism was Home Rule. Despite the failure of Gladstone's efforts in the previous century, the proposal was revived by the Liberals in the new. The Tory party, the House of Lords, and the Protestants of Ireland (especially those in Ulster) were bitterly opposed. Nevertheless, by January 1913 a bill to grant Irish Home Rule had obtained its third (i.e., final) reading by the House of Commons, the Lords having been stripped of its veto earlier. Meredith concerned himself with the mode of election to be used in returning an Irish assembly. In August 1912, he published the first of two articles in *The Irish Review*. The second, dealing specifically with the list system of returning members that he advocated, followed in April 1913. His recourse to the *Review* indicated a degree of fellow feeling with its organizers and editors, including the poets

Padraic Colum and Thomas MacDonagh; its founder, David Houston, a scientist, agnostic and northerner, had not yet been jostled out of the saddle. In the summer of 1913, Meredith consolidated his scrutiny of proportional representation at book length and probably at his own expense. Comparing systems of parliamentary election in Belgium, France, and parts of Australia and Switzerland, he also noted in some detail the scheme advanced by Victor D'Hondt in 1878.[133]

It may seem quixotic to impose a philosophical interpretation on Meredith's preferences in electoral matters, even if he was even then becoming a recognized authority on Kantian texts. Nevertheless, an argument could be made that, in the field of politics, proportional representation constituted a minor implementation of the categorical imperative, that is (as Kant formulated it), "Act only on that maxim whereby thou canst at the same time will that it should become a universal law."[134] In defense of this argument's relevance, one might note that Kant himself observed that "if we collected votes [on] whether pure rational knowledge . . . or whether popular practical philosophy is to be preferred, it is easy to guess which side would predominate."[135]

Meredith was certainly a convinced nationalist by 1913. Though he joined the Irish Volunteers, he probably never wore their uniform. A backroom drafter of complex documents, he served on the seventeen-man Standing Committee; this had been devised to be more effective than the huge Provisional Committee that arose from an awkwardness between the parliamentarians (under Redmond) and the Volunteers (under MacNeill).[136] His contribution apparently was the constitution adopted on 25 October 1914. While it was a firm principle of the IRB that a rebellion to establish an independent republic should take place while the European war preoccupied the government and the mass of the population, the Irish Volunteers' stated objectives were broader and less predetermined—"to secure and maintain the rights and liberties common to all the people of Ireland." Meredith's legal expertise helped to ensure that the organization did not violate the law of treason or the recently enacted Defence of the Realm Act. Unlike Plunkett and MacDonagh, Meredith did not graduate to the IRB; that is to say, he was not wanted, and did not wish to be wanted.

Pearse was a barrister too, but did not practice. Meredith was a busy lawyer, with a scholarly cast of mind. At the age of thirty-five he completed a translation of Immanuel Kant's *Critique of Aesthetic Judgment* (1790), duly published by the Clarendon Press (Oxford) in 1911 and warmly reviewed in *Mind* by John Marcus O'Sullivan (1881–1948), an Irish nationalist like Meredith, trained in German philosophy, but later a fervent upholder of Catholicism as the nation's infallible guide.[137] In the preface, Meredith acknowledges the assistance of various individuals including Bernard, Macran and T. K. Abbott (all of TCD), and Harold Joachim of Merton College, Oxford. Bernard had published his own translation of Kant's third critique back in 1892, and it might be wondered why the younger man, not attached to an academic institution, ventured a successor, albeit of the first, aesthetic part only. Meredith finally completed his translation when Clarendon issued his *Kant's Critique of Teleological Judgment* in 1928. By that date, his political activities were long concluded, and he sat as a judge in the High Court of the Irish Free State.

What might seem an eccentric detail in the mental world of the Irish Volunteers—a Kantian in the committee room—requires a larger framework. TCD's active interest in German critical philosophy went back at least to 1873, when Longmans of London published Abbott's translation of Kant's second critique. His association with this respectable commercial publisher had begun almost a decade earlier with his modestly styled attempt to refute Berkeley's subjective idealism.[138] Better known to the general reader was J. P. Mahaffy (1839–1919), whose *Kant's Critical Philosophy for English Readers* appeared under the same imprint in 1872, and again in 1889 and 1915. Essentially a scholar of classical Greece, Mahaffy also published "Kant and His Fortunes in England" for American readers. According to him, a veritable "school" of Dublin Kantians arose after 1862 through the influence of John Toleken (1803–1887, a professor of medicine), who set TCD fellowship examination papers drawing on the previously neglected critiques.[139]

Kant, then, had numerous advocates in the University of Dublin at the opening of the twentieth century, despite a renewed interest abroad in its alumnus Berkeley's version of idealism. If we were to attempt a comparison of Meredith's intellectual training with J. M. Plunkett's in the years running up to Easter 1916, the exercise would be complicated by the latter's youth, his lack of formal education after Stonyhurst, and his apparent nonapplication to UCD for a place in the nondegree metaphysics course. UCD would in time concentrate its philosophical teaching within a scholastic curriculum, Aristotle as mediated through Thomism, and so forward. As an undergraduate O'Sullivan cofounded a student academy devoted to Thomas Aquinas, and later won a fellowship from the Royal University of Ireland that funded research in Heidelberg. His doctoral dissertation, "Vergleich der Methoden Kants und Hegels auf Grund ihrer Behandlung der Kategorie der Quantität" (1908) (A Comparison of Kant's and Hegel's Methods Based on Their Treatment of the Category, Quantity) reached an Irish readership under the nativized title *Old Criticism and New Pragmatism* (1909), to which Meredith directed his own readers.[140]

During the first two decades of the twentieth century, philosophy in Ireland underwent significant changes of alignment vis-à-vis the public world of higher education and the active world of social debate and political conflict. One sees a microcosm of the larger pattern in the concerns of Meredith, O'Sullivan, and Plunkett, all of whom played their part in the active world. What the trio scarcely indicate is the lively presence of Bergson in the contemporary clash of ideas. His influence is acknowledged in early numbers of *The Irish Review*, and fleetingly in Plunkett's diary. In academic terms, however, Bergsonism only reaches Irish lecture halls with the appointment in 1911 of A. A. Luce (1882–1977) to a fellowship in TCD. Luce, an Englishman by birth who served on the western front during the Great War, became a world-renowned authority on Berkeley's immaterialism, but initially lectured on Bergson. In 1916, on leave in Dublin from the front, he witnessed the Irish Volunteers' seizure of the General Post Office (GPO), and took part in the defense of his college against the rebels. Luce's volume of lectures, published in 1922 by the Society for Christian Knowledge (London) as *Bergson's Doctrine of Intuition*, was sympathetically noted in the *Journal of Philosophy*, though the reviewer added "of background, of critical temper, of philosophical significance it contains nothing."[141] Berkeley was to prove a worthier and more congenial protagonist.

The more strictly philosophical understanding of Plunkett's actions in the years leading up to the Easter Rising will be attempted in *Enigmas*' final part. Some parting comments on Meredith and, to a lesser extent, O'Sullivan will be unavoidable in demonstrating the diversity of potential in the Irish situation of that time.

Action or Absence at Kilcoole, August 1914

Is it technically possible, is it intellectually desirable, to distinguish the word and the deed? Is it not required of the distinguisher to acknowledge that, in marking off one from the other, he or she also relates them, the one to the other? "Other," we should note, has two distinct meanings—(1) different, and (2) additional and similar. A case in point illuminates these points within the broad context of Plunkett's career.

On 1 August 1914, a small quantity of German guns was landed on the coast of Wicklow at a place named Kilcoole, in effect completing the larger importation of weapons effected by the Irish Volunteers at Howth, just north of Dublin on 26 July. The yacht belonged to Sir Thomas Myles (1857–1937), an accomplished surgeon, amateur boxer, and sailor. He had been recruited to this venture by Meredith on the strength of Myles's earlier support for Home Rule and C. S. Parnell, his sympathy for locked-out workers in 1913, and his friendship with the mastermind of Irish Volunteers gunrunning, Erskine Childers. Those actively involved at sea included Meredith, Myles, Diarmuid Coffey (1888–1964) with, less predictably, a British army (future) general named Shephard, and Kilkenny-originating Captain Hervey de Montmorency of the Dublin Fusiliers. Indian-born and Eton-educated Gordon Strachey Shephard (1885–1916) was a founding member of the Royal Flying Corps, and a skilled yachtsman in which latter connection he too was a friend of Erskine Childers.[142]

The prompt to the Irish Volunteers' arms importation, indeed to their establishment in November 1913, was the creation of a much larger Ulster force dedicated to resist the imposition (by Parliament) of Home Rule. Myles's involvement at Kilcoole demonstrates how tenacious constitutionalists could find common cause on the eve of the Great War with a defensive but armed organization. Meredith's position one may assume to incorporate similar feelings. The presence of de Montmorency indicates a degree of support among country gentlemen, Kilkenny in particular having been exhorted toward a vigorous conservative patriotism by the novelist Standish James O'Grady. Later, he turned decisively against Irish separatism, worked as a British undercover agent in Dublin, and eventually published a memoir, *Sword and Stirrup* (1936). Coffey presents a different aspect. His background was both Catholic and Protestant; he became a barrister (like Meredith) but had little need to practice; he moved in literary circles, Gaelic and Anglophone. On Achill Island, in 1913, he had met (and eventually married) Cesca Trench (1881–1918), granddaughter of Richard Trench, archbishop of Dublin during the disestablishment debates.[143] A member of the Irish Volunteers, Coffey did not turn out on Easter Monday, having recognized in the "Castle Document" (see appendix 3) a forgery perpetrated by the Plunkett family. Shephard remains, for obvious reasons, the least explicable hand on the deck.

The gunrunning at Howth succeeded in landing just over half the shipment acquired from the Germans. The remainder was still at sea. The talkative yachtsman Conor O'Brien approached Frank Cruise O'Brien and a solicitor (W. C. Lloyd) with a view to rescuing the situation. They in turn approached Meredith, who was put in touch with Sean Fitzgibbon by Eoin MacNeill. These convolutions indicate how relatively open were relations between different shades of nationalist politics in immediate prewar Ireland, open, insecure, and vulnerable to opportunism. In a history of the Irish Volunteers serialized in a newspaper shortly before his death, Maurice Moore (1854–1939), brother of the novelist, provided an unusual account of the Kilcoole episode. The guns, having been safely brought ashore and stored in a small fleet of motorcars, disappeared from his view there and thereafter. He strongly suspected they had been hijacked by the Plunkett family.[144] In some respects, this was a plausible story. The semiabandoned semi-industrial site that the countess had acquired at Larkfield provided an ideal hiding place for arms; within a few weeks of the Great War beginning (on 4 August), it became home camp for numerous Irish refugees from England, keen to avoid enlistment in the British army. But none of the surviving accounts of the Kilcoole incident mention Joe Plunkett as a participant. He was not yet an IRB member, though he did attend the secret meeting on 9 September at which Thomas Clarke, Sean MacDermott, and others determined to organize a rebellion before the Great War ended. Independent of them, Connolly also resolved on a Citizen Army "rising," partly to provoke the Irish Volunteers into active support of the workers.

With reference to peacetime 1914, two questions arise simultaneously. Why was Meredith actively involved in an event later enshrined in the proto-history of an insurrection he strikingly distanced himself from? How, if at all, was Joseph Plunkett implicated in the matter? Much has been made of Protestant involvement in the gunrunning. A booklet produced for the centenary of the Kilcoole incident mentions Erskine and Molly Childers, Darrell Figgis, Alice Stopford Green, Meredith, and Sir Thomas Myles, but ignores de Montmorency and Shephard. In the *Irish Times*, Peter Murtagh emphasized "the leading role played by Protestants" in the entire operation while maintaining the same discretion about the British army officers. A similar discretion resulted in silence concerning Colonel Moore's views of the Plunkett contribution. The two publications, however, differ sharply on a crucial question of control—for the pamphlet's authors, the IRB is everywhere in charge, while Murtagh never mentions it.[145]

To disentangle the questions and provide an answer to both, one needs to reconsider the political outlook of the historian Alice Stopford Green and the genius yachtsman Childers. The historiographer Ciaran Brady once summarized Mrs. Green's objective for Ireland as "English law without the English." Arthur Conan Doyle much earlier characterized Childers and his associates as "imperialist Home Rulers," a term also applied to Redmond's parliamentary party by some latter-day radicals.[146] Neither Brady nor Doyle, each in his generation, thought he had coined the abracadabra of Anglo-Irish conflict, but each drew attention to the primary issue that led to the Irish Volunteers' foundation in November 1913 and the gunrunning incidents of July and August 1914; that is, the threat to Home Rule posed by the well-armed Ulster Volunteer Force (UVF) and its powerful sympathizers in the British army's senior officer corps. Not all British officers took the view demonstrated in the Curragh Mutiny of March 1914—that the army would refuse to put down an Ulster Protestant uprising, for not all officers held the parliamentary approval of Home Rule in contempt. Thus, the importation of arms at Howth and Kilcoole was undertaken to oppose the UVF and in defense of Home Rule legislation, not as a deliberate step toward complete Irish separation or sovereign independence. In 1909, an Imperial Irish Home Rule Association had been encouraged by Sir Anthony MacDonnell, who, in becoming undersecretary for Ireland, frustrated the ambitions of Count Plunkett. Doyle's characterization of Childers and others was not a personal or eccentric one, but the underscoring of a short-lived or briefly viable proposal to keep Ireland unified and, to a limited extent, self-governing albeit within a larger imperial constellation.

One could hardly resist the argument that, on 4 August 1914, such a possible solution became impossible. But as Meredith and the others supervised the unloading of German guns into Irish Volunteers hands, the immediate threat lay to the north in the extensive areas controlled by the UVF and a complacent civil administration of law and order. Many of these hands were, by secret oath, also IRB hands—Cathal Brugha (1874–1922; IRB 1908), Joseph MacGrath (1887–1966; IRB, c. 1916?), Liam Mellows (1892–1922; IRB 1912), Sean T. O'Kelly (1882–1966; IRB 1901), and others. Neither Sean Fitzgibbon nor Joseph Plunkett was a member, though the latter was inducted later in the same month. In connection with Kilcoole, Plunkett is nowhere mentioned in Fitzgibbon's memoir of the period nor in the recent centenary publications. Maurice Moore, in 1938, accused the Plunkett family of spiriting away some at least of the cargo, but named no individual. Yet Desmond Greaves in 1971 felt able to record an Irish Volunteers inquiry into the disappearance: "Joseph Plunkett was subjected to a gruelling cross-examination . . . but kept his head and his guns."[147]

Even with these details, he remains an enigma. His sister's memoir makes little reference to Kilcoole, from which it can be safely deduced that he was not an active participant. From Fitzgibbon we know that he was not in Meredith's house on 4 August to consider what positive opportunities the outbreak of war might bring to Irish nationalists. Nevertheless, an association with the gunrunning, however distant or discreet, can be assumed. Moore's reference to the Plunkett family can hardly mask activity by the sixty-three-year count, a consciously dignified public figure in 1914, not one for leaping round the back lanes of Kilcoole. The younger boys, George and Jack, turned twenty and seventeen in 1914. Geraldine Plunkett Dillon should not be ignored in considerations of illegal activity; her future husband Thomas Dillon had drawn Joseph into the Industrial Peace Committee the previous autumn. Among the organizers of the Howth landing, MacDonagh was certainly in a position to steer contraband firearms toward the Plunkett stronghold at Larkfield. Plunkett's admission to the IRB sometime in August 1914 makes sense only if he had contributed materially to its objectives. Kilcoole is the only candidate for this role.

After the British declaration of war, Meredith called a meeting in his home, at which Fitzgibbon, Sean MacDermott, Sir Thomas Myles, Seamus O'Connor, and (less certainly) Bulmer Hobson contributed. When Fitzgibbon arrived, the discussion of Irish opportunities had evaporated with the news that Redmond had declared the country's faithful support of Britain.

"Meredith was so annoyed that he could not discuss the matter." Myles, on his arrival, was more positive, declaring that the Volunteers should take over the island's defense under Thomas Kelly-Kenny (1840–1914), a retired Irish general with plenty of Boer War experience.[148] However, Edward Carson had already published a statement in the London *Times*, committing the UVF to the defense of Ireland, if required. Once again the nationalists had been beaten to the punch.

In all of this, the motives of Childers, Montgomery, Myles, Shephard, and—perhaps to a lesser extent—Meredith, were purely to arm the Irish Volunteers in the face of Ulster Unionist militancy. The gun landings at Howth and Kilcoole were ostensibly designed to protect the defensive policy adopted by the Irish Volunteers on their formation in the autumn of 1913. The open organization was infiltrated by the IRB, whose objectives went much further than defense. Ironically, Bulmer Hobson (1883–1969), who had formulated much of the broader defense strategy, had chosen Kilcoole as a safe landing place and, as a senior IRB member, directed operations on land. Within less than two years, he would be kidnapped by the "advanced" faction while the insurrection he strongly advised against was inefficiently launched. By that date, Plunkett had moved firmly behind the insurrectionists.

When the European conflict was not over by Christmas 1914, as predicted by many, the scale of mass destruction and mass slaughter became apparent. In January 1915, East Anglian ports were bombed by a German airship. The SS *Lusitania* was torpedoed off the coast of Cork on 7 May, with a great loss of life. Italy and Turkey became embroiled. *The Irish Review*'s founder, David Houston, was so appalled by German submarine ethics that he tried to enlist aged well over forty. In July, "Perpetual Peace and the Doctrine of Neutrality" appeared above Meredith's name in the Chicago-based *International Journal of Ethics*. Whether or not these immediately preceding events stimulated the essay cannot be readily decided. Its central portion robustly questions Bertrand Russell's antiwar pamphleteering, and quotes Theodore Roosevelt with some ease. In neither of these positions does the author appear in the pacifist colors he later took on, though his detestation of the war in progress is unmistakable. Ireland scarcely features at all in the argument. Readers familiar with Kant's political writings will recognize in Meredith's title an allusion to "Toward Perpetual Peace" (1795). Twentieth-century warfare bore little resemblance to the phenomenon Kant had hoped to eradicate, and Meredith's three specific references to the essay fail to mobilize any philosophical substance for his argument. The first of these is, predictably enough, the categorical imperative as advanced by Kant in the "Groundwork for the Metaphysics of Morals": Meredith had it to hand in his mentor T. K. Abbott's translation.[149] If to universalize the obligations of states with reference to a conflict between a very few of them may have seemed feasible in the late eighteenth century, the attempt was quixotic in the age of high capitalism, the race for Africa, and airborne warfare. Moreover, Meredith occupied an uncomfortable position from which to make an argument. As an Irish nationalist, he could refer to no sovereign state except, perhaps, the United Kingdom of Great Britain and Ireland. As author of the Irish Volunteers' constitution, he had fixed their objectives at securing "the rights and liberties common to all the people of Ireland" without reference to sovereignty or independence.

On the question of neutrality, he could state with professional confidence that international law was recent and ambiguous. Kant was no help, if Meredith's ultimate objective was to undermine arguments for noninvolvement, for he concedes that "Kant . . . seems to have regarded the right of neutrality as an inherent right of nations." He then proceeds to quote a passage on the unjust enemy:

> This is one whose determination publicly expressed, either by word or deed, betrays a maxim which, if reduced to a universal rule, would preclude the possibility of a state of peace among nations, and inevitably perpetuate a state of lawless nature.[150]

What Meredith does not do is disclose that, some six or eight sentences above this passage, Kant briefly discusses the relationship between Great Britain and Ireland in the eighteenth century.

In short, "Perpetual Peace and the Doctrine of Neutrality" represents its philosopher-author at a point of extended perplexity within an unfolding military crisis, international and local. Meredith never styled himself as anything more than a translator, yet, among the company he kept in Irish affairs, he approximated to the full profession of thinker well beyond any of his colleagues, Plunkett included. In 1915 and after, the issue of neutrality was acute in these circles. The *Lusitania* incident almost brought the United

States into the war, a development that would complicate Irish-American efforts to foment insurrection at home. American neutrality provided a safe zone from which the separatist conspirators (and Plunkett especially) could nurture German support. In the autumn of 1914, Connolly launched an Irish Neutrality League, arguing that "the enemies of England were not necessarily the enemies of Ireland. It was their duty to gather together the forces in Ireland so that they might place their country in the position it ought to occupy—a position of neutrality." Thus, in July 1915, Meredith was facing two ways, subliminally critical of American neutrality and silent on the Irish Neutrality League. The prospect of conscription into the British armed forces translated the "doctrine of neutrality" into a practical unreason. To oppose conscription Connolly headed up a meeting in Liberty Hall, center of Dublin's trade union movement, on 18 July.[151] Action was speaking louder than thought. Plunkett was in Germany for much of the year.

Kilcoole may have been the first active step in the undermining of Irish Volunteers policy by the inner IRB cabal. The professed objective in obtaining arms—defense against the UVF—dissolved within days. The Great War did not so much dictate the plotters' strategies as provide a huge morally neutral backdrop against which their incomparably minor actions would be undetectable. Nationalists before and beyond professing republicanism, to them the political forms and institutions of others meant nothing. "Others" in this context were categorically different, not additional and/or similar. The Irish-American legacy of dictatorial governance within Clan na Gael, foolish escapes such as the Dynamite War in England, and murderous infighting brought little reassurance that an independent democracy could be obtained on such credit. Among those who increasingly gave Plunkett models for emulation Clarke, who came from that background as recently as 1907, was a prematurely old man in a hurry. His ally MacDermott, a young, polio-stricken man in a hurry, has been described as a physical-force separatist, "hostile towards trade-unionism and socialist internationalism as . . . diluting national feeling."[152]

Accounting for any connection between physical frailty and political extremism would require more expertise in the psychology of ideological compensation than I would wish to possess. Yet the characteristics of Kilcoole provide some justification and guidance. The incident, altering within hours of its apparent completion, united innocence and ambiguity in each and all the participants. Yeats's exculpatory distinction in *The Countess Cathleen*, between the intention and the deed, serves one or two of them better than others. But Meredith, acting for the Irish Volunteers as he believed that organization to be, unwittingly ceded weapons to the IRB. At the other end of a hazy spectrum, Captain Montmorency committed acts that, three days later, would have constituted treason against George V. Diarmuid Coffey, in his joint capacity as yachtsman and volunteer, would later decline to turn out for the insurrection, recognizing the Plunketts' involvement in forged documents. And, on 1 August 1914, no one knows where Joseph Plunkett was. Perhaps neither with the intention or the deed, though shortly to join the frail hard men in their determination to rise.

Such an unfortunate combination of conditions in men bound also by a strongly held ideological position embellished a lure of the sacrificial role. Each had suffered—in English jails, or in the grip of polio, or from the longer ravages of tuberculosis. Yet for evidence of sacrifice's appeal among the insurrectionists one would not look first to Clarke, MacDermott, or Plunkett. Pearse was its self-anointed priest, James Connolly a late but ardent disciple. Rebaptism was the name Pearse gave to the experience. In Connolly's case, the urge to "rise" with his tiny band of proletarian Citizens was recognized in some panic by the IRB leaders as a commitment to spontaneous action on the syndicalist model perfected in contemporary France.

France and the Irish Logic of Sacrifice

It is generally accepted that France ranks high among the Catholic nations of Europe. Yet the claim requires modifications. If France went through a golden age of eloquent preachers, learned and profound theologians, and could boast of a devout faithful, the countertruth is that the country was wracked by religious wars during the latter half of the sixteenth century. In addition to the significant Protestant minority (Huguenots), a factor qualifying the near-hegemony of Catholicism was the existence of a distinctive and stubborn Jansenist movement inside the Church of Rome, centered on the Port-Royal convent in Paris. Here Pascal, Racine, and other sympathizers found refuge and, under Jansenist influence, elaborated a dialectical world vision (in Pascal's *Pensées*) and a tragic vision (in Racine's drama). The movement was finally eclipsed in the early eighteenth century, though its later influence has been traced in the nineteenth-century Irish church, with particular reference to doctrines of man's helpless depravity.

Any comparison of the two nations must bear in mind that, however fractured French religious life may have been, Catholic France knew nothing like the official persecution suffered by Irish Catholics from the late sixteenth century until the early nineteenth. In Irish circumstances, no school of refined preaching or contemplative theology could establish itself. The best religious minds of the time found refuge on the continent in numerous Irish colleges, for example in Antwerp, Douai, Paris, Prague, Rome, and Salamanca. From these seminaries, priests returned (clandestinely, in the earliest years) to minister to their people at home. Only with the establishment of Maynooth College in 1795 did the British government tolerate clerical training in Ireland, and then only to bulwark the population against Jacobin influences from Paris.

Early in his study of religion, French nationalism, and social thought between 1880 and 1920, Ivan Strenski describes a long religious history producing "a school of Roman Catholic theology defined by its determination to articulate a theory of sacramental sacrifice." In support of his argument, he claims that at the height of nationalist agitation, France possessed a rich and elaborated literature of sacrifice in poems, novels, plays, and diatribes.[153] Items from this canon were noted or reviewed in Irish Catholic periodicals. Maurice Barrès (1862–1923) and Paul Bourget (1852–1935) among the novelists visited Ireland. In the summer of 1916, Yeats immersed himself a study of work by Charles Péguy (1873–1914), Francis Jammes (1868–1938), and Paul Claudel (1868–1955).

Even non-Catholic Ireland paid attention to this cultural efflorescence, looking back to earlier French apologists for sacrifice. With reluctant approval a Victorian Irish-Churchman noted that the final words of Joseph de Maistre's last book proposed "salvation by blood." Ferocious advocate of Catholicism and political absolutism though he had been, the author of *Eclaircissements sur les sacrifices* (1821) developed a posthumous talent in assisting hostile causes at difficult moments. The collocation of enlightenment with sacrifice in the same book title may puzzle readers accustomed to thinking of the former as a coolly rational outlook, removed from passionate and deliberate self-destruction. However, the advocate of papal absolutism had his Freemasonic interests also, and the joyful approver of the Spanish Inquisition also investigated the necessary separation of morality from church or state.[154] His relationship with an Irish fellow antirevolutionary of equally contrary genius, Edmund Burke (1729–1797), awaits a fuller treatment than that ventured by the Reverend William Alexander in 1859.[155]

Nor have apologists for Yeats's authoritarianism dared to measure any possible debt. Yet there are discernible footprints across the interval. A namesake (and no doubt kinsman of the Savoyard Count) served on the early board of management for Mungret College in county Limerick; another of the line, Stephanie de Maistre, contributed fiction to *The Irish Monthly* and *The Catholic Bulletin*.[156] In 1871, *The Dublin Review*, a journal admittedly more Catholic than Irish, published a brief piece titled "The Opinions of Joseph de Maistre." I have found no trace of a direct influence on the Plunkett family, who were, like the master, devoted to the Jesuits. To judge by the records of Stonyhurst, the English Jesuits were not seduced by the continental revival of interest stimulated by publication of a biography in 1894.[157] Further west and two decades later, Yeats's lesser poem about Easter 1916, "The Rose Tree," is a dialogue between Patrick Pearse and James Connolly in which the clinching words echo a dictum of de Maistre's:

> "But where can we draw water,"
> Said Pearse to Connolly,
> "When all the wells are parched away?
> O plain as plain can be
> There's nothing but our own red blood
> Can make a right Rose Tree."[158]

In Alexander's summary of 1859, de Maistre "writes theology like a politician, and politics like a theologian."[159] It took half a century for the poets of 1916 to demonstrate the point.

Before proceeding to seek out sacrifice among the tropes of Irish insurrection, we should make a number of distinctions which many writers on the topic (including Strenski) are inclined to ignore. The word in English (and French) exists in both noun and verb forms. Thus we can say, "The mother sacrificed her career for the children's sake." And, "The sacrifice of his right arm prevented him from working in peacetime." There are also intransitive verb usages—"they made them a calf and sacrificed thereunto" (Exodus 32:8). While biblical practice functioned within accepted codes of propriety—A and B were objects properly sacrificed to God for this purpose or that, respectively—modern instances (generally secular in appearance) allow for almost any item to be "sacrificed" in any cause. In chess for example, "He sacrificed a pawn in order to protect his queen" or (in business) "That well-earned promotion, it was a big sacrifice."

It is a universal assumption that sacrifice is a voluntary undertaking. If the following sentence used by Strenski were to pass without complaint, then the assumption would be jeopardized: rituals of commemoration sought to handle "the enormity of sacrificial mass death and the unbearable loss of life during the First World War." As most of the combatants who died were conscripts, to whom no choice was available (however cheerfully they left home), they cannot be said to have *sacrificed* their lives: theirs was no case of self-sacrifice. It might be argued that an individual soldier who ran forward in order to let injured comrades escape did in fact sacrifice his life for others. But some analysis of his chances of survival, had he not acted so, would be in order.

This latter case arises poignantly in O'Casey's play about Easter 1916. In act 2 Bessie Burgess, a Dublin Protestant whose son is at the front, deplores the situation of "young men . . . layin' down their white bodies, shredded into torn an' bloody pieces, on th'althar that God Himself has built for th' sacrifice of heroes." In the final act, while trying to keep a demented neighbor out of danger from British troops on the street, she is herself shot:

> BESSIE: Merciful God, I'm shot, I'm shot . . . Th' life's pourin' out o' me! [*To Nora*] I've got this through . . . through you . . . through you, you bitch . . .

Dying, she begins to sing a hymn, "I will believe . . . Jesus died . . . me; th' cross He shed . . . blood, From sin . . . free."[160] Here, what we might take as a true act of self-sacrifice is marked by incidental mild vituperation and the ironic breakup of a sacred text piously approached.

These distinctions may help to clarify ideological problems arising from the insurrectionists' exposing civilians, including children and the aged, to risk of violent death. Here, the extreme case of human sacrifice cannot be avoided. Jesse Goldhammer, in a nicely worded account of de Maistre's *Sur les sacrifices*, writes that he was "loath to believe that human sacrifice achieves the same redemptive effects as Christ's crucifixion." Yet the possibility endures because, "*life* being guilty, a less precious life could be offered and accepted for another."[161] Here the component actors should be distinguished. If life itself (via man's utter depravity, as the Jansenists insisted) is guilty, then all are guilty without distinction. Or, if a distinction (precious, less precious) is made, it is made by the beneficiary of the sacrifice who offers it. By whom it is accepted is another matter. To quote Beckett, "God is a witness that cannot be sworn."[162]

Accounts of Easter 1916 have repeatedly employed a quasi-religious terminology in which the words "martyr" and "sacrifice" are frequently used. In order to appreciate how this Irish political phenomenon relates to a wider contemporary frame of reference, we should begin by looking closely at the domestic history of rebellion, an exercise that takes us back no further than 1798. There had been earlier armed campaigns suddenly to alter (or at least influence) the regime, most notably in 1641, but none of these aimed to establish an independent republic. Some victims of political trials were executed primarily on religious grounds, Oliver Plunkett among them. In a few of these cases, the term "martyr" might have been deemed appropriate. Its heyday was yet to come and, when it arrived, the causes of conflict were religious only at a secondary level. While the rhetoric of early twentieth-century Irish separatism sometimes invoked heroes from the remote past, the usual dramatis personae were inheritors of French revolutionary ideas and/or more insular national feeling.

Prior to 1916, it had been a tale of repeated failure on the insurgents' part. Historical recollection of the events varied in its language from the recitation of individual names to the commemoration of battles and other disasters. The transmission of this material profoundly affected its shape and tonality; for example, the name of Theobald Wolfe Tone (1763–1798) emerges into prominent liturgies of commemoration after the publication of his *Journals*, posthumously by his son, in 1826.[163] The several insurrectionary campaigns of 1798—in Leinster, Connacht, and Ulster—were not readily convertible into the achievements of a few singular leaders; neither Tone nor Lord Edward Fitzgerald had been able to take the field. Five years later, the Dublin rising associated with Robert Emmet took a more concentrated (and more hopeless) form, with Emmet's person highlighted in a trial leading to public execution. Even in his case, where a commemorative iconography had grown up during the nineteenth century, personalized veneration was greatly intensified by the impact in 1898 of the centenary commemorations for Tone and his fellow United Irishmen. Pearse was nineteen, and Plunkett ten, at the time of the 1898 commemorations.

The year (1848) of revolution in France was eclipsed in Ireland by the enormous and anonymous catastrophe of famine. In 1867, a Fenian rising had taken place in Ireland, supported by a number of diversionary incidents abroad. Inevitable military failure did not produce a Fenian hero; on the contrary, James Stephens (1824–1901) was despised by some of his followers for the style in which he survived Parisian exile. Only when three men were executed in Manchester for the killing of a policeman did Fenianism acquire memorable names; Henry Boylan's *Dictionary of Irish Biography* (1978) has a collective entry under Manchester Martyrs, rather than individual entries for Larkin, Allen, and O'Brien. The prompt establishment of a collective and religiose identity for the trio can be judged by the young Swinburne's publication of a slim volume, *The Manchester Martyrs* (1867), in suitably green wrappers.[164]

But the Manchester executions provided an impetus for the intensification of personalized commemoration through ballads, through the naming of clubs, and (in time) through fine literature also. What was gradually called "tradition" might be more revealingly analyzed as the operation of new modes of communication, including a vibrant Catholic press, the engagement of religious orders in education, and an increasingly populist dialogue in politics. Cultivating the mystique of banditry, subversive movements became "represented" by figures from the past, whose activities (suitably edited) conformed to the notion of "dying for Ireland" or "giving their lives." Thus, in one renowned song, "Roddy MacCorley has gone to die / On the bridge of Toome to-day."[165] Retrospect becomes intention in these celebrations of individual heroism.

Two quite different, larger engines of analogy gave further resonance to the commemorative strategy just described. One was the ecclesiastical history of persecution from the reign of Elizabeth onward; the other was the interpretation of the Great Famine (1845–1847) as the deliberate work of British policy, that is, its reinterpretation through concepts of intentionality.

Irish Catholicism provided a long list of notables and a more anonymous body of humble victims, killed because of their religious attachment if not always for it. The term "martyr" could be applied in some cases, according to the rulings of canon law. In its transference to the political, and especially nationalist-political, domain, "martyr" was far more loosely used. When executed at the age of eighteen for his part in the killing of six soldiers, Kevin Barry (1902–1920) became in the ballad immediately written to commemorate him "Another martyr for old [*sic*] Ireland, another murder by the crown," though few if any of the canonical requirements for the status of martyr were to be found in his conduct.

The pervasive enmity toward Britain that transformed the initial hostility of Irish local opinion in 1916 into a positive commemoration of the executed leaders arguably did not arise from strictly political (or even military) causes. Certainly, the pathos assembled round Joe Plunkett, and his eve-of-execution marriage, arose from no appreciation of his genius as military strategist. Older, more atavistic powers were at work. The Famine had decimated the rural population and launched a practice of migration, and general population decline, only checked during the Celtic Tiger (or Bubble) years. From the days of John Mitchel to Gerry Adams, this historical experience inspired generations of Irish-American exiles to support a separatist policy by any means available, and—most potent of all—left a deep seated fear of renewed scarcity or "proximate famine," conditioning the social body for well over a century and a half. Three of the most remarkable, and irreconcilable, products of this extraordinary psychic complex were the Land League (founded in 1879 by Michael Davitt); an early play, *The Countess Cathleen*, by W. B. Yeats (1892), and (more subtly) "The Dead," the final story in James Joyce's *Dubliners* (1914). Joe Plunkett's sketchy notes toward a political teleology take cognizance of a possible famine, or rural crisis, suggesting that change on the scale inaugurated in 1845 was what he longed for.

At least equally influential as the Great Famine itself, the writings of Mitchel combined unrelenting excoriation of Britain as the deliberate agent of mass starvation in Ireland with a philosophical egoism derived from Gottlieb Fichte (1762–1814) through Thomas Carlyle (1795–1881). Mitchel's name occurs early in surviving records of Plunkett's reading and also in what will amount to Yeats's last poetic will and testament, "You that Mitchel's prayer have heard 'Send war in our time, O Lord.'" The years between 1911 and Yeats's death in 1939 can be marked off in successive stages of Irish nationalist endeavor—1916 (the insurrection), 1921 (the Anglo-Irish Treaty), 1931 (the Statute of Westminster), 1937 (de Valera's constitution)—to break the link between Ireland and Great Britain.[166] A neat sequence of dates obscures the fact that some of the events encoded represent modification and adaptation rather than linear progress toward a link-less, immaculate nonrelation between the two countries. More significant, however, is the manner in which the internalizing of these relations generates the myth of an exclusively-Irish agency—we did this, we alone (or Sinn Féin), we like no other.

The convergence of nationalism with popular Catholicism (not forgetting nationalism's secondary role as an internalizing of political relation), and the increasingly personalized form of historical memory all led to a widespread use of "sacrifice" as a term to describe the individual's role in violent action. Sean O'Casey's pamphlet *The Sacrifice of Thomas Ashe* (1918) encapsulates much that is essential in this rhetorical phenomenon: Ashe (1885–1917) had not only died young and as a republican prisoner of the state, he had died at the end of a hunger strike upon which he had voluntarily embarked. The term accurately conveys the sense that he chose to give up, surrender, or destroy something intimately close to him—his own life—with a view to serving (by publicizing) a cause he held to be more important.[167] The iconoclast O'Casey's interest in Thomas Ashe was politically inflected by their shared commitment to the labor movement; in other regards, the two men differed. Ashe's amenity to the rhetoric of sacrifice was underscored by his religious effusion: in prison on an earlier occasion, he had written a poem (or political hymn), "Let me carry your cross for Ireland, Lord," in which the religious and nationalist mutual substitutions are clearly displayed.

The hunger strike as a form of self-sacrifice that doubles as a political statement recurs in Irish nationalist strategies until the early 1980s. Among those who employ the threat of fasting to death was at least one member of the Plunkett family, though the authorities under pressure were to be Irish and not British. Joe Plunkett's bodily condition as he marched into the GPO on Easter Monday 1916 was so wretched through severe ill health, and his expectation of life so poor, that the notion of his sacrificing it is severely compromised. More generally, claims that the insurgents were prepared to make "the supreme sacrifice" rarely absorb the implication of the insurgents' willingness to see many others killed also. Training in warfare, seizing public buildings, holding prisoners, usurping elected authority—not to mention shooting civilians and soldiers—do not logically constitute the preliminaries of self-sacrifice. Invocations of self-sacrifice across such a retrospect possess more than a tincture of violent sentimentalism. Having directly or indirectly killed numerous others, the claimant seeks to transform his own inevitable (juridical) death into an end chosen by himself. That such invocations were made, and made successfully as far as the transformation of public opinion is concerned, can only be understood through wider perspectives.

The long tradition of Irish nationalist historiography, with its calendar of heroes and villains, martyrs and self-sacrificing redeemers of ignoble generations, is (by denied definition) shorter than it declares. Dermot MacMorrough (1110–1171), who allegedly brought the Normans to Ireland in the twelfth century, was in important emotive respects a construct of nineteenth-century nationalist thought. Only after 1800 do historians castigate him as a traitor. The foreign potentate, to whom he addressed his complaints, saw himself as a French Angevin king, and not an English or Anglo-Norman one. The invading Cambro-Normans were opposed in the field by the Vikings of Waterford, not the Gaelic chiefs. The mix of gender politics and cultural nationalism that infused this latter-day representation of the catastrophe unleashed by MacMurrough is well represented in Daniel Maclise's *Marriage of Strongbow and Aoife* (1854), which hangs in the National Gallery of Ireland like a colossal altarpiece. Other instances of retrospective national martyrdom could be instanced. The earls, whose Flight (1607) has become a milestone in the catastrophic version of Irish historical experience, had no conception of a unified state at home. Theobald Wolfe Tone, as an influential propagandist, was the late child of his own posthumously issued *Journals*. Emmet's famous Speech from the Dock (1803) reached its accepted textual form more than ninety years after his execution. This accelerating consolidation of a constructed Irish history is expressed increasingly through the invocation of personal names—Parnell (died 1891), O'Donovan Rossa (died 1915), Thomas Ashe (died 1917)—through whom funeral rites become political portents either of division or other disturbance. At the burial of Jeremiah O'Donovan Rossa in August 1915, Pearse spoke "on behalf of a new generation that has been re-baptised in the Fenian faith."[168] The religious terminology of his address has been often noted, less so Pearse's mixture of biologist and moral commentary on generation and generations, de-generation and re-generation.

In the preface (dated Christmas Day, 1915) to his essay "Ghosts," Pearse boldly acknowledged borrowing his title from Henrik Ibsen's play of 1881. Certainly, Dublin was familiar with the Norwegian dramatist: Edward Martyn, John Synge, and James Joyce were powerfully drawn to his relentless truth-telling, though, in Synge's case, the possibility of *reversing* the plot of *Ghosts* was preferred. It must be wondered whether Pearse really knew the play, with its ultimate revelation of illicit sex between master and servant, and of venereal infection transmitted through the legitimate line. "Give me the sun," a congenitally deranged Osvald pleads in the full blaze of day, for whom no miraculous Easter will dawn.[169]

By comparison, Pearse's ghosts are comparatively restful company—Wolfe Tone, Thomas Davis, James Fintan Lalor (1807–1849), and John Mitchel. The first three all died young, adding pathos to the severity of their political condition. Pearse juxtaposes their moral stature against that of the ascendant generation, and employs an unexpectedly strong metaphor for the latter. "One wonders what sin these men have been guilty of that so great a shame should have come upon them. Is it that they are punished with loss of manhood because in their youth they committed a crime against manhood?"[170] So pervasively familiar are the religious, theological, and ecclesiastical metaphors of Pearse's exhortations that the intrusive biological question, about sins against *manhood*, is in danger of being ignored. From this acknowledgment of an irreversible etiology in the political body follows a determinism sometimes negative, sometimes almost carefree. "Even had the men themselves been less base, their failure would have been inevitable . . . the national demand of Ireland is fixed and determined."[171]

A conviction that Redmond's Parliamentary Party was compromised, politically corrupt, and out of touch with the depths of national feeling permeated the minds of those who established the Irish Volunteers in 1913. Consciously or unconsciously, the poet and novelist James Stephens echoed Pearse's motif and metaphor—"Ireland must in ages gone have been guilty of abominable crimes or she could not at this juncture have been afflicted with a John Redmond."[172] Sins or crimes, damnation or punishment, the language consistently invokes an inexorable process of cause and necessary effect. *John Bull's Other Island* (1906), Bernard's Shaw's comic play on national stereotypes, pokes fun nervously at the idea; Yeats's stylized drama *The Dreaming of the Bones* (1917) advances a relentlessly occult version of the same logic, invoking the ghosts of MacMurrough and his fallen woman, with the events of Easter Week as mundane background. One view of the sudden outbreak of insurrection might see it as the unexpected breaking of iron chains, or at least a link in the iron chain of a determinist culture. The Great War was already recognized by some as a monstrous demonstration of such a culture's self-destructive unity. In England, a few brave literary spirits (including D. H. Lawrence) opposed the thanatic fervor of the establishment.[173]

Cynicism about established political systems was widespread, not only in Ireland, but elsewhere in the United Kingdom and also in France (to go no further). The nineteenth-century liberal faith in progress had turned sour, even rancid. If Marxism offered a counterprophecy, it nonetheless regarded the progressive immiseration of workers as a necessary step in their emancipation. The dialectic had a disconcerting facility in supply of the misery, without any comparable swiftness of the emancipation. Evolutionary science had produced a bastard called Social Darwinism according to which the strong devoured the weak. Pearse, in "Ghosts," did not resist this hard doctrine, merely acknowledged a delayed gratification. He concluded with quotations from his four chosen spirits, and the last word was left to Mitchel quoting the Old Testament: "that thy foot may be dipped in the blood of thine enemies, and that the tongue of thy dogs may be red through the same."[174]

The apocalypse in France had commenced some seventeen months earlier. The Great War remains the nonnegotiable clause in any sufficient account of the Easter Rising's many sources and contexts. The precise relation between the war and the Rising has proved elusive of definition—were the events of Easter a protest at, or extension of, the greater conflict? No recruiting officer on behalf of His Majesty's forces spoke with greater enthusiasm than Patrick Pearse, for whom it was the end of a degenerate epoch. Positive ideas of nobility and apostolic succession fit oddly amid the official paraphernalia of an Irish egalitarian republic, and their presence (at times uncertain, shimmering, even spectral) may indicate the influence of other ideologies. Frankly antimodernist, Pearse detested cosmopolitan and greater-urban ways of living; he evinced no approval of technological advance, and viewed the past as a model for the present and future. Plunkett certainly had an magpie interest in the sciences, biological and physical, but his literary models were hopelessly antiquated or just plain quaint. Connolly's arguments with both Pearse and Plunkett are discussed elsewhere. It has yet to be fully acknowledged, I feel, that the several differences between components of the Easter 1916 project surely indicate the influence upon them of external factors and experiences.

The American contribution is the best known, though a tendency to regard it as Ireland Overseas, or to treat exile communities as if they continued to be Irish before they were American, has led to a neglect of important questions. The nationalist Irish were only one "exile" community in the United States; their relations with other Catholic groups—the Italians and the Poles—would bear examination in terms of attitude toward the dominant American culture, capitalism, pragmatism, secularism, bitter dreams of ruralist secession, and so on. In repeating the nostrum that nationalism in exile tends toward extremism, or self-congratulatory purism, one is in danger of losing sight of its multiple contexts.

The German dimension to the Easter project is, at one level, obvious. It is facilitated by diplomatic activity in Washington; perhaps it could only have been constructed through a non-German and non-Irish intermediary channel. The interest of Clan na Gael in German military support was not based on any notion of the proposed Rising as self-sacrificial; John Devoy wanted effective sufficient support from Wilhelmstrasse, and found Roger Casement a far from reassuring emissary. Joe Plunkett, whom he met briefly after the latter's visit to Berlin, can hardly have impressed as a hardened revolutionary. As their performance demonstrated, armed support for the rebels was a minor consideration in the Germans' war strategy. In search for some explanation of the very limited results of German-Irish cooperation, one should not ignore the absence of any sustained cultural or social relations between Ireland and Germany in the decades or century preceding the Great War. The *Kaiserreich* was then a new and not very accessible force in continental politics; at its inception, Irish feeling had been decidedly pro-French, not pro-Prussian. In historical, religious, literary, and linguistic spheres, Germany had not enjoyed anything like the same intimacy with Ireland as France had.

Leaving aside the Vatican, and Italy with it, we inevitably meet France as nationalist Ireland's spiritual resource. The IRB had brooked no interference from Catholic clergy and, as for Italy, its relatively recent unification provided energies for ambitions to the east and south (Abyssinia), not in the Atlantic west. France had been home to Irish exiles ever since the Reformation; its twin historical chronicles of Catholic power and revolutionary patronage could bind together in the eyes of Irish antimodernist conspirators. In its third monthly issue (May 1911), *The Irish Review* published an open letter in French that, quite apart from its content, indicated a confidence on the editors' part that readers would regard the exoticism as a bonus, not a challenge, to their literary sophistication. George Moore's reply to his cousin (a Carmelite nun for twenty-three years) treated the conflict between art and belief; in doing so, it recalled the novelist's debt to the impressionist painters and naturalist writers of France. These debts were not Moore's alone but, with little modification, could be charged against the accounts of Oscar Wilde, J. M. Synge, Celtic scholars such as Richard Best, a brilliant eccentric like Stephen MacKenna, and even perhaps Patrick Pearse himself. While in Algeria, Joseph Plunkett had turned to translation from the colon's tongue.

Ancient sacrifice, more particularly the Abramic willingness to kill the son, is transformed by the Christian doctrine of Easter into sacrament. In early twentieth-century French literary culture, these themes arose in new political garb, notably in Barrès's novel *La Colline Inspirée* (1913), ably written up in *The Irish Review* by Jean Malye, who, in one contemporary account, is described as a Breton nationalist.[175] Georges Sorel, who has featured earlier, certainly looked forward to a spontaneous rising of the workers, through which all might be changed, "changed utterly." Yeats's poem is now so familiar that we fail to weigh up the implications of its mantric lines. The individuals named (which did not include Plunkett) are finally gone; in their place is a general condition, nameable only through the complex vacancy of the phrase "all changed," or through the complex negativity of "all changed," or through the complex kinetic energy of "all changed." Position, sequence, time, instance—these markers of the ordinary way of things are dissolved in what Yeats apprehends as the outcome of Easter 1916. In the end, all other codes being inadequate to the insurrectionary novelty, Yeats reverts to one of his earliest religious preoccupations—the Annunciation. A collapse or (equally well) explosion of organic time is evident when the Annunciation coincides with Easter, though, if one thinks of the Blessed Virgin's pregnancy, it *must* have begun nine months before Christmas, that is (roughly),

March/April. For this reason, the final word of "Easter 1916" reinaugurates the incarnation, not now of a God, but of "a terrible beauty."

Again, familiarity breeds contentment with the phrase. The birth three times announced in the course of the poem is of beauty itself. Supporters of the view that fascism renders politics aesthetic have been slow to draw on these lines by a poet who, twenty years later, will unquestionably approve aspects of Nazi legislation, suggest the elimination of blacks from "our civilisation," and make two or three anti-Semitic jokes. Yet it is not quite possible to regard beauty itself as the offspring of Easter 1916. "A terrible beauty" is at once more than, and less than, beauty itself per se. I do not think that Yeats's adjective is simply a descriptor, which might be replaced by "shocking," or "dreadful." What is truly and fully terrible is terror itself; paraphrasing Keats, one might say "Beauty is terror, and terror beauty." This is no more satisfactory as a theory of art than the young Cockney Romantic's original proposition, but it is in keeping with Yeats's developing interest in terror as a component in his philosophical system.[176] It is not an original conjunction: Yeats's eighteenth-century mentor, Edmund Burke, wrote of the sublime in not dissimilar fashion.

"Too long a sacrifice / Can make a stone of the heart." What does Yeats suggest in these lines? His own response is to assign the issue (question, topic) of sufficient sacrifice to heaven. Our part, however, is to "murmur name upon name, / As a mother names her child." The anticipation of a biological issue (offspring, birth) is paralleled with the upward relegation of sufficiency in sacrifice. What is the issue of sacrifice, in this second, biological sense, but terrible beauty, beauty as terror. Yeats's poem is notoriously cautious on the politics, and future politics, of Easter 1916. Central to this caution is an uncertainty as who is (so to speak) the agent of sacrifice—those who died or those who executed them?

The long, if not very old, tradition of Irish nationalist insurrection is in many ways an awkward framework into which to fit Easter 1916. Pearse volubly invoked Wolfe Tone as his John the Baptist, yet a careful comparison with the events of 1798 might show the later insurrection in a strange light.[177] Instead of reworking these historical precedents and justifications, one may learn more of the inner character of Easter 1916 by making connections with developments elsewhere, both contemporary and historical. Jesse Goldhammer's account of sacrificial violence in modern French thought inevitably looks back to Machiavelli, before concentrating on figures closer to our own time. Of these, Joseph de Maistre and the ubiquitous Sorel bear directly upon the present argument. In one critic's summary, their relationship turned on a transvaluation of the sacred and profane: "Sorel radicalizes and secularizes [de] Maistre's hope that Christ's sacrifice and return will obviate the need for endless cycles of accumulated guilt and purifying bloodshed . . . [by] imagining that final human redemption will be achieved through the proletariat and socialism, not Christ and his Second Coming."[178] But this is to take us toward dreaded abstraction, where most reading angels fear to tread.

Where do we find Plunkett, the man of specific place and time? Though his friend MacDonagh's widow was shortly to die in lamentable circumstances (thus underlining the funereal descent from words spoken at O'Donovan Rossa's graveside into the postinsurrectionary world), it was Plunkett among the signatories and other executed men who most intimately brought revolution and "the body" into dramatic relation. If the affair with Columba O'Carroll had never existed for her, the end of it was scripted with a unique solitariness by Joe himself in New York. Within days of this extraordinary self-denial—extraordinary, because what he denied himself had never been available—he had embarked on a conqueror's invasion of another human territory, one where no resistance was likely. Grace Gifford wanted to become a Catholic, and he would accomplish this objective by proposing marriage. Good Friday would have been ideal, when the veil of the temple was rent.

What survives on paper of this sadly brief relationship provides evidence of conventional feeling and strangely retracted emotion. The earliest preserved letter (29 November 1915) strives to reassure her that anxiety on some topic—very likely, his health—was mistaken. "It is not what you thought—it is something quite different but perhaps more serious." Did this hint at lymphatic cancer, Hodgkin's disease? Enclosed with the letter were some "colorless . . . crude and stilted notes on the kind of mysticism I hold to be true but I will ask you to believe that they are not more like to the reality than a death-mask to the living lover."[179]

The notes cover some of the same ground so awkwardly trampled in the unwritten letters to Columba a few weeks earlier. The document sent to Grace is organized along lines that a Jesuit might have approved. The tone is academic: "It follows that love is something greater and deeper than an emotion. It is a true act of the will and may be emotionally expressed." And, a little later, "Acts of the will are the life of love." Well might he have warned his reader against mistaking these mystical, sophistical annotations for any sort of reality.

Plunkett's anticipation of his own death can be linked to several concerns—his extremely poor health, his taste in fin de siècle literature, and his commitment to violence. He was simultaneously capable of directness. In the next letter (2 December 1915, proposing marriage) he began with two unremarkable declarations: "Since yesterday everything is different. What was the truth then is not true now." There followed a few more sentences of self-deprecatory feeling, and then a postscript describing himself "actually a beggar." From pardonable hyperbole, he moved to a potential cancellation of the marriage proposal: "there are other things more desperate, practically speaking to prevent anyone marrying me."[180] Perhaps he meant the IRB and their plans for insurrection within months, though "desperate" does not sound like Joe Plunkett's account of these factors. Before long he would insist to Grace that they should marry on Easter Sunday, in jail if necessary—hardly the decision of man who regarded these as rival commitments.

When he turned to write without reservation—"this is what I mean (I hope it is now)"—Plunkett headed his letter in bold capitals HONI SOIT QUI MAL Y PENSE (Shame on whoever thinks evil), the renowned motto of England's Order of the Garter. The escape from reservation continued to elude him. "I cant, I mean partly I cant and partly I mustn't dip my pen in blood and fire and write deep into your heart." The age-old conceit about lovers' exchanging hearts leads to an uneasy report of his whereabouts: "This family cant make out whats wrong (?) with me because I've been shouting and roaring all day and scribbling scraps like (see next page) I mean when here though I haven't been but at headquarters and heartquarters and such." The page that follows is devoted to touching personal declarations of love and impatience, ending with a suggestion of meeting at Sibley's stationery shop in Dublin the next day.[181]

One shouldn't complain if no more of this correspondence survives, except a terse note written on Holy Saturday 1916 to accompany a little gun, some money, "and all my love forever."[182] At least one quasi-formal inscription from the intervening months deserves notice. On New Year's Day 1916, Joe presented Grace with a copy of *The Circle and the Sword*, the collection of his poems issued by Maunsel in 1911. In many ways, these were now texts from a lost world. The phrase he chose to use in signing the book for her described them as "these dragons of the primal day." The primal day in question may simply have been 1 January 1916—his last New Year's Day, as it was to prove. The phrase resounds beyond merely calendric functionalism; it gestures at a private society of imaginary or heraldic beings in whose company, or against whose resistance, Joe and Grace will approach the brief future. "To Grace with all my love," Joe writes, but does not add his name.

Another inscribed copy of *The Circle*, though bound in stiff buff paper rather than the strong blue boards of Grace's copy, was given to Thomas Dillon, shortly to be the poet's brother-in-law. Its inscription reads with masculine plainness—"Thomas Dillon M Sc. / Nil admirari / Joseph Plunkett."[183] The Roman poet Horace's advice that, to be blessed, one should marvel at nothing may commend a middle course in life, but that was hardly Plunkett's intention for 1916. Dillon, as an intimate fellow conspirator, was of the same mind; indeed his influence may have directed Joe's steps toward the covert conspiracy against (when necessary) the Irish Volunteers' leadership. As a comment on the contents of the book, Plunkett's choice of Latin tag has a touching modesty.

Grace Gifford endured a variety of harassments after Easter 1916, and her personal possessions doubtless suffered waste. She may also have filleted her correspondence before handing it over for daws to peck at. She and Joe may not have exchanged many letters between December 1915 and Easter, enjoying the fuller record of each other's company. Sexual intimacy occurring on 1 December is implicit in the letter written immediately afterward in which he, however, speaks defensively of his "sort of love . . . a poor thing beside the splendours of your heart." The second page written on 4 December speaks eloquently of his "only home," which is being "in your arms." In crudely factual terms, Joe should have had no difficulty commandeering one of his parents' many houses as his own home—about twenty were empty at the time—even if sustained cohabitation was unthinkable. The headquarters of the "advanced" IRB at Larkfield increasingly became his domestic base, with Mrs. Quinn's Nursing Home as second best. At twenty-eight, Joe Plunkett knew connubiality had passed him by. This was a truth he could embrace.

A wedding, an insurrection, sexuality, violence, disease, conspiracy—Joe Plunkett's life between the sudden proposal to Grace and the less-sudden attack on the GPO was patterned on the repeated overlapping of two strands, like the twisting of a rope. Pearse's rhetoric exhorted Irishmen and women to accustom themselves to the sight of blood. In advance of the insurrection, nobody in the leadership did more than Joe to carry out orders. Instead of a comfortable bourgeois home on Fitzwilliam Street, he lived in an armed camp. There, he suffered at least one accidental gunshot wound at the hands of his sister. But home, either with this same sister as kindly attendant, or with the larger and parental family, he knew domestic violence with casual frequency. Habituating himself to a regime designed for violence, he merely stepped up a routine he had observed in more than shadow play. Alternating between one of these homes and the camp at Larkfield, or between one of these three "digs" and Mrs. Quinn's Nursing Home, Joe shifted also between the rifle range and the surgeon's table. Engaged to Grace, he stood at the entrance to a different kind of domestic future, and sacrificed it. If, as seems certain, he knew that his illness had reached the terminal stages, he could only make a sacrifice before the insurrection and not (like Tone or Emmet) perhaps after it, in the openness of a possibly liberated future. Having plunged into the engagement to marry, he began to overlap it with other commitments, making of that particular commitment the traditional sacrifice of the nationalist. It would not be said in his case, that "some woman's yellow hair / Has maddened every mother's son."[184]

Yeats's poetic eloquence did much, then and now, to enforce an interpretation of 1916 in strictly traditionalist terms, even if he never held exclusively to an Irish perspective on reality. Readers of "Easter 1916," who are not hypnotized by the murmuring of name upon name, detect decidedly external influences, including that of Nietzsche.[185] Like Richard Wagner before him, Nietzsche became the one "need-to-know" German of his generation whom advanced Anglophones took seriously. In practice, Nietzsche reached the British Isles through French intermediaries, a factor all the more important in Yeats's case, with his limited continental experience and poor linguistic abilities. Translation from French of Daniel Halévy's influential biography was the work of Joseph Hone, who, in time, became Yeats's biographer. For students of the Nietzsche-Yeats relationship, the central focus has rested on tragedy and heroism, or the mask, rather than on notions of sacrifice for all that these are articulated in "Easter 1916." In some regards, however, Nietzsche resurrected a concern with sacrificial ritual more explicitly related to a political context by de Maistre. Significantly omitted in this implied outer history was the Commune of 1871, with its explicitly socialist agenda. For Irish nationalists of Pearse's and Plunkett's kind (though not Yeats's), French conservative thought was more congenial precisely because it offered some assurance of Catholic orthodoxy.

Influence at this level does not travel on personalized documentation. The author of *Zarathustra* may have known nothing of de Maistre, though Halévy certainly did, and Hone after him.[186] One line of dubious continuity drawn in the difficult years of Vichy linked de Maistre to Charles Péguy (1873–1914), whose poetry Yeats studied after 1916.[187] Yeats's return to the great political crisis of his early maturity, in "Parnell's Funeral" (first published 1932) is also a remobilization of sacrificial ritual at a time of public turbulence in Ireland and—far more gravely—in Germany. Only in 1936, with a temporary excitement about Roger Casement's diaries, does Yeats return to the theme of Easter 1916.

Observation of this broken continuity, or line of discontinuity, may help in challenging the accepted and self-advanced theory that the nationalism of 1916 stands in direct succession to that of previous Irish insurrections. The secrecy into which the United Irishmen were driven tended to intensify their resemblance to Freemasonry in which Reinhart Koselleck and others detect the growth of an effective opposition to the Absolute State.[188] But, if the latter-day IRB invoked the United Irishmen as a model, the state they sought to overthrow had ceased to be absolute while falling short of anything like representative democracy. In this evolution of political institutions, the role of the secret society shifts from opposition to absolutism into a potential for its replication.

Between the pathos of Thomas Davis and William Smith O'Brien in the 1840s and the sacrificial rhetoric of Pearse in 1916, there unquestionably arose with the Fenians a new and tougher mentality. By the same token, Fenianism had little time for sacrifice, a predicament to be avoided rather than a strategy to be embraced. Attracted by the Parnell trauma of 1890–1891, and the convulsing of nationalist Ireland on the dichotomy of loyalty/betrayal, a renewed French ideology of sacrificial violence attached itself to a semi-moribund Irish political movement. If as one commentator has expressed it, "Sorel became dedicated to the idea that a few martyred workers could animate a world-historical, anarcho-syndicalist movement capable of regenerating, but not founding, politics," what happened in Dublin bore more than a passing resemblance.[189] No *new* politics was to be established, and whatever socialist revolution Connolly might have looked forward to was to be serially postponed. Plunkett, as far as one can make out from the scant remains, had no politics, except a generalized nationalism and contempt for the populace.

Goldhammer's philosophical tendency runs from de Maistre to Georges Bataille (1897–1962). The Irish parallel knows nothing quite as exotic as the latter, and earlier exemplars (including Sorel) will prove more helpful in any comparative exercise. Before looking in any detail at the ideas of these thinkers, we may be advised to consider how their influence operated, even how it reached Ireland. In the case of de Maistre there had been a long process of absorption since his death in 1821, including the posthumous publication of important works that served to maintain a dynamic. Cogordan's biography in 1894 topped off the historical edifice, and handed it over for contemporary use and occupation. De Maistre was ready to become a supporter of L'Action française and of Maurice Barrès. As these names indicate, literature and polemic were strategic zones of combat in which the French Catholic Revival operated. Unlike British idealism or German neo-Kantianism, this French school of thought did not rely on technically abstruse philosophy, but on fictional narrative, poetry, and the exposition (perhaps also distortion) of traditional Catholic values and practices.

These were modes of expression and avenues of intellectual exchange that the newly educated Irish middle classes could assimilate. The Royal University, the Catholic public schools (many with French origins), journals such as *The Dublin Review*, all provided training and confidence that encouraged a breadth of interest in foreign cultures. Irish painters had taken up plein-air opportunities at Fontainebleau, in Brittany, and elsewhere. The Celtic studies movement, no longer an Anglo-Irish monopoly at home, was in communion with scholarship at the Sorbonne. A carefully disguised pleasure in outmaneuvering London and Britain occasionally broke the surface. Anticlericalism in France paradoxically fed Irish Catholic awareness of a universal basis to the conflict of values articulated with Parnell's fall in 1891. Disillusion with parliamentary democracy, and with the corruption that appeared to be part of the system, grew at home and abroad. Reaction and irrationalism acquired an aura of dignity.

Although he spent remarkably little time in Paris, Joe Plunkett followed in the footsteps of Irish exiles, political and literary, stretching from Fenian days to the apprenticeship of Stephen Dedalus. His close associates on *The Irish Review*—MacDonagh, Maguire, Colum, and Pearse—all acquired a greater familiarity with the City of Light than the *Review*'s last editor and proprietor. Illness and convalescence were his rough guides, which took him further south. It is worth noting again how Henri Bergson and Barrès all but monopolize the French contribution to Plunkett's magazine; both were irrationalists, though of contrasting temper. No contemporary British or Irish literary thinker is given anything like the same liberty of exposition in its pages, not even Yeats, who is all but excluded.

Prewar London had proved keenly receptive to Bergson as translations appeared, through a small flood of English books dealing with his philosophy from 1909 onward. Among the more substantial contributors to the debate were William James (1909), George Santayana (1913), A. O. Lovejoy (1914), and Bertrand Russell (1914). British insularism was enduring an indulgence in American openness, even in the literary sphere—young T. S. Eliot and older Ezra Pound were exploding the canon. Home-bred, brilliant, and ill-fated T. E. Hulme (1883–1917) had been in touch with French literary opinion since 1911, when he met Pierre Lassere, L'Action française's critical theoretician—his account is significantly entitled "Mr Balfour, Bergson, and Politics."[190] This was the moment (January 1911) when Joe was beginning to read Bergson's *Time and Free Will.* Back in London Hulme, who also translated Sorel's *Reflections,* delivered a series of lectures on Bergson in 1913.[191]

This was not to be Dublin's source, at least far as one can gather from the sparse evidence. In 1912 Tom Kettle referred confidently to "Bergson's brief authority" in the field of French philosophy.[192] Learning Gaelic in Kerry, Desmond Fitzgerald regaled Ernest Blythe with stories of the Imagist circles he had moved in, including stories about Hulme and Pound. No mention of Bergson. The Imagists had included Plunkett's friend and teacher, Joseph Campbell, in their number. Fitzgerald's memoir of those days speaks of his *intuitive* conviction that a national revival was imminent, but the Bergsonian concept should not be overinterpreted.[193] The French intellectual influence, deemed proper company for a new generation of Irish writers, is openly embraced in *The Irish Review* but not thanks to any English mediation. For the first time since the 1790s, Irish insurgent thought was directly in touch—at least through Bourgeois and Malye—with a contemporary philosophical and cultural movement abroad. French on both occasions, and radical in the first instance, this influence deserved to be regarded as radical *and* reactionary in the second.

Until the articles by Maurice Bourgeois appeared in *The Irish Review*, Plunkett's reading of January 1911 was the sole (traceable) contact he had established with the French philosopher whose name does not appear in the lengthy booklist compiled in a Stonyhurst notebook (see appendix 1). The exhaustive roll call of book titles by Herbert Spencer that feature in the notebook indicate how Plunkett stood in relation to the issue of Bergson versus Spencer that one philosopher of science has located at the heart of *L'Évolution créatrice* (1907).[194] Joe's widespread interests in science, including physiology and wireless, were ostensibly practical; they also marked his position on an indeterminate line between past and future, between established knowledge and speculative thought.

Bergson arrives into the *Review* long before Plunkett took control of it. Barrès, on the other hand, can be confidently assigned to his influence. The plot of *La Colline Inspirée* (1913) culminates in a near-schismatic division between local piety and Roman authority. At one level, it exploits the familiar self-confidence of French Catholicism; at another, it intensifies notions of a spiritualized landscape, even of a neopagan divinity associated with place, and indeed with attachment itself. It is no accident that the novelist's own background, and the setting of the novel, is that of disputed territories, those of Alsace and Lorraine, lost by France to Germany in 1871. Nor is the allusion to Jeanne d'Arc on the opening page a mere historical gesture, for the Maid of Orleans is at once a martyr to English power and to Burgundian treachery. In such conflicts as the novel repeatedly excavates and projects, the pious man is divided.

The Bergsonian philosophy is remote from these particularities and their acidic inscription on the literary page. Nevertheless, Bertrand Russell had no trouble in confirming that Sorel, in *Réflexions sur la Violence*, "used Bergsonian irrationalism to justify a revolutionary labour movement having no definite goal." Russell's opinions are valuable, not only as those of a professional philosopher, but as the response of a man who was active as a conscientious objector in 1916, making his own protest (like D. H. Lawrence) against the war. Thirty years later as the Second World War ended, he may have been too close to events to strike an exact balance between intellectual influence and material cause when he wrote that "the main effect of Bergson's philosophy was conservative, and it harmonised easily with the movement which culminated in Vichy"—that is, in French collaboration with Nazism.[195] His endeavor, to link philosophy to its social circumstances and consequences, deserves respect. In regard to Bergson, what may be relevant to the activities of Plunkett and the other conspirators of Easter 1916 is his systematic dualism of intuition and intellect.

Bergson impressed Bernard Shaw when they met at the Savile Club in October 1911, despite the substratum of questionable political tendency later detected by Russell. However, Shaw's touchstone would be *L'Évolution créatrice* (in English as *Creative Evolution*, 1911) whereas we know that Plunkett acquired a copy of *Time and Free Will* at the end of his Stonyhurst period. Whereas the first-named of these books will give rise to, or at least feed, various kinds of vitalism, the other is a more technical work dealing essentially with problems associated with human memory. According to it, events in the external world and those of consciousness occur in noncomparable ways. Russell's summary of Bergson's central tenets was written with no political or historico-political intent, least of all one directed toward an elucidation of the behavior of Plunkett and his colleagues in 1916:

> Pure duration is what is most removed from externality and least penetrated with externality, a duration in which the past is big with a present absolutely new. But then our will is strained to the utmost; we have to gather up the past which is slipping away, and thrust it whole and undivided into the present. At such moments we truly possess ourselves, but such moments are rare. Duration is the very stuff of reality, which is perpetual becoming, never something made.[196]

If Plunkett in January 1911 read anything of which this is a considered summary, he did so at a time when his relations with J. J. "Ginger" O'Connell were not those of rival military strategists but of neighborhood friends of similar social background. We do not know, with any precision whatever, how much of Bergson's philosophy Plunkett read, when he might have read (or even reread) it, and with what mental responses. Despite these handicaps of ignorance, we should not fail to observe a resemblance between the process described by the French thinker and the presuppositions accepted by the signatories of the Proclamation of the Irish Republic. Whether any relationship between the two turns out to be one of analogy or affinity or influence may prove difficult to establish with conviction. Yet the effort is worthwhile.

The Proclamation deserves close scrutiny in many regards—its authorship, its political antecedents, even the circumstances of its printing and publication. Its ultimate sponsorship is boldly expressed in what might be termed a zeugmatic figure—"the name of God and of the dead generations"—the two parts of which only avoid mutual cancellation by the intensity with which they are conjoined, either in the mind of the author(s) or reader(s). Whether the dead (e.g., Fintan Lalor) are in any proper sense comparable to the Almighty, the Divine Majesty, the Creator, the Lord of Hosts, is a question to which answers may differ. But they will differ upon two distinct issues: (1) the special importance accorded to the dead, and (2) the special importance assumed in being (as these dead allegedly were) "Irishmen and Irishwomen."

The particularly religiose form of nationalism that inspired the signatories in 1916 inclined, almost vertiginously, to presume Ireland as being, in some essentialist and not merely descriptive way, Catholic. This is difficult to reconcile with the roll call of heroes—Tone, Emmet, Davis, Mitchel, Parnell—which was all too often a list of Protestant individualists, agnostic in almost every case. But the Irish paralleled to God in sponsorship are characterized very particularly as "dead generations," a phrase that unites completion and process, the absolute condition of being dead with the continuity implied in the concept of generation. In short, the Proclamation expresses its sense of history as (in Bergson's French) *une durée*, though the English words used are "her old tradition of nationhood."[197]

Russell, in his summary of 1946, quickly moved to describe the Bergsonian *durée* as something "in which the past is big with a present absolutely new." The implied metaphor of pregnancy—compare big with child—does nothing to discourage a continued examination of the 1916 Proclamation with its strongly gendered language, the first sentence of which refers successively to "her old tradition . . . her children . . . her flag . . . her freedom," a feature maintained in the following paragraph through "her manhood . . . her secret revolutionary organisation." While this may reflect a feminism often attributed to James Connolly, it remains true of Ireland than "her secret revolutionary organisation" was exclusively male, a tension vividly encapsulated in "her manhood," where the noun shifts uneasily between an abstract and a collective usage. Russell is severe on Bergson's reliance on metaphors and similes, and several that he cites uncannily anticipate the conflict of old and new methods in the Great War.

> The animal takes its stand on the plant, man bestrides animality, and the whole of humanity in space and in time, is one immense army galloping beside and before and behind each of us in an overwhelming charge able to beat down every resistance and to clear many obstacles, perhaps even death.[198]

The apparent suspension of chronological or topographical order in this evocation of the élan vital is clarified in a different treatment or simile, according to which life is like a bursting shell, the parts of which become other shells; in other words, consequence becomes a species of multiple cause. Russell's attempt at a more abstract summary describes the Bergsonian subject as a kind of grammatical plural—"our will is strained to the utmost; we have to gather up the past which is slipping away, and thrust it whole and undivided into the present"—with a re-presented past offering something whole and undivided (i.e., nonplural).

It may be that Russell neglects to acknowledge the extent to which Bergson's concept of time is biologically, and not historically, modeled. But then, the phase of Irish nationalist thinking with which we are engaged was distinctive precisely for its employment of biological imagery, and especially the triangle of generation(s), degeneration, and regeneration. The rhetoric of "land and the dead," associated with Barrès but traceable in at least one regard to Edmund Burke, does not lack a sanguinary dimension. Blood flows from the dying into the land; the living derive their blood from the (now) dead who lie buried in the land. Irish nationalist rhetoric could readily accommodate a new theory of time without disturbing its "age-old traditions" of revolution.

Certainly, an obstacle to reading the Proclamation in Bergsonian terms arises precisely on the distinction between the individual and the collective subject. Here the rhetoric and practice of sacrificial violence becomes relevant. Modeling themselves on the behavior of Christ, the more articulate rebel leaders—essentially MacDonagh, Pearse, and Plunkett—seek to expiate the offense of earlier generations and to invoke the dead generations in acts of what they regard as self-sacrifice. In doing so, they do so each as an individual—their profession as poets is here crucial, and (perhaps) a knowledge of Sorel's *Réflexions*.[199] Their action as individuals is not, however, solitary: its deliberately martial character necessitates the participation (and, hence, death) of others.

Discussing Sorel's application of Bergsonian ideas to the state of the working class, Jesse Goldhammer stresses the appropriation of Christ as an exemplar of sacrificial violence. At this level, any French influence on the IRB's intellectual wing came from the *Réflexions* rather than *L'Évolution créatrice*, and this possibility is enhanced by the international interest in syndicalism as a vehicle of revolution, shared by Connolly and Larkin, the trade union leadership, and the ICA. It is the confluence of several different influences that proves critical, rather than the dominance of one. Catholic Revivalism in the English-speaking world did not truck with violent labor strikes or the state violence always already present on such occasions; its literary productions seem tame compared to the works of Barrès or Péguy, though Wilde's *Salome* (produced May 1905 for the first time in England) cannot be omitted from a survey of sacrificial violence as cultural trope. But this insular Catholic Revivalism, reinforced in Ireland by popular religious practice, provides a medium of reception for continental ideas of coarser stuff. Alongside the French material in *The Irish Review*, bilingual (Gaelic and English) poetry drew the current toward the past. For example, the issue of July 1913 included "The Song of the Whiteboys" (an eighteenth-century agrarian movement) presented with a translation by Seán Mac Giollarnáth; Jean Malye's article on Barrès's *Colline Inspirée* immediately followed; in the next issue, Pearse's serial anthology of "Songs of the Irish Rebels" commenced.

Salome in 1905 (and again in 1906) may have influenced Plunkett's own efforts at orientalist drama, *The Dance of Osiris*, the crude moral of which is the futility of high-minded political schemes. The same disillusion invades MacDonagh's *When the Dawn is Come* (1908), where a military Committee of Seven makes its first appearance in the numbers game of cultural nationalism. These amateur exercises in drama explore, perhaps unwillingly, the difficulties inherent in sacrificial violence, as if the plays were rehearsals for the real performance of Easter Monday 1916. The passing of time, the deliberate filling of time with distracting action, is a main concern of Plunkett's, as far as one can tell from the surviving play manuscript. Sacrificial violence in its "real" manifestation revolutionizes time itself, just as the Sorelian myth replaces history. It is a consummation of time past, or history, worked by the supposed consuming of time itself. The plot laid down by the Military Council of April 1916 will pay scant attention to *future* success for the very reason that its own defeat is a success more neatly assimilable to its ideological origins. Here Sorel's catacomb reflections appear particularly apposite.

Some notes of caution before closing. The present chapter constitutes (I think) a first attempt to elicit a *philosophical* coherence from the language and behavior of Plunkett and his coconspirators. Their relationship with a secret society (the IRB) required a doctrine of time if action was to be predicated upon assumption. The rhetoric of sacrifice has of course featured prominently in many historical and political analyses of the Irish rising, though these have rarely shown an interest in external influences (apart from the German arms). Among Plunkett's papers and published writings, there is little of substance upon which to elaborate. From the period under discussion, only James Joyce has been read in the light of René Girard's influential criticism. Bill Johnsen's scrupulous reading of Joyce's early writings, up to and including *A Portrait of the Artist as a Young Man* (1916), sets an example which close readers of other authors might follow.[200] Even in the Joycean rebuff to the overtures of dedicated nationalism, one hears echoes of a sacrificial dialogue—that in which Christ is bought or sold, betrayed or enabled. Against the institutionally powerful influence of the 1916 myth, and its mélange of poetry and gunfire, it is possible to trace a counterversion of blood sacrifice or sacrificial violence. Joyce's preoccupation with betrayal (usually linked to Parnell) is only one strand of a typology; another can be found in George Moore's novel about a Jesus who did not die on the cross, *The Brook Kerith*, published in August 1916. Nor did Bergson fade passively from the Dublin scene. In 1921, toward the end of the Anglo-Irish War (or War of Independence) public lectures on his idea of intuition were delivered in TCD in a series devoted to the Christian religion.[201] The lecturer, A. A. Luce (1882–1977), had spent part of Easter Week 1916 on top of the college's frontage shooting at Plunkett's fellow rebels. But that is to run ahead of events.

CHAPTER 2

Actions of This Kind or That

The Pale Cast of Thought

The fin de siècle witnessed a turbulent confluence of literary and philosophical energies, a clash of scientific and irrational preoccupations in which William Shakespeare featured on either side. Oscar Wilde's "Portrait of Mr W. H." (1889) set out to endanger the distinction between science and the irrational and, in acknowledgment, the most recent *Complete Works* persists in classifying it as fiction.[1] The scholars were at work with important publications coming from E. K. Chambers, Sidney Lee, C. F. Onions, Arthur Pollard, and others in the decade or so following. Some of this was taken to be dry-as-dust, for example Pollard's *Shakespeare's Folios and Quartos: A Study in the Bibliography of Shakespeare's Plays, 1594–1685* (1909). Behind this important piece of English scholarship lay the labors of Dublin-born Edmond Malone (1741–1812), the son of an Irish MP. Malone's edition of Shakespeare (1790, 10 vols.) established new procedures and standards in editorial practice, and opened up research into the playwright's life. Irish contributions to this field were not numerous, but we should note W. J. Craig's edition of 1904 (Oxford University Press) and, with greater influence, Edward Dowden's work as critic in *Shakespeare: A Critical Study of His Mind and Art* (1875), *Introduction to Shakespeare* (1893), and as general editor of the Arden series.

Malone had contributed to other areas of Shakespeare studies in the eighteenth century. Certain zones of his drama, both the speech and the action, were treated as dangerous, beyond discussion. In 1923, members of a London audience fainted at the staging of Roman and Goth violence in *Titus Andronicus*: the previous production of note had occurred in the 1850s (with an Afro-American lead actor) and, before that, in 1720. At a less visceral level, Dr. Johnson regarded Hamlet's behavior as inexplicable and, in effect, unspeakable. Among others, Malone proposed ways of reading the play that brought to light immanent meanings. However, "mining the text for a justification . . . mystified by its surface" involved risks or unforeseen counterparts, not unlike the spectral existence of plays forged by other, later hands, but attributed to the bard.[2] Wilde's "Portrait of Mr W. H." (1889) observes the traffic between forgery and interpretation, pursuing a theme that will be found to pervade discourses in Anglo-Irish relations and cognate political affairs from Parnell's alleged (but forged) endorsement of terrorism in the 1880s to the controversy about Roger Casement's diaries in 1916 and after.

Much of this could be pushed to the margins of the present argument were it not for another development in British academic thought and practice occurring alongside the growth in Shakespearian scholarship. Idealism is nowadays associated in the popular mind with the work of F. H. Bradley (1846–1924) rather than recognized as a broad and diverse movement in British thought. I say British rather than English because Scottish thinkers were prominent, including A. C. Fraser (1819–1914), whose 1871 edition of the *Works* brought Kilkenny-born George Berkeley (1685–1753) into the center of philosophical debate in timely fashion. In Oxford, where Fraser's edition was published, idealism took up its headquarters in the college founded by John Balliol, king of the Scots from 1292 to 1296, and named after him. Andrew Cecil Bradley (1851–1935), youngest brother of the philosopher and a fellow idealist, had a long association with Balliol, first as an undergraduate, then as fellow, and then as a lecturer in English (1876). The teaching of English literature in Victorian universities was far from well established; in some eyes it was hardly respectable. The first chair had been Dowden's in Dublin (1867). On the larger island, the Oxford professorship in poetry (founded in 1708) was essentially a part-time and short-term appointment that A. C. Bradley held from 1901 to 1906.

In 1909, he published his *Oxford Lectures on Poetry*. The best known of these—"Hegel's Theory of Tragedy"—contains a sentence that very neatly draws his philosophical idealism and his literary critical faculty into collaboration. Having summarized German *Sittlichkeit* as "ethical substance," Bradley declares that tragic conflict occurs "between powers that rule the world of man's will and action . . . [that is,] the family and the state, the bond of parent and child . . . of citizen and ruler, of citizen and citizen." Then, in the next paragraph, with un-German pithiness, he concludes, "The essentially tragic fact is the self-division and intestinal warfare of the ethical substance, not so much the war of good with evil as *the war of good with good*" (emphasis added).[3]

The phrase took wings in unphilosophical Ireland. An Ulsterman, who had been a Balliol undergraduate in 1889–1890, died before seeing into print *The Two Irish Nations: An Essay on Home Rule* (1913). W. F. Monypenny (1866–1912) had been a journalist in South Africa and London, in every situation a fervent imperialist abroad and a defender of the union at home. Through his connections with the *Times*, he had been commissioned by the publisher John Murray to write a lengthy biography of Benjamin Disraeli, two volumes of which appeared before his sudden death. The following year Murray issued *The Two Irish Nations*, in which Monypenny adopted and modified A. C. Bradley's phrase to characterize Irish history as "a constant tragedy, a tragedy in the deeper sense, not as the clash of right and wrong, but as the clash of two rights."[4]

Hegelians of the Strict Observance would hardly recognize this as an application of the master's dialectic. Hegel was concerned with ancient tragedy, which is to say drama rather than political conflict. Monypenny's *constant* tragedy offered little prospect of a dialectical synthesis and, even with reference to the Bradleys, his substitution of right for good merely added confusion. For "right" may lean toward duty and probity, but it also carries overtones of legal entitlement, formal rather than inherent. The Bradleyan emphasis on ethics was part of the British idealists' wider concern with matters of social amelioration, among which Irish nationalist aspirations did not rank high. Nevertheless, through this passage *The Two Irish Nations* indicates that contemporary philosophy did have a purchase on constitutional and political conflict. Arthur Balfour (1848–1930), whose premiership is best remembered in Ireland for the Wyndham Act (1903) and on the prewar international stage for the Entente Cordiale (1904), was also a serious follower of philosophical debate—his sister was married to Henry Sidgwick—and an active member of the Society for Psychical Research. In 1911, he tackled the growing reputation of Henri Bergson in an article, "Creative Evolution and Philosophic Doubt" published in the *Hibbert Journal.* In the present context, a question might be: did the vigorous Irish cultural movement of the years 1890 to 1921 harbor a mind attuned to abstract reasoning or intuitive generalization?

The period from Victoria's death in January 1901 to the outbreak of war in August 1914, often referred to as an "Indian summer," was marked by a high-voltage sense of the penultimate. Something was always about to happen. The Boer War ended in 1902; the Russo-Japanese War flared up in 1904. The Moroccan crisis (1905) was followed by nationalist disturbances in Egypt (1909) and the Agadir crisis (1911). Events taking place off the western stage were essentially concerned with the global influence and ambition of the great European powers. The action was elsewhere. Subsets of these occurred within domestic realms. In the United Kingdom, parliamentary approval for Irish Home Rule was repeatedly sought, only to be frustrated by the House of Lords. In the years 1912–1914, this obstacle was overcome and the measure was awaiting implementation when war began. Action on the western front postponed activation of Home Rule, leading to the republican insurrection of 1916 in the planning of which Plunkett played a major part.

Throughout his short life, the movement from planning (or intending or inaction) to external impact was problematic. Personal reasons, including ill health, were at work. But more abstract problems pervaded the period and the class to which he belonged. Wealth precluded vulgar work, just as peace denied change. The British idealists worried about the relationship between thought and social reality; some of them even engaged in good works and programs of amelioration (in housing, education, etc.) Literature, especially tragic literature, was scrutinized for examples, for lofty advice. Racine did not rank high—this was also a period of British imperial introspection. The cult of Shakespeare ensured that *Hamlet* was not forgotten. The famous soliloquy in act 3 posed the fundamental question of being or not being. Close readers might have noticed that the speech proceeds by stages that are marked off by a very few words ending *-ion*. "That is the question . . . 'Tis a consummation . . . the native hue of resolution . . . lose the name of action." The rhymed movement from one of these words to the next advances a paradoxical retreat from the wish to the loss. Strangely, when C. T. Onions published his glossary in 1911, he did not cite *Hamlet* 3.1.88 to illustrate the word *name*. And neither does the *Oxford English Dictionary*. So we must improvise to propose that this phrase, "the name of action," means "designation under *action*" or, more fully to Hamlet's position, to fail the requirements for such designation.

Plunkett's career repeatedly encounters this moment of likely failure, and only crosses it in the days before his death. One could argue further that the entire enterprise of Irish insurrection in 1916 was bedeviled by the same elusive control or utterance of "the name of action." Would the Germans intervene, would the Irish-Americans pay up, would Casement arrive, would MacNeill believe the forged document? The desire to rise, or rise out, precisely on Easter Sunday sprang from a deep-rooted fear that only a divine precedent would suffice to overcome the inertia of an allegedly colonial situation—Joyce's center of paralysis may deserve comparison, though his metaphor springs from neurology and pathology rather than Christian doctrine. But the Easter Sunday plans lost the name of action, and Bank Holiday Monday had to serve. An imperfect mimesis, or botched blasphemy.

From Poetry to Propaganda in *The Irish Review*, 1911–1914

Joseph Plunkett's name is invariably associated with the events of Easter 1916, and especially with the interpretation of those events as becoming ultimately successful. In reassessing his input to the insurrection, one should bear in mind earlier activities and achievements less prone to ideological appropriation. Contrary to general belief, his poetry did not conform to a nationalist prescription, and so is open to critical evaluation without direct reference to his political and military objectives. Nor was his literary activity confined to poetry; although he published little as a journalist or essayist, he was a major influence in shaping Irish public opinion through his role in *The Irish Review*.

The first decade of the twentieth century saw the growth of a new sophisticated literary journalism in Ireland, much of it associated with Yeats and his circle. *Beltaine* (1899–1900) and *Samhain* (1901–1908) were official publications of the Irish Literary Society, appearing with great irregularity but making available work of the highest quality. Their origin lay in the bitter dispute arising from clerical opposition to Yeats's play *The Countess Cathleen*. Across the two journals, contributors included many names who would feature in *The Irish Review*, including Douglas Hyde, Edward Martyn, George Moore, George Russell, and of course Yeats.

Contemporaneous with *Beltaine*, the Gaelic League began to publish *An Claidheamh Solais* (Sword of Light), a bilingual paper edited by Eoin MacNeill. In its first year, it carried Patrick Pearse's attack on the Abbey Theatre for projecting a false image of Ireland. Pearse became editor in 1903, and Sean Mac Giollarnath (1880–1970) succeeded him in 1909. Both men were members of the IRB, Pearse much later than 1903. Both also contributed to *The Irish Review*. In 1913 MacNeill's essay in *An Claidheamh*, "The North Began," led directly to the formation of the Irish Volunteers, with Thomas MacDonagh and Joe Plunkett among the earliest recruits.

In May 1904, the first issue of *Dana* appeared, subtitled *A Magazine of Independent Thought*. The leading figures were William Kirkpatrick Magee (1868–1961; using the pseudonym John Eglinton) and Frederick Ryan (1876–1913). They drew contributors from a wider social and literary circle than the Abbey and its supporters. Though it debated the merits of the Gaelic League, *Dana* stood apart from the language revival movement, while its politics (or Ryan's at least) was of a more international and socialist kind than was common in Irish journalism. Despite these differences, between *Dana* and *The Irish Review* an extensive overlap of contributors was to develop—Padraic Colum, James H. Cousins, Maurice Moore, Seamus O'Sullivan, Russell, and Ryan. *Dana* only lasted eleven months, its final issue appearing in April 1905. Its demise can be explained in terms used by John O'Leary advising the young Yeats—nothing succeeds in Ireland without either the Fenians or the Catholic Church onside. *Dana* scorned both.

Far more directly political, *The New Ireland Review* ceased publication in January 1911 after fourteen years. When David Houston proposed launching a magazine with Thomas MacDonagh, he was probably aiming to fill the void.[5] The older journal had begun when the land issue was still lively, the

Parnell split bitter, and the endless Victorian era intact. Houston's venture characterized a new century, and the presence of Science in *The Irish Review*'s subtitle bespoke a confidence shortly to be vaporized in the Great War.

When *The Irish Review* was established in 1911, Plunkett was not among the founders. These were Thomas MacDonagh, James Stephens, Padraic Colum, and Mary Maguire. The first editor (1911–1912) was Houston, assisted by MacDonagh, who had become his tenant at Grange House Lodge, Rathfarnham. An associate of Horace Plunkett in the cooperative movement for some time, the founder-editor remains a shadowy figure. He was succeeded (for 1912–1913) by Colum, and finally Plunkett, who reigned from July 1913 to September/November 1914. MacDonagh acted officially as associate editor throughout, and his influence is readily traced at least up the point where Plunkett takes over. With a degree of commercial professionalism not found in many other literary magazines, ownership was vested in a registered company, The Irish Review Publishing Company with an address at No. 12 D'Olier Street, Dublin. The firm of John Falconer (55 Upper Sackville Street) acted as printers.[6] The relatively long life of the *Review* saw it maintain a consistent quality of design and production.

Change of editorship arose at times of financial difficulty. When Houston, as backer to the tune of £88 per quarter, grew tired of the Colums' impractical handling of affairs, MacDonagh evidently swung his support behind Plunkett as successor. The printers also demanded greater security, and the obvious wealth of the Plunkett family had its own effect. Presciently, Colum felt uneasy about the prospective editor's attitude to the freedom of opinion that had characterized the *Review* in its early years.[7]

The family's account of Joe's involvement offers some additional details to the bald recital of facts. According to Geraldine, the *Review* "was published by Ernest Manico, who owned a printing works in Temple Bar. The printer, Mr Lachford, was an artist at his profession and had perfect taste in layout, printing and centering poems on the page."[8] Certainly, the *Review* presented verse elegantly, and Latchford's guidance can also be detected in the more finished items among the Columba Press's output.

Most discussions of *The Irish Review* emphasize its inclusiveness as indicated by the range of contributors, with Lord Dunsany (John Moreton Drax Plunkett, 1878–1957, 18th Baron of Dunsany) at one end of the scale and Frank Skeffington at the other. Certainly, there was diversity of social background and, to a lesser extent, of political opinion. Ticklish questions were sometimes debated under pseudonymous names—Albanach, An Ulster Protestant, Sorca, Another Irish Protestant, and the intriguing Sechilienne. Many of the now revered big names were also present—Roger Casement, Maud Gonne, Arthur Griffith, Douglas Hyde, Edward Martyn, George W. Russell, W. B. Yeats. If painters are included, whose work featured in a series of frontispieces, then the list grows impressively, with Augustus John, John Lavery, William Orpen, Sarah Purser, Estella Solomons, and (on no fewer than three occasions) Jack Yeats. In the context of Joe Plunkett's life, the appearance of graphic work by Grace Gifford (July 1911, and September/November 1914) deserves notice, and likewise a picture by her brother, Gabriel Gifford (December 1913).

Like most successful literary magazines, *The Irish Review* thrived because it could rely on a supply of work from a few prolific writers of a consistent standard. Colum, Dunsany, and James Stephens were important here. There were notable absentees, for example Augusta Gregory (a friend of Martyn's) and James Joyce, whose friends Skeffington and Fred Ryan did contribute. As on other occasions, Joyce acted as a barometer of tolerance, and the *Review* (for all its merits) declined to endorse the moral and aesthetic modernism implicit in the stories that become *Dubliners* (collected in book form in June 1914). Bernard Shaw, a bête noire of Plunkett's, did not feature either.

The appearance of Pearse in the first issue (March 1911) became an omen of the trajectory the *Review* was to follow. MacDonagh alongside Pearse must seem to confirm that interpretation. However, the editor of "Sliocht Duanaire Gaedhilge—Specimens from an Irish Anthology" is Pearse the educationalist more than it is Pearse the insurrectionist. The changing relative importance of these vocations is reflected elsewhere in the columns of *The Irish Review* during its three-year survival, but one should not be taken as an alibi for the other. Pearse contributed to eighteen of the forty-two numbers issued between March 1911 and September/November 1914, principally as an editor and translator of Gaelic poetry from the past, occasionally as a writer on education per se, and only rarely as a political commentator.

Gaelic material was contributed by several other hands, the most eminent being the scholar Osborn Bergin (1873–1950), then a lecturer in University College Dublin, and Padraic Ó Conaire (1882–1928), an innovative short-story writer from Connemara. In all, thirty-two numbers included material of this kind, usually incorporating sufficient extensive Gaelic text to give the *Review* a bilingual character. Ó Conaire apart, the preponderance lay with historic rather than contemporary literature and, within the former, a secondary preponderance lay with mediaeval or very-early-modern texts. Thus the Gaelic aspect of *The Irish Review* did not contribute to any apocalyptic vision of the future, except to emphasize the dolefulness of Ireland's past and, by implication, the need for a more assertive nationality. A tincture of Jacobitism is evident.

Less prominently, the editors accommodated articles, stories, and poems from other cultures—Bengali, French, and Yiddish. There was surprisingly little commentary on German affairs, and none on British or English culture. (Unionism with its related politics was unavoidable in the context of the Home Rule debate, but great efforts were made to avoid every other aspect of life on the bigger island.) America featured hardly at all, again a surprising omission given the close relations between separatist Irish nationalism and the Irish-American community.

The Irish Review paid far greater attention to its French theme. At a commercial level, the *Review* had taken steps to establish an address in Paris—c/o F. Tennant Pain, at 18 rue Favart—which did not survive after February 1912, having provided a link with professional distribution of some Anglophone magazines. Nevertheless, a pronounced French influence in this premier journal of Irish cultural nationalism calls for closer examination. Fifteen issues of *The Irish Review* carried substantial articles deserving attention:

- George Moore, "La Réponse de Georges Moore à son Cousine Germaine, une Carmélite depuis 23 Ans quit lui a Demand de Brûler ses Livres" (May 1911)
- Maurice Bourgeois, "A Great Modern French Thinker: Henri-Louis Bergson" (August 1911)
- Bourgeois, "A Great Modern French Thinker: Henri-Louis Bergson," cont. (September 1911)
- Bourgeois, "A Great Modern French Thinker: Henri-Louis Bergson," concl. (October 1911)
- P. J. Sheridan, "The Renaissance of Alsace-Lorraine" (February 1912)
- Ellen Duncan, "Modern French Pictures at the United Arts Club" (May 1912)

- Thomas Bodkin, "Modern French Poetry" (October 1912)
- Sechilienne, "Correspondence" (January 1913)
- T. B. Rudmose-Brown [while reviewing Thomas MacDonagh's *Thomas Campion and the Art of English Poetry*] (March 1913)
- Sechilienne, [A letter to the editor on] "Art and Life" (May 1913)
- Sechilienne, "Art and Life II" (June 1913)
- Madeleine Reynier, "La Mentalité Féminine Française" (June 1913)
- Jean Malye, "Maurice Barrès, La Colline Inspirée" (July 1913)
- Malye, "Chronique de France" (January 1914)
- Malye, "Le Mouvement Philosophique en France" (March 1914)
- Malye, "Le Home Rule et La France" (July/August 1914)

The contributors were both Irish and French (four of each), aided by Rudmose-Brown, a lecturer in French at Trinity College, English (or Scottish) by birth. The accidental origins of this extensive dialogue may lie in MacDonagh's summer-long retreat to Paris after an unhappy affair with his fellow editor, Mary Maguire (later Mrs. Padraic Colum). Another contributor who subsequently flourished as a critic in America, Ernest Boyd, published on Irish theater in the *Revue de Paris* of September 1913, and married Madeleine Reynier, who was published in the *Irish Review* (June 1913).[9] As the essays on Bergson and Barrès indicate, French intellectual life possessed magnetic attractions that cannot be reduced simply to personal influence. MacDonagh, Stephens, and (of course) Joyce all took their Irish grievances to Paris, but the traffic moved in both directions. Bourgeois spent time in Dublin researching the first biography of J. M. Synge, some of whose plays he also translated. For example, he joined a band of Dublin *literati* in Colum's Donnybrook home in June 1913, and corresponded with Joseph Holloway in connection with his work on Synge.[10] Bourgeois was particularly keen to demonstrate Synge's familiarity with French literature, even proposing a resemblance between *The Well of the Saints* and an obscure play by Georges Clemenceau, "our former premier."[11]

Bergson, as we shall see, unwittingly conceived a diverse and highly fractious progeny. For Bourgeois introducing him to an Irish readership, the salient points of his thought constituted an argument linking contemporary philosophy, the history of Irish thought, and the interaction of French poetry and politics. In the first of three articles, Bergsonism is defined "less a closed-in system of thought, a philosophical doctrine, than a method, or rather a mental attitude applicable to all questions." The specific topic is time, about which "the libertarian and the determinist" adopt contrastively absolute positions; they are "equally wrong, because they both explain the action when it is over, because they both adopt an attitude of retrospection, not of living."[12]

The contribution of September 1911 opened with a passing comparison of Bergson with Maine de Biran, a philosopher of spiritualist leanings back in Napoleonic times. With greater attention to detail, Bourgeois relates his master's thought to that of George Berkeley, "the Irish metaphysician" who died in 1753.[13] This was no groundless allusion designed to flatter readers in Dublin. At the beginning of the twentieth century, Berkeley was regarded in British and Irish academic circles as an (unusual) empiricist, certainly not a metaphysician. Bergson had lectured on Berkeley's *Siris*, *Principles of Human Knowledge*, and *Three Dialogues* at the Collège de France. The Frenchman's relations with William James brought the discussion to a contemporary conclusion.

The final instalment of Bourgeois's introduction of Bergson to the Irish reading public focused on contemporary or near-contemporary artistic affinities—with Stephane Mallarmé, Maurice Maeterlinck, Claude Debussy, and more sweepingly, with the modernist movement within the Catholic Church. The crucial mediating figure in the latter connection was Father George Tyrrell. But the ultimate ideological point of reference in this pocket map of the Bergsonian milieu is socialism, with Georges Sorel singled out for special mention. On this note, Bourgeois wonders if "some great thinker" in Ireland might find a solution to the country's problem through an applied Bergsonianism.[14]

The French theme was sustained, especially during the period of Joe Plunkett's editorship. After Bodkin's article of October 1912, none of the writers on French matters were Irish but (apart from Rudmose-Brown) French. Three articles in French by Malye, a young student of modern Irish literature, appeared in 1914. These were of a distinctly more political character than those devoted to Bergson three years earlier. By the same token, they attended closely to literature. Malye had spent a year in Dublin (1911/1912), and had also been a guest at Maud Gonne's Normandy home. His future (he hoped) lay in the role of secretary to Maurice Barrès, novelist and politician of the Right. His first contribution to *The Irish Review* served to introduce readers to Barrès's recent work, especially *La Colline Inspirée* (1913). The novel was not generically estranged from abstract thought. In March 1914, Malye (like Bourgeois before him) commended "Le movement philosophique en France" to Irish minds. The prestige enjoyed by Bergson stemmed not only from his professional achievements as a thinker, but also from his public lectures in the Sorbonne. Likewise, the Bergsonian philosophy posited two realms—that of an external physical world of rigorous causality, and that of consciousness, ever moving and flowing, within which free will may yet be exercised. The grim and guilt-haunted determinism discernible behind Patrick Pearse and James Stephens's sour commentaries on conventional Irish politics might be released and redirected under such tutelage. But Malye was no prophet; his third and final article in *The Irish Review* attended to "Le Home Rule et La France," appearing in the very month the Great War canceled all expectations, and shortly after the Plunketts were mixed up in smuggling German guns to the IRB.

Amid these diverse and Francophone contributions to Irish public debate in advance of the war, Malye probably hit his target with the following (translated): "Just as national energy [or spirit, *l'énergie nationale*] has gone from public and economic activity in France, so the same has ceased to inspire literary and artistic creation." What is important in this account of exchanges between the political ("public and economic") sphere and that of the arts is not some irreversible decline in the nation's *ésprit*; on the contrary, the striking relationship is the mutuality between the political and the artistic, reliant on *l'énergie nationale*. While the passage laments the present depleted condition of French culture, the dynamism implicit in terms used to describe an essential resource for the nation posits a renewal, even a revolution. This was not to be a social, but a national revolution.

In this light, the *Review*'s broader treatment of political issues makes more sense. George Russell had identified a central problem of Irish society when, in the first issue, he wrote "The Problem of Rural Life." The problem for some at least of the *Review*'s contributors was that they were attracted to a primitivism inconsistent with Russell's analysis. In May 1911, Fred Ryan assessed the possibilities in "The Prospects of Democracy in Ireland" but did so from a socialist viewpoint that the editors did not share. They were closer to Arthur Griffith—and, after Easter 1916, he would move closer to them—who wrote "True and False Imperialism" in August 1911. In what was perhaps the editors' most signal act of broad tolerance, Ernest A. Boyd's "The Jingoism of the Gael" was included in April 1913. Education provided firmer ground for extensive complaint and some progressive suggestions: contributors included Maud Gonne, Hanna Sheehy Skeffington, Stephen B. Walsh, E. T. Culverwell, and of course Pearse. The January 1913 issue published an editorial about Pearse—referring to him as H. P. Pearse. Afforestation, suffragism, proportional representation, and (inevitably) Ulster were regularly debated.

With Dublin's labor crisis of the late summer 1913 came a small flurry of articles. James Connolly was admitted to the ranks of the contributors with "Labour in Dublin" (October 1913), neatly balanced by James Bertram's "Liberty Under Capitalism." Tom Kettle's "Agony of Dublin" appeared in the next issue. By now, Pearse's second series of translations, headed (in English) "Songs of the Irish Rebels," was in full swing. The decision to establish a nationalist armed force was immediately reflected in the publication of MacDonagh's "Marching Song of the Irish Volunteers" and an anonymous "Manifesto of the Irish Volunteers" (both December 1913). In the same issue, a contributor named J. Justin Dempsey shrewdly detected the arrival on the scene of a discontented lobby, neither labor nor capitalist in essence, in "The Revolt of the Middle Classes." Plunkett, as editor and proprietor, changed the subtitle of the *Review* with the next issue. From January 1914 to the end, it was *A Monthly Magazine of Irish Politics, Literature and Art*. Politics had displaced Science to take pole position.

Like all magazines maintained by young people, *The Irish Review* lost contributors whose careers took them out of the editorial circuit. Colum and his wife emigrated to the United States. James Stephens tried living in Paris. Fred Ryan died young, having gone to Egypt as a campaigning journalist. Even allowing for such departures, the eight issues of 1914 contained few distinguished contributions. Stephens appeared once (April 1914), likewise Colum (June 1914, reviewing Dunsany). In addition to Pearse's serial anthology, poems were contributed by Roger Casement (March), Thomas MacDonagh (March, April, May), Geraldine Plunkett (June, September/November), and the editor himself (January, February, March, April, May, June). There was virtually no poetry published in the penultimate issue (July/August), while the critical standard of the final issue was reduced to

MacDonagh's declaring Alice Milligan "The Best Living Irish Poet." So much for Yeats, or Russell, or Stephens. Unlike them, Milligan (1866–1953) was thoroughly sound on the national question.

Plunkett's role in this politicization can be traced. In the summer of 1913, David Houston found that he had incurred debts on the magazine's behalf that he could not personally meet. Plunkett was offered ownership of the enterprise, in return for a payment of £200 to meet these debts and thus clear *The Irish Review* of encumbrances. In the words of his sister, the offer "was an acceptance of his standing," though perhaps sterling outweighed standing. As with most of the major decisions in his life, this new development occurred while the countess was away—on holiday in England with Mimi and Moya. Nevertheless, it was her money that secured the magazine for Joe. The drawing room of No. 17 Marlborough Road became his editorial office, with Geraldine assisting in the book review department. In her account, the assessment of books for review made Joe more critical of his own prose style. The changes wrought in the *Review* under his leadership are explained by his sister in terms of a general tendency of the age. "As time went on poetry and literature always seemed to lead to politics, and in the writings of our friends the ideas of art and patriotism became so mingled that we would not imagine them as separate."[15] It was this confusion of related but distinct realms that outraged Yeats but which also chimed with the aesthetic politics of Barrès and others in France.

Between July 1913 and the year's end, political life in Ireland was convulsed by the Dublin Lockout. Though Joe may have taken the decision to invite contributions from Bentham, Connolly, and Kettle for the October issue, his late summer had been passed in Cloghaneely, county Donegal. The Gaelic Summer School there had been patronized by Casement since 1907; in autumn 1912, the hero of the Congo found himself marooned by an attack of lumbago while staying at the school.[16] Once in control of *The Irish Review*, Joe encouraged Casement, said to have been long a friend of Count Plunkett, to contribute. "Ireland, Germany and the Next War," appearing under a pseudonym in July 1913, was the harbinger of an entirely new alliance for Irish armed nationalism, one in which all three men—Casement and the Plunketts *père et fils*—played striking roles. But Joe's purpose in staying at Cloghaneely in August 1913 was (again) to be close to Columba O'Carroll, whose family had their summer house nearby.

According to Geraldine Plunkett Dillon, her brother took the IRB oath early in August 1914.[17] The extinction of *The Irish Review* can hardly have been unconnected with the outbreak of war, yet the secret commitment of its owner-editor was also decisive. Sundry manifestos from the Irish Volunteers had appeared in the *Review* since December 1913, and shortly the conspiracy-within-conspiracy would begin to crystallize. The last day of the year brought typesetting of *Sonnets to Columba* to completion. Literature was now about to be eclipsed by the militant politics with which literature had already been merged. "From this time on all Joe's interests began to lead, directly or indirectly, to the overpowering question of Ireland's freedom."[18] If there is any wisdom in the suggestion that literary modernism aspired to the condition of a secret society, or coterie, then the 1916 poets applied themselves to the task with a dedication unrivaled even by Yeats or Pound, except that their work was in few (if any) ways sympathetic to modernist techniques. For Joe, *The Irish Review* might go by the board if the success of a Military Council so required.

In 1914, he had done a deal with Manico by which the printer obtained possession of unsold back numbers and—it seems—also agreement on "Joe's own poems" in a last-minute bid to keep the *Review* alive. By the summer of that year, the monthly issue had been adjusted to cover a two-month period, and the guns of 4 August cannot be blamed for the magazine's problems of late spring onward. Houston had long ceased to be a backer. One cannot help but wonder if another kind of generous, but secretive financial backing was quietly in retreat. Geraldine Plunkett was inclined to blame falling sales on the reluctance of persons employed by the state to be identified as subscribers or readers of a journal now avowedly the mouthpiece of Volunteerism. Her observation that civil servants constituted a sizable proportion of the *Review*'s early readership tells us more about levels of sophistication in the public service than about political loyalties. Immediately after the Rising, Manico sold all back numbers for half a crown apiece. A week later they fetched thirty shillings.[19] It is still a collector's item.

There was a brief future. In October 1922, Bulmer Hobson, Eimar O'Duffy, and Colm Ó Lochlainn launched a new *Irish Review* that lasted a mere six issues. A country caught up in civil war had little time for luxuries, despite some evidence of official backing for the magazine. In literary terms, its nemesis came with Eimar O'Duffy's contorted efforts to review

Joyce's *Ulysses*, noting its genius, deploring its vulgarity.[20] Hobson, the editor, represented a viewpoint in 1916 that was now losing ground, and indeed Ó Lochlainn had declined to "turn out" on Easter Monday. The surviving Plunketts were all on the antitreaty side of the civil war, republicans to a man and woman.

The Theater of Ireland

Young Plunkett may have been conceited and also, due to illness, undereducated. Money at a good address, and personal charm with a supportive network of local contacts were more than enough to compensate for a poor show in Belvedere or garrulity at dances. On his return from Africa, the family strove to find him an opening in professional society, even to the point (it seems) of encouraging an application to the Royal College of Surgeons. For middle-class Catholics in Ireland, these Indian summer years before the Great War were shortening days, foreclosing prospects, sharply contrasted evening lights. Some of his contemporaries were launched into parliamentary politics, others into the respectable professions of law and medicine. An academic career became increasingly attractive as the new National University fulfilled the implied change of orientation from the old Royal institution. MacDonagh chose this route to advancement, only to have a brilliant career guillotined by the firing squad. Joe Plunkett's brother-in-law, Thomas Dillon, also active in the IRB, taught chemistry at UCD, before moving by promotion to Galway. Dillon's wife, Geraldine, author of *All in Blood*, had every reason to look forward to a similar appointment, till motherhood and onset of The Troubles canceled her rightful ambitions.

What were her eldest brother's rightful ambitions?

◆ ◆ ◆

Ever since 1899, when Augusta Gregory, Edward Martyn, George Moore, and W. B. Yeats came together with the intention of devising an Irish literary theater, advanced thinking about national identity placed drama and its performance high on the agenda. In 1904, the Abbey Theatre came into being, based in premises near the eastern end of Lower Abbey Street, Dublin. Hostile public reaction to Yeats's *Countess Cathleen* (1899), J. M. Synge's *Playboy of the Western World* (1907), and—much later—Sean O'Casey's *Plough and the Stars* (1926) confirmed rather than challenged the centrality of theater in the emergent political movement.

This was something other than a mere continuation of the nineteenth-century pursuit of parliamentary independence that, in turn, had marked itself off from the radical (or Jacobin) initiatives of the United Irishmen at the end of the previous century. The latter were explicitly republican and separatist, as was the IRB (founded in 1858). Despite some well-publicized doctrine to the contrary, all Irish republican movements were nationalist in mood; not all nationalists favored the establishment of a separate republic. By the end of the nineteenth century, parliamentary nationalism had split and had become little more than the pursuit of concessions.

The New Nationalism, as I wish to term the movement of which Thomas MacDonagh, Patrick Pearse, and Joseph Plunkett were prominent advocates, drew on continental models of national action, forged a stronger bond between political and religious identity, and paid far closer attention to cultural propaganda than had ever been previously thought wise. Discourses of race played some part in the New Nationalist rhetoric, though never to the extent witnessed in France and Germany between 1890 and the Great War. Language provided a less toxic potion through the imbibing of which an elusive oneness of the collective and the individual, the archaic past and the eager present, might be achieved. What becomes desirable—the amalgam of (1) a processive move towards an object always still unreached with (2) that object itself—is the collective individual, the essence of those totalitarian systems of the Right (those of the Left are different, not better, at least not necessarily better) with whom some Irish republicans collaborated in the 1930s and after.

Plunkett never became more than functionally communicative in Gaelic, unlike Pearse and MacDonagh. Except on the issues of education and female suffrage, Irish New Nationalism was illiberal or antiprogressive and antimodernist. The two issues in question were championed by eloquent signatories of the 1916 Proclamation (Pearse for education, Connolly for feminism), with little room for Plunkett to choose a third. Yeats's rejection of "the filthy modern tide" may serve as an ideal, though Yeats was never wholeheartedly of that party. The socialist contribution to Easter 1916 arrived despite the nationalist program, and not in replication of it; the socialist priority did not survive.

What Yeats had done, even in the 1890s, was to demonstrate the potency of theater as a form of resistance to metropolitan (that is, British) values. Rational utility, consensus, personal "getting on," could never satisfy a nation awakened in the theater of its own longing. The tragic, the heroic, the sacrificial and ritualistic—all these could be engaged with through participation-in-observance at the theater. If it is too often said that the 1916 Rising was the work of poets, one notes with greater relevance that at least four of the signatories to the Proclamation—Connolly, MacDonagh, Pearse, and Plunkett—had written plays. William Pearse and Plunkett were experienced, if amateur, actors. Plunkett and MacDonagh had become fully engaged in the workings of theater companies.

Though the Abbey has achieved a worldwide reputation as Irish national theater, it had no official status until well into the 1920s, and it experienced a series of defections or "splits" that compromised any claim comprehensively to represent the nation. The grandly named Theater of Ireland came into existence in 1906, largely as a result of fission in Abbey Street. It drew considerable talent to its cause, including Padraic Colum, Edward Martyn (1859–1923), and George Russell. As president of the new group, Martyn was an unlikely heresiarch or breakaway pioneer. A devout Catholic and a landowner, he championed the work of Henrik Ibsen. What he had come to dislike at the Abbey was the emphasis on "peasant drama." He sought a theater that would be intellectual, psychologically acute and—in a word—European. In Dublin, the problems his Theater of Ireland faced were crudely basic. The demarcation between amateur and professional acting was unclear. The availability of suitable premises was complicated not only by architectural demands, but also by a licensing system that was, at heart, a form of intermittent political control exercised by Dublin Castle.

Late in 1910, a primary school in north Dublin once the property of the Jesuit order came on the market. Josephine Plunkett bought up the sixty-nine-year lease, acquiring a number of rentable apartments into the bargain. The Dun Emer Guild, a craft enterprise run by Yeats's sisters, gained accommodation at the rear. The idea of basing a new company in Hardwicke Street may have arisen from the practice in the Dun Emer rooms of playing Charades on Sunday evenings. The main auditorium was converted into a theater for renting out to visiting companies. It was also used by the Plunkett family for private entertainments; apart from dances, the nature of these cannot now be recovered.[21] From the firm of Strahan, the countess was persuaded to buy some leftovers from the Exhibition of 1884, and with them gilded ornaments and striking serpents. These provided the bare stage with an exotic framework. The location in Hardwicke Street was close to Belvedere College, in an area scarcely better than a slum. The entire street has now disappeared in the course of a housing renewal program.

From November 1911 onward, the new Irish Theater of Martyn, MacDonagh, and Plunkett used what Joe came to term "our hall"—meaning the family's. The first production under these arrangements was James Stephens's one-act, tenement-set *Julia Elizabeth*, a copy of which survives in the Plunkett Papers. Joe had no association with Yeats, Synge, and Gregory or their company and so, unlike the Fay brothers, he cannot be considered to have rejected the Abbey style or revolted against that impressive "anti-establishment." His engagement with theater went hand in hand with his mother's commercial enterprise. He had taken part in a production of Ostrovski's *The Storm* in February, using the stage name Luke Killeen—the surname derived from a suburban road in which the family owned considerable property.

The authorities had moved against the Theater of Ireland's production of the Russian play in the unlicensed Molesworth Hall, after which the Plunketts' Hardwicke Street hall was used. Tickets were not sold; instead, annual membership fees of ten shillings were sought, guaranteeing admission to five productions. "The performances thereby became private, members-only entertainments outside the jurisdiction of any licensing body."[22] An experiment in club-theater or, in another perspective, the drama of the coterie, was under way. An acknowledged influence was the Moscow Arts Theater. Joe wrote an exotic play set near Karnak in the Pharaonic Egypt of "B.C. 950 (about)," played in May 1913 after MacDonagh's *Metempsychosis, Or a Mad World* (with a present-day Irish setting).

Later, in June, *The Dance of Osiris* was given three additional performances in "our hall."[23] Staged this time with a revival of Stephens's *Marriage of Julia Elizabeth*, the Egyptian play was produced as a benefit for two charitable causes—Saint Enda's School (run by Pearse) and the Connemara Islanders Relief Fund, the latter an attempt to counteract distress in the West of Ireland. Both could be loosely termed political causes, though the drama offered by Plunkett in support was, on the surface, exotic, remote, and ancient. One motive was experimentation with the antirealist stagecraft of Edward Gordon Craig (1872–1966), whose *Towards a New Theatre* appeared in 1913. Geraldine Plunkett painted hieroglyphs on temple pillars made of hessian.

The plot revolves round an attempted assassination delayed when a priestess is required to dance as a prologue to the bloody act. (Some influence of Wilde's *Salome* is clear.) Her agreement is conditional on the presence of gods-in-effigy, from which spring soldiers who kill the would-be assassins. As in the fragmentary schoolboy fiction, Plunkett's theme is homicidal. In retrospect, it is possible to read the play as an inquiry into the fate awaiting conspirators, and the implications were hardly encouraging. Indeed, in however so slight a degree, *The Dance of Osiris* contributes to a premonition among the signatories of Easter 1916 that they were doomed to more than failure.

William J. Feeney noted that the play-script was signed Luke Killeen and that the players were identified as the Luke Killeen Company. Stage names are commonplace, though Plunkett's growing list of pseudonyms and disguises deserves attention. Considered alongside his evasive/ostentatious behavior as a suitor, they might prompt questions about the self behind the names. After *The Dance of Osiris* Joseph Holloway, an inveterate first-nighter in Dublin theaters, recorded how customary calls for the author "only produced the apparition of one of the figures of the gods" between folds of the stage curtain.[24]

Plunkett's choice of an Egyptian setting reflected the extraordinary length of his Egyptian reading list entered into a Stonyhurst notebook circa 1909. He had (perhaps) been to Egypt once and, at the close of the later Algerian visit when the weather turned very bad, Moya had considered moving eastward along the North African coast to Cairo. Nothing happened to realize a second (or perhaps first) visit to the land of the pharaohs, and that possible first has disappeared from the preserved family chronicle. Joe used Rameses II as a joke-signature, and deployed fragments of Egyptian allusion here and there throughout his notes. The play was never published, despite his having direct access to the pages of *The Irish Review*. It remains an exotic detail in the Irish Theater's brief history.

A Franco-German Club, bringing together respectable individuals with an interest in drama, had been established in Dublin before the new century began. Edouard Cadic, a Breton professor of French in UCD, played a leading role: he had taught both Joyce and Pearse. The Club met in suitably large private houses, including Cadic's in Pembroke Park. Once again an important function was the mixing of young people, male and female, with adults more experienced in the arts. Members prepared for reading-rehearsals even without an intention of seeing a script through to production. Joe prepared *L'été de Saint Martin* by Henri Meilhac (1831–1897), a librettist who had worked with Bizet and Offenbach. Cadic was pleased with his efforts, and an added pleasure for Joe was Columba O'Carroll's presence. (Though she rejected him, clearly she did not totally avoid him.) When about sixty members of the club gathered at No. 26 Upper Fitzwilliam Street on 23 January 1911, the Plunketts staged a grand show with lines of Irish harpists playing music disinterred by the count from his basement archive. Joe was racked by a persistent cough at this time; he also broached the Young Ireland branch of the United Irish League and Bergson's *Time and Free Will*.[25]

In this little world of amateurs and overlapping small companies, Plunkett played the player with considerable flair, using a variety of stage names. The Theater of Ireland included Grace and Kathleen McCormack, who worked in the Dun Emer enterprise as designer and weaver respectively. Teams of siblings characterized their social world; Joe, Mimi, and George Plunkett; John, Joseph, and Thomas MacDonagh, and three Reddins of Belvederian background. Patrick Pearse's brother, Willie, contributed with distinction, and Tommy Dillon's brother, Andrew. Outsiders included Bethel Solomons, a young Jewish gynecologist, and R. M. Smyllie, later a famous editor of the *Irish Times*—well, famous in Ireland. Despite the presiding and subsidizing figure of Edward Martyn, this was Tír na nÓg, a pretend Land of Youth. It created *esprit de corps* in advance of the insurrection to which several leading players would contribute with their lives.

Formal arrangements for the theater were drawn up in the summer of 1914, as *The Irish Review* (under Joe's editorship) was visibly failing. A holograph (with many corrections) of the agreement between MacDonagh, Martyn, and Plunkett has recently been discovered in the Aidan Heavey Library, Athlone. While much of the cash burden was to fall on Martyn, Plunkett undertook to provide the essential services, including upkeep of the premises and employment of a caretaker. Clause 22 curiously insisted that "the details of the agreement shall not be made public," in the interests perhaps of keeping the countess in the dark about her son's assuming control of what was strictly her property. The triumvirate "shall, acting collectively, have a power of veto in all such matters as the casting of plays," and—previous clause—"shall choose the plays to be performed." In this version of the MacDonagh-Martyn-Plunkett agreement, no one director had a veto over the choice of a play, an issue that arose in 1916 when Plunkett disapproved of Strindberg's *Easter*.

It had been an axiom with Martyn that his theater would banish the Irish peasant, and the program in which Joe Plunkett participated remained true to that ordinance. A degree of metadramatic irony could be discerned here. At least three of his associates were actively plotting a rebellion that invoked an Irish history of revolt in which peasant participation had been recruited—1798, for example. The Land War (1879–1882) had brought the rural economy to the fore, and successive Land Acts had created a powerful class of smallholders whose votes counted heavily in national politics. What Plunkett was planning was a revolt that also eschewed peasant drama, a revolt in which the seizing of important urban buildings would constitute the initial act. The theatricality of Pearse's oration in front of the GPO on Easter Monday 1916 has often been noted, less so his turning his back on rural Ireland, which had borne the brunt in all previous rebellions, save Emmet's in 1803. Obsessed with Emmet's "martyrdom," Pearse neglected to study the Land War. Constantly evoking a pastoral, or at least ruralist, vision of an Ireland not only free but Gaelic, not only Gaelic but free, he knew little of farming or the countryside except his chosen retreat in south Connemara. The detailed plans for rebellion, however, were Plunkett's work, not Pearse's. And Plunkett knew less about the homes of Tipperary than Pearse did. Is it too much to suggest that the planning, like the theater, was antirealist?

Journey to Berlin and Casement, Spring 1915

Plunkett's mission to Germany on behalf of the Military Council was masked by the plausibility of his desire, as a well-to-do victim of tuberculosis, for treatment at an Alpine sanatorium. As far as the war was concerned in the spring of 1915, Spain remained neutral and Italy had not yet joined the Allied side. Nevertheless, his determination to reach Berlin through neutral Switzerland complicated any casual maintenance of a traveler's aide-mémoire.

Details of railway timetables, comments on hotels and fellow passengers all contributed to the image of a holidaymaker with medical needs. As a useful record of serious business accomplished, the codes adopted for addresses and personal names seem naive. It is difficult to conclude what intentions and motivations lay behind the document. Perhaps because it would have had to pass muster with the British authorities on Joe's homeward trip through Folkstone, London, Liverpool, he left the journal in Berlin; it was returned to Ireland by Casement's cousin, Mrs. Bannister, after the war. Less obviously, it would have had to satisfy the German ones while he traveled in the Reich. In neither case was use of the Gaelic language likely to reassure.

Geraldine Plunkett Dillon published the diary in 1956, amounting to seventeen pages of text, and two interpolated photographs.[26] The opening eight pages take him from Dublin (Saint Patrick's Day, 1915) to the Swiss-German frontier (19 April). These cheery accounts of travel include Plunkett's first encounter with the Great War when the Italian boat from Barcelona to Genoa is twice halted by the French navy. Entries for 20–30 April continue in English, increasingly terse and employing initial letters to indicate his contacts. Pages 41–48 are inscribed in Gaelic, with several poems in English among the brief diary entries. Most of this material is reprinted in Honor O Brolchain's account of her great-uncle's life, the Gaelic summarized in English.

In France he had the advantage of speaking the language, while arousing more curiosity as a stranger in a land partly occupied by foreign troops. French, and indeed British, intelligence can hardly have regarded civilian foreigners with equanimity. The latter was well aware of Casement's movements. On Good Friday (2 April) he arrived in Florence, where he met up with family friends, learned how to identify Italian plainclothes police ("a useful accomplishment"), inspected Michael Angelo's *David* (1504) in the Galleria Accademia, and read sixty-six of the Psalms. "He was some writer as well as some fighter. I wonder which chilled me?"

Throughout the diary, the writerly side of Plunkett found scope for expression. Six poems are inscribed: (1) some nonsense lines about Saragossa ("Fever Rimes"), (2) an imitation Shakespearean sonnet (untitled), (3) "The Lady Elect," (4) "The Mask," (5) an untitled, irregular, unrhymed, and unfinished poem, and (6) "The Spark." All but the first two were written in Germany. On Sunday, 11 April, while still in Berne, he had gone to

Mass in the Dreifaltig Keitskirche on Taubenstrasse. The encounter with a street named after doves sent him into several ecstatic recollections of Miss O'Carroll, whose code (dove) features in the sonnet and in "The Lady Elect," with blood, fire/flame, and hearts more frequently repeated among the diary poems.

Two points deserve attention. Item five deals prosaically but frantically with "the back of your neck." Lines 5–10 read, "Years ago—before you were grown up / It was hidden by your hair. / But I used to catch glimpses of it / And go crazy; / I used to walk behind you on purpose / And feel like a criminal." Line 14 (unfinished or unpunctuated) reads, "And I swore." These lines deal more openly with sexual obsession than any others Plunkett ever wrote, preserving a smart juvenile vocabulary (go crazy, criminal) but abandoning the theme exactly where what he swore or might have sworn could have been written.

Item six is a more polished performance, consisting of seven five-line stanzas of some complexity. Written on 7 June 1915, it appears as the final item in the "Occulta" section of the 1916 *Poems*, with, however, a number of small discrepancies between the two versions. The poem might properly be titled "Renunciation," and certainly earns that title better than Pearse's of the same name, though there are similarities. The Columban obsession with "your name" is, in the diary version, overcome or at least moderated—the parallel phrase is "my name."

Now shall I shout my name
Now shall I seek to die

By any hands but these
In battle or in flood,
Whether I burn or freeze
No more shall I spare ease,
No more shall I spare blood . . .

Now death and I embark
And sail into the dark
With laughter on our lips.

A thanatic resolution of his sexual crux provided its own code for disappointment with diminishing German interest in an Irish campaign, while his lingering hope for such external support erased the lure of suicide (lines 20–21) by a commitment to a more general spilling of blood (line 25). On his return Plunkett did little to dispel the conspirator-insurrectionists' reliance on German support. Later, Sean Fitzgibbon told an inquirer that Plunkett "gave the impression that his visit abroad had made him sane"—a diagnosis Fitzgibbon had not always entertained. On reflection Fitzgibbon, a member of the Volunteer Executive but not an IRB man like Plunkett, came to the conclusion that "his moderation was a pose assumed to deceive."[27]

From the outset, Casement was Plunkett's objective, because the former had traveled to Germany more or less on impulse after war began, had negotiated in New York, but had not been back in touch with Dublin. Casement had contributed to *The Irish Review*, and had written poetry. En route for Berlin, Plunkett was supposedly an invalid hoping to take the waters for his tuberculosis. Naturally he required reading matter and conversation. Early entries in the diary record a variety of literary connections. The opening paragraph offers little of interest, except for Plunkett's noticing a Dublin police detective whose presence on a wartime boat was unexceptional. A more familiar reference draws in Gerald Gurrin, whom *The Monitor* listed as a Stonyhurst prize winner.[28] The two eldest Plunkett boys only reached the school in 1906, though Thomas Henry Gurrin (godfather to Fiona Plunkett in 1896) had recommended it to the countess. According to Mrs. Plunkett Dillon, Gurrin senior was employed by the British Foreign Office as a handwriting expert. This was probably just an occasional service; in 1898, Gurrin made international news when he demonstrated that the handwriting on the bordereau supposedly written by Alfred Dreyfus was identical to that of Major Esterhazy. More banally, Gurrin (1848–1913, Norfolk-born son of an Irish father and English mother) was a professional graphologist who also wrote textbooks in Spanish for students of English. The Gurrins were assisting Plunkett's passage with introductions in northern Spain.

The diary's second paragraph reports on Parisian matters:

> After an enormous dejeuner in the Gare D'Orsay (more like a cathedral than a station—as my friend Chesterton says "What poet-race Shot such

> cyclopean arches at the stars.") bought Edmond About "Le nez d'un notaire" (which is good fooling) and a map of Paris. Studied both of these for a short while and then with my sole piece of luggage (a black portmanteau) in the cloakroom, set out on my feet and my adventures. I turned to my right coming out of the station and walked down the quays till I came to St. Michel. Then up the whole length of the Boul' Miche' and again to the right into the Bould. Montparnasse. On the left side of this, a little way up is a narrow street called Rue Campaigne Premiere and up this I walked till I came to No. 11 on the left side, where I rang and asked the concierge if M. James Stephens lived there. To my great surprise she pointed out a door and said, "au premiere." I went up the winding stairs and knocked at the first door. It was answered by Mrs Stephens and two small children, a boy and a girl. Mrs Stephens told me that she was to meet Seumas at 3.15 in front of L'Opera so I went there and met them and we had talk and coffee in the Cafe de la Paix. Stephens is writing things about the war as he sees them. He seems to have become orthodox (in the right sense) in his opinions about Irish affairs but otherwise is lamentably concerned with ideas (pur et simple) instead of realities, i. e. things that may (or may not) be or become instead of things that are.

Chesterton and Plunkett had no known personal contact. The line quoted comes from "King's Cross Station," which appeared in *The Wild Knight and Other Poems* (1900). The original dealt with the London railway terminus in some postcalamitous ruined scenario. Edmond About (1828–1885) was a French novelist and farceur, whose politics went somewhat radical toward the end. *Le roi des montagnes* (1856) told the story of a Greek brigand chief who turned his business into a registered limited liability company. *Le nez d'un notaire* appeared in 1862. James Stephens, poet, novelist, and author of *Insurrection in Dublin* (1916) was well known to Plunkett as a contributor to *The Irish Review* and as an actor-dramatist in the Theater of Ireland. Mrs. Stephens, however, was another matter. Millicent was a married but deserted woman, with a daughter by her husband; a son, by Stephens, was born in 1909. The poet's views lay well to the left of Plunkett's: in the early years of the war, he was contributing to *The Irish Citizen* and the Larkinite *Irish Worker*.

In Italy he decided to buy some further "necessary books"—including

C. L Leland's *Legends of Florence*. On the day he discovered Taubenstrasse in Berne, he finished reading Shaw's *Perfect Wagnerite*. Four days later he "went on a bust in a book shop," buying H. G. Wells's *An Englishman Looks at the World*, George Moore's *Vale*, George Borrow's *Romany Rye*, and Arnold Bennett's *Hilda Lessways* (one of the Clayhanger novels). Bennett he had long approved of. Wells had taught him how to fight little wars; here he was entering the battlefield to end all battlefields, while posing as the invalid he actually was. The reading list suited his declared purpose of recuperation in a Swiss resort, a magic mountain in Thomas Mann's later parable. It also signaled his isolation. His diary records steady drinking, of wine mainly, but also a mix of cognac and Malaga. Occasionally, poor health provides a context for the indulgence, but lack of company also features. What one does not find, even when he has reached the *Kaiserreich*, is an interest in German literature or even German scenery. Casement's company does not alter things. In the Gaelic portion of the diary, Plunkett records his reading of books acquired from the older conspirator and his associates—work by Robert Browning, George Meredith, Moore again, and Christina Rossetti. By necessity if not by choice, the IRB's representative in Berlin remained a middle-class reader of English literature. Even the Gaelic diary entries, numerous enough but using a transparent code for addresses and political contacts, was written in what Seamas Ó Síocháin calls "a very unidiomatic variety" of the language.[29]

Ó Síocháin's exhaustive biography of Casement provides the best contextualization of Plunkett's German mission. Negotiations with military and diplomatic personnel about an Irish Brigade to be formed out of prisoner-of-war camps, and about a substantial German involvement in the planned insurrection did not bode well. Nor did the changing international scene. Italy entered the war on the Allied side in May, and a new cabinet in London appointed Edward Carson as attorney general (bad news for Irish nationalists). Plunkett regarded the Italian decision as "accomplished treachery," a phrase some (including Irish nationalists) might think worthy of him. In the prisoner-of-war camps, he met a former Dublin associate, Robert Smyllie, an occasional player in the Hardwicke Street theater. Casement's view of the conspirators' plans for an insurrection in Dublin—"criminal stupidity"—reflected his steadily diminished reliance on German aid. By the time G. N. Plunkett communicated with him from Berne in April 1916, mere days before the zeppelin would go up, confidence had turned to despair. Nevertheless Casement promised his own personal engagement should an Irish flag be raised in rebellion.

Strindberg's *Easter*, in Dublin 1916

On Good Friday and Holy Saturday 1911, the pupils of Saint's Enda's College staged a Passion play in Gaelic at the Abbey Theatre. The script by Pearse incorporated some traditional Irish songs into the dramatic narrative. Few alliances of liturgy and language-revival struck a more prophetic note. Colum reviewed *Cluiche Trí Rannach* favorably in *The Irish Review*. The intensely local character of the occasion promised a resurrection of Ireland's "soul" on terms of its own creation. Though Catholicism pervaded Irish nationalism like air through a snare, external sources of influence were few; or, to say something different, few external influences were acknowledged. Five Easters later, Pearse directed another drama, though by then it was possible to speak of the Republic's "gallant allies in Europe," that is to say, the Hapsburg and Hohenzollern empires.

It is unlikely that Joseph Plunkett read Miguel de Unamuno's *El Sentimiento trágico de la vida* when it was published toward the end of 1912. Its distribution in the English-speaking world was limited and its appeal to Catholic intellectuals problematic, while Plunkett's knowledge of Spanish was poor at best. Somewhat more likely is Plunkett's encountering an article in an American magazine the Spanish philosopher cites toward the end of his book:

> I have just this very day read in the *Nation* (July 6, 1912) an article, entitled "A Dramatic Inferno," that deals with an English translation of the works of Strindberg, and it opens with the following judicious observation: "If there were in the world a sincere and total pessimism, it would necessarily be silent. The despair which finds a voice is a social mood, it is the cry of misery which brother utters to brother when both are stumbling through a valley of shadows which is peopled with—comrades. In its anguish it bears witness to something that is good in life, for it presupposes sympathy . . . The real gloom, the sincere despair, is dumb and blind; it writes no books,

and feels no impulse to burden the universe with a monument more lasting than brass."[30]

As the last phrase alludes to Horace, so the account of modern despair echoes Dante, an author with whom the young Plunkett had complex relations. These were compass-bearings to which he paid strikingly little attention after 1914. A poor showing at Belvedere, illness at Saint George's (Weybridge), some brio and little discipline at Stonyhurst, and failure to matriculate for UCD, had left Plunkett a high-flying academic nonperformer.[31] His reading in contemporary literary was distinctly middle-of-the-English-road, well below the classical standards implied in *The Nation*. A notebook (see appendix 1), which he described as a "bibliography," gives a clear indication of his taste in modern fiction; a list of ten authors includes the following novelists—George Brown Burgin (1856–1944), G. K. Chesterton, Georg Moritz Ebers (1837–1898), Maurice Hewlett (1861–1923), Maarten Maartens (1858–1915), David Christie Murray (1847–1907), and Elizabeth Robins [Pennell] (1855–1936). The three remaining names are Belloc, Shaw, and Fiona Macleod. Apart from Shaw, of whom Plunkett disapproved, it is an entirely non-Irish list, notable for the oblivion to which most of its names have now been consigned. No mention of enduring reputations—Hardy or Conrad or Ford Madox Ford. An editor, later proprietor, of *The Irish Review* can hardly have remained ignorant of *The English Review* (founded 1908), which in its first years published work by Hardy, D. H. Lawrence, Wyndham Lewis, and H. G. Wells. (*The English Review* bought advertisement space in its Irish counterpart, at least in the early numbers.) Pitting G. B. Burgin (author of *Galahad's Garden*, 1908) against George Moore (cf. *The Lake*, 1905) or Conrad (cf. *The Secret Agent*, 1907), one cannot classify Plunkett's choice as anything other than bourgeois and provincial—English provincial at that.

The preliminaries inscribed in the bibliography notebook highlight the compiler's determined contrariness. The top line reads: "Homo sum humani nihil in me alienum puto," a phrase from the Roman playwright Terence (died 159 B.C.) meaning "I am a human being, I consider nothing that is human alien to me." Below this admirably balanced self-definition, a column of names or signatures begins "Joseph Plunkett" and descends in equally large writing:

- Ramessu II
- Cheops
- Gothmus
- Idiotes
- Memphes[32]

Of the five terms, three are distinctive of ancient Egypt, if a trifle vague in transliteration. Rameses II (1303—1213 B.C.) was the greatest military pharaoh of the nineteenth dynasty. Cheops was the second pharaoh of the fourth dynasty. Memphis is the site of a magnificent sphynx. But these terse dictionary identifications perhaps miss the list's significance. Taking Joseph Plunkett as the first name, then the second is an ancient military leader, the second to bear the name. The follow two non-Egyptian pseudo-names (Gothus and Idiotes) carry negative connotations unless (in the first case) the Swedish family of theologians and professors is implied. In the second case (Idiotes), the Greek meanings of a private person as opposed to magistrate or ruler; common soldier as distinct from a military officer; and, finally a writer of prose as opposed to a poet, are inconclusive.

The strikingly bifurcated character of Plunkett's mind is well illustrated in two brief and incomplete documents that sit side by side among his papers. The first is a short story, "Snakes in the Back Attic," attributed to Birdy German Haux.

> It was a snowy evening in July. Under the naphta flares, Guinevere hurried anxiously towards her humble home. The young man under the lamp raised his hat and came forward . . . Silently he took up his position at her side. Silently they walked together saying no word. The sidewalk seemed to glide beneath their feet. The Sky-signs glowed and glimmered past them and seemed to bear a message for the two whose destinies were to be so closely interwoven. Suddenly the heart beats of the mighty City suffered a change. It seemed to be swiftly stricken with palpitation.

The second document, untitled, consists of ten numbered points:

1. Suspension Act.
2. Arms Prohibition.

3. Foot and Mouth Restrictions removed. Proximate Famine.
4. Redmond's offer accepted but no steps taken to arm or train the Volunteers.
5. Misrepresentations of Irish recruiting.
6. Pressure by threats and intimidation upon employees through their employers.
7. Ill treatment of recruits and their dependents.
8. Depopulation of Ireland.
9. Desertion of Parnell's principles of Nationality.
10. British historic response to trust and self-sacrifice.[33]

One's first inclination is to contrast the two documents as being (the first) fictional and (the second) historico-political. Rather than impose these terms absolutely, let us refer to them in turn as "A" and "B." Undoubtedly, in "A" there is a clear reference to English literary tradition through the name Guinevere, who, in the legendary material concerning the Knights of the Round Table, is the wife of King Arthur, central to plots of seduction and fidelity, chivalry and betrayal. The Knights, as a surviving remnant of the departed Roman order, exercised a fascination for Victorians anxious about the future, the upward invasion of *demos*, and a decline in shared religious belief. In Plunkett's generation, this material was familiar through Alfred Tennyson's epic poems and, long behind that, the work of Thomas Malory (d. 1471). However, the implied landscape of "A" is far removed from the idyllic, courtly rural world of Camelot. The sidewalk and "sky-signs" of the mighty city strongly suggest New York, or some other American metropolis. That the setting is in fundamental ways anomalous in itself is conveyed in the opening phrase about snow in July. German Haux may transmute to German Hawks. Nature is out of joint, and human society is a distant vast organism subject to unannounced change.

The bullet-point structure of "B" also presages vast change. Though the proper-name vocabulary—Redmond, Ireland, Parnell—gives the document the appearance of a political analysis, there are odd unexplained features. The "Suspension Act" might refer to the decision in Westminster to postpone implementation of Home Rule for Ireland until after the Great War. The term, however, is highly general and, historically, has been used to describe successive suspensions of the habeas corpus provision under common law.

Far more inscrutable are references to foot-and-mouth disease and depopulation. An outbreak of the disease (affecting pigs and cattle) had occurred in 1912, with the effect that farmers were unable to send livestock to the Irish market in Liverpool, instead placing them in quarantine at Birkenhead.[34] The loss fell upon the Liverpool dealers. It did not bring proximate famine to Ireland, which did not then suffer especial depopulation. It is true that the removal of restrictions on movement of people from affected areas would have aided recruitment to the armed forces.

Point six appears to refer to the labor troubles of 1913, though the phrasing strangely transfers responsibility away from the employers and on to an unnamed power exercising pressure *through* them. The state in 1913 had found the Irish employers a more than adequate repressor of workers—backed up, of course, by the police. However, Connolly wrote in the *Worker's Republic* of 15 January 1916 about "Economic Conscription," defining this as *more than* the "enforced utilizing of all the manhood of a country in order to fight its battles." Instead, by this term Connolly meant what would later be called "the war economy"—"the enforced use of all the economic powers of a country to fight its battles."[35] It is possible that "B" could be read as an outline of Plunkett's shifting politics, toward a syndicalist antistate position of the kind associated with Georges Sorel, whose legacy was to be more fascist than socialist. In support, there is the syndicalist influence of Jim Larkin in Ireland, though Larkin's training was American and not French and, in the longer run, he became a member of the Comintern executive (1924).[36] Against this reading of "B," one must stack up Plunkett's aversion to "the populace," his position as the heir presumptive of very considerable wealth, and the absence of leftward tendencies. British army recruitment after August 1914 was doubtless conducted through a variety of means including an appeal to employers: Point 6 is an extreme formulation of the procedure, if that is what is referred to. The ten points conclude in a restatement of nationalist doctrine—that Britain always fails to appreciate Irish generosity (or chivalry).

Although these ten points rather vaguely trace the origins of a sharp division between Britain and Ireland, probably focused on the autumn of 1914, they also possess an active, constructivist quality. It may be excessive to suggest that they resemble headings for a futuristic novel. Plunkett certainly toyed with such a fiction, to be called "The New Power," and set in a period round 1920. Both Tennyson and Wells could be counted *accoucheurs* in the very limited process of sketching the book. This was a popular genre from the 1890s onward, when the fear of (or desire for) conflict with Germany began to infiltrate fiction and propaganda.[37] Erskine Childers's *The Riddle of the Sands* (1903) is pertinent to Plunkett's literary training because, after 1916, the novelist will become director of propaganda for the Irish separatist cause (and later be executed by comrades for his trouble). More renowned names—P. G. Wodehouse, "Saki" (H. H. Munro), and Charles Doughty—also made their contributions. From Plunkett's "bibliography" notebook, we know that he interested himself in at least one of these fantasy prophets, the prolific novelist David Christie Murray, who contributed to the highly influential *Great War of 189-: A Forecast* (1892).[38]

It would be wrong to force "A" and "B" into too close a relationship, violating their individual characteristics. For example, a deleted passage in "A" refers to Guinevere's mother, waiting at home for her daughter to return. The deletion may at some level reflect the relationship between the countess and her children, and the strange distance that opened up between mother and son when they were both in America. The author's pseudonym probably echoes the word "hoax" (as much as hawks) while also giving a learned international flavor. Nothing like a domestic or individualized human focus emerges from "B," which is, of course, a mere sketch where "A" purports to be the actual opening paragraph of a work in continuous prose. Where "A" hints at personal destinies, "B" is a blueprint for crisis.

Irish literature had few obvious links to this theme, neither its chivalry nor the "coming war" motif. Nevertheless Standish O'Grady's fiction strove to create images of Celtic and Gaelic nobility, while D. P. Moran's magazine, *The Leader*, proclaimed an inevitable conflict between two civilizations, of which Ireland was clearly the superior. When O'Grady ventured a science fiction tale about Chinese warlords achieving world domination (in A.D. 2179), he did so under a pseudonym.[39] Irish literature would have liked to stand apart, despite the success abroad of *The Playboy of the Western World* (1907). A critic in *The English Review* of December 1912 drew Synge's *Riders to the Sea* into comparison with August Strindberg's *The Crown Bride*.[40] Although *The Irish Review* largely restricted itself to literature produced locally, it published a few impressive articles on Scandinavian drama. In April 1913, Strindberg had been treated in a pair of articles by Mary Colum (née Maguire) and Bryan Cooper, in response to an Abbey Theatre production. *There are Crimes and There are*

Crimes, a comedy that opens in a cemetery, had been the first Strindberg play staged in Ireland.[41] Martyn, a partner with Joe in Hardwicke Street, wrote on Ibsen during the period of Plunkett's dominance as editor/proprietor.[42] Martyn's own plays were strenuous applications of Ibsenite practice to Irish conditions.[43] Ibsen in old age was becoming an acceptable point of reference, a giant of theatrical history. He died in 1906, the same year as Davitt, founder of the Land League, a "politics of conviction" Irishman out of tune with the increasingly narrow convictions of the New Nationalism. Among the tributes paid to Ibsen in Ireland, few were more unexpected than that of Pearse. What he particularly commended was the dramatist's commitment to a new language, or at least a language rescued from its dependence on a foreign tongue (Danish) and now employed in the cause of a national literature. The Ibsenite position was more complicated than Pearse's tribute suggested, but the tribute was nonetheless remarkable in itself.[44]

Davitt's death, though little remembered in the circles where Plunkett was becoming influential, had silenced an emergent trend in Irish politics for which the term *democracy* had been central. Although the founder of the Land League remained an Irish nationalist, he was capable of international sympathies, even advocating an alliance between British workers and Irish separatists. Plunkett's only links with Davitt-ite ideas had been established through short-lived friendship with Frank Skeffington and W. J. Moloney, through—that is—the Young Ireland branch of the United Irish League that Thomas Dillon succeeded in distracting him from. Davitt too was capable of sturdy independence when it came to disagreement with the Catholic Church. Pearse's appreciation of Ibsen as a northern exemplar for the Gaelic Revival depended on a studied neglect of some fundamental differences. The literary movement of which he became the best-known member had emerged from a sharp conflict between anticlericalist and peasant-focused visions of the Norwegian future. Ibsen's dramatic language was no recovery of an ancient tongue, more an adaptation of demotic speech to radical dramatic ends. If, at a distance, he seemed to provide a model for Irish emulation, there were other Scandinavian writers who might yet intrude on plans for an Irish insurrection.

Approval of Strindberg's *Easter* for production by the Theater Company of Ireland can be assigned ultimately to Edward Martyn, who combined Ibsenite enthusiasm and Catholic piety in unique combination.

MacDonagh's positive support can also be assumed, though we know painfully little of his attitude toward foreign literature. The two directors stood in total contrast in their expectations for the coming Easter: MacDonagh joining the IRB's Military Council in April while Martyn remained outside of both the conspiratorial Brotherhood and the openly armed movement while acting as a figurehead in Sinn Féin. The MacDonagh brothers—John was a professional, employed by the Theater of Ireland—were the practical team, with Martyn and Plunkett taking on other responsibilities.

We know even less of Plunkett's attitude. His scattered notes on literature, his reading lists and diaries, give no indication of an interest in Ibsen, though Shaw and Joyce had been vocal in celebrating the Norwegian iconoclast. He did not lack an interest in contemporary developments in the theater, for he admired Edward Gordon Craig's theory and practice. *The Irish Review* had attended to Ibsen's posthumous reputation, but the theater in which Martyn and Plunkett were active as directors did not go out of its way to prove the point. There had been two phases to Ibsen's long career, the first characterized by plays with a poetic or even idealist character—*Brand* (1866) and *Peer Gynt* (1867), notably. In the second phase, a strongly realist and socially critical perspective is adopted, evidenced powerfully in *A Doll's House* (1879) and even more powerfully in *Ghosts* (1881). It was this latter play that gave Pearse a title for his essay of Christmas 1915, the undisguised annunciation of imminent revolt.[45] Between the two major phases of Ibsen's development, he wrote *Emperor and Gallilean* (1873), a vast reading-drama in ten acts based on the career of Emperor Julian "the Apostate" (c. A.D. 331–363). The play turns on a possible return to paganism, and simultaneously on the idea of a total transformation of reality, anticipating Nietzsche's transvaluation of all values, and the skeptical pessimism of the early twentieth century. However loftily, Ibsen's near unproduceable pivotal work takes its place with and above the multitudinous novels and plays of epochal conflict, end-of-an-era anxieties, and wars between civilizations. These were themes evident in Plunkett's middle-brow reading list, as well as in the manifestos of rarefied experiment. As Toril Moi has pointed out, *Emperor and Galilean* "is a play about war, terrorism, religious fanaticism and religious persecution" written (or at least conceived) at the end of the Franco-Prussian War and the bloody conclusion forced on the Paris Commune.[46] Today, we might note with a rueful smile that the tragic ending of the near-global conflict occurred in what is now Iraq, with a Christian general proclaimed emperor. In the Dublin of 1916, such members of Sinn Féin who might be thought familiar with the play (Martyn certainly) and others, (members of the IRB, Pearse, and MacDonagh, possibly) would have noted the long action's commencement on Easter Night.

In retrospect, the occurrence of the IRB Rising on Easter Monday has been accepted as uncomplicatedly symbolic. The IRB were popularly known as Fenians, a term partly deriving from the pre-Christian sagas (such as *Na Fianna*) and partly from the Phoenix Clubs of the mid-nineteenth century devoted to national rebirth. Thus, to rise at Easter was fitting. But to rise at Easter in a military enterprise known to be futile raises questions about the nature of symbolic action itself. Whereas Easter in the Christian calendar commemorated and reenacted the triumph of Christ over death, in modern literature Easter had become a profoundly ironic point of reference. One could trace a graph of implication, from Goethe's *Faust* to—say—Anton Chekhov's short story "Easter Eve" (1886) or Thomas Hardy's *Jude the Obscure* (1895). Maurice Barrès's historical novel *La Colline inspirée* (1913), which was warmly commended in *The Irish Review*, set part of its action within the framework of Holy Week, as if to recover the possibility of a fulfillable belief. Yeats's poem "Easter 1916" would shortly consider whether England "might keep faith after all." It was, crucially for Yeats, a question of keeping faith, nor merely honoring one's word. Perhaps, after the executions and the "all changed" of Irish public opinion, General Maxwell might have been advised to murmur words from Swinburne's "Hymn to Proserpine":

> Thou hast conquered, O pale Galilean; the world has grown grey from
> thy breath;
> We have drunken of things Lethean, and fed on the fullness of death.
> Laurel is green for a season, and love is sweet for a day;
> But love grows bitter with treason, and laurel outlives not May.

More confidently one could detect a rewriting of Swinburne in Yeats's response to Irish treason, the stone abiding in the midst of all, and the sleep that might be death. That is to anticipate the executions, the decision to revolt acted upon, the choice of Easter Monday, and the deceptions practiced by Plunkett and a few others upon their fellow volunteers. In the middle of the Great War, these actions aspired to the totalizing merger of end and/as beginning, however localized their political idiom. For a mind like Plunkett's, sensitive to death's clock ticking within the body, thought of Easter was an alarming necessity.

Just a month before the insurrection that would cost him his life, Plunkett became embroiled in a row about Strindberg. The Irish Theater Company chose the Swede's *Easter* to play between 3 and 7 March 1916, a work never previously acted in Ireland and generally thought of as uncharacteristically mellow. The chief promoter of the idea was MacDonagh, also to die for his (lesser) part in the insurrection. Martyn, as the third director, was a strong advocate of continental drama. The directors in various combinations could foresee the immediate future. Though a leading member of Sinn Féin, Martyn was no confidant of the Irish Volunteers. MacDonagh and Plunkett were not only leading volunteer officers, but they also were committed to rise, even (as it turned out) against the wishes and express orders of their commanding officer, Eoin MacNeill. As a close friend, MacDonagh knew something of Plunkett's deteriorating health, even something of the surgical procedures the younger man would undergo in Holy Week. Plunkett alone knew the exact ratcheting of disease against the commitment to take up arms. This would shortly be the season of Lent during which it was impossible to marry his fiancée, as he nonetheless had suggested.

Sometime in June, after the executions, Geraldine Plunkett Dillon wrote that "towards the last six months my brother disagreed with the other directors for not abiding by the spirit of the agreement, and definitely dissociated himself from the theatre on the production of Strindberg's *Easter*."[47] According to the account provided by John MacDonagh, a director-playwright of some ability, Joe Plunkett resigned his directorship in protest at "this piece of contemptible profanity." Quite when the resignation occurred is difficult to pinpoint. Grace Gifford was at the opening night on 3 March. An undated note from her to Joseph Holloway, complaining, "Isn't the play at Hardwicke St horrible!" can be assigned to the following week. It seems unlikely she would have attended and complained after her fiancé's resignation, and thus Joe's protest would appear to have been made after the curtain went up.[48] Certainly his action came too late to keep it off the stage. Not yet returned from New York, the formidable countess was unable to deprive her son's opponents of a platform for their oddly chosen piece.

Far removed from the hectic spiritualism and violent misogyny for which Strindberg's drama was infamous, the Swedish *Easter* took its characters through a modern Holy Week. Instead of an Inferno, the action moves through Maundy Thursday, Good Friday and Easter Saturday. The Irish Theater Company was staging it some seven weeks short of a military takeover of the religious calendar, with Plunkett, MacDonagh, and their comrades in charge. Juxtaposition of a literary theater and a dramatic politics might have been sharp enough to nag the mind of a sensitive conspirator. Strindberg's plot involves seven characters (as indeed the IRB's did). Through an unpunished financial crime Mr. Heyst has injured six persons close to him, including his wife, son, and daughter, a boarder in the Heyst household, and (finally) one Lindqvist who is a deus ex machina rescuer despite being the main victim of the embezzlement.

Plunkett's only recorded reaction spoke of profanity. Not enough of his opinion comes down to us to allow for a full understanding of what he objected to in Strindberg's *Easter*. One might translate his "profanity" into secularism, that is, might regard the ordinary world of the play as lacking any possibility of a transcendental (or fifth) dimension, while utilizing the once sacred calendar of Holy Week. Read in the same light, Strindberg's offense was not very different from that of the Military Council. Among the sociological complaints voiced by the insurgents or their cultured apologists, the drab, compromised, and unpoetic nature of Irish politics—its sordid ordinariness—was often condemned. Yeats did it sublimely in "Easter 1916"; Geraldine Plunkett Dillon more prosaically in her memoir complained of "the political prostitutes who surrounded us" and from whom escape could only be achieved by violent means.[49] An allegedly corrupt parliamentary system was not to be reformed, but simply overthrown by other means. Inadequate democracy was to be remedied by less, rather than more, of that political mode. The Proclamation of the Irish Republic made no mention of democracy or representation. According to an obituarist, Plunkett detested the "fugue of parliamentiarism."

Strindberg's *Easter* disturbed him because it suggested forgiveness and not redemption, continued living rather than sacrifice. Odd though its place in the dramatist's oeuvre remains, it aligns itself with Joyce's *Ulysses* in its ultimately triumphant negotiation with bloodshed, vengeance, and scapegoating. In an all-too-slender tradition reaching back to Goethe, these few works could be classified under the heading Avoidance of Tragedy.[50] As the compact, representative titles of both play and novel suggest, such precarious triumphs are won against the pressure of an entire worldview, Christian or Hellenic, contemporary or inherited. Ibsen's midcareer epic drama encoded both sides of a radical choice, or both sides of a radical totalizing alliance, *Emperor and/or Galilean*. The writers of Dublin 1916 scarcely feature in such breathtakingly rapid surveys. However, there were local sources through which an archaic world might be invoked. Yeats in old age asked, "When Pearse summoned Cuchulain to his side, / What stalked through the Post Office?" The Iron Age world of Na Fianna and (in Ulster) Cuchulain and Deirdre is absorbed by the rebel poets into an enterprise actively and piously Christian. The summoning of Cuchulain, insofar as this can be deemed a component of the Rising, took place "in the name of God and the dead generations." As the time was a day past the anniversary of Christ's rising from the dead, so in time, the monument to commemorate the event represented the dying Cuchulain, tied to the stump of a tree (as, in a sense, Christ had been too) by his own hand. The Easter envisaged by Cuchulain-admiring Catholic members of a secret society condemned by the church mixed pagan and Christian with insouciance. Oliver Sheppard's bronze sculpture (cast preinsurrection in 1911/1912) was eventually installed in the GPO, roughly where Plunkett's motorbike had been parked throughout Easter Week.

As a conventionally good Catholic, Joe Plunkett might well have been disturbed by these travesties of holy doctrine. In his own work, he did not indulge the Gaelic-pastoral of Pearse or the Last-Romantic-Iron-Age visions of Standish O'Grady and Yeats. But the solitary evidence available, suggesting a hesitation in the prelude to the tumult for which he was director of military operations, relates to Strindberg's mild *Easter*. It is possible to extend acknowledgment of this hiatus in two directions. In domestic-biographical terms, Plunkett could read it as an unintended, remote but disturbingly affective commentary on bourgeois life as he knew it in Kilternan, Upper Fitzwilliam Street, Marlborough Road, and other family properties. The deceptions required in the management of money, the subjection of women and the young to the imperious needs of a *pater familias*, commerce as a self-regulating ethic, appearance as substance—these were common knowledge to the alert among the Plunketts, with only minor derogations required to accommodate the countess. In political terms, however, Strindberg (with

Ibsen behind him) also conjured up vague memories of the 1905 crisis between Sweden and Norway, a crisis in the monarchical union that resulted in Norwegian independence. Unlike the crisis that Plunkett was urgently promoting in Dublin, the Scandinavian breakup occurred without bloodshed. Political and constitutional impasses had been reached, ultimatums promulgated. But when the Norwegians effectively seceded, the masters in Stockholm did not call down Thor and dynamite. And when the Norwegians resisted, they did so through resolution and internal resource, without foreign aid and without conspiratorial violence.[51] It was possible to achieve national independence without bloody insurrection just as (in *Easter*) the crisis in family could be resolved through forgiveness and a resolve to face the truth. Plunkett, however, was masterminding a very different Easter, just some four weeks in the future. Strindberg's play was a rebuke, preemptive, indirect, and intolerable.

Joe's role as director of military operations was echoed in his role as director in the Theater of Ireland. In the domestic sphere, he was by no means the only Plunkett alert to the approaching chariots. His sister Geraldine was well aware of his IRB membership and of conspiracy within the Irish Volunteers. His brothers were energetically preparing the bombs in Larkfield. A future brother-in-law was in charge of explosives, assisted by Rory O'Connor. The count was sworn into the IRB to seek papal benediction for the Rising. George Noble Plunkett's poem "Sursum Corda," appearing in the March 1916 issue of *The Catholic Bulletin*, looked forward to a transformation of Dublin that was much closer and ruddier than punctual readers of that journal can have imagined.[52] Against the Plunketts in combination, Strindberg stood no chance.

All the same, Joe's protest at *Easter* came very late. Had he, through ill-health or other preoccupations, failed to note what was in rehearsal at "our hall"? What was it about Strindberg's play that Grace Gifford thought horrible and Plunkett profane? Did she simply echo his rejection? Or were these foot-lighters so attuned to a different, imminent Passion that no happy ending was tolerable? Birth or death, marriage or execution lay ahead—absolutes all. '"The Dark Way" is among Plunkett's better poems, and inevitably came to be read as prophetic of his passively violent death. Its concluding stanzas plainly alternate the names of the two women who had dominated Joe Plunkett's emotional life:

Now have I chosen in the dark
The desolate way to walk alone
Yet strive to keep alive one spark
Of your known grace and grace unknown.

And when I leave you lest my love
Should seal your spirit's ark with clay,
Spread your bright wings, O shining dove,
—But my way is the darkest way.

Papal Feints and Secret Orders

In nationalist accounts of the 1916 insurrection, a crucial point in the unfolding drama is said to be Plunkett's dispatch of his father to Rome, just before Holy Week, to seek the approval of the pontiff for events planned by the secret Military Council. To secure confidentiality, G. N. Plunkett had been sworn into membership of the IRB immediately before leaving Ireland. Little or no comment has been made on this Chestertonian adventure, apart from commendation of the younger Plunkett's foresight. Yet the whole business begs half a dozen questions or more.

First, at what level and when did the IRB agree to the proposal? The Fenians, in March 1916, were still unreconciled to the church, and jealously guarded their secrecy. If the idea arose from within the IRB leadership, it seriously compromised the Proclamation's imminent avowal of civil liberties in religious matters. While it is clear that the Military Council had been granted a good deal of scope for maneuver, the use of so prominent a nonmember as the papal count would have broken secret (and near-sacred) precedents on the most important occasion in the IRB's career. It is true that Plunkett had earlier used his elder sister, Philomena (Mimi), to carry messages from the Military Council to Devoy and other Clan na Gael leaders in New York. But a previous family involvement in relaying confidential material to known allies could scarcely justify an uninvited descent upon the Vatican, in the busy week before Easter, of all times.

Second, bluntly, who did G. N. Plunkett think he was? The papal title he bore had been awarded in 1884 by Leo XIII, for assistance in financing a convent in Nottingham. It brought no diplomatic privileges, nor is there any evidence that he had busied himself in church affairs over the intervening thirty or so years. Indeed he was long disinclined to use the title. He was, however, a fluent speaker of French and Italian, familiar with European culture, impressive in appearance and demeanor, though with little practice in formulating the Irish separatist ideal. According to his daughter, he—a barrister by training—was generally "struck dumb during court business."

Third, what did G. N. Plunkett intend to convey to Pope Benedict XV (1854–1922)? As the Proclamation was not yet written—or, certainly, was not yet finished and agreed—on leaving Dublin, he cannot have been in a position to say precisely what the insurgents stood for, though he certainly would have known of the means at their disposal and—probably—the additional foreign aid they expected. Benedict's understanding of these insular complexities could not be easily relied on. At the outbreak of the Great War, he had declared the Holy See neutral, had referred to the conflict as "the suicide of civilized Europe," and generally worked for international peace. Some important leaders among the French (e.g., Georges Clemenceau) and sections of the German population (Lutherans, mainly) distrusted him. Influential Irish clerics in Rome attempted to steer him toward an improved view of Irish nationalism.[53]

Fourth, what was Benedict's known attitude toward the issues likely to be raised in any meeting with Plunkett? In July 1915, he issued an exhortation, declaring how he

> on turning a fearful glance on the blood-stained battlefields, felt the anguish of a father, who sees his homestead devastated and in ruins before the fury of the hurricane. And thinking with unspeakable regret of our young sons, who were being mown down by death in thousands, We opened Our heart, enlarged by the charity of Christ, to all the crushing sorrow of the mothers, and of the wives made widows before their time, and to all the inconsolable laments of the little ones, too early bereft of a father's care.

It may be supposed that Count Plunkett prepared himself for the desired papal audience by refamiliarizing himself with this unambiguous statement on issues of bloodshed and war that Pearse had also addressed in "The

Coming Revolution" (November 1913), though with a different emphasis. It is true that Benedict's exhortation later took a somewhat different turn:

> Lay aside your mutual purpose of destruction; remember that Nations do not die; humbled and oppressed, they chafe under the yoke imposed upon them, preparing a renewal of the combat, and passing down from generation to generation a mournful heritage of hatred and revenge.
>
> Why not from this moment weigh with serene mind the rights and lawful aspirations of the peoples? Why not initiate with a good will an exchange of views, directly or indirectly, with the object of holding in due account, within the limits of possibility, those rights and aspirations, and thus succeed in putting an end to the monstrous struggle, as has been done under other similar circumstances? Blessed be he who will first raise the olive-branch.[54]

While these sentences can be read as offering hope to subject peoples or nations, the papal advice and plea run counter to Pearse's fin de siècle pessimism about Irish national degeneration and imminent extinction of the national spirit.

Fifth, who might G. N. Plunkett have met, or bumped into, while awaiting the pope's summons? Commendatore Samuel Walker O'Neill, Chamberlain of the Cape and Sword, a few days earlier had escorted Asquith into the pope's presence. The wily secretary of state, Pietro Gasparri, was essentially a canon law expert rather than a diplomat. Below this, Vatican civil servants would have been unlikely to respond in any specific way to the representative of an Irish secret society or even to someone posing as the representative of the Irish Volunteer movement. As, inevitably if however reluctantly, Plunkett would have arrived as a subject of His Britannic Majesty, he must have expected some contact (however indirect) with Sir Henry Howard (1843–1921), who had been appointed in December 1914 as minister plenipotentiary to the Vatican. Educated at Downside, Howard was an aristocratic Roman Catholic, an experienced diplomat, and (evidently) a charmer in the best English tradition. He remained in office till August 1916, when he retired. He and his American wife remained in Rome. A distant cousin, Sir Esme Howard, had gone to Dublin Castle in 1885 as assistant secretary to Lord Carnarvon. There was little wiggle room for a recently inducted Clongowes Wood Fenian.

Sixth, how did G. N. Plunkett fare on his mission? The family chronicler, Geraldine, provided no indication of when her father left Dublin, how long it took him to reach Rome under wartime conditions, or how he reached home. He was, however, back in Ireland by Easter weekend. While he might have been expected to attend Geraldine's wedding on Easter Sunday, he was "still down the country visiting the bishops, telling them about his meeting with the pope." From this it would seem that the family were fully aware of his mission, despite the oaths of secrecy imposed on IRB members. The two G-men (special branch police) who gate-crashed the wedding ceremony noticed the absence of the bride's principal male relatives, her father and her eldest brother. Mrs. Plunkett Dillon clearly states that the papal count met the pontiff, but perhaps nothing more than a public audience was required to meet the requirements of her strict truth. In one form of the occasion, the visitor moves forward close to the pope, out of earshot of perhaps scores of other visitors who wait their individual turn; such an occasion might last *a total* of two hours, providing privacy for each. No papal endorsement (or condemnation) followed the insurrection, either before or after the executions. Catholic support locally was plentiful, first through the friars who tended the wounded and dying on all sides, through *The Catholic Bulletin* with its extended obituaries and tributes, and in less concentrated fashion, through the reactions of individual clergy, for example Edward O'Dwyer, bishop of Limerick. On 30 April—that is, before the executions—the papacy telegraphed Michael Logue, archbishop of Armagh, asking for news and expressing the wish that Ireland might be spared further bloodshed.[55]

Some answers to these questions are provided by Honor O Brolchain, granddaughter of Geraldine Plunkett Dillon. She places the Roman journey in two political contexts—one created by Prime Minister Asquith's meeting with Italian politicians on 31 March 1916 in Rome, and his subsequent audience with the pope; and the other by Joe Plunkett's need to communicate with Casement in Germany. It appears that G. N. Plunkett first traveled to Berne in neutral Switzerland, where he committed to paper a letter memorized back in Dublin. This was successfully dispatched via the German consulate and the Foreign Office in Berlin, to a Casement increasingly dissatisfied with German responses. Only with the Swiss business concluded did he turn south and travel down through Italy to the Eternal City. His journey (absorbing two days at least) took place in the aftermath of the Fifth Battle of the Isonzo River, with Italy playing an aggressive role on the Allied side. Though the railway route lay west of the war zone, we must admire the sixty-four-year-old's courage and tenacity.

It is worth adjusting our focus to consider (in stages) a still unconfirmable schedule that makes such an expedition plausible. A mere mention of Asquith's imminent Roman diplomacy appeared in the *Irish Times* on Friday 31 March. Assuming that the Plunketts, father and son, promptly agreed on a plan, the count could scarcely have begun his journey—through Britain, France, and Switzerland—in less than twenty-four hours, a journey of some three to four days (by a reasonable calculation) . Staying overnight in Berne, and traveling for two days to reach Rome, he could have hoped for nothing earlier than an audience with Benedict XV on 10 April, a Monday. Ms. O Brolchain avers that he "had a right, as a Papal Count, to have an audience with the Pope." Right or no right, the thing could hardly have happened pronto—Italy was at war, the pope was greatly concerned about the conflict, and additionally (so to speak) had Lenten commitments. It is more or less agreed that Plunkett was back in Dublin by Holy Thursday, 20 April, having again taken four days to travel. His Vatican window of opportunity can be dated to 10–16 April, not impossible if his powers of persuasion with the gatekeepers were successful. But the assertion is that the letter to Casement reached him on 6 April, which places the earlier portion of this deduced schedule under renewed scrutiny. Furthermore, at the audience, the pope said "Asquith had informed him some months [*sic*] before that the Irish now had Home Rule and the Irish question was settled." The count then "gave the Pope a more accurate view of Irish affairs and told him that the Irish Volunteers intended insurrection and that 'the prospects were desperate.'" Of course, the volunteer leadership did not intend insurrection, though a minority of the middle-officer class did. Leaving aside the omission of any reference to the pope's more recent meeting with Asquith, we must note that no pope, no canon lawyer, no conscientious Catholic could approve a resort to arms in conditions providing no hope of success. The Plunketts, neither of them a fool, must have known this principle before any decision to travel was considered.[56]

This account of the papal contact emerges from family tradition, and has the value of indicating how such opinion consolidates and edits itself over a century. In keeping with the principles of the *16 Lives* series, it is light on traceable references and avoids self-criticism. Fortunately, another summary is available, drawing on stated sources and incorporating critical commentary. About the audience, Charles Townsend (a military historian), writes that the count

> delivered a letter purporting to come from Eoin MacNeill, "President of the Supreme Council of the Irish Volunteers," informing the Pope that "we have an effective force of 80,000 trained men, and the people, the Catholic nation, is with us."[57]

What about the non-Catholics one might ask, who accounted for more than 26 percent of the island's population in 1911? If they were largely concentrated in Ulster, were there not significant numbers of Protestants also in counties Dublin, Wicklow, and Cork? Or did nation transcend demographics?

Enough confusion arises from the mix of Volunteer and IRB terminology, the impossible number of trained men claimed by Count Plunkett, his special pleading of sectarian distinctions, and so forth. Behind detail lies a larger improbability—that G. N. Plunkett, while instructed to memorize a seemingly innocuous letter to Casement, would carry so incriminating a letter from the volunteers' chief of staff through the territory of three hostile (for him) states—Britain, France, and Italy. It is possible that he devised the letter off his own bat, on his arrival in Rome, the confusions therefore being his distinctive contribution. One way or the other, what supposedly occurred was inept in the extreme as an approach to the Supreme Pontiff. Undeterred, Joseph Plunkett in Dublin told MacNeill that he had received a message direct from Rome to the effect that the pope had sent his blessing to the Irish Volunteers and also to MacNeill in person. This cut no ice with MacNeill.

Fortunately, a late contribution to the debate appeared in 1933 with an air of authority. The *Irish Press*, a newspaper closely allied to the Fianna Fáil party, carried on 26 May a front-page story headed "A Pope Who Blessed the Men of Easter Week," which incorporated material sent to the editor by

G. N. Plunkett himself—"one of the most stirring disclosures ever given to the Irish people," as the journalist described it. The count had pledged the Irish Republic to fidelity to the Holy See and the interests of religion. In his verbatim account, piously dated Ascension Thursday, he explained:

> About three weeks before the Rising, I was through my son Joseph, commissioned by the executive of the Irish Volunteers (the Provisional Government), to act as their envoy on the Continent. One task given to me I need not particularise here. When it was carried out, I went on to Rome, according to my instructions.
>
> There I was received in private audience by His Holiness; for nigh two hours we discussed fully the question of the coming struggle for Irish independence . . . The Pope conferred His Apostolic Benediction on the men facing death for Ireland's liberty . . .
>
> Back in Dublin on Good Friday 1916, I sent in my report on the results of my mission, to the Provisional Government. In the General Post Office, when the fight began, I saw again the portion of that paper relating to my audience with His Holiness.[58]

Whatever merits this document possesses, a barrister's understanding of sovereignty is not one of them. Whatever legitimacy the Proclamation could claim depended on its sponsors' relationship to the IRB of the 1860s (a nonlegal body of course) and the succession of Supreme Councils intervening. The Executive of the Volunteers was not the IRB council, though a majority on the Executive was (covertly) made up of IRB members. And the claim that this Executive actually *was* the Provisional Government blithely ignores the fact that the Proclamation had not been uttered at the time of which G. N. Plunkett spoke. None of this is more implausible than the notion that the portly sixty-four-year-old papal count was among the armed party who occupied the GPO on Easter Monday. What is more likely is that Joseph Plunkett "commissioned" his father, either on behalf of the IRB's semiautonomous Military Council or simply on his own behalf, to perform certain acts in Europe. Even if much of the muddle was the father's doing, responsibility lies with the son, not simply for (1) yet another deception of MacNeill (his commanding officer in the Irish Volunteers) but also for (2) a personation of MacNeill in his relationship with the pope, their spiritual leader and vicar of Christ. It follows that Benedict also was deceived by young Plunkett in being led to believe that MacNeill's representative, a person commissioned by the Irish Volunteers' executive, was before him. MacNeill replied in the same paper on 2 June, simply denying the very existence of a Provisional Government on the date proclaimed by Plunkett and, more personally, denying any of the actions attributed to him by the count's communications. The Plunketts practiced what the Belfast novelist Brian Moore called "lies of silence," if not more.

Unfortunately, for the count, other versions of his *Irish Press* communication emerged, even if these suffered from the fault of authenticity. The rival *Irish Times* printed a text that included a paragraph explicitly stating that "Mr John MacNeill . . . signed the commission given to this Republican Envoy [i.e., the count]."[59] There was now no doubt that MacNeill was the discreet object of antagonism, not to say hatred. Years later, Geraldine Plunkett Dillon joined an exchange of letters in the same newspaper during which she claimed that Joe told his father to go to Rome *on Pearse's instructions.*[60]

Some evidence from the continent is extant, Roman and German. Jérôme aan de Wiel, first in a lengthy article of 1999 and then in his full-length book, *The Catholic Church in Ireland, 1914–1918* (2003), deals with the Plunkett mission to the Vatican. He treats the letter from the count to the pope in some detail, translating the original French into English. The absence of a date, and the nature of the contents, suggest that it was composed before G. N. Plunkett's arrival in Rome and probably before his departure from Dublin. In the opening paragraph he presents himself as an appointed envoy acting "on behalf of the President and the Supreme Council of the Irish Volunteers (national troops.)" The president, "Prof. Jean MacNeill," had given him a document for the pope, which "present circumstances forced me to leave in Ireland." We are to believe that the Council had "unanimously supported the liberation of the Holy See [in 1870!] and the restoration of its ancient rights." Six further paragraphs followed, "justifying the future rising" (aan de Wiel's interpolation). Of these six the historian chooses, in his article, only to translate numbers seven and eight, the latter providing an exact time for the insurrection—evening of Easter Day—surely grounds for a charge of treason had the count been apprehended in any Allied state—British, French, or Italian. Paragraph 7 lists Irish nationalist grievances—"we are oppressed . . . we run the risk of being massacred . . . war taxes will naturally engender famine" and concluding, "it is during the war that we have the greatest chance of success to obtain the freedom of rights and of worship for our Catholic country.'[61] Finally, aan de Wiel supplies a near-exact date for the audience—"round 8 April"—that is, immediately after contact with the Germans in Berne. This and other details strongly suggest that the audience had been arranged in advance of his leaving Dublin.

The German material, published by Reinhard R. Dorries, confirms aspects of the evolving timetable. He refers to Plunkett's rapid departure from Berne for a "planned audience" with Benedict, though he also notes that, on 11 April, "the count gave another letter for Casement to Minister Romberg," the German ambassador to Switzerland. From this, it appears that Plunkett traveled back to Switzerland, and returned home via Paris and London. In the letter of 11 April, he gives the date of his departure from Dublin as 29 March, and tells Casement that "the Supreme Council of the Irish Volunteers desire [*sic*] to associate Germany, in this marked way, with the liberation of Ireland." Casement, who was in great distress about his collapsing German mission, could not but note this unforced confusion of the IRB and the Irish Volunteers, here attributable only to the count, even if papal staff might miss its significance.[62]

The material that the Plunketts had assembled or drafted in Dublin, allegedly with MacNeill's tacit approval, contained similar confusions. One key to precise authorship may be found in the complaint of imminent famine listed in the letter to Benedict as edited by aan de Wiel. Among the Plunkett papers in the National Library of Ireland (NLI) is a longer list of omens-cum-grievances related to the possible onset of rebellion. The fourth of these refers to John Redmond's brief involvement with the Irish Volunteers; the third deals with agricultural matters and the (supposed) threat of "proximate famine." In lexical terms, the phrase is matched by "proximate apocalypse" in one of Plunkett's hyperbolic poems, its meaning for him evidently being "immediate" or "imminent." The undertones are eschatological, concerned with the Last Days, and so on. Even without the adjective, famine was a highly emotive term in Irish nationalist discourse, its use calculated to catch the eye of a benign and caring prelate, irrespective of prevailing economic conditions. The younger Plunkett's hand is at work at least in part of, if not throughout, the letter ascribed to the Supreme Council.[63] If, as seems inescapable, full responsibility for the escapade rests with him then, as aan de Wiel has established, the most dangerous secret of all (a date for insurrection) had been communicated in advance not only to the pope but also to three Irish churchmen based in Rome and, astonishingly, a journalist on the *Melbourne Advocate*. MacNeill knew less and was lied to more. Aan de Wiel also establishes from Irish sources that, while G. N. Plunkett may have traveled to inform some Irish bishops (Dwyer is a likely case) of his mission during the Easter weekend, he was in Dublin on Easter Monday attempting (unsuccessfully) to gain access to Archbishop Walsh of Dublin. At noon, his sons took part in the seizing of the GPO.

◆ ◆ ◆

In 2006 the Dublin-based lawyer Peter Charleton published a reflective book-length essay on evil and deceit, which dealt with major political catastrophes of the twentieth century. Its preface began, "this book is about the transformative power of hatred."[64] The first and last of the three un-verities are very strong terms; for evil, many deep thinkers would argue that a belief in the existences of both God and Satan is necessary. Pearse, on Christmas Day 1915, wrote of the words inscribed above Parnell's statue by politicians who would settle for Home Rule, "It is as if a man were to write on a monument 'I believe in God and in Life Everlasting' and then to sell his chance of Heaven to the Evil One for a purse, not of gold, but of I.O.U.'s."[65] Though the image is effective, Pearse's Evil One is not a metaphor.

Of deceit we have just considered several impressive instances for which the Plunketts, son or father or both, are responsible. The relationship between hatred and deceit, or hatred and evil, is more difficult to pin down. "A Prayer for My Daughter" (written during the first half of 1919, when the Anglo-Irish war began) has Yeats brood on the place of hatred in deep human affairs. Of its ten stanzas, each of the final four includes the word itself. It is associated with the "thoroughfares," public bustle, public life, politics of the (to Yeats) turbulent kind. By contrast, the infant daughter is repeatedly imaged as a tree that survives Atlantic storms, rooted in "one dear perpetual place." More specifically, it is a laurel, that is, the protective vegetative form into which the nymph Daphne was transformed when pursued by lustful Apollo. The infant then is cast as a survivor not so much of hatred as violent sexual love. ("Sociologically," laurels grow rapidly along the avenues of "big houses," emblems of Yeats's chosen class identification.) Stanza 8 opens:

An intellectual hatred is the worst
So let her think opinions are accursed.[66]

And here the crux is reached and never abandoned, despite elegant conclusive benedictions. Hatred is to be condemned, though its victim is delicately encouraged to curse its summary in this form or that. In the process, the intellect is by implication reduced to the manufacture of opinions. The poem, one of Yeats's finest achievements in stanza building and interlacing of images, reflects a historic moment when growth and permanence contend. Elizabeth Bowen's *The Last September* catches the local politics of the war when Lois, from the big house, glimpses a rebel gunman cross her avenue without him seeing her, so intent upon his mission is he.

◆ ◆ ◆

In discussions of suspect documentation pertaining to the Easter Rising, pride of place has been given to the so-called Black Diaries of Roger Casement. The controversy, launched by W. J. Maloney in 1936, deserves historical reflection on its merits, even if, since the technical examinations of 2002, it is generally accepted that all the diaries held in the National Archives at Kew are genuine. However, the question of forgery is not monopolized by Casement. There is also the so-called Castle Document to be considered. Ahead of a detailed account of it, we should note the occurrence and the allegation of forgery on a wider political stage.

In Ireland, the activities of Richard Pigott came to light in 1889, as a forger of letters supposedly written by Charles Stewart Parnell and published in the *Times*. Seven years later, Captain Alfred Dreyfus was degraded from the French army, tried for treason and imprisoned on Devil's Island for years, on the basis of a bordereau wrongly attributed to him, though further suspect documents would follow to bolster the original crime. In September 1899, the Parnellite *Weekly Independent* editorialized against Dreyfus's conviction, declaring that a nation that depended on forgery and human sacrifices for its honor was in a sorry plight.[67] More than one item was forged in the long course of the Dreyfus Affair, and we may return to France in search of a terminology to describe the Dublin Castle Document. In a less intensively focused instance, the virulently anti-Semitic *Protocols of the Elders of Zion* was fabricated and disseminated from 1903 onward, its origins being Russian.

(Henry Ford subsidized the printing of half a million English language copies in the 1920s.)[68] In 1924, publication in Britain of a letter urging intensive communist agitation, and supposedly issued by Gregor Zinoviev and Arthur MacManus, was declared genuine by the incoming Tory government but is now universally taken to be a forgery. Finally, let us not forget a much earlier incident, the Bad Ems dispatch sent by Bismarck on 13 July 1870.

And so, back to Dublin and Holy Week, 1916. While G. N. Plunkett was traveling home from Rome and his duplicitous audience with the pope, circa 15 April the Castle Document was printed on the handpress owned by Joseph Plunkett and located at Larkfield, near Kimmage, south of Dublin. It consisted of a single small sheet of off-white-to-yellow lightweight paper, printed on one side, with thirty-eight lines of text. Those said to have set up type or carried out the printing operation included Joe Plunkett, his younger brother George, his even younger brother John (aged eighteen or nineteen), Colm Ó Lochlainn, and Rory O'Connor (all public school boys). The quality of typesetting was quite high, the design simplistic. The text is headed "Secret Orders issued to Military Officers." It was said to have been supplied by Eugene Smyth, a telegraphist in Dublin Castle. It is undated. Not a single personal name appears in the text.

Accounts of the document's emergence differ. Honor O Brolchain's deserves quotation at length:

> Eugene Smith [*sic*] had access to a document from General Friend to the Chief Secretary, Augustine Birrell, in London. Smith believed the document was a response to questions about the actions of the armed forces when conscription was introduced. The document was lengthy but as he dealt with it himself, he had enough time. He was "deeply interested in the political situation in Ireland and in the threat of conscription to Ireland." He decided to give the document to those whom it would affect and, having memorized it, he wrote it out and gave it, complete, to one of his contacts—he wasn't sure which—but probably one of Seán MacDiarmada's agents—he dealt with several. It is likely that Smith's contact passed the document to MacDiarmada who put it into a "cipher," a simple mixture of shorthand and word contractions. The IRB could not risk a document like this if the carrier were arrested. The document was delivered to Plunkett in the nursing home where he "de-coded" it with Grace [Gifford] sitting

> on his bed and writing the contents down. Plunkett then brought it to Larkfield, where there was a meeting of the Military Council, and George Plunkett, Rory O'Connor, and Colm O'Lochlainn were told to print it on Plunkett's small handpress. Colm left after a while, but the other two carried on. They had no experience of printing, and found it slow and difficult, passing the time singing ballads and God Save the King. They ran out of punctuation and capital letters almost immediately, but continued anyway. They found that the wrong name "Ara Coeli" had been given to Archbishop House and sent Jack Plunkett across to Joe, who was now back in Mountjoy Square and Joe told them to change it to Archbishop House. As tiredness grew, a tray of ready type was knocked over and they had to start again, but at last it was done and on the orders of Plunkett and the Military Council copies were sent to all the papers on 15 and 16 April, and to many prominent people.[69]

On Spy Wednesday 19 April, Alderman Tom Kelly read the document to a meeting of Dublin Corporation. He had learned of it earlier in the day from Arthur Griffith, and may have obtained a copy from the pacifist Frank Sheehy Skeffington, who feared it would provoke bloodshed if left unchallenged. In essence, the "Secret Orders" outlined plans for a martial law regime to arrest numerous leaders of nationalist organizations, seize their buildings, and generally stamp out all political activity unsupportive of government and the war effort. From the outset, there were divided views about the document's authenticity.

It is tempting to assume that this latter issue could be resolved to the unambiguous yes or no. Indeed, the implications of its dissemination over a week or ten-day period (including the first stages of the insurrection itself) are so extensive that the present moment is not long enough to deal with them adequately. So, if only by default, we should concentrate on the question, What is Forgery?—with specific reference to the "Secret Orders."

Let us begin with the heading, and the following two lines of print. "Secret Orders issued to Military Officers" might be taken as the title, part of the text. Then comes an explanation that "the cipher from which this document is copied does not indicate punctuation or capitals." What follows as the body of the text amounts to thirty-six lines divided visually into two parts by an ellipsis (. . . . .) of five dots. Conventionally, an ellipsis was used by printers to indicate the omission of some material from a text being quoted. If we take the five dots in this sense, then the printed document is not a full copy. And with this comes the implication that the printed document is based on a process of selection from an original or originals that were (temporarily) in cipher. Here, a strictly material point should be made. The Castle Document exists in at least two printed states—one with an ellipsis of five dots, and the other with just three dots. What this implies for the production of the document is this—the type was set and copies run off; and then, after a pause of unknown duration, more copies were run off again, after more than one alteration of the type.

At this point, the court of enquiry might hear from Otto von Bismarck. In July 1870, the king of Prussia was confronted at Ems, a spa resort, by the French ambassador to Berlin, and a political discussion resulted. The king's secretary wrote up a report sent later in the day to the Iron Chancellor with approval for release. Bismarck edited the report, removing phrases that indicated the king's conciliatory tone, and generally sharpening the import of the exchange. Once released, the Ems telegram provoked Napoleon III to declare war on Prussia, with calamitous results for France, and world-historic ones for Germany. Was the victorious Bismarck's communication a forgery?

Curiously, none of the Ems reports appears to have been encoded, whereas the Castle Document passed through an enciphered stage. On this point, there are two witnesses, both recording their views years after the incident. Eugene Smyth claimed that "he was in a position to know, at first hand, the entire contents of the suggested plan of operations, and I can definitely confirm the truth of the contents of the document."[70] If this is relied on, it follows that a junior clerical member of the civilian staff in the Castle had some knowledge of official ciphers as used on behalf of the undersecretary and the general officer commanding the forces in Ireland. Not a plausible scenario. Smyth, however, also stated that the contents had been *abstracted* from Castle files, suggesting more than one source and, consequently, indicating that the document was not a single unitary one. The second witness to the enciphered form of the text as it reached the Plunketts was Grace Gifford, who married Plunkett on the eve of his execution. In a later statement, she recorded that she had watched and heard her fiancé decode some of the material. This firsthand evidence is, by the same token, compromised. Plunkett was a show-off and a puppeteer; Grace was no superintellect. Her statement vindicates her late husband, loyally, that's all. Others more closely involved in the printing of "Secret Orders" deserve consideration. George Plunkett, aged twenty-one, was his brother's no less loyal shadow. At Larkfield, Rory O'Connor was busy making bombs, and unlikely to do more than pull the press's lever when the others tired. Colm Ó Lochlainn presents a very different case.

Aged twenty-three at the time of the Rising, Ó Lochlainn had graduated in Celtic studies at UCD under the guidance of Eoin MacNeill. He had joined the IRB in 1913, and was a founding member of the Irish Volunteers. In addition, he was the son of a professional printer and familiar with the intricacies of typesetting. In the wake of Alderman Kelly's public reading of the document, and the various responses of Sheehy Skeffington, MacNeill, and others, Ó Lochlainn aligned himself with MacNeill, deploring the efforts of Pearse, Plunkett, and Clarke to rise without further thought. Later, he concluded that the document he had helped to print was a forgery perpetrated by Joe Plunkett.

This judgment of course raises the problem of definition. If Eugene Smyth had delivered intelligence from the Castle, and if Plunkett edited this (in the Bismarckian manner), was the result a forgery? Charles Townshend, usually a stern critic of "street-savvy" language, has declared that Plunkett had "sexed-up" the data, which, nevertheless, was no forgery in the professor's eyes. The question now shifts to one of intention. What did Plunkett and company intend when they printed and distributed "Secret Orders"?

After months of Irish Volunteer demonstrations, deportations by the authorities, threats of conscription, and inflammatory rhetoric from Carson, Connolly, Kitchener, Pearse, and others, it was reasonable for all to assume that Dublin Castle had contingency plans to suppress opposition whenever it deemed drastic action necessary. However, military action, of the kind implied in "Secret Orders," lay beyond the Castle's control. Plunkett's document was undated, and so impacted on the public as an ever-immediate threat. It was also unconditional and comprehensive: no mention of specific circumstances that would trigger the drastic action, no limit to the number of individuals to be rounded up. The result could be calculated to stampede moderate nationalist opinion and its leadership. Bernard Shaw, writing from Weymouth before the month was out, was in no doubt about the document's status and intent:

> it purports to be an official military set of instructions for the capture of the Sinn Fein barracks throughout Dublin & the disarmament of the S. F. Volunteers. Just the thing to take the poor devils in and manufacture a rebellion. It is much too clever to be German: only an Irishman could be at once clever enough and scoundrel enough (or bigot enough) to have planted such a trap.[71]

A week later, in the *New Statesman*, he claimed to have "a copy of the fabricated document" and also a letter from Sheehy Skeffington to the London press warning of a defensive-offensive response by Sinn Féin. Shaw regarded the minor pre-Easter crisis as romantic folly that "made those unfortunate Sinn Feiners mistake a piece of hopeless mischief for a patriotic stroke for freedom."

This public argument, less forthright than private denunciation of scoundrel forgers, curiously if ironically echoes Charles Maurras's defense of J.-H. Henry's conduct at a late stage in the Dreyfus Affair. Some detail is unavoidable. Colonel Henry had fabricated a handwritten document, seemingly exchanged between German and Italian diplomats, by taking pieces of two letters that had been torn into fragments, and constructing a third incorporating parts of the original two. Thus assembled, the document compounded Dreyfus's apparent treason. Unfortunately for Henry, the apparently identical paper in both differed slightly in color when scrutinized in subdued light. Though Henry confessed to the deception in 1898 (and committed suicide), some fellow anti-Dreyfusards regarded him as a virtual hero. For Maurras, royalist, anti-Semite, and ultraconservative, this was "patriotic forgery." Was the Castle Document also a patriotic forgery, circulated with the intention of justifying in advance the Rising led by the forger and others?

The details of Colonel Henry's activities are helpful in one important regard; they concentrate attention on the materiality of certain kinds of fabrication. Minute differences of paper color and of handwriting led to the exposure of a complex dossier of falsification of which Dreyfus was the victim. Nearer home, a textual detail, Pigott's inability to spell the word "hesitancy," led to his exposure as forger of the letters approving violence over Parnell's name. This latter instance, though less material than the Henry case, is still closer to the physics and chemistry of classic forgery than Bismarck's edited telegram or Plunkett's pale-yellow flier. The technology of print, whether the state-machinery generating telegrams or the privately-owned handpress used most often for verse, complicates judgment about forgery.

William Blackstone's *Common Laws of England* (1765–1769) offers a workable definition—"the fraudulent making or alteration of a writing to the prejudice of another man's right"—though it doesn't distinguish between manuscript and printed material, and doesn't anticipate the telegram or computer. It may, however, dispatch Professor Townshend's finesse to the margins of historical debate, provided it can be shown that "Secret Orders issued to Military Officers" prejudiced some person's right. To this end, let us glance at the method of distribution adopted.

The first individuals to hear of the Castle Document included Griffith, Sheehy Skeffington, and Thomas Kelly. The latter stated that he got his copy from P. J. Little. None of these were members of the Irish Volunteers, the ICA, or the IRB, though Griffith and Little were members of Sinn Féin. In the evening of 25 April, the first full day of the Rising, Diarmuid Coffey (a volunteer who did not take part) was given a copy by Douglas Hyde that is now preserved in Trinity College Library. In his diary, he referred to "the supposed orders of General Friend which may have been the spark which fired the whole business." (We know, and Benedict XV knew then, that a spark had already been lit.) Thomas MacDonagh (IRB and Irish Volunteers) claimed the document was genuine, and that it had been put into his hands by friends in Dublin Castle, a remark that may simply restate the account of Eugene Smyth's providing the originals, MacDonagh having been close to the Plunketts. From this, one might conclude that distribution was aimed at initiating public discussion through individuals *not* identified with the advanced separatist position, people whose independence of mind would be acknowledged, notably Kelly, who was called Honest Tom even by his opponents. In addition to the alderman, Little publicized the document through *New Ireland*, a weekly paper of which he was editor. Some might claim that these tactics amounted to a clever manipulation of public opinion at a time when opinion was firmly policed through censorship. More specifically, however, it prejudiced the authority of Eoin MacNeill on two distinct but successive occasions. The first occurred when he accepted the document as genuine, and advised the Irish Volunteers to ready themselves against suppression. The second occurred when he was obliged to countermand orders, having decided that it had been forged by his subordinates.

Other deceptions had taken place, including the misrepresentation of MacNeill to the pope. The seven-man secret Military Council of the IRB manipulated the Irish Volunteers and Citizen Army rank and file; indeed the Castle Document was only part of that larger betrayal of the volunteer leadership, connived at by the Citizen Army leadership in the person of Connolly. Pearse lied to MacNeill when visiting his home; MacDonagh backed him up, perhaps innocently. These are the men who, as deceivers or deceived, issued the Proclamation with others on Easter Monday. In this explosion, the "Secret Orders" had acted as a catalyst would in a chemical reaction. The effect-metaphor had contemporary force. Three years later, when T. S. Eliot published "Tradition and the Individual Talent," he wrote:

> There remains to refine this process of depersonalization and its relation to the sense of tradition. It is in this depersonalization that art may be said to approach the condition of science. I therefore invite you to consider, as a suggestive analogy, the action which takes place when a bit of finely filiated platinum is introduced into a chamber containing oxygen and sulphur dioxide . . . the newly formed acid contains no trace of platinum, and the platinum itself is apparently unaffected.[72]

Eliot in 1916 had been lecturing on Georges Sorel and writers of the French cultural Right, cautiously approaching the doctrines of Conservative Revolution that he later expounded more directly. Like the argument in his essay of 1919, the republican Proclamation of Easter 1916 sought to restore a living understanding of the dead generations and "old tradition." Yeats spent much of April and May in London, with access only to censored news from home. On 30 April, he wrote to the younger of his sisters, "the whole thing bewilders me for Connolly is an able man & Thomas MacDonagh both able & cultivated. Pearce [*sic*] I have long looked upon as a man made dangerous by the Vertigo of self sacrifice."[73] Later in the year, when he began to compose "Easter 1916," he found it necessary to characterize or symbolize that element which, unchanging in itself, results in "all changed, changed utterly." The catalyst in his poetic account was a stone in the midst of all.

Abduction and Insurrection, January–April 1916

Plunkett was sworn into the IRB late in 1914, following the successful landing of German arms at Kilcoole, an incident after which he probably acted as a helpful gate-man when the consignment was brought to the family stronghold at Kimmage. Such service would have earned the IRB's gratitude and (perhaps) trust. Already a leading member of the Irish Volunteers, his recruitment certainly advanced a takeover of the open organization by the clandestine. The construction of a military committee, later a seven-man Military Council, created a tiny but powerful third force through which the Council effectively controlled the volunteers' Executive Committee, a state of affairs unconsciously fostered by Eoin MacNeill's irregular attendance in the chair. Of the Military Council Thomas Clarke and Sean MacDermott remained IRB ultraloyalists, without any volunteer role. In turn Connolly and MacDonagh were sworn in during the early months of 1916.

Well before the end of 1915, the ICA leader had been keen to bring out his several hundred men and women without delay, regardless of the Irish Volunteers' response. Though MacNeill detected a "mystic" component in such thinking, others ascribed it to the belief (shared by Pearse) that their generation was in danger of shamefully failing to maintain an insurrectionary tradition (1867, 1803, 1798 etc.). The issue of shame is no less important than that of motivation. The preferred phraseology at the time was that action of some sort was better than no action. Feelings of shame may have been at work, buttressed by the knowledge that hundreds of thousands of men were fighting and dying in Austria, Belgium, France, Italy, Russia, Serbia, and so on, for causes good, bad, or negligible. When Bulmer Hobson attempted to discuss the matter with Connolly in a restaurant, "his conversation was full of clichés derived [from] Europe."[74] These were (it seems) proletarian clichés or the slogans of communists, socialists, and anarchists. Of the candidates available (Blanqui, Engels, Kropotkin, Marx, Sorel, and others), Sorel offers the best fit. An active contemporary of Connolly's, he too felt that demoralization had struck the working-class movement, that spontaneous action would redeem it even if victory did not result. A recent historian has followed tradition in translating the argument into explicitly Christian and biblical terms. Fearghal McGarry quotes a latter-day text to the effect that the insurrection "fits into a powerful strand of separatist thinking, one of a series of moments that should cause *a communal epiphany*."[75] Matthew Kelly offers more: the split of 1890 was "Parnellism's epiphany, revealing the violently contradictory forces that had structured home rule's support base"; closer to our point of interest, he also notes Pearse's "mechanistic hope of provoking an epiphanic exposé" of British oppression. These extraneous epiphanies, together with the nicely phrased "apostolic succession of Irish failures," testify to the deeply embedded religious terminology of the insurrection, and also to the historians' difficulty in extricating themselves from its deep structure.[76]

Bearing this intellectual viscosity in mind, consider Hobson's restaurant conversation with Pearse, of much the same date as the conversation with Connolly. As Pearse rose from the table, he said, "I cannot answer your arguments, but I feel that we must have an insurrection." Recalling this later, Hobson noted that Pearse "had evolved a strange theory that to keep a national spirit alive it would be necessary that there should be a blood sacrifice in every generation. He had visions of himself as a scapegoat for his people." Hobson regarded the Old Testament as a source for Pearse's scapegoat preoccupations. This is unlikely, though indeed the practice is described in Leviticus, for Catholics of that period did not often read the Bible independently and, additionally, Pearse was not fervent in his devotions. Hobson, brought up a Quaker, was far more likely to have recognized Pearse's blood sacrifice ideology as a perverted offshoot from the Leviticus account of driving one goat into the wilderness and sacrificing a second in the temple. "The goat, on which the lot fell to be the scapegoat, shall be presented alive before the Lord, to make an atonement with him, and to let him go for a scapegoat into the wilderness" (Leviticus 16:10).

I am not aware that Pearse used the biblical term in his writings, though the deplorable state of Pearse's texts in his centenary year makes certainty nigh impossible. It is possible that he came across the widely circulated work of Henri Hubert and Marcel Mauss, *Essai sur la nature et la fonction du sacrifice* (1898) either in the original or in English translation. Here he would have found a discussion of the scapegoat in anthropological terms. Freud's *Totem and Taboo*, discussing sacrifice more broadly, appeared in 1913 and, in English, 1918. It is more likely that Hobson read Hubert and Mauss, for he was greatly perturbed by the influence of Pearsean blood-sacrifice rhetoric in Irish nationalist circles.

Differences between various overlapping groups—the IRB and the Irish Volunteers—and between them and the clear-cut Left (the ICA)—involved urgent questions of timing as well as loftier issues of motivation, objective, and inspiration. In January 1916 some members of the IRB Military Council decided to advance matters by abducting Connolly. Joseph Plunkett was one of them. Every biographer of Connolly, and they are many, devotes several pages to this brief incident, yet unanimity remains elusive—except on the outcome. The accepted dates are Wednesday 19 to the evening of Saturday 22 January. Early lives refer to Connolly's "disappearance." The recent, synoptic, and lengthy work of Donal Nevin specifies that he was unexpectedly met outside Liberty Hall by two IRB men who also were volunteers. They had orders to take him by motorcar to a brickworks in Dolphin's Barn for discussions with MacDermott, Pearse, and Plunkett. Austen Morgan adds a confirming detail to the effect that an IRB man, John Cassidy, managed the brickworks.[77] Plunkett, on the other hand, specified "a house near Chapelizod." Neither of these locations is far from the Plunkett stronghold at Larkfield, though Dolphin's Barn is the nearer. Larkfield could scarcely be used as a place to hold the ICA leader, due to the large number of returned exiles (the "Liverpool Lambs") quartered there for training as volunteers.[78]

Evidence about the substance of these day-and-night discussions emerges with a variety of emphases. Desmond Ryan (a sympathetic critic), and C. Desmond Greaves (a Stalinist Saint Paul) admitted Connolly's mental desperation in midwar. On a crucial point Ryan, however, is an exception to the rule just stated: in his little study of 1924, the incident of Connolly's three-day disappearance is ignored.[79] Ostensibly, the issue was timing. Connolly was anxious to strike against the authorities (Dublin Castle, the military establishment, and less directly, the economic system) as soon as possible, despite the fewness of his armed followers. He argued that the country would be inspired and that the Dublin working class in particular would recognize its opportunity. One imagines that some of the IRB men pointed out the condition of the city's workers, exhausted by the events of 1913 and, since 1914, systematically reduced in numbers through economic conscription into the British army. In Desmond Ryan's words, "workers stung to madness by low wages and evil conditions remained aloof from the Sinn Féin organisations."[80] The IRB men countered with reasons for a limited delay. They were prepared, had outwitted the Irish Volunteers' leadership, but awaited support principally from Germany. Plunkett could speak to this factor with authority; he had been in Berlin six months earlier, had met high-ranking military and diplomatic staff, had perfected with Casement a German Plan, and could now report the level of support sought—a U-boat in Dublin Bay, a sizable expeditionary force of soldiers, and large quantities of arms and munitions for the Irish Volunteers. Some arms had arrived back in 1914. What he almost certainly did not report was German reluctance to commit on a larger scale, and a looser sense of Germany's limited interest in an Irish campaign. The objective was to persuade Connolly, not to inform him fully. Plunkett's contribution is a fine example of what Fearghal McGarry has termed "ruthless duplicity" among the Military Council members. Even Plunkett's specification of Chapelizod, in telling his sister where he had been, may be an instance of their systematic deception.

He returned home (probably to nearby Larkfield) exhausted but elated by the three nights of tactical dueling with Connolly. Behind the impatience of one and the measured urgency of three, the negotiators were engaged with more than timing. The uncertainties of German support, the fewness of ICA active members, the internal divisions within the Irish Volunteers combined to raise the level of risk. Inevitably, sacrifice entered into the consciousness of those who knew. The possibility of success existed, though remarkably little was planned for that eventuality. Plunkett's response was to embark on two private enterprises of sublimely ruthless duplicity—his father's mission to Rome, and the forgery of "Secret Orders." But the Dolphin's Barn conference had its immediate results; Connolly was recruited to the Military Council and perhaps sworn into the IRB. It is legitimate to think that membership of the Military Council was a condition imposed by Connolly in return for his forbearance. Nevin is guarded on the question of induction into the IRB; there are some who hold that Connolly may have been a member early in his life and merely needed "rebaptism."

The Military Council proceeded with its plans throughout the early spring. MacDonagh, Pearse, and Plunkett categorically denied to Eoin MacNeill, their chief of staff, that this was the case, in keeping with the practice of ruthless duplicity. Undercurrents of unease should have brought the 1873 Fenian constitution to mind, for it had stipulated that no military action could be taken without an express mandate from the Irish people. In vital theoretical terms, this requirement jeopardized the Council's wish to proclaim an actual sovereign state to replace or activate the republic "now virtually established" of the Fenian oath. It is striking that the Proclamation as finally uttered on Easter Sunday used *sovereign/ty* no fewer than three times in its very short text, *democratic* or *democracy* (like *labor interests* or *socialism*) not once. All concerned were now living through "the time that remains." On Palm Sunday, Hobson spoke at a nationalist concert, taking the opportunity to utter cautious, veiled, but recognizable warnings against precipitous action. A meeting of the Military Council took place the next day that approved both a draft of the Proclamation intended for Easter Sunday and circulation of Plunkett's "Secret Orders." Hobson's biographer considers that the same meeting decided to kidnap Hobson. On Good Friday, he was lured into effective captivity that lasted four days. Release only came after the insurrection had begun and his power to frustrate it had fizzled out. He was held at gunpoint and, at one stage, the option of shooting him arose. Thereafter, he found himself steadily propelled into the office of scapegoat.[81]

Easter Monday being a bank holiday, Dubliners were slow to notice the unprecedented events unfolding in Sackville Street. They strolled in the parks, wheeled the babies in their prams, contemplated the afternoon's race-cards, and generally took their ease. By far the most ironic account of a citizen's learning the facts is Joseph Holloway's. The inveterate first-nighter was walking through the south city area when, near the quays, he came upon a fresh poster:

> I passed a hoarding and read a Proclamation pasted up which caught my eye at once. It had a Gaelic heading and went on to state that Ireland was now under Republican Government, and they hoped with God's help etc etc., to do justly to their own country's people.[82]

Three aspects of Plunkett's behavior during his last week of freedom have been generally noted, his exotic appearance, his enfeebled physical state, and his personal courage. Roddy Connolly, only son of the ICA leader, summarized all of this in a recollection of the GPO on Easter Monday:

> There he was gorgeously apparelled in his uniform with a long sword and a silk scarf around his neck . . . someone procured a mattress and put it in front of the stamp counter and he lay down on it. I thought he was rather

> out of place, lying on a mattress in the middle of a revolution. I didn't think he was much of a leader. Of course as soon as I could I asked my father about him. My father said, and I remember his remark, I think it was very striking. "That's Joe Plunkett and he has more courage in his little finger than all the other leaders combined."[83]

During the week, Plunkett entered a brief account of events in a British army field message book; his record begins on page 52, the previous (serrated) pages having been removed probably for use as dockets. At some early point, his doctor turned up in the GPO to check on the patient. In the notebook Plunkett noted the occupation of the GPO at about 12:15 P.M., and the Proclamation of a Republic. About an hour later, a detachment of Lancers tried to force their way down O'Connell Street from the northern end but were repulsed by the rebels. This action took place in full view of Geraldine Plunkett Dillon's wedding party in the nearby hotel. On the second surviving page of his record, however, Joe proceeded: "simultaneously our operating positions were successfully taken up in the front and rear of Dublin Castle and troops in that strong hold prevented from coming out."[84] Here was positive material for a radio broadcast or other announcement. But the situation was quite different; the rebels' attack on Dublin Castle had faltered and failed despite the unpreparedness of the small guard on duty. His alleged insider, Eugene Smyth, had curiously failed to notify any of MacDermott's many agents (or Plunkett) of the near absence of troops on the premises over the Easter weekend. The near-defenselessness of Beggars' Bush barracks, close to Commandant de Valera's headquarters also escaped rebel intelligence.

Desmond FitzGerald, writing during the Second World War, provided a remarkably serene account of conditions in the GPO. Pearse was greatly worried. Plunkett "looked appallingly ill but at the same time very cheerful . . . supremely happy." All three of them discussed the nonarrival of substantial German support. FitzGerald records his own fantasy about a wider German victory and the prospect of a German prince—he names Prince Joachim—as head of an Irish state. "For the first generation or so, it would be an advantage." Plunkett was able to divert their thoughts by discussing writers and literature, though by Thursday a main topic among the leaders was the prospect of execution—would it be by shooting or hanging?[85]

Once Pearse's surrender had been accepted, the rebels rounded up and disarmed, the army lost no time in organizing legal retribution under military law. Plunkett was court-martialed on what was a conveyor-belt of death sentences. The public knew nothing of the proceedings, until the first phase was completed, though, in most cases, the prisoner was allowed to see some members of his family before execution. Even during these exceptionally high-charged wartime courts-martial, certain rights were acknowledged. Prisoners were examined, records of question and answer were written down, and the formulas of trial procedure observed. Snatches and versions of these events were circulating in Dublin by midsummer.

Plunkett was the unmarried eldest son of exceedingly wealthy parents, who managed to marry Grace Gifford between condemnation and execution. The charge was that he "did an act to wit did take part in an armed rebellion and in the waging of war against his Majesty the King, such act being of such a nature as to be calculated to be prejudicial to the Defence of the Realm and being done with the intention and for the purpose of assisting the enemy." A plea of not guilty was entered, though it cannot be known whether the prisoner spoke any words to this effect. Witnesses were then called—Major Philip Holmes (attached to the Third [reserve] Battalion of the Royal Irish Regiment, based in Clonmel, county Tipperary); Sergeant John Bruton of the Dublin Metropolitan Police; and Lieutenant-Colonel H. S. Hodgkin (Distinguished Service Order) of the Sherwood Foresters (a regiment that had suffered heavy casualties during the fighting).

The evidence amounted to little more than sampling of the obvious, imprecisely phrased. Holmes identified the prisoner as "one of the leaders of a large company of Sinn Feiners" who surrendered on the evening of 29 April. "Sinn Feiners" was repeated several times in the officer's brief account, though the movement known as Sinn Féin had nothing to do with organizing the insurrection. From Holmes's evidence, it is established that, during the court-martial, Plunkett was wearing the same green uniform he had worn in the Post Office—the rank markings of a captain may have been removed in the interim.

Bruton stated that he knew the prisoner, having seen him on two occasions entering and leaving the Irish Volunteers' headquarters at No. 2 Dawson Street. He added that "his name appears on the Proclamation issued by the Irish Volunteers & I believe him to be a member of the Executive Council of that body." Plunkett did not passively accept the policeman's evidence. Cross-examining Bruton, he asked, "How do you know the Proclamation was issued by the Irish Volunteers?" The reply was scarcely rigorous, simply associating the prisoner with Pearse, "Edmund Kent" (Eamonn Ceannt), and MacDonagh, who were members and whose signatures were attached to the Proclamation. Neither prisoner nor witness made any allusion at this point to Connolly or the ICA.

Hodgkin appears to have said little beyond stating that he saw the prisoner when he surrendered. "He was wearing a sword and pistol." And so it was time to hear the defense. The single sentence entered in the trial record can hardly represent in full what Plunkett argued, but it is enough to indicate his political cast of mind at that crucial juncture:

> I have nothing to say in my defence but desire to state that the proclamation referred to in Sergt Brutons [*sic*] evidence is signed by persons who are not connected with the Irish Volunteers & the Proclamation was not issued by the Irish Volunteers.[86]

Although this can hardly have been all that Plunkett said, it still provides food for analysis. By stressing that the Proclamation was signed by persons additional to those who were Volunteers—for example, by Connolly of the ICA—he may have hoped to shake the court's reliance on the fact of his long-known association with the Volunteers. But, in point of fact, there was a double accusation—that he was a senior member of the Volunteers and that he had signed the Proclamation. It is more likely that Plunkett was making a different point—that the Proclamation was the responsibility of those who had signed it—"the glorious seven," as they would become in tradition. Here a strong sense of egoism, or of individual consciousness, may be detected, though underlying that there remain two striking political silences. The ICA is nowhere alluded to in the meager record; Plunkett's distance from Connollyite Marxism never wavered. And neither is the IRB, into which Connolly (perhaps) and MacDonagh had been sworn so that they might qualify for posthumous glory.

Nothing is known of his demeanor toward the court-martial. As with the many, not wholly convergent, reports of Robert Emmet's speech from the dock in 1803, cold print preserves little if anything of the atmosphere, especially print or script edited by the prosecution. Plunkett too endured very considerable bodily hardship—surgery a few days before Easter, five days of little sleep and great stress under fire in the GPO, the isolation and rigors of military confinement, and trial for his life. His perception of a flaw in the case presented against him—no, not a flaw, an inelegance or asymmetry—had no screen upon which it might be projected.

His mercurial personality, complicated by the effects of advanced tuberculosis (or cancer), made him perfectly capable of either tight-lipped compliance or colorful eloquence. The organization that had determined on an Easter Rising was not limited to the Seven. While James Stephens's on-the-spot account of Dublin rumor during Easter Week pithily testifies to the lure of speculation, make-believe, and desperate hope—the Chilean navy was on its way—the stories that later circulated to suggest what the prisoners had said in their defense did not arise under any such immediate psychological pressure.

Count Plunkett was held in Richmond Barracks while the authorities decided what to do with him. Much depended on what was known of his mission to Rome and his connections with Germany. In confinement, he made notes on scraps of paper—unused envelopes, visiting cards, and so on—he found in his pockets. On Tuesday, 16 May, he was allowed write to the provost marshal "for facts of tragedy in my family (Joe, George, Jack & Mammy)."[87] The same cache of prison notes contains a postcard, not in the count's hand but in his wife's, recording a version of their eldest son's last moments that has become widely quoted:

> The priests were called upon (with a lorry) to say that 4 men were about to be shot and 4 priests went immediately. When they arrived at Kilmainham a prisoner was led out to be shot. The warder seeing the priest brought his prisoner into a cell that happened to be open on the ground floor. The priest went in to hear the man's confession. The man knelt down with his hat on. The priest thought that is a strange penitent who goes to confession with his hat on. Just as he was about to hear the man's confession, the warder [went?] into the cell and removed the prisoner's handcuffs whereon he immediately took off his hat.
>
> Father Sebastian heard Joe's confession . . . Father Albert was in the cell with two of the other men who were to be shot when Joe to whom he

> had never spoken, walked over to him and said, "Father I want you to know that I am dying for the glory of God and the honour of Ireland![''] Father Albert said to me (Josephine) that he was admiring this noble-looking youth just before Joe spoke. In speaking of him Father Joseph of Mount Argus said ["]there was more courage in his little finger than in others that were being made much of."[88]

From the hasty manner of the memoir, one can readily conclude that the countess was writing shortly after the events described had been in turn described to her, and writing in awkward circumstances. Nevertheless, it possesses a literary construction that takes it beyond the class of naive facticity. The point about the hat is difficult to reconcile with the treatment of a prisoner on his way to the execution yard, unless the item in question was a hood. One can understand how that detail might be withheld from a mother's ears, as the touching action of the warder releasing the handcuffs permits the bareheaded man receive the sacrament of confession and absolution. Spun out this way, the narrative on the postcard's first side resembles *by contrast* one version of "The Croppy Boy," a ballad about 1798, in which an unscrupulous officer dons the priest's cowl to elicit an incriminating confession.

The second side of the postcard provides a narration in which the priesthood is shown to be everywhere in support and comfort of the condemned men and their relatives. Their names are duly recorded, though, in contrast, none of the other prisoners with Joe is named in his mother's little memoir, not even William Pearse, who had acted in the same companies with Joe and who was on the "intellectual" side of the insurrection. As it is told by his mother, Joe presented himself before two of his comrades and Father Albert (to whom the two had been talking on their own) to make his spoken apologia aloud: "Father I want you to know that I am dying for the glory of God and the honour of Ireland!" Hard for any condemned man to better that, and hard now to regard the remark as less than inflated and distastefully self-centered. The priest from Mount Argus wraps up this spiritual showing-off by making little of other condemned men that were "being made much of"—by others, not themselves.

Of course, there is also some reason to qualify the total verisimilitude of the postcard's account of events in the final minutes of Plunkett's life. His mother has written down, and to some inevitable degree, shaped what she has been told directly by Father Albert and perhaps also by others. The motives stated for Joe's death are those a mother would wish to hear rather than those a man, just shrived, might utter in all humility. "I want you to know" serves the purpose of allowing the priest to utter these words for her solace. In the 1960s, Richard J. Loftus described how "each of the Rising poets chose the deed—and the deed for Pearse, MacDonagh and Plunkett meant violent insurrection—and each of them set about to justify that deed by invoking religion."[89] As the postcard demonstrates, religion willingly undertook its side of the bargain.

Mrs. Geraldine Plunkett Dillon recorded a memoir of these events in 1951. Her thirty-five-year-old allusions to "sincere cowards" and "a few completely dishonest people" preserves a bitterness toward consensual nationalism only matched by the offhand impracticality of any alternative to the seizing of Dublin buildings—"there was, of course, the plan to fall back on Maynooth & to defend the whole block of buildings & to disregard the fury which this would provoke amongst the Bishops . . . The bother about this was that artillery could be used freely against Maynooth."[90]

So there we had it, in the version of 1951. No plans for the country as a whole, until the success (or failure) of Dublin was known; if failure, then a retreat to Saint Patrick's College, Maynooth, twenty miles west of Dublin, where a last stand might have been made in the national headquarters of the Catholic Church. Even with this fantasy of a Gaelic Masada in mind, Plunkett's poetry does not easily fit into the patriotic mold. *The Poems* (summer 1916) was naturally seen into print by members of the family, with access to unpublished manuscripts. Fellow writers rallied to the cause. Padraic Colum edited *Poems of the Irish Republican Brotherhood* (1916) and was also responsible for *The Irish Rebellion of 1916 and its Martyrs: Erin's Tragic Easter* (also 1916). Both of these were published in the United States, where an edition of Plunkett's *Poems* appeared before 1916 was closed, under the imprint of Frederick Stokes (a fellow Belvederian).

It was possible to beef up his prerevolutionary activities in a way that foreshadowed the hero. *Studies*, a Jesuit magazine that cautiously adjusted its assessment of 1916, published an article in December allowing Peter McBrien to encapsulate a life "of marvellous grist." The general tone was an unconscious anticipation of Flann O'Brien's mockery of Celtic heroic virtue—"ill-health, absorbing study and hard poet-work." These burdens somehow could be implied for every stage of Plunkett's development, with the GPO (where Plunkett sported jewelry) serving as the Mount of Transfiguration:

> In his school days at Passy; with his dear friend Asphar at Malta; with the Algerians with whom he was held in such affection; with Stäckler, the tall dark companion who taught him Arabic (it was Stäckler's habit to go out of nights amongst the different tribes of the hinterland disguised as one of themselves and be hail-fellow-well-met with the strange guardians of the fringe of the Sahara—a real life Strickland); in the Cercle Republicaine in Algiers, where Plunkett often danced, and where when a shot went off in the cardroom alongside to punctuate a charge of cheating, no one girl or gentleman, even turned to look; in the half-French, half-Moorish skating rink (Plunkett was a finished skater), where there occurred accidents too full-bodied, too near the elemental edge of things, to be allowed to redden the pages of a stately review.[91]

This is mythmaking stuff, for if one bears in mind that Plunkett only spent a few months in Algiers, and recalls also that his own private diary records no expeditions to the hinterland or even its fringe; its principal activity is the filling of a vacuum with scarcely perceptible suggestions of danger, courage, and full-bodied incidents. The "half-Moorish" skating rink becomes a veritable bullring on the edge of the ineffable. Clearly McBrien is filling out an allusion in Geraldine Plunkett Dillon's foreword to the *Poems*, but he gives the game away with a climactic character assessment of the poet-martyr that collapses into zeugmatic mawkishness—"the Spartan type, contemptuous of lambency or paw." To borrow a term from Roy Foster's entertaining survey of this generation, McBrien's Plunkett best gets by in homosocial environments. It is not wholly surprising that Edith Balfour, an Englishwoman visiting Dublin in January 1922, encountered faded rumors of Plunkett's homosexuality.[92]

CHAPTER 3

Affinity and Mimesis

Affinity in Philosophy's Rattle-Bag

The third part of the critique is even less concerned with chronology than its predecessors, though these investigated certain sequences of events, personal or public. The brevity of Plunkett's public career—an almost Christlike three years—argues against too much reliance on any stage-by-stage analysis of cause and effect. In contrast, this chapter presents a number of largely discrete investigations the order of which is neither random nor absolute. Each is intended to illuminate a facet of the sacrifice enigma as it intermittently discloses itself through Joseph Mary Plunkett, antipolitical insurgent and religious poet.

The most persistent question generated by the combined insurrection of the Irish Volunteers and the Irish Citizen Army in April 1916 focuses on the relationship between the two forces, both founded in the autumn of 1913. The objective in the first case was to form a counterpart to the armed Ulster Volunteers who threatened and offered military resistance to Home Rule; the Irish Volunteers' motive was explicitly nationalist. In the second case, James Larkin created the initially unarmed Citizen Army to protect striking workers from police violence during the Lockout; the motive was expressed in terms of class conflict, or at least class defense. Relations between the two bodies fluctuated. When an offer was made to affiliate the Citizen Army to the larger Irish Volunteers, it was firmly rejected. Later, Connolly advised his comrades to hold on to their weapons for possible future use against what he regarded as the militia of a petty bourgeoisie. Some Volunteers characterized the armed workers as little better than scum, slum-dwellers, social riffraff. Nevertheless, on Easter Monday they "rose" together.

The salient features of a chronological explanation are provided. This accounts for little more than *what* happened, to the neglect of *why*. Austen Morgan has argued that Connolly was always a nationalist at heart even when campaigning vigorously for a socialist revolution. Others, Desmond Greaves the most influential, argue that an independent nation-state was an essential prerequisite for any radical change. Neither of these polar opposites, nor the variants lying between them, explains the thirty-month-long and active relationship between the two bodies. As a preliminary contribution to some deeper analysis, we might look at a term used in today's political theory.

Affinity politics arises where two or more movements or pressure groups recognize that, beyond their highly specific and unrelated objectives, a common interest offers the basis for a loose or informal kinship network. For example, feminism and radical ecology do not occupy common ground, though they may well identify a common obstacle or foe. Affinity politics necessarily arises in situations where a powerful or compelling one-issue politics has already established itself. In the United States, the civil rights movement of the 1960s is such a case. Earlier, the campaign for female suffrage in the United Kingdom had its links with Irish separatism but also with socialist objectives more broadly. Affinity in this practice is often short term. In the present context, the objective will be to clarify how affinity is regarded as a politico-philosophical concept, with reference to the events, issues, and personalities surrounding Joseph Plunkett.

Bearing in mind the preoccupations of J. C. Meredith and (less doggedly) J. M. O'Sullivan in this period, we should note German thought of Kant's late eighteenth century and the Romantic period as a possible source of guidance in considering how affinity might be considered. Kant himself will make a contribution, but the more obvious text is Goethe's novel of 1809, *Die Wahlverwandtschaften*, translated either as *Elective Affinities* or *Kindred by Choice.* Here a metaphor for human passion is drawn from chemistry. Four characters, that is, two couples (one a married couple, the other made up of a retired captain and a young single woman) come together on an estate described in detail along the lines of chemical theories of compounds and affinities.

Later in the nineteenth century (and after) Max Weber employed the metaphor of elective affinity in much of his work, of which the most relevant here is *The Protestant Ethic and the Spirit of Capitalism* (1905; English 1930). H. H. Gerth and C. Wright Mills in 1948 were among the first to draw attention to Weber's deployment of affinity and, as late as 1975, R. H. Lowe found it advisable to bring together evidence supporting the debt to Goethe and the Kantian background to Weber's thought.[1] It is consequently advisable to underscore the philosophical substance of affinity as such, rather than casually perpetuate the common-sensible view that affinity (like taste or influence) is an everyday term requiring no great scrutiny. For Werner Stark, elective affinity is Weber's theoretical alternative to mechanistic causation and quasi-organological functionalism.[2]

These latter two forms of argument are pervasive in Irish debates about history and nationalism. Weber, for the most part, is not directly relevant, except through his association with neo-Kantianism. With reference to the philosophical options under consideration in the Ireland of 1916, Kant himself is the more immediate concern. In Mellin's multivolume *Encyclopädisches Wörterbuch der kritischen Philosophie* (1797), the term *Affinität* is treated over eighteen pages, all the more significant for appearing years before Goethe's novel gave it a novel charge. Recently, Howard Caygill's *Kant Dictionary* (1995) observes that the concept, though enigmatic, secures the objective validity of associations between phenomena such as cause and effect.[3] The reassurance in one regard is genuinely that—a reassurance about the world; in another regard, however, it remains a technical one, concerned with the relationship of phenomena to each other, these accessible by conceptual means. The author of an article in the *Stanford Encyclopedia of Philosophy*, detecting a gap in Kant's theory of judgment, writes, "there remains the real possibility of relatively or absolutely chaotic aggregates of sensory appearances or objects that are not subsumed or even in principle cannot be subsumed under the transcendental affinity of the manifold, i.e., the real possibility of the categorical anarchy of rogue objects." Here, the language of the world as we know it—chaos, anarchy with rogue items of one sort or another—is admitted. Does this in any way illuminate the relation between thought and action in the experience of Meredith or Plunkett?

Before proceeding to consider the latter's recorded views on literature and philosophy, we might remind ourselves of his interest in the sciences, including electricity, Hindu chemistry, physiology, wireless telegraphy, and so on. Usually assigned among the poets of the 1916 insurrection, he might also considered one of the less celebrated whose education was acquired in science faculties (including medicine). His sister Geraldine and her husband, Thomas Dillon, trained in chemistry; his colleague in Larkfield, Rory O'Connor, was an engineer. There were others. What affinity existed between these fields? T. S. Eliot, in his canon-shaping essay "Tradition and the Individual Talent" (1919) resorted to a new term in chemical description to illustrate his theory of depersonalization because, through it, art may be said to approach the condition of science.[4] Thus the word *catalyst* entered the vocabulary of literary criticism. Eliot's quest for depersonalization had its domestic context, but that in turn (and much more) is not explicable without reference to the Great War. His academic prospects, concentrated in a Harvard dissertation on the British idealist F. H. Bradley, supervised by Harold Joachim, did not survive the crisis. British idealism did not entirely collapse in the wake of the slaughter, but its critics (including Bertrand Russell) emerged as a sharper phalanx than any it had faced in Edwardian or Victorian times. Philosophy, poetry, and science discovered affinities—some of them antagonistic, but nonetheless affinities—in these years, and Plunkett offers a specific, local case for deeper consideration.

Plunkett on the Just State

Tom Kettle's farewell to the Industrial Peace Committee appeared in *The Irish Review* of November 1913. Although increasingly the victim of chronic alcoholism, he was a prolific and effective writer. Leaving aside professional work on economic topics, the list displays his active interest in European thought. He wrote an introduction to Louis Paul-Dubois's *Contemporary Ireland* (1908), translated Karl Alois Kneller's *Christianity and the Leaders of Modern Science* (1911), and contributed an introduction to Daniel Halévy's biography of Nietzsche as translated by Joseph Hone (1911). While J. M.

O'Sullivan was writing his Kant and Hegel dissertation in Heidelberg, Kettle and he took extensive walking holidays in the German countryside. "The Agony of Dublin" opened with a downbeat account of class conflict only partly enlivened with a plaintive joke—"Wherever Hegelianism may fail, in this field at least it triumphs. There is always a 'Yes!' for which something can be said; there is always a 'No!' for which something can be said."[5]

Plunkett's writings are fragmentary in several senses, brief and unfinished in a tantalizing way, scattered and internally unfocused in a less pardonable fashion. In September 1913, he wrote a short note on what his biographer called "the necessity for a just and egalitarian state." A month later, he was involved (though not centrally) in the Industrial Peace Committee established to mediate in the Lockout of workers by Dublin employers. The text as published by Honor O Brolchain reads:

> It should be (but unfortunately isn't) obvious that the sole objects of government should be the peace and prosperity in the fullest sense of all the individuals composing the nation—that all other objects, such as the furtherance of law and order, the cultivation of relations with other powers and peoples, the extension of boundaries, the building up of trade, the development of resources, the subjection of enemies, the pursuit of the arts, sciences and philosophies, the promulgation of ideals should entirely and completely subserve those first named. It should also be evident (but here there is more difficulty) that the destinies, the habits of life and labour, the ideals and religion of the individuals composing the nation should as far as possible be their own free choice. This alone is liberty. It was not only the great Emperor Otto whose mind wavered between "*l'état c'est moi*" [I am the state] and "*Ich dien*" [I serve.] The Fabian Society does the same. The collectivist theory of government makes the state (as embodied in the government) more important than the governed—which is precisely the fallacy of oligarchy and aristocracy.
>
> Put in these terms the absurdity is manifest therefore these terms are never used. The nearest approach to them is the statement of the position one logical step back. One is permitted to say that the difference between the democratic theory of government and all the other theories is that the former supposes that the opinions and desires of the governed should prevail even when they run counter to the ideas of those in power, while

> all other theories of government assume as axiomatic the proposition that only those possessing power know how it should be used.
>
> There is always, moreover, the double subsumption that those who know how power should be used will thus employ it and that those who do not know could not be trusted to find out.

The note or essay is divided into three paragraphs. The first is concerned with the nation rather than the state, at least up to the reference to Otto I (912–973), a Holy Roman emperor who did indeed attend to the extension of boundaries and the subjection of enemies. He cannot be intelligently compared to Louis XIV (1638–1713) of France supposed author of the quip *L'état, c'est moi*. There is no affinity of concept or maxim here, apart from the crude fact of monarchy in the long age of monarchy. *Ich dien* is the motto of the Prince of Wales, from a date in the fourteenth century, again post-Otto. While these phrases added color to the mini-essay, they did not obscure Plunkett's assumption that the nation is made up of individuals whose liberty in matters of conscience ought to be fundamental: this notion would have meant nothing to Otto, and would elicit little but ridicule from Louis. Nevertheless Plunkett grapples with a central problem for modern democratic theory. However, he shows no enthusiasm for "collectivist" government, recognizing that above or beyond democratic institutions are those who hold power.

This is a shrewd if hardly original criticism. The succeeding brief paragraphs proceed to convert it into a theoretical logjam. The absurdity of democratic government (no example cited) is such that it is never stated openly. One (that is, the individual) is permitted to think up to a point immediately prior (logically, not chronologically) to the absurd. The double "subsumption" of the concluding paragraph amounts to statements (1) that those who know how power should be used actually possess it and will employ it; and (2) that those who do not know how power should be used should not be allowed to gain it. These are the constitutive subparts of the more general argument of the first paragraph.

The attempted proof of the necessity for a just state demonstrates some efforts toward systematic organization. In its subject matter it sadly lacks any familiarity with the ideas of J.-J. Rousseau, Kant, Mill, the British idealists, or indeed with the course of Irish debates on these matters from the eighteenth century onward. An ethical concern is evident throughout, principally through repetition of "should"—eight times, neatly, in eight sentences. However, the first of these is promptly jeopardized by the admission that *what should be obvious* isn't. There is, from the outset, an instability in the search for necessity through moral or ethical imperative, an instability that appears at two levels of description: first, the nation is regarded as a sum of individual persons without any thought as to how the collective relates to the constitutive; second, collectivist (or, perhaps, democratic) government may exist even while power is possessed, exercised, and monopolized elsewhere *and here*, its possessors apparently lying beyond description or particularization.

Plunkett on Obscurity as Criticism

In the February 1914 issue of *The Irish Review*, Plunkett (by then both proprietor and editor) reviewed two recent collections of verse, one by his close friend and coeditor, Thomas MacDonagh, the other by George William Russell (known as AE), a poet of Yeats's generation who had contributed six articles on "The Problem of Rural Life" to early numbers of the *Review*. The notice constitutes Plunkett's longest published statement and, as such, deserves attention.[6] When Plunkett's sister, Geraldine, compiled a posthumous selection of his work, she included "Obscurity and Poetry" as the sole example of his prose.

> There are two kinds of obscurity—the obscurity of Art and the obscurity of Nature. They may be called the obscurity of mist and the obscurity of mystery. They have nothing in common. They are as opposed as the poles.
>
> A thing may be hidden by Art in two ways. It may be overlaid with irrelevancies, or its expression may be restrained to the point of poverty. The effect is the same. The essentials are hidden. In Nature also (but by Nature we mean not so much apparent Nature as real Nature) there are two ways by which things may be hidden. They may become so common as not to be regarded, or they may be so uncommon as not to permit regard. They may be as universal as light or as unique as the sun. Observation involves comparison, and that which is entirely universal or absolutely unique—or both—cannot be compared with anything.
>
> An artist is one who has the power of unveiling Nature, only to

substitute the veils of Art. Indeed it is by imposing the veils of Art that he is enabled to show the real qualities and relations of things. For the veils of Art need not be obscure. The vision of the artist is of such a kind that it penetrates these veils and thus can view the realities underlying them that otherwise could not be confronted. It is through his Art that the artist sees.

The artist's task, however, is to make others see; for all Art is revelation. This he does chiefly by the great instrument of inspiration, Choice. He chooses the portion or phase of Truth that he is to reveal, and he chooses the veils that he must impose in order to make that Truth visible. Here it is that the artist is liable to obscurity. He is apt to lose the consciousness of his purpose of revelation to others in the overwhelming devotion that the vision requires. Then is it that the quality of his inspiration decides the nature of the obscurity that is certain to result. If his vision be powerful and his inspiration deep he will choose to scale the topless peaks of beauty and attempt to set down the splendour of the spreading plains of Truth. He will fail to clothe his vision with the necessary veils. His work will have the obscurity of Nature. If, on the other hand, his inspiration be more subtle and superficial, running hither and thither in intricate mazes of wonder, he will multiply veils on detailed portions of his subject, adding one to another according as the various points of view and possible relations of parts come within his cognizance. His work will have the obscurity of Art.

As the principle of all Art can be exemplified in the production of any Art, and as poetry is the most satisfying of all the Arts, better examples could not be chosen to demonstrate the obscurities of Mist and Mystery than two poets in whose works these opposite tendencies exist. It so happens that something of one of each of these tendencies to obscurity may be observed in two books of poems that have just been issued. They are the *Collected Poems* of AE and *Lyrical Poems* by Thomas MacDonagh.* AE has followed the two Arts of painting and poetry, and in both of these has manifested the rhythmic creation of beauty. If sometimes we have been in doubt as to which of these arts we ought to attribute some of his work,

---

**Collected Poems* by AE. Macmillan: 6s. net. *Lyrical Poems* by Thomas MacDonagh. "The Irish Review": 6s. net.

our confusion is not an arraignment of his methods, but rather an assertion that by means of the two arts sprung from the same necessity, and appealing to like faculties of appreciation he has contrived to satisfy us of their unity and origin and essential identity of purpose. Though many have remarked on the unusual similarity of AE's poetry and his painting—a similarity which leaves his poetry easily the superior from the point of view of craft, as it never has the faulty draughtsmanship nor the glaring crudities of colour occasionally visible in his pictures—none seem to have mentioned the outstanding difference always and everywhere observable on comparison of these two media of expression. It is simply this, that one is never in doubt as to what is on the canvas, but one is very frequently in doubt as to what is included in AE's poems. Now let us be very careful and very clear. One might say "We know that there is on the canvas a certain amount of paint, and in the poems a certain number of syllables." But we know much more of what is on the canvas. We may not know the ulterior meaning of the picture, if it have one; we may not know whether the figures wading in the light-flooded sea are illusions of flesh and blood or realities of the spirit; we may not know the secrets of the symbols, but we do know the symbols. But in the poems we sometimes know nothing more than the suite of the syllables. We taste the honey of their sound, but we get no milk of their meaning. They may call up flashes of colour and shape, but these always fade and pass

And burning multitudes pour through my heart too bright, too blind,
Too swift and hurried in their flight to leave their tale behind.
(The Winds of Angus).

We do not know these symbols—if they are symbols. We could not be trusted to recognise them again. This may be due in some measure to our limitations, but it is these limitations that the artist must take into account. We have, however, some reason to believe that much of AE's obscurity is deliberate, or at least conscious. For when he is roused to rage he becomes cold and clear. When he wishes to express anger or disgust towards men and conditions, all his immutable immensities go by the board. He ceases to be the prophet of pantheism, seeing the universal in the smallest of things and the immortality of Nothingness at the end of all. He denies the kingship of the beggar and the divinity of the worm. He becomes Nietzschean in his contempt for humility:

He does not love the bended knees
The soul made worm-like in his sight.
(Faith).
He asks with the Old Aristocrat:
How came this pigmy rabble spun,
After the gods and kings of old?
(The Iron Age).

He feels the reality and hates the oppression of death:
The worship of the dead is not
A worship that our hearts allow.
(On behalf of some Irishmen not followers of Tradition).

The portion of Truth that he will have is that which seems to be cut off from the body of Truth, and then he prefers to hold it as a heresy—which is the last cold profanity of Pride:

No blazoned banner we unfold—
One charge alone we give to youth
Against the sceptred myth to hold
The golden heresy of Truth.
(Ibid).

With the withdrawal of his superimposed beauties of imagery, his obscurity vanishes and his meaning stands clearly forth, freed from the mist of his Art.

As this is the first issue of Thomas MacDonagh's *Lyrical Poems*, it is primarily necessary to tell something of its quality. There is a quiet depth of meaning and a calm splendour of expression throughout the great poems in this book that unquestionably raise them to the region of essential poetry. Tried by any of the touchstones of criticism, clarity, lyrical beauty, perfection of imagery, effortless rapture, sympathy of human feeling, profundity of Vision—everywhere we catch the glint of perfect gold. Witness this passage from "The Golden Joy": [thirty-six lines are quoted].

In his essay on Coleridge, Francis Thompson says: "There is not one great poet who has escaped the charge of obscurity, fantasticalness, or affectation of utterance," but we may ask, Is there one great poet who has not deserved the charge of obscurity? If we limit the charge to that kind of obscurity that we have called the obscurity of Nature or of Mystery, then to our knowledge there is none. Certainly in some of his poems Mr MacDonagh deserves the charge. Much of "The Book of Images" is difficult if not impossible to interpret, but the Vision is not less clear for that, and the one thing that we must insist on is clarity of Vision. Without clarity of Vision there can be no certainty of inspiration. It is only in utterance that the great poet is obscure. And it is only in utterance that Mr MacDonagh is obscure. This is not because he does not speak plainly, it is because he speaks too plainly to be understood. Nor is it because all utterance is inadequate. It is not that his words do not mean enough. It is that they mean too much. When he says:

The phases of the might
Of God in mortal sight
I saw, in God's forethought
Fashioned and wrought,
Now wrought in spirit and clay,
In rare and common day,
And shown in symbol and sign
Of power divine.

he is claiming inspiration and prophecy as it is claimed in the Book of Wisdom. He is like Blake, holding infinity in the palm of his hand. He is stating his Vision of all Being in eight short lines. He makes a verse of the Universe. He fills all the heavens with a syllable and with a word holds the gates of hell. His is the true dominion of the mystic. In his symbolism Mr MacDonagh shows the same power:

The flowers of heaven and earth,
The moons of death and birth,

> The seasons of the soul,
>
> are three clear images which illustrate and illuminate the obscurity of his form and the precision and plenitude of his meaning. And indeed the first of these serves to remind us of the essential teaching of all the great mystical poets from Solomon to Francis Thompson—the doctrine that binds AE and Thomas MacDonagh in the same service of beauty, the creed subscribed to by all who have experienced the divine vision; for the flowers of heaven and earth are the same flowers.

In attempting to distill Plunkett the critic's underlying principles, one could do worse than list the poets whom he invokes—William Blake, S. T. Coleridge, and Francis Thompson, an English trio made up of a radical antinomian Protestant, an Anglican, and a Catholic (though all three might also be described as converts to those positions). Coleridge features only in passing, and so we are left with two ill-matched figures—the experimentalist Blake and the metrically hidebound Thompson. Like Russell whose *Collected Poems* are under review, Blake was poet and painter, yet Plunkett attempts no comparison. All of these men are said to be mystic poets (not forgetting Solomon), but the acknowledged mystics of English literature—Richard Crashaw, George Herbert, Henry Vaughan, for examples among the poets—nowhere feature. It is difficult to excavate for intellectual or aesthetic foundations.

In contrast, a method or procedure is immediately obvious. There are two kinds of obscurity; a thing may be hidden in either of two ways: there are two arts, poetry and painting; and two poets, MacDonagh and Russell. The review advances by offering the reader alternatives in pairs. Geraldine Plunkett Dillon, in gathering material for the commemorative volume, compared "Obscurity and Poetry" to MacDonagh's own (far more extensive) critical writings, referring to "a curiously painstaking method of discussion" that she attributed to the fact that both were dealing with what was to them "an exact science for which they had no exact terms."[7] Most readers of MacDonagh's book on the Elizabethan Thomas Campion (1913) or his posthumous *Literature in Ireland* (1916) appreciate his critical sensitivity maintained within an increasingly nationalist interpretation of poetry and literary language. Few would classify it under the heading of science, even linguistic science. The pairing of Plunkett and MacDonagh as critics is as artificial and forced as the former's declarations about the two obscurities, the two arts (what about music?) in his opening paragraph.

One should not dismiss considerations of science as irrelevant to the Dublin events of April 1916 and their leading sponsors. There is, however, a protean term utilized prominently in the review, which gestures decisively away from any scientific concern. It appears first as mystery, and jokingly associated with mist. The origins of this opening gambit lie in a remark much in circulation during the late Victorian age, that mysticism begins in mist and ends in schism, sometimes attributed to Chesterton or even Cardinal Newman but without proof. Late in the essay, Plunkett moves from mystery to the mystic poets and their mysticism, having associated his friend MacDonagh with that school, while conspicuously declining to reward AE in the same coin. Given G. W. Russell's reputation as a learned student of Celtic and Indian pagan religions, not to mention voluminous writings in prose and verse, this is a bold step. Whereas MacDonagh was a close friend, a fellow editor of *The Irish Review* whose little book appeared under the *Review*'s imprint, Russell and his *Collected Poems* lay outside the pale. And whereas Plunkett's treatment of MacDonagh is less scientifically critical than effusively vapid, his response to the senior poet is decisively polemical. The crucial passage reads:

> When he wishes to express anger or disgust towards men and conditions, all his immutable immensities go by the board. He ceases to be the prophet of pantheism, seeing the universal in the smallest of things and the immortality of Nothingness at the end of all. He denies the kingship of the beggar and the divinity of the worm. He becomes Nietzschean in his contempt.

In Russell's case, anger about conditions arose specifically in his lengthy response to the Lockout, published in letter form on 7 October 1913, and addressed to Dublin's employers:

> Your insolence and ignorance of the rights conceded to workers universally in the modern world were incredible, and as great as your inhumanity. If you had between you collectively a portion of human soul as large as a threepenny bit, you would have sat night and day with the representatives

> of labour, trying this or that solution, mindful of the women and children . . . Cry aloud to Heaven for new souls! The souls you have got, cast upon the screen of publicity, appear like horrid and writhing creatures enlarged from the insect world.[8]

This, it would seem, was too partisan for the recent assistant secretary to the Industrial Peace Committee, whose parents owned vast swaths of high-class suburban property—and some tenement or slum property also. Plunkett's complaint is religious, alleging that Russell has been unfaithful to his supposed Buddhist doctrine of reincarnation and the blessedness of the humble and meek. More specifically, he quotes from his elder's *Collected Poems*, taking particular exception to one of the longest, "On Behalf of Some Irishmen not Followers of Tradition":

> They call us aliens, we are told,
> Because our wayward visions stray
> From that dim banner they unfold,
> The dreams of worn-out yesterday.
> The sum of all the past is theirs,
> The creeds, the deeds, the fame, the name,
> Whose death-created glory flares
> And dims the spark of living flame.
> They weave the necromancer's spell,
> And burst the graves where martyrs slept,
> Their ancient story to retell,
> Renewing tears the dead have wept.
> And they would have us join their dirge,
> This worship of an extinct fire
> In which they drift beyond the verge
> Where races all outworn expire.
> The worship of the dead is not
> A worship that our hearts allow,
> Though every famous shade were wrought
> With woven thorns above the brow.
> We fling our answer back in scorn:
> "We are less children of this clime

Than of some nation yet unborn
Or empire in the womb of time.
We hold the Ireland in the heart
More than the land our eyes have seen,
And love the goal for which we start
More than the tale of what has been."
The generations as they rise
May live the life men lived before,
Still hold the thought once held as wise,
Go in and out by the same door.
We leave the easy peace it brings:
The few we are shall still unite
In fealty to unseen kings
Or unimaginable light.
We would no Irish sign efface,
But yet our lips would gladlier hail
The firstborn of the Coming Race
Than the last splendour of the Gael.
No blazoned banner we unfold—
One charge alone we give to youth,
Against the sceptred myth to hold
The golden heresy of truth.

Plunkett had quoted two brief passages with detrimental intention. The first (lines 17–18) touched on a doctrine of the New Nationalism imported from France, a cult or worship of the dead (cf. Maurice Barrès's fervent invocations of "la terre et les morts") with its concomitant preoccupation with martyrs (line 10) whom Russell thinks entitled to undisturbed rest. Russell, theosophist and scholar of metempsychosis, does not take up the French invitation to resurrect and remobilize the dead because, for him, death-created glory dims the living flame (lines 7–8). The cult of self- (and other-) sacrifice, martyrdom, and veneration of the dead will blossom within Irish nationalist rhetoric in the years leading up to April 1916. Russell's mystical learning and his engagement in contemporary politics (not simply in October 1913, but more extensively through the Agricultural Co-operative Movement) relies on a quite different understanding of how past and present engage.

A key term, tradition, is deftly placed at the end of the poem's title. The celebration of martyrs, and the recitation of historic dates (whether of defeat or, less often, glory) had become the liturgy of the new Irish nationalism, an ideology shaped and articulated in the nineteenth century, no earlier. By tradition, Russell means that political doctrine which speaks of a continuous Irish nation, existent in 1169 (when the Normans came) and despite oppression existent ever since. His view is substantiated by reference to dim pageantry and repetition, "renewing tears the dead had wept." The rhetoric of Easter 1916 employed the tropes of self-sacrifice, glorious violence, and "the dead generations." What is striking in Plunkett's review is his recognition of Russell's politics as dangerously antagonistic to the emerging project of armed insurrection blessed by the Catholic Church.

A sectarian line of argument, however obscured by Plunkett's heavy style, is discernible. Quoting the poem's last four lines, he writes that Russell's portion of Truth "seems to be cut off from the body of Truth . . . he prefers to hold it as a heresy—which is the last cold profanity of Pride." Heresy is active deviation from the church's teaching; the church in question can only be Rome. Independence of mind, even on religious topics, is profane, evidence of pride, the trademark of Satan. Russell, born into a Primitive Methodist family in Ulster, opens by noting that such people are regarded as "aliens," less on grounds of their presumed foreign origins than on a refusal to merge into the tradition of ageless Irish nationhood. These were uncomfortable distinctions for the leaders of 1916: Patrick and William Pearse's father had been an English agnostic turned Catholic in Dublin for business reasons; Thomas MacDonagh's mother had been an English dissenter who also converted, though from higher motives. Connolly's wife was brought up in the Protestant Church of Ireland. Thomas Clarke's father was a member of the same.

Within the review, the comparison of MacDonagh and Russell involves more than one asymmetry. Quite apart from age and literary reputation, plumbing the religious or philosophical dimension involves a recognition of nonpolar differences. Russell grew up in a branch of Irish dissent known for its emphasis on the laity's role in the church, but MacDonagh's mother had been brought up in the even looser community of English Unitarianism. Russell's wife, Violet North, was an English occultist. MacDonagh's, Muriel

Gifford, was the child of a fractiously mixed marriage between Catholic and Protestant. She cleaved to the Protestant faction. When she and MacDonagh married on 3 January 1912, something clandestine about the ceremony prompted the officiating priest to advise them, "if you intend publishing the marriage—*leave out church and place*."[9] As late as May 1915, MacDonagh confided to an emigrant friend in the United States that "Muriel and I are of the same religion, which is neither Catholic or protestant nor any other form of dogmatic creed."[10] Plunkett's review of his friend's *Lyrical Poems* has its deliberately obscured stratum; below the highly ornamented commendation one can read a stern persuasive against "the golden heresy" and a call to orthodoxy.

Plunkett on The Unimportance of Philosophy

J. M. Plunkett's surviving papers are doubtless incomplete to a more than commonplace extent by reason of military imposition on his family and his household in the years after the insurrection. It would, however, be a flattering of Military Intelligence to conclude that all his sophisticated and completed work on literature, religion, and philosophy was confiscated or destroyed, leaving unrepresentative fragments, uncharacteristic notes, and superseded juvenilia behind. Within a few months of his death, a full collection of poems was in print, but no companion volume of prose whether fictional or discursive. One is obliged to conclude that what is accessible is not untypical. Naturally enough, problems of a theoretical or perhaps hypothetical kind arise from such a situation, especially with a thinker given to approving Silence. Is it not possible that Plunkett's profounder ideas remained unuttered yet powerfully influential through his actions and the impact of these on other people?

Among the papers, one finds individual sheets carrying two, three, or more individual inscriptions, some divided by emphatic lines, sometimes following each other without any guidance to a reader. Their author scarcely envisaged a reader, and it is greatly to the credit of his latter-day relatives that the collection is preserved in the NLI. The contents, as with Plunkett generally, can be surprising and contradictory, complicated by a paucity of dates. When, for example, did he write in a larger than usual hand, "Damn the populace! There is no such thing," at the bottom of a box shape with double lines to close it off from the material below? An answer of sorts lies to the right, outside the side line—29 November. What follows, immediately in space but not necessarily in time, is a verse:

> Fire and flame, my sister and my brother
> Fire of consuming flame of {our cremation} tribulation.
> {?} the hid spirit {than} and the manifestation
> Each {?}, of the other

These three and a half lines are enclosed in a rough border. Below again, an aphorism: "If you understand Woman you are a mystic, if you understand women you are a lunatic, {if you understand one woman you are a wise man}." Taking the added, if incomplete, date with the sentence about women, one might conclude with some confidence that the page was written up in the month following his visit to New York in the autumn of 1915. Such a conclusion makes no allowance for his dismissal of the populace, nor does it explain the incomplete verse about fire and flame, sister and brother.

In earlier pages of the present study, close analysis generally has focused on correspondence, letters, poems, and short reflective observations (often whimsical). To turn to an intellectually substantial essay on a topic of acknowledged importance would greatly assist our understanding of an unquestionably intriguing and mobile intelligence, whose impact on Irish affairs in the second decade of the twentieth century (and beyond) cannot be denied. Does such a document survive? Did one ever exist? "The Unimportance of Heraclitus" must serve as a test case, for want of better. The manuscript, on two sheets of paper, is very brief, amounting to just over three hundred words.

> Two men have reinterpreted Heraclitus. Acting {separately} independently their interpretations clash so {frequently} completely and so often that the {opposition of their views and their} contrast cannot fail to be illuminating. If the light so generated throws a powerful shadow on the Philosopher of Aphorisms himself it cannot be helped—it {will} may at least {show he made to} show up in strong relief the teachings of his strong interpreters. For, the early followers of this strangest of Philosophers—if indeed he was

> a Philosopher and not a Mystic Prophet—enjoined Silence, believing that his doctrine was beyond the power of true verbal expression.* Whereas, the predominant characteristic of his modern exponents is garrulity.
>
> Now it is readily conceded that there are but two chief types of garrulity {?} familiar to the majority of the inhabitants of these islands,† Saxon (including German) garrulity and Gallic garrulity. Saxon garrulity consists in saying too much in a great many words. Gallic garrulity consists in saying too little in a great many more words. The interpreters (pardon the misstatement) of Heraclitus writing . . .
>
> At this present date are admirable presentations of these two types. The Teutonic representative is a Briton (modern) bearing the typically Saxon name of Wells. The Gaul on the other hand wears the surprising superlabel of Bergson. From this it will be understood that they are representatives not of races but of things infinitely more pathetic if far less real, that is to say, tendencies. {A tendency may be said to be a predisposition to act; an ethnotendency, a linked series of predispositions to act in accordance with a race-habit or national habit.}[11]

The word *garrulity* provides a starting point. Together with its adjective, there are seven occurrences. The authors named—H. G. Wells and Henri Bergson—were prolific writers who also entertained audiences at public lectures. However, on the topic of Heraclitus, they had relatively little to say. In the former's *Modern Utopia* (1905), the "philosopher of aphorisms" is mentioned only twice, though "that lost and misunderstood giant may be coming to his own."[12] In *First and Last Things* (1908), he devotes two short paragraphs to "The Resumption of Metaphysical Inquiry," concluding:

> In the past half century there has begun a more systematic critical movement in the general mind, a movement analogous to the Pre-Raphaelite movement in art—a Pre-Aristotelian movement, a scepticism about things supposed to be settled for all time, a resumed inquiry into the fundamental laws of thought, a harking back to positions of the older philosophers and

* There is reason to believe that some {of} who pretended to understand Heraclitus sought to give him expression in symbolic and imitative movement.

† Celts are only garrulous when intoxicated.

> particularly to Heraclitus, so far as the surviving fragments of his teaching enable one to understand him, and a new forward movement from that recovered ground.[13]

This is positive and stimulating on the issue of Heraclitus's place in modern thought. But hardly garrulous. Neither of these publications appears in Plunkett's book lists; indeed Wells's name is oddly absent. Plunkett did study *Little Wars* (1913), published after the lists were compiled. But *Little Wars* has nothing to add on Heraclitus. So much for German garrulity. It is true that German scholarship in the late nineteenth century devoted much time and thought to the publication of Heraclitean texts and commentary, but Plunkett has not indicated any awareness in this field.

So, to the French contribution. In the nineteenth century, Heraclitus featured as a comic character, often partnered on stage by Parmenides. The degree of scholarly attention appears considerably lower than the German, yet far from inconsiderable. Much changes with the emergence of Henri Bergson, who, while teaching philosophy in a Clermont-Ferrand lycée, wrote a Latin dissertation on Aristotle's concept of place. Toward the end, the young Bergson cites a passage from *On Generation and Corruption*, with the comment, "I am not sure whether it is a recollection of a statement of Heraclitus."[14] The dissertation was approved in June 1889, in which year the author also published his first book, translated into English as *Time and Free Will*. This we know Plunkett commenced to read: it contains no reference to Heraclitus. The canonical text of Bergsonian philosophy, *L'Évolution créatrice*, appeared in 1907 and was translated into English as *Creation Evolution* in 1911: it too contains no reference to Heraclitus, though, in writing, "the movement of the stream is distinct from the river bed, although it must adopt its winding course. Consciousness is distinct from the organism it animates, although it must undergo its vicissitudes," Bergson may be drawing on the best known of Heraclitus's aphorisms.[15] In 1913, *Creative Evolution* was added to the reading list for final year undergraduates in Trinity's mental and moral science department, together with William James's *Pragmatism*. Dublin's ancien régime of intellectualism was officially under pressure.

Creative Evolution created of Bergson a "superlabel," in Plunkett's sardonic phrase. Among Anglophone enthusiasts was G. B. Shaw, inventor (for his language) of *Superman*. Even before it had appeared, Bergson was credited with a New Philosophy. For several years, the journals and newspapers—garrulous by their calling—featured reviews, overviews, tributes, and submissions. The hard-headed and word-pinching T. E. Hulme wrote two pieces, brought together in a posthumous volume—he was killed in France in 1917. A central declaration was, "Man's primary need is not *knowledge* but *action*. The characteristic of the intellect itself Bergson deduces from this fact."[16] A militarist by faith—the diagnosis is Herbert Read's—Hulme had something in common with Plunkett, director of military operations for the IRB. But no citation of Heraclitus. That Bergson became known as the latter-day Heraclitus is undeniable, for their concentration on the metaphysics of change made the point unavoidable.

In our analysis, the Ephesian has been sidelined by attention paid to Wells and Bergson. Perhaps this vindicates Plunkett's highlighting of the *unimportance* of Heraclitus, the bulk of whose aphorisms, and whatever else he wrote, disappeared in antiquity or before. What was available of them at the beginning of the twentieth century involved some scholarly disputation. For the present, an American publication of 1889 serves our purpose. The young American scholar G. T. W. Patrick compiled an edition of 130 fragments, published in Baltimore, Maryland. The too familiar observation about stepping into a river occurs in fragment numbers 41, 42, and 81 in significantly different formulations, the most challenging being 81–"Into the same river we both step and do not step. We both are and are not."[17] The river's mutability (to use a Renaissance term) is matched/outmatched by the mutability of self, the identity of nonidentity.

Patrick's edition was available when Plunkett visited New York. No evidence survives that, amid his active concerns with John Devoy and Clan na Gael, and passive concerns with Columba O'Carroll, he took time off for early Greek philosophy. He might have been impressed by Heraclitus #3 "Those who hear and do not understand are like the deaf. Of them the proverb says: 'Present, they are absent'" partly because the intermediary source offers a biblical parallel to the first sentence: "He that hath ears to hear, let him hear" (Matthew 11:15). This well-known verse occurs in "Seals of Thunder," which opens *The Poems of Joseph Mary Plunkett*, edited by his sister after the executions.[18] Other aphorisms adopt positions apparently relevant to Plunkett's military and political intentions, for example, #100, "The people must fight for their law as for their walls."

With Heraclitus, however, every position has its counterposition. In the final pages of *Fragments*, three entries are devoted to a notion fully central to the strategies and ideologies of Easter 1916—sacrifice. These are preceded by #127 with its commentary on lasciviousness and ritual celebration of the sexual organs: "Were it not Dionysus to whom they institute a procession and sing songs in honor of the pudenda, it would be the most shameful action. But Dionysus, in whose honor they rave in bacchic frenzy, and Hades are the same"—this attributed to Heraclitus via Clement of Alexandria. Then follow immediately, in Patrick's arrangement, the aphorisms on sacrifice. The pithiest, together with its scholarly cladding of provenance and transmission, is

> And Heraclitus, making sport of these people, says, "When defiled, they purify themselves with blood, just as if any one who had fallen into the mud should wash himself with mud!" For to suppose that with the bodies and blood of the unreasoning animals which they offer to their gods they can cleanse the impurities of their own bodies, which are stained with vile contaminations, is like trying to wash off mud from their bodies by means of mud.[19]

Plunkett's notion of blood sacrifice was conditioned by his awareness of imminent death from tuberculosis. A devout if also intellectually errant Catholic, he found Patrick Pearse's utterances calmly acceptable—"Blood is a cleansing and sanctifying thing, and the nation that regards it as the final horror has lost its manhood . . . there are many things more horrible than bloodshed, and slavery is one of them!" Or, more surprisingly, the near-Marxist Connolly: "Without the shedding of blood there is no redemption." This strand of thought is readily placed under the broader rhetorical shroud thrown over the Great War, indeed prepared before the war in the ratcheting up of nationalist fervor and the celebration of violence as renewal. On the other hand, *pace* songs honoring the pudenda, he found Strindberg's *Easter* profane.

Plunkett, we may be sure, was the only signatory of the Proclamation who read Heraclitus—with the just possible exception of his friend MacDonagh, who was constitutionally less inclined toward sacrificial politics. "The Unimportance of Heraclitus" establishes the fact of his awareness, but little more. The author has not graduated with a distinction from the philosophy class in Stonyhurst. The essay's internal organization offers little insight into Plunkett's mode of thinking. Its contents—the comments on Wells and Bergson—are not well informed. However, the final (canceled) sentence unquestionably picks up the Zeitgeist (as much English as German) of racial difference: "A tendency may be said to be a predisposition to act; an ethnotendency, a linked series of predispositions to act in accordance with a race-habit or national habit." The first clause limpidly expresses a view expounded by Hulme of the North Staffordshire Regiment, acknowledging Bergson—"not knowledge but action." The second, however, aims to go much further by extending the range of words employing an "ethno" stem.[20] It seems that the argument has by now shed any connection with Heraclitus and, perhaps for that reason, Plunkett crosses it out to conclude or abandon his essay.

"The Unimportance of Heraclitus" is not the only composition in which one finds the writer unable to keep to the point, and equally unable to relate with ease new themes to the first one. Instead, connections emerge between apparently disparate pieces of writing. Heraclitus dwelt on the centrality of fire to all reality; Plunkett's few lines of verse just quoted make repeated use of fire and flame, using family relationship (sister and brother) as some kind of metaphor. As far as we can tell after several thousand years, Heraclitus generally held the common people in contempt; Plunkett once exclaims, "Damn the populace" and offers a partial dating of this outburst. Though we are grateful for the marginal hint, we might also puzzle over the footnote about Celts, "only garrulous when intoxicated." In search of an Irish enthusiast for Bergson, note Shaw, who took up creative evolution / élan vital / life force in support of his plays, *Man and Superman* (first performed 1905) and *Back to Methuselah* (1922). Shaw is not mentioned; Plunkett disliked Shaw.

"The Stars Sang in God's Garden" and "I Saw the Sun at Midnight"

These poems appear in the second portion of Plunkett's posthumous collection immediately following the still remembered "I See His Blood Upon the Rose." The first of the pair keeps to a pattern of simply presented metaphors not unlike "I See His Blood." The second, in marked contrast, opens with that grand paradox of cosmology and time stated in the title. That metaphor is also at work here emerges plainly enough in line 9—"O Sun, O Christ, O bleeding Heart of flame!"—which serves powerfully to confirm the earlier analysis of imagery in the "Occulta" part of *Poems* (1916) as a dispersed representation of the Sacred Heart. Dispersal is not noted here as a fault but—for whatever reason—an emphatic, elusive feature. Plunkett, a poet of Christian mysticism, is confirmed in that thematic, if remaining suspect in the matter of sufficient diction, address to his contemporary readers, and spiritual maturity.

There is, however, an alternative, profane source from which the paradox of the sun at midnight may have been taken, *The House by the Borderland* (1908), a fantasy set in or below the landscape of north county Clare, by the English novelist William Hope Hodgson (1877–1918), killed in the dying days of the war. Plunkett's sonnet contrasts favorably with the length of the cosmic horror story, and neatly uses the two-part division of the classic sonnet, first to describe and then to address the all-encompassing imagery of transcendent light at midnight. And yet Hodgson is a learned horror-fantasist, drawing silently on Dante as J. M. Synge and Charles Louis Philippe also do.[21]

An emphatic detail of the poem is the use of an uppercase initial in every appearance of the word, "it," where It refers to the sun / Christ / "bleeding heart of flame." (This can be read as taking over a typographical convention whereby God becomes "He" not "he." Other distracting or discordant words include "dearth / Of rights" for the inadequacy of the sinner's calling on "Thy Name." A term (*rights*) drawn from constitutional or legal language must surely be itself inadequate: here it is does not strike my ear as an attempt at deliberate inadequacy. A related phrase, "Thou pawnest Heaven as a pledge," at least has the age-old use of "redemption" behind it. But most striking of all is the description of the Sun "heavy with the stain / Of blood-compassion." If my hunch that Plunkett had read Hodgson carries any weight, these poems can be reinterpreted as approaches to a theme not necessarily mystical or theological—the end of the world, atrophy, dissolution of matter. Grammarians might note that both poems open in the perfect tense—"the stars sang" and "I saw the Sun"—yet quickly move into the present tense, differentiating between a moment of profound even mystical insight (an epiphany?) and the later (that is, present) elaboration of the moment in sequential time. On the other hand, the shift in tense may signify a merger or slippage whereby past and present lose their distinctiveness, as in the world's end, apocalyptic or otherwise. In a sense, this coming together is an at-one-ment comparable to what is said to happen in the Roman Mass. Whether the poem qua poem lives up to this possible interpretation is another day's work.

Influences at Sea off Dublin: Kant and Bergson Refloated

The generally underdeveloped or, overparticularly concentrated, state of philosophy in Edwardian Ireland has been noted already in connection with study of the subject at the Dublin colleges. The small scale of Irish higher education, and the peculiar conditions under which intellectual reflection was conducted, tended to throw exaggerated colors over the history of ideas. These were too readily labeled foreign or native, especially in the era gradually dawning in the mid-Victorian years. With Cardinal Cullen (1803–1878), the triumph of ultramontanism led to a steady naturalization of Roman ideas as Irish tradition. Fenianism was condemned by the Vatican in 1870. Control of education became a central issue in church-state relations, and the milieu of Trinity College increasingly regarded as alien in the eyes of the Catholic hierarchy.

We have already noted the involvement of Kant's translator, J. C. Meredith, in the events leading up to Easter 1916. Somewhat earlier, we spotted Plunkett's reading of *Time and Free Will*, and the *Irish Review*'s wider three-part summary of Bergson's philosophy. Beyond these different contributors to the Dublin events of 1916—Meredith and Plunkett—it is difficult to attach philosophical labels to the major actors. Discretion played a discreet role. Connolly has been repeatedly hailed (or condemned) as a Marxist. Unquestionably, his prodigious writings provide an analysis of conditions under capitalism entirely consistent with Marxism. But that is not all they contain and, indeed, Marx's name is rarely invoked. Two points deserve attention.

First, there is a question of rhetoric and tactics. The Irish bishop-philosopher George Berkeley observed that, in certain situations, one needs "think with the learned and speak with the vulgar."[22] As with Marx and Hegel, a standing-on-the-head inversion is necessary: Connolly may have thought with Marx, but avoided naming him to a popular readership heavily policed by Christian (and, in his case, mainly Catholic) functionaries. Hence, for instance, the economy of truth, the acutely limited citation of *Das Kapital*.

Second, however, the national question. In 1869, Marx and Engels commended the Fenian campaign for Irish independence on the grounds that it would accelerate the breakup of the British Empire. There were more positive motives also: "The English working class will *never accomplish anything* before it has got rid of Ireland. The lever must be applied in Ireland. That is why the Irish question is so important for the social movement in general."[23] Note the disposability of Ireland in this future broad circumstance or that. A few years later, in 1874, Engels examined the Home Rule movement in terms of alternative strategies. "Violent insurrection had no prospect of success for many years, at least until such time as England would again be involved in serious difficulties abroad."[24] This latter observation became gospel for militant Irish separatists with the onset of the Great War, not necessarily through Engels's influence.

There were actual connections between Berkeley's nonphilosophical writings and Connolly's nationalist side. In the interrogative mode, *The Querist* (1735/37) opened up multiple defects in the workings of Ireland's economy and, by implication, proposed solutions. Editions and modifications proliferated, in the first instance in Scotland, also in Philadelphia (1839), but significantly reemerging through trenchant modern Irish nationalism. The firebrand John Mitchel produced an edition in 1849. In the twentieth century, Richard Best (1930), Bulmer Hobson (1933), J. M. Hone (1936), and Joseph Johnston (1970) played variations on the theme. Eamon de Valera was also an admirer.

In this continuity, the relationship with history is traditional rather than progressive, which, in turn, is further evidence of the ahistorical aspect of nationalism as a body of thought. Tactics may have persuaded figures as opposed as Connolly and Hobson to invoke Berkeley, with a view to reassuring non-Catholics in twentieth-century Ireland (especially those with roots real or imagined in eighteenth-century landownership) that they had a reserved place in the future. Yeats, assisted by Hone, was enchanted to comply; Meredith, with a similar family background in the Church of Ireland clergy, was perhaps the shrewder. Yeats conceded Meredith's capacity as a possible reviewer of a book about Berkeley, adding by way of qualification that the judge was, at that moment, hearing a case about a Battersea ice-cream vendor.[25] Tradition is not a matter of pure transmission, whether Neoplatonic or folk-based. It involves change, misrepresentation, alienation, betrayal, *traison*, though it is not reducible to any of these. Its operations are wisely scrutinized through the lens of irony. When Meredith invoked Kant in July 1914, he cited texts that stood at the latter end of an eighteenth-century European enquiry into republicanism as a theory of government. He, however, stood among activists for a very different kind of republicanism, which was based on nationalism and content (as events quickly proved) to collaborate with the universal Church to the detriment of civil rights provision, not to mention socialism. If one substituted Wolfe Tone for Kant, others associated with the Irish Volunteers (notably Pearse) performed a rhetorical version of the philosophical crux upon which Meredith squirmed. They advanced a tradition of Irish separatism "in the name of the dead generations" as if it were an intellectual or cultural lineage, whereas their campaign was nearer to being a colonization of the past through the cult of blood sacrifice sublimely exemplified by Jesus on the cross. Plunkett mocked Wells on Heraclitus, but studied his *Little Wars*. When the guns began their work in August 1915, Wells published *The War that Will End War*, as ironic a reworking of Kant's search for perpetual peace as any imaginable.

Seen in this context, and with that of Abbott and Bernard still visible in the receding past, Meredith's Kantianism must appear anachronistic especially in so young a man. However, other and wider perspectives are available in which Kant appears renewed and reinterpreted for the twentieth century. The German school of neo-Kantianism of Hermann Cohen (1848–1918) was preeminent during the reign of Wilhelm II. However, Meredith's preface to his edition of *The Critique of Aesthetic Judgment* (1911) suggests that the Dublin school was playing catchup. His commentary provides a valuable guide to the line of transmission. Having discussed authoritative German editions of Kant's collected works, he admitted to a rapid substitution of that published from 1902 onwards by the Könlich Preussische Akademie der Wissenschaften for Gustav Hartenstein's much earlier one. Given that the text he was translating did not appear until 1908 (in volume 5 of the Academy edition), Meredith had very little time to adjust. Its existence he "only became aware of shortly before sending the work to press."[26] He then proceeded to record that "through this edition I also learned of the existence of Dr. Schlapp's valuable work, and was further induced to procure a copy of the extremely suggestive work of Hermann Cohen, whom previously I had only known by name." Cohen by this time was over sixty. In such tortuous details one establishes the relatively sluggish intellectual environment from which Meredith hoped to emerge. The College Library does not appear to have acquired anything by Cohen during his lifetime, and Otto Schlapp does not feature on its radar at all, though he had studied Kant's familiarity with English literature, especially John Milton's poetry, matter surely of interest to a translator of Kantian aesthetics. Whereas Mahaffy's Princeton essay had celebrated the growth of a school of Kantians within the Victorian college, evidence from the library catalogs tells a different tale. Scholars in those days could afford to stock their own bookshelves to a degree unthinkable for many years now, and did not always serve up the best tidbits to their undergraduate audiences. Yet it seems that Abbott, Bernard, and Mahaffy between them were unable to guide the translator to the most authoritative (and recent) edition of his chosen text.

That Cohen's best-known work, *Kant's Philosophy of Experience*, appeared as early as 1871 would seem to underscore a diagnosis of Dublin's laggard interest in contemporary thought. However, German philosophy was not the only area of research in the TCD department and, alongside or above Kant, Hegel occupied a prominent position; English and Scottish philosophy was taught also, not to mention the classics. Elsewhere in the college, John Kells Ingram held office as professor of this and that in succession, and as librarian; in addition to his official duties, he was a major disseminator of positivist philosophy to the Anglophone world. *Passages from the Letters of Auguste Comte*, translated by Ingram, appeared in 1901: Comte had died in 1857. Mahaffy, who became provost just in time (1914) to ban Pearse speaking on college premises, pioneered what would now be described as the sociology of ancient Greece.

The academic-intellectual milieu of Dublin was both advanced and marginal; in addition, influential movements of thought stimulated people outside the universities. The Gaelic League (founded 1893) proclaimed itself nativist in accordance with German Romantic notions of language from the eighteenth century onward. Irish feminism, though sharing much with the British movement, had more success in generating alliances with other progressive groups, Cumann na mBan (League of Women), for example, founded in 1914 as an auxiliary to the Irish Volunteers. Experimental theater flourished under the leadership of powerful minds such as Augusta Gregory, Edward Martyn, and, of course, W. B. Yeats. The Plunkett family contributed to this renaissance with the Theater of Ireland, performing in premises shared with the Irish Volunteers.

Much of this is taken for granted in independent Ireland, a foundational history open to all except those who might revise it. Douglas Hyde's scholarly *Literary History of Ireland* (1899), devoted to Gaelic material, makes extensive use of German research academic and other, but nowhere mentions the philosopher Johann Gottfried von Herder (1744–1803), without whose work on language and anthropology modern Celtic scholarship would be unthinkable. Antiquity, and the archaic world before it, were accessible through philological procedures, though these in themselves remained above scrutiny. Hyde quoted Heraclitus via Lucian of Samos, to the effect that "men were 'mortal gods,' gods were 'immortal men.'" This served his purpose of clarifying the status of heroes: "certainly Cuchulain and Conor and probably . . . other famous Red Branch chiefs, *whatever they may have been in reality*, are the equivalent of the Homeric heroes."[27] The original Greek, which Hyde very properly supplied, was a good deal more laconic and paradoxical: in Patrick's translation quoted earlier, "Immortals are mortal, mortals immortal, living in their death and dying in their life."[28] Plunkett's reading of Heraclitus may not have delved very deeply, but the play that he set in Pharaonic Egypt played with these notions inside a politico-conspiratorial plot. A more capacious and determined thinker, Yeats wrote in his final year, "To me all things are made of the conflict of two states of consciousness, beings or persons which die each other's life, live each other's death."[29]

Yeats's Cuchulain preceded Hyde's *Literary History* by several years, and endured into the poet's final years. The theme of heroism, including tragic heroism, finds its most concentrated expression in plays and poems of 1938–1939. It is linked, though not by adamantine chains, to the theme of sacrifice, including (human) blood sacrifice not always of the self. From his remarks on the Great War in 1915, and more diffusely from his attitude to the Irish Volunteers, we can with some confidence deduce that Meredith did not share this perspective on life and death. The neo-Kantianism that he discovered in Cohen's last decade can only have confirmed his position. The

Stanford Encyclopedia provides a succinct account of Cohen's life and work, opening with the statement that his "ethics and political theory provided the foundation for a non-Marxist, Kantian democratic socialism that informed his more popular and topical writings. He argued publicly for universal suffrage and for the rights of workers to organize democratically-constituted collectives."[30] This alone earned Cohen a hostile reception by a significant contributor to Kant's revaluation.

Lucien Goldmann, in his Genevan doctoral dissertation of 1945, treated all varieties of neo-Kantianism with scant respect. In neutral Switzerland, the Romanian-born Marxist may have seen the Red Army's westward victorious advance as a likely harbinger of even better things to come. If so, he quickly adapted his Marxism on arrival in France. Yet, even in 1945, he had identified one factor in the neo-Kantian debate relevant to the Dublin "school"—the interest in aesthetics. In his view, the new concern in Germany was limited to the aesthetic only as treated in *The Critique of Pure Reason*.[31] This, he argued, was intrinsic to the neglect of perhaps Kant's most famous conception, the unreachable thing-in-itself. Quoting from an 1877 book by Cohen, he proposed that the youthful neo-Kantian quite simply thought that "the law is the thing in itself."[32] In relation to Kant himself, Goldmann had two major affirmative emphases: (1) "that Kant in aesthetics takes the decisive step which Feuerbach and Marx were much later to take in ethics and epistemology: the humanisation of the transcendent," and (2) that Kant's philosophy is a dynamic system which assumes and works towards a future.[33] In ways unimaginable to their Reverends T. K. Abbot and J. H. Bernard, Kant potentially informed a progressive politics for Meredith and his colleagues in 1915–1916. Since Goldmann, Kōjin Karantani offers a sensitive treatment of Kant and Marx, while R. J. Bernstein takes up a neglected Kantian notion in an attempt to cast a glimmer of philosophical light on Auschwitz.[34]

Mitchell Cohen, in his 1994 study, argues that Goldmann was not so far from the neo-Kantians he had, as a doctorand, lambasted. He nonetheless retained the central place given in Goldmann's investigation of culture, class, and politics to "tragic vision" or "tragic worldview." The concern with tragedy had been introduced into the 1948 French version of his Kant dissertation, in advance of *The Hidden God* (*Le Dieu caché*) his magisterial examination of Pascal's contribution to dialectics completed by 1955.[35] It remains a challenge, perhaps a will-o'-the-wisp, for an intrepid thinker on Irish brains and blood to devise or discern a homology relating literary form and social individualism of the kind postulated in Goldmann's *Towards a Sociology of the Novel* (*Pour un sociologie du roman*, 1964), which might consider if "tragic vision" possesses any meaning in the circumstances of 1916.

The Dublin novel of 1916 surely is *A Portrait of the Artist as a Young Man*, published in December of that year by a philosopher superior to any of his contemporary countrymen so far named. Difficult to name a work of fiction more remote from the tragic vision except, for the year in question, George Moore's *The Brook Kerith* (August 1916), an equally nontragic tale of Jesus's survival of crucifixion. Joyce, like MacDonagh, J. M. O'Sullivan, Pearse, and Geraldine Plunkett, emerged from the Royal University of Ireland; indeed a photograph survives capturing Joyce and O'Sullivan side by side. The latter took his Kantian interests into print several years before Meredith's translation of the *Aesthetic*. Supervised by Wilhelm Windelband (1848–1915), O'Sullivan's dissertation appeared as a monograph in the Kant-Studien series (1908) as *Vergleich der Methoden Kants und Hegels auf Grund ihrer Behandlung der Kategorie der Quantität*. On his return to Ireland, the author prepared an English translation, augmented by three new essays, to appear collectively as *Old Criticism and New Pragmatism* (1909). Like Abbott and Bernard, he relied on Longmans for distribution in England, though his primary publisher was the eminently Catholic house of M. H. Gill in Dublin. The author was clearly in pursuit of an academic post at home.

Old Criticism and New Pragmatism amounts to more than three hundred pages, with the Heidelberg dissertation occupying more than two-thirds of them. (The term "criticism" here stands for the critical philosophy, or critique, introduced by Kant.) It was dedicated to William Magennis, who taught philosophy in a Catholic teacher-training college, and later became the backbone of censorship in the Irish Free State. The book received appreciative reviews in *The Journal of Philosophy*, *Mind*, *The Monist*, and *The Philosophical Review*, largely on the strength of the long first essay. The second essay in *Old Criticism and New Pragmatism* (207–48) also focuses on Kant, his treatment of causality, which O'Sullivan finds unsatisfactory. The two remaining essays virtually abandon Kant to investigate contemporary pragmatism. Though they are slight compared to the work on Kant, through them O'Sullivan discloses his reading in contemporary philosophy—principally John Dewey's *Studies in Logical Theory* (1903), William James's *Pragmatism: A New*

Name for Some Old Ways of Thinking (1907), Henri Poincaré, *La Science et L'hypothèse* (1902) and F. C. S. Schiller's *Studies in Idealism* (1907). In *The Philosophical Review*, G. W. Cunningham concluded his notice of *Old Criticism and New Pragmatism* by declaring that what was needed there and then in 1910 was "an unsparing pruning of philosophical doctrines in the light of the lessons taught by the development of philosophical criticism."[36] If this looks forward to some aspects of Wittgenstein's early work, it more starkly contrasts with H. G. Wells's comments on the rediscovery (as he thought it) of Heraclitus.

O'Sullivan's book appeared too soon for review in the Jesuit journal *Studies*, founded in 1912. It did come to the attention of one Irish reviewer, R. A. P. Rogers (1874–1923), writing in *Mind*. What is noteworthy in the present context is that Rogers was a fellow of TCD and a mathematics tutor. Such enduring ecumenism between the Irish universities would soon diminish to famine levels under native rule. The younger Irish Kantians, Meredith and O'Sullivan, occupied different, but equally exposed, positions and, while the former completed his translation of *The Critique of Judgment* in 1928, neither man adopted an engaged or active relationship to Kantian or neo-Kantian thought. O'Sullivan lost the chair of philosophy at University College to a Jesuit rival candidate—Kant's *Critique of Pure Reason* had been prohibited for Catholic readers by the papal Index Librorum, and pragmatism was dangerously relativistic. O'Sullivan got modern history instead. In 1926, he became minister for education in the southern government. Meredith had become a judge.

The Index Librorum exacerbated relations between thoughtful and philosophically inclined persons in Ireland. Bergson, whom the *Irish Review* of 1911 publicized in three articles, was placed on the list in 1914. Berkeley, then enjoying a revival of interest in Britain, Germany, and Italy, had been prohibited many years earlier. Thus, when A. A. Luce abandoned Bergson in favor of Berkeley as the subject of lectures in TCD, he remained equally cut off from students in UCD, where Jesuit control of philosophy was consolidating. In Dublin the Contemporary Club (founded 1885) provided its members and occasional visitors with a forum for intelligent discussion, but the numbers were small and public indifference increasingly effective. Little intercourse between the colleges was possible until the late 1960s. With reference to the events of Easter 1916, one has to report that exceedingly few (if any) graduates of TCD participated on the rebel side, though some (R. M. Gwynn, John Joly, C. H. Oldham, and of course Meredith) were well disposed to the Irish Volunteers in 1913. Whereas the future count had been able to take a TCD degree in the 1870s, the prospect was wholly discounted in the next generation of Plunketts. If dialogue between opposing points of view is essential for the health of philosophy, then the Irish situation was near-chronic. Polarization, far from being a dynamic, led to stagnation.

The condition of Dublin, famously characterized by Joyce as the center of paralysis, was more agitated by labor demands and police repression than Joyce (who had left in 1904) ever admitted. The lockout of 1913 prefigured in some respects the Rising of 1916; indeed the ICA, which participated in the events of Easter 1916, was formed in the aftermath of the Lockout. Behind the cracked heads and the batons, philosophical ideas and activities were at work. A reviewer in *The Irish Monthly*, a Jesuit periodical aimed at middle-brows, noted "several interesting pages on the connexion between the Syndicalism of [Georges] Sorel and the Evolutionism of Bergson." Three months later, *The Hibbert Journal* carried an article on same topic by the liberal Congregationalist Thomas Rhondda Williams.[37] Through the politico-industrial movement of syndicalism, Bergson's name and his prioritizing of intuition over reason acquired a degree of popular recognition. Others associated with syndicalism advocated spontaneous revolt, sacrificial politics, and a cult of the dead, all French grist to the neo-Fenian mill.[38]

It is as well to review the state of Irish public opinion at this time. Politics affected virtually every household. In the northeast, a vigorous attachment to the Union with Great Britain grew increasingly vocal in opposition to the prospect of Home Rule: this opposition was to all intents and purposes grounded in the Protestant churches and congregations and, of course, in the Orange lodges. Among Irish Catholics, degrees of conscious nationalism prevailed, with significant non-Catholic individuals (Yeats, the most renowned) joining in. But neither "party" articulated a unanimous, unchanging doctrine. Unionism, for obvious reasons, could refer to no earlier date than 1801 in vindication of its primary conviction. Nationalism, by its nature, invoked lineage and tradition in elaborate historical constructions. Its ordinary adherents invoked heroes and villains, events and failures—Cromwell, Sarsfield, Penal Law, Daniel O'Connell, the Famine, the United Irishmen in 1798. Its leadership in the early twentieth century, however, was open to new theoretical perspectives, suitably dressed, of which France was to be the principal source.

Herein lies the paradox of Irish opinion in the period. Unionism spoke with pride of the empire, the dominions, and the colonies, but learned little from them. Nationalism, by contrast, absorbed practices and ideas not only from France, but also from the United States and even Britain. As Irish Unionism gradually concentrated its attention in Ulster, its relations with Great Britain changed. Historical and geographic links with Scotland became more clearly delineated. Yet one might formulate a quasi-proposition, based on the Unionist relationship with the empire (including Scotland): affinity inhibits influence, where influence is measured as an inward movement (that is, toward Ulster from—say—Australia). The test case would involve Canada, and for two reasons. First, Protestant emigration from Ulster to Canada was substantial, permanent, and articulate; second, Canada experienced problems of religious and linguistic diversity not wholly different from those confronting Irish Unionists. This observer is not aware that Edward Carson or James Craig studied the Quebec situation in an attempt to understand the need to parlay with minority as such.

The attempt to formulate a similar proposition about nationalism involves a greater number of moving parts. Irish nationalists supported the Boers in resistance to imperial policy. A significant body of Irishmen went to South Africa to fight as an Irish Brigade. One of these (John McBride) later took part in the Easter Rising, and was executed afterward. Arthur Griffith, founder of the Sinn Féin movement, had worked for years in the Transvaal as a journalist. A third figure, Colonel Maurice Moore, had participated on the British side of the conflict and was so appalled by Kitchener's brutality towards noncombatants that he later helped to organize the Irish Volunteers.

Nonaffinities between Ireland and South Africa hardly need to be tabulated, in terms of distance from Europe, climate, mineral wealth, and ethnic diversity. Nationalism tended to emphasize a common anti-imperialist endeavor above these factors, paying little attention to the fate of nonwhites at the hands of Boer and British alike. Griffith chose an even less obvious analogy in *The Resurrection of Hungary: A Parallel for Ireland* (1904), which recommended dual-monarchy as a model for self-sufficiency. This did not go unnoticed by dissidents from his view. In *Stephen Hero*, the gimlet-eyed heresiarch saw through this selective myopia, casting himself as any young skeptic "who was aware of the capable aggressions of the Magyars upon the Latin and Slav and Teutonic populations, greater than themselves in number."[39]

Griffith's developing policy essentially extended the practice of boycotting to national economic and national cultural levels as an effective alternative to armed resistance. He was also a stern critic of parliamentarianism. These are salient policy points, but the foregrounding of an Irish *resurrection* in the pamphlet's title uncannily anticipated the religious idiom that would pervade the supportive rhetoric and later vindication of 1916. Griffith, one might add, was as indifferent to the imperialistic sway of Hungarians over Slovaks and other populations as he was to the Boers' treatment of Zulus.

We might look at just one further pamphlet, less for its contents than for specific rhetorical devices employed in the title. The author, Bulmer Hobson, had already come to our attention as a senior member of the IRB whose policy for the achievement of independence stood in the way of Clarke, Pearse, and Plunkett as Easter approached in 1916. A Belfast man by birth, and a Quaker by upbringing, he published *Defensive Warfare: A Handbook for Irish Nationalists* in 1909, anonymously and under a Sinn Féin imprint. Despite the first two words of the title, the policy advocated is not armed conflict. "Failing in military insurrection to assert her independence[,] Ireland at the word of her politicians has assumed that all doors were closed to her save submission and beggary."[40] What is recommended instead is not constitutional agitation but a thorough and sustained campaign of economic, social, and cultural passive resistance. "It is the negative side of war, and its aim is, that where it cannot overthrow a foreign power by force of arms it will render government by that power impossible."[41] Much detail follows. The purpose of these quotations is to provide material for the examination of metaphor in Hobson's argument. Two further are necessary—a passing reference to "incoherent warring factions" in debate and the declaration "Defensive Warfare is in reality war."[42]

Is it possible on this initial characterization of central nationalist positions to formulate a proposition similar to that offered in connection with Unionism? To begin, one should emphasize that these heuristic devices have no universalist application; the (revised) proposition that affinity inhibits influence where influence is measured as an externally originating movement has its exceptions or instances of nonvalidity. The most obvious, in relation to Irish Unionism, would concede that an affinity between that constituency and the values or interests of the military elite did result in at least one visible inward supportive movement—the Curragh Mutiny of March 1914. Here, however, "inward" is compromised as a term because the army was that of the United Kingdom (though called the British Army) operating inside the United Kingdom). Consequently, Unionism presented itself as "natural," pertaining to all, unaffected inwardly or outwardly.

Similarly what one may venture as a proposition about Irish nationalism—and perhaps about nationalism more widely—makes no claim to be comprehensive. Nonaffinity allows for influence mobilized by the group to be influenced may serve for the moment. Philosophical glosses on this elementary proposal could be sought through one further weary return to Hegel's discussion of consciousness in *The Phenomenology of the Spirit* (1807). The principal, perhaps only, merit in looking back to the metaphor of lordship and bondage is to be reminded that, for Hegel, the uneven partners in labor (the lord and the bondsman) were the mere vehicle by which the tenor (consciousness) is described: Marx in due course inverted the metaphor's components. In the present context, however, a little more can be gained. J. N. Finlay's summary of the relevant passage reads:

> Self-consciousness exists in and for itself inasmuch, and only inasmuch, as it exists in and for itself for another; inasmuch as it is *acknowledged*. It is therefore essentially one only in duplication, and reveals itself in a number of traits which have to be kept firmly apart, and yet reveal themselves as always melting into one another, and dissolving this apartness.[43]

If, impertinently, we were to borrow again from Hegel and characterize the position of Unionism as happy unconsciousness and nationalism as "unhappy self-consciousness," there would follow an obligation to pursue the dialectic. A more urgent point would insist that the to-be-influenced term in J. N. Finlay's proposition is not an indicator of chronological order, but of dependence, or need, or—we shall argue at greater length—*desire*.

The Anxiety of Succession

Though the interconnection between Catholicism and Irish nationalism is generally accepted, sometimes stressed, and rarely denied, there has been little attempt at any conceptual analysis of the relationship. The same claim could be made about Poland or Croatia, where recitations of history are said to make the point blindingly obvious. Blinding is right. In the Irish case, the largely Protestant origins of what is called colonial nationalism, and the mixed legacy of that movement in the figures of Thomas Davis, John Mitchel, and C. S. Parnell temper the assumption. These historic debts are recited later in the era of the Free State, Eire, and the Republic even though the most notable Protestants in Irish public life were essentially decorative—the aging Douglas Hyde as Gaelic icon, and Erskine Childers the younger as political token. The moral and cultural preponderance of Catholicism within independent Ireland came from alliances established in the immediate aftermath of Easter 1916. W. F. Monypenny's 1913 essay *The Two Irish Nations* had been vindicated within three years when—at the symbolic level—the Plunketts *père et fils* laid the emergent polity at the feet of a deceived pontiff. *The Catholic Bulletin*'s rebaptism of the neo-Fenians, from the summer of 1916 onward, completed the task.

In 2006, Jonathan Githens-Mazer published the ill-named *Myths and Memories of the Easter Rising*, originally a dissertation written for the London School of Economics. Based on "ethnico-symbolism" in its approach to nation, state, and church, the book provides a number of innovative perspectives on familiar topics. The most previous to the insurrection is the allusion, bare of commentary, to the disestablishment of the Catholic Church.[44] When did this event take place, if it did? Nothing comparable to Gladstone's Irish Church Act of 1870 can be traced in the reformation period to which such an event would seem to belong. The issue, though anachronistically phrased, has its worth. When Henry VIII of England was declared "supreme head in earth of the whole church of Ireland" in May 1536, little of any theological significance changed, though the break with Rome was seismic. Many Irish bishops continued in their sees. Henry, following continental developments, introduced the concept of divine right of kings into his realms, by which the king was subject to no authority except God. Only in 1541 was Henry declared king of Ireland, as distinct from the inherited mediaeval title, lord of Ireland. When a Protestant theological reformation got going, these fundamental changes to the king's position had already taken place. As a matter of contemporary developments in England, one should note that, a few months after Henry assumed headship of the church in Ireland, the northern "up-rising" or "rising-out" known as the Pilgrimage of Grace broke out in the north country.

Henry died in 1547 with his kingdoms facing into a decade of rapid change and uncertainly. Elizabeth succeeded in 1558. A Catholic lawyer, Sir Edmund Plowden (1518–1585), brought to the attention of Tudor England, in settlement of matters relating to the duchy of Lancaster, what became known as "the king's two bodies" account of succession and (ultimately) sovereignty. While it might be treated as a proto-secular restatement of apostolic succession (the uninterrupted transmission of spiritual authority from the Apostles through successive popes and—then—metropolitans and bishops, taught by the Roman Catholic, Orthodox, and Anglican churches), this was essentially a medieval fiction, applied to the Lancastrian triumph in the Wars of the Roses. We are far from myths and memories of the Easter insurrection. Nevertheless, the claim to sovereignty made in the Proclamation of the Irish Republic by its seven signatories is a wayward collateral descendant from Plowden's *Reports* (1571) just as, in other respects, their rhetoric is indebted to Jean-Jacques Rousseau's *Social Contract* (1762). Pearse, as the solitary lawyer among the seven, may have been on nodding terms with both authorities, but the 1916 Proclamation's collective authorship worked under (self-imposed) pressures of time, without pausing for reflection or over precedent.

The locus of powerful ideas lies in their reception, sometimes obscuring or obliquely altering their origination. Today we appreciate the medieval king's two bodies, because of a dense volume by an exiled Germano-Polish scholar, Ernst Kantorowicz (1895–1963), published in 1957. *The King's Two Bodies: A Study in Mediaeval Political Theology* is remembered half a century later in the Anglophone world partly for the light it casts on Shakespeare's drama, especially *Richard II*, which Kantorowicz discusses at length but, by extension, on the English history plays generally, and also on *Hamlet* and *Lear*. As the prince of Denmark cunningly knew, it was not a case of "the play's the thing" but, more exactly, its reception, the responses of an implicated audience. Kantorowicz may have been very marginally implicated in the celebratory drama of his book's enthusiastic reception. While its meticulous historicism was acclaimed by many reviewers, one or two readers with longer memories linked its subtitle to the *Politische Theologie* (1922) of Carl Schmitt, Hitler's erstwhile favorite jurist. Kantorowicz, of course was a Jew who had to flee Germany in 1938. True to cussed form, he refused to sign a McCarthyite affirmation required by the University of California.

The central fiction underpinning the political doctrine, which he extricates from its medieval proto-versions, states that the king possesses a body natural and a body politic, and by these is maintained both the independence of his "being a king" from his "being a mortal," and an interrelationship between these. The distinction transcends natural death and so allows for uninterrupted succession in "being a king"; it is, however undesignedly, a universal metaphysical distinction even if Kantorowicz's argument glances aside on occasion to mention not only James Ussher (1581–1656), archbishop of Armagh, but also so minor a figure as William of Drogheda (died 1245). In his fifth chapter he advances to add a *corpus mysticum*, related to the church and then to the *res publica* (or commonweal). "It first came into existence in Carolingian times and gained some importance in the course of the controversy about the Eucharist . . . the Church was compelled to stress most emphatically, not a spiritual or mystical, but the *real* presence of both the human and the divine Christ in the Eucharist."[45] And so, there follows in late medieval western Christendom an exchange-and-intensification of roles of the kind that Weber detected at the root of capitalism's appropriation of Calvinist doctrines for its transformation of the world. While "the Pauline term originally designating the Christian Church now began to designate the consecrated host[, and] the notion *corpus mysticum*, hitherto used to describe the host, was gradually transferred—after 1150—to the Church as the organized body of Christian society united in the Sacrament at the Altar," this was not a mere swap of descriptors. "It was the beginning of the so-called secularization of the medieval Church . . . balanced by an all the more designedly 'mystical' interpretation even of the administrative body and technical apparatus of the hierarchy . . . to hallow the secular polities . . . This does not imply causation."[46]

Kantorowicz's formidable argument, however firmly rooted in late medieval specifics, bears upon the background cloth of God and gold against which the leading insurrectionists fought for an Irish republic, and does so in threefold.

First, it indicates precedents both within western Christendom and within the western system of kings and kingdoms for displacement-accrual between the sacred and the profane domains. These precedents to Easter 1916 might be thought remote in time, but for the interest in pre-Reformation life in part stimulated by the Catholic Revival in Victorian England, and in part also indulged by Chesterton and Belloc, whom Plunkett revered. Yeats's longing for "unity of being" is a refined version of a medievalism he first learned from William Morris.

Second, it recognizes the consecrated host (*corpus verum*), not simply as the central emblem within the bi-valve medieval system, but as an active component in the sense that the capacity to display it conferred power and authority in *unum*. This too might be dismissed as remote, were it not for developments in religious art through the baroque and rococo styles, allowing for the seventeenth-century cult of the Sacred Heart initiated by Sister (now Saint) M. M. Alacoque, renewed in the nineteenth century by a Portuguese nun, and astutely observed for Ireland by James Joyce. The Society of the Sacred Heart was founded against a revolutionary background in Paris in 1800; its school system, reaching Ireland in 1842, is extensive. Private devotion to the Sacred Heart was (and remains) highly popular in Catholic Ireland.

Third, it provides an exemplary account of undying legitimacy and—more important—sovereignty, king to successor king (or queen, as also happened in the Tudor dynasty, complicating theological change with gender difference). Further prolonged upheavals in Western culture and society, most obviously the Enlightenment and the French Revolution, call for persistence as well as care in seeking continuity. The example does not obviously fit the IRB profile of inspirational precursors, but the IRB has never conceded that (native movements apart) it had found external inspiration, American, French, or anything else. Kantorowicz's king's-two-bodies theory cannot be a model in the present context, and yet may be instructive.

Having noted these cardinal points, we need to expand on the third. The R in IRB had originally been Revolutionary, with Republican slipping in to indicate limited radicalism. Nevertheless, a lineage joining Sir Edmund Plowden to Tom Clarke or G. N. Plunkett would stretch credulity to its limits, at first view. The establishment of modern democracy, first in the American colonies, then in France, was followed with the greatest interest in Ireland. Daniel O'Connell was recognized as building a pioneering mass organization to achieve parliamentary reform, the admission of Catholics to Parliament in 1829. The renewal of French democracy in 1848 lasted only three years, when the dictatorship of Louis Bonaparte followed, leading into the Second Empire. For Irish politics, the significance of this period was the development in France of conspiratorial politics.

In December 1848, the socialist Louis Blanqui (1805–1881) was in prison but, at a celebratory gathering, his toast was raised, "*To the Mountain of 1793! To the Pure Socialists, its true heirs!*" In this instance, the business of transmitted political identity related to the revolutionary party (La Montagne, les Montagnards) of half a century earlier. Despite the stoutly proletarian attendance, the speech includes numerous references to Jesus, to "the daughters of the gospels," to draining the chalice, and so on.[47] Blanqui believed in revolutionary organization through secret cells, much as the Fenians would a decade or so later. After Blanqui's death, his movement split into an adventurist wing led by General Georges Boulanger and a form of syndicalism committed to spontaneous action.

In 1873 the Fenian (IRB) constitution was amended following comprehensive military failure. The Brotherhood was to be governed by an eleven-man Supreme Council (internally and only partly elected): all members would swear allegiance to it as the government of the Irish Republic. The existence of this republic, and indeed the government alluded to, depended on a republican version of the king's two bodies. That is, while the membership of the Council would alter decade by decade (largely by natural death) to a point where none of the original members survived, the Council itself was unchanged with respect to oaths of loyalty to it. None of this would have been difficult for a corporation or limited liability company, whose board of directors altered frequently. But for a secret society, essentially a nonlegal entity, the business of a transmissible identity was more complicated for the relatively small numbers involved. From the declaration that the Council constituted the government of a declared republican state, the issue is raised from the fuzzy notion of identity to the internationally recognized concept of sovereignty. While the IRB was committed to a republican future, and eloquently denounced monarchy, its fundamental commitment was to the nation. The relationship between nation and republic, and between the nation and the population, posed other (largely neglected) problems.

Of course, the 1916 insurrection (though approved by the Supreme Council) was in practice organized by a Military Council so secret that even the Supreme Council did not know all of its decisions and doings, the most fundamental of which was the drafting of a Proclamation in which sovereignty was several times proclaimed. Denis McCullough, Supreme Council president, remained in ignorance of much that was decided in his name. The impossibility of a kings-two-bodies legitimation emerges coincident with its necessity. The Military Council, initially made up of Ceannt, Pearse, and Plunkett, had been rapidly expanded during 1915 to include Clarke, McDermott, and—even later—MacDonagh and Connolly. In the last two cases, induction into the IRB almost coincided with appointment to the Military Council. MacDonagh was acquired for his ability to liaise with Eoin MacNeill, Connolly out of a need to control the ICA. All these persons were based in Dublin, Connolly less continuously so than the others. The proclaimers of the Republic, who also constituted the provisional government and the Military Council, existed at some considerable distance from the Supreme Council (selected on a regional basis, including Scottish and English regions) to which alone all oaths of allegiance were made. The Blanquist system of revolutionary cells had eventually led to a semidetached organism capable of, but not answerable for, a coup d'état with a difference. The objective of 1916 was not to take over the state, as Napoleon had done in 1799, and as General Boulanger contemplated in 1889, but to break all dependency with and within the state of the United Kingdom and to establish a separate entity, an independent Irish republic. The Proclamation declared this most radical of innovations on the basis of Ireland's "old tradition of nationhood." Philologists might point out the congruence here of *tradition* and *trahison* and thereby underline the anxiety of succession. Historians nostalgic for a metaphysical dimension of the king's two bodies might recall the discussions among the Dublin republicans as to which German princeling might agree to head up the new Irish (republican) state—a Catholic, some would hope, unlike the gallant but plainly Protestant kaiser—in the event of victory.

Plunkett was party to the Proclamation's drafting, though he was inactive due to rapidly declining health for most of Holy Week. Much of his energy was given to overseeing from Mrs. Quinn's north-city nursing home the forgery of a *texte provocateur* in the Larkfield armed camp. Little in his surviving papers indicates interest in the history or origins of Fenianism, apart from a poem entitled "1867," awkwardly memorable for "jaws of the gallows" and its relentless repeated addresses to "ye" in a high-school hieratic style.

His poetry may disclose greater concern with a central image of occult Christianity, in part already explored by Yeats through the *rosa alchemica*, for example in poems gathered as *The Rose* (1893), and in prose *The Secret Rose* (1897). The greater part of Plunkett's verse posthumously edited by his sister Geraldine was entitled "Occulta," twenty-seven poems written (it seems) between November 1911 and July 1915. A simple analysis of these establishes that the word *heart* occurs in fifteen poems; in most of these it occurs more than once. The heart is so well-established a lyric trope that its prominence is hardly remarkable in a young writer. Deserving more attention is the cross-currence (to coin a term) of heart/blood/flame, with *dove* added as a personal cryptic for its Latin name, Columba (O'Carroll). As shown in the figure "Dispersed Image of the Sacred Heart in Plunkett's 'Occulta,'" certain cognate words (e.g., *fire* for *flame*) are absorbed; references are to page numbers in *The Poems of Joseph Mary Plunkett.*

What can be deduced from these figures? A start should be made with columns 4 and 5. References to the dove may be read at a low level of significance as allusions to Columba O'Carroll, with whom Plunkett had been obsessed for years to no avail. The Latin origin of her name relates back not only to the early Irish saint Columba, but also to biblical doves, symbols of purity and particularly associated with women. When Jesus was baptized by John, the Holy Spirit descended in the form of a dove (Matthew 3:16).

Superficially, this looks uncomplicated. The most ungarnished reference to Columba O'Carroll, however, is cloaked in pseudo-translation. In "Nomina Sunt Consequentia Rerum" (the title comes from Section XIII of Dante's *Vita Nuova*) he wrote "Nuala and Columba did I see / Coming towards the place where I was lingering." The Latin title embodies a philosophical maxim of the thirteenth century, deriving from the *Institutes* of the Byzantine emperor Justinian (A.D. 483–565), meaning roughly that names follow (take after, reflect) the things that are named. Elsewhere, Plunkett worked on translation of *Vita Nuova* Section XXIV, including the line "Vanna and Beatrice did I see / Coming towards where I was lingering," a scene illustrated by the British artist Henry Holiday in a painting of 1884.[48] These excursions at least indicate that Plunkett had thought deeply and read Dante, if not Justinian. In the 1890s J. M. Synge struggled to adapt the *Vita Nuova* to his own needs, literary and personal.[49]

Column 5 indicates the most explicit involvement of the Holy Spirit

Dispersed Image of the Sacred Heart in Plunkett's "Occulta"

(1) *Blood*	(2) *Fire/Flame*	(3) *Heart*	(4) *Dove*	(5) Other
2		2		Paraclete Pinions
	3			
4, 4	4			
6				Pinions
11				
	12	12		
				13 pucelle
				14 Maid
		17	17	
		18		
	19			
20	20	20		
	22			
		23, 23, 23		
			25	
		26		
		27	27	
	28	28, 28, 28		28 wings of God
		29, 29, 29		
		31, 31		
				32 grace
		33, 33		
	34	34		
35, 35		35, 35, 35		
36				
			37	37, 37, 37 grace
	38	38, 38		
		39, 39, 39		
40	40	40	40	
			41 bird of peace	41 pinions
42, 42	42, 42			

(the Paraclete) in Plunkett's concerns. Through its traditional representation in bird form, *pinions* (portion of feather) and *wing* occur infrequently and perhaps inconsistently. Allusions to Joan of Arc (c. 1412–1431) are explicit in "La Pucelle" (11–12), not only in its title but also in the phrase "the banner of the Maid." The banner motif recurs in "Heaven and Hell" (the poem that most clearly discloses anxious religious uncertainty) with phrases such as "You are the Standard of high Heaven, / The Banner brave." As Joan was inspired by her voices, so Columba should be inspired by Plunkett's songs, all this under the aegis of the Holy Spirit. But Columba, the songs concede, is not inspired thus. Insofar as the "Occulta" poems constitute a suite assembled by the poet himself, the *amour courtois* directed toward the ideal Dove/Columba is vitiated by four occurrences of the word *grace*. While grace is a central term in Christian theology, and is compatible with the thematics under consideration, it features in Plunkett's life as the Christian name of the woman he married the evening before his execution, Grace Gifford. Even more fully than Columba, the word/name exemplifies the maxim, *Nomina sunt consequentia rerum* in Plunkett's effusive use of it.

By apparent contrast, columns 1–3 list the occurrence of words all too frequently found in apprentice poetry. Blood, fire, and heart are the staple diet of romantics in every sense of the term. In the case of *heart*, it can be observed without animus that Plunkett overindulges (thirty-seven instances). However, the cross-currence of heart/blood/fire provides a larger lexical context. Encouraged by some evidence of thematic coherence in columns 4 and 5, and in Plunkett's attempt to apply Dante, we should look to an art-historical framework in which to explicate columns 1–3, with a little assistance from Ernst Kantorowicz. If this move seems unjustified by anything as yet discovered of Plunkett's education or private study, it should be borne in mind that his father, G. N. Plunkett, was an art historian with a short book on Botticelli to his credit, and strong interest in early printed books, and a large reference library.

Discussing a variety of artistic forms and material, Kantorowicz pointed to a concurrence of realms in a *volto santo* crucifix and in the frontispiece of the Aachen Gospels (c. A.D. 975). Of the first he says that it shows "at once the regal and sacrificial [*sic*] character of the God-man." The Aachen image "shows the emperor in the *maiestas* of Christ." In a mosaic depicting the coronation of Roger II of Sicily, there is "a striking facial resemblance between Roger and Christ." Here is a fragile link to Plunkett's expressed interest in the Holy Roman Empire, for Kantorowicz relates these images to the Ottonian period generally, while Plunkett had briefly mentioned Otto I in his mini-essay on the just state. Here, in plenty, are visual representations of the medieval king's dual nature, "human by nature and divine by grace."[50] With the dogma of transubstantiation (1215), an additional focus for the visualization of duality arose. The consecrated host now officially was the very and true body of Christ (*corpus verum*). It was displayed in the monstrance (or ostensorium) that provided a chalice-like frame in which the Real Body became a visual object of devotion. With its processions, the feast of Corpus Christi (instituted 1264) ostentatiously presented it to the faithful.

From the history of art, it is advisable to skip epochal developments associated with the Reformation, the Counter-Reformation, and what became known as the Renaissance in order speedily to reach a later period in which religious art took on more popular forms. (Plunkett as a hesitant writer might be classified under Populist Occult.) As an early consequence of the French Revolution, clerical life and secure public worship came under severe pressure with, eventually, the growth (for economic reasons and others) of domestic piety. Following the establishment in 1800 of the Society of the Sacred Heart with its many schools, the iconography of the cult spread widely through popular print, small in size, and plainly colored.[51] The heart is depicted flaming with divine light, pierced by a Roman spear, bound in thorns, surmounted by a cross, and bleeding. A living Christ, pointing to it outside his body, or within his transparent flesh, appears to present it as the priest presents the host for adoration, or—"take and eat." From the late 1870s onward, devout Catholics were encouraged to wear a scapular of the Sacred Heart with the familiar image to the front and another, showing the Virgin Mary, at the back. The commercial distribution of these devotional objects extended the cult, while additionally transmitting the domestic visual icon into a bodily or clothed intimacy. Perhaps more than a million images of the Sacred Heart existed in Ireland at any moment in Plunkett's life, primarily but not exclusively, in relatively humble homes, but also in schools, convents, parochial buildings, and churches.[52] New churches were dedicated to the Sacred Heart. The Pioneer Total Abstinence (from alcohol) Association of the Sacred Heart was established in Dublin (1898), and its very numerous members identified themselves by wearing a Sacred Heart lapel badge. Abstinence was deemed "the heroic sacrifice." In January 1911, *The Catholic Book Bulletin* announced *The Golden Treasury of the Sacred Heart*, "printed and bound by Catholic hands on our own premises." By Catholic hands" at this point in Irish time was meant "non-Jewish hands."[53]

In the absence of any other attempt at a comprehensive statement about

Plunkett's verse, the central role of Sacred Heart iconography can be essayed. This, however, encounters issues of duality, the coexistence but noncongruity of the mystic poet and the nationalist conspirator. (Plunkett personally denied that he was a mystical writer.) In search of a bridging text, we find no equivalent of Pearse's "I am Ireland" or MacDonagh's "Marching Song of the Irish Volunteers" (December 1913). Indeed, it seems that Plunkett abandoned poetry when his engagement with the IRB intensified. The poems analyzed here were gathered under the Latin title, "Occulta," which might casually be read as indicating hidden or concealed matters, for example in esoteric or cultic doctrines. More specifically, the form is either feminine or neuter, depending on the noun thus qualified. Given the traceability of two identifiable women's names among the heavy freight of words, it seems reasonable to suppose that Columba and Grace are the concealed (perhaps unreleasable) concerns of the text, both in their names doubling as theological references of the most desirable kind. "Nomina sunt consequentia rerum," as a poem's title, is no casually mobilized trophy of Plunkett's diligence: it encapsulates a maxim with which he struggled repeatedly—the issue of whether Columba (O'Carroll) by necessity is an emblem or harbinger of peace and purity, whether Grace (Gifford) by an even higher necessity exemplifies the grace that only God confers. The surnames appear intrusive, and the personalized "drama" vulgar compared to Dante's luminously distant Lady in the *Vita Nuova* and, more luminous and more highly distant again, in the *Divine Comedy*.[54] Nor is this a covert attempt to boost Plunkett's standing in the Irish poetic canon by indicating the gravity of his themes. The phrasing, with its leaden gravity—"Sing all ye mouths of music" (2), "Braver is she than ruby" (15), "the smoky mists of blood" (20), "the wine-bag of the bee" (21), "the windy wastes of death" (34)—sinks the ambition even before it can be launched.

What if the Latin maxim is transferred from the pseudo-Dantean sphere to the Pearsean? Applied to the IRB and to the Proclamation of which Plunkett was a signatory, it immediately raises the question of sovereignty. If, in 1803 (Emmet), or 1867 (the Fenians), or 1916 (the signatories) declared a Republic of Ireland, not to state an objective but as what J. L. Austin described as a performative statement, then a sovereign state has been brought into existence. This, it may be argued, is contingent on the new state's being formally recognized by other existing states. (For contrast, consider the Republic of Northern Cyprus, which is only recognized by Turkey.) In the process of recognition, the issue of authority arises—by what authority is the performative statement made? Pearse, Plunkett, and the other 1916 signatories took the precaution of claiming to act "in the name of God and of the dead generations." The 1867 proclamation made no such concessions. Its fourth paragraph, in declaring that "All men are born with equal rights," stayed traceably close to Rousseau and to the American Declaration of 1776. The nearest it approached metaphysics was in the phrase "Nature's god." As for Emmet, he settled for expectations of "the national will," and "the blessings of divine providence."[55] In search of the national will, he could vividly recall what approximated to a countrywide rising in 1798; neither the Fenians nor the men of 1916 could invoke any such tacit endorsement. Thus, between God and the dead generations, the living were passed over in silence. "The right of the Irish people to the ownership of Ireland, and to the unfettered control of Irish destinies, to be sovereign and indefeasible" falls short of acknowledging or bestowing sovereignty in the people, the nation, or the provisional government. What is said to be sovereign is a right to ownership—whether corporative, private, or otherwise remains unstated. Evasive, enigmatic, and then repetitive, the Proclamation which Plunkett set his name to is no clearer on the crucial issue than his poetry is on thematics of faith and sexuality.

Sir Edmund Plowden is not much remembered today except, among academic lawyers, for the expression, "The case is altered; no priest, no mass." He had appeared in a case where it seemed that the Roman Mass had been illegally celebrated. But, having discovered that the celebrant was actually a layman and no priest, Plowden declared that no Mass had been truly celebrated, no offense committed. The issues concerning the 1916 insurrection are in the process of altering as its centenary approaches, especially issues involving religious motivation, popular authority, and forms of proposed government. Central to each is the notion of sacrifice and, while Pearse expounded the theme with confidence, Plunkett through texts that might be attributed to "the devotional unconscious"—apologies to Fredric Jameson again—explored dangerous cross currents.

Two famous Irishmen, larger figures than Plunkett, can be drawn into comparison. Michael Davitt, Fenian jailbird and founder of the Land League, wrote in his diary for 17 June 1894:

> Twenty-five years ago I was in Leeds and had an arms depot there for the "Irish Republic virtually established"! I sent hundreds of rifles from there to different parts of Ireland hoping and believing they would some day—and not at a too distant date—be shouldered & used against "the proud insulting foe." There will be a strong apparent difference between the Fenian soldier of 1869 and the Irish constitutionalist of 1894. The methods are totally different but what about objects & motives? I feel myself to be a *stronger* enemy today of all I conspired against twenty five years ago than I was then. My then means to an end played into the hands of Dublin Castle and Irish landlordism. Conspiracy & impotent insurrections only strengthened the enemy's hold and wasted the spirit & resources of Irish national sentiment. The methods of the Land League have told a different story. The enemy is no longer saved by the blunders of its foes.[56]

The other figure is Yeats. "Parnell's Funeral," written in 1932–1933 and published in 1934, is divided into two parts. The earliest drafts include a baffling line soon abandoned—"In my heart I long to cry—Had Jesus peace who slew his master." In the long process of composition, Yeats eliminated and inserted, rewrote and rethought the inky web of nearly illegible words. Jesus disappeared early. A provisional title emerged, "Somebody at Parnell's Funeral." The uncharacteristic anonymous-personal recurs in the drafts themselves—"Somebody has drawn the tragic buskin on . . . somebody here / Thinks of the god whose heart became a star." Substitution-for-name is followed by an avoidance of names, until the proposed name-heavy line "England killed Tone, Emmett [*sic*], Fitzgerald" is modified by the substitution of "The stranger" for England. This sets up the drama Yeats so often seeks—who "killed" Parnell? Answers collide: "we" (repeatedly), "hounds in their rage," "contagion of the throng," And then comes another baffling line: "what blood star hounds the stranger tarring them on[?]"[57]

In the earliest draft to bear the drab "Somebody at Parnell's Funeral" title, the question is asked (echoing Keats and the Grecian urn), "What is this sacrifice?" With Yeats a question does not solicit an answer; it requires choice between answers with a consequent obligatory renunciation of worth or value—even kinship, truth, or a life. As to who killed whom, the victims are fully and ostentatiously named—Emmet, Fitzgerald, Tone, already commemorated in "September 1913." Plus Parnell, why not? In the poem's canonical state and, indeed, in the available manuscript materials, the "uncrowned king" is never named except in a possessive phrase—"Parnell's funeral," "Parnell's heart," and (again) "Parnell's heart." After the repetition, "Parnell's heart" is replaced by "Jonathan Swift's dark grove." Swift was not killed.

Before pursuing the list of names, we might return to Lucien Goldmann and the preliminaries to *The Hidden God*. The Pascalian dialectic struggled, like Jacob and the Angel, between "the whole and the parts." Goldmann deals with literary texts, but describes them as (or containing, embodying) empirical facts. Yeats constructs miniature texts in names and, in Parnell's case, allows the oneness of text and name (whole and part) to expand and also to partly disappear: we have "Parnell's funeral" and "Parnell's heart," the part or attribute or occasion, without Parnell. This is the possessive case, grammatically, without a possessor. He is the *dux fortissimus absconditus*. Sean O' Faolain, the literary inheritor of a Parnellism Joyce and Yeats used, wrote his study of the twentieth-century novel under the title *The Vanishing Hero*.

Despite all these higher perspectives, in the average historian's mind, Fitzgerald, Tone, Emmet, Parnell were none of them killed by strangers. The first died of wounds inflicted during his police arrest in Dublin. The second committed suicide. The third was tried in Dublin, executed by the local hangman (and perhaps decapitated by ditto). The fourth died in Brighton, in bed, of pneumonia probably complicated by cancer of the stomach. "Stranger" is another version of "somebody," a distanced somebody, not one of "we." One can nearly smell the intervening hygienic absence. However, Yeats's direct ancestor (William Taylor, 1747–1817) worked in Dublin Castle at the time of the United Irishmen insurrections of 1798 and 1803. His position required him to keep secret service money in his desk. And, we may presume, to hand it out. Didn't Taylor pay the informers (McNally and Armstrong) who betrayed the United Irishmen? And if the poet also tells us that Major Henry Sirr (1764–1841) was godfather to "several of my great-great-grandfather's children," should we not add that Sirr arrested Lord Edward Fitzgerald, who died as a direct consequence? Among "we," the stranger is a circulating scapegoat.[58] The hygienic absence directs us where not to look.

"Parnell's Funeral" is generally explicated with reference to ancient myth and ritual, involving Cretan and Sicilian references and a cult of the Great Mother. The modern names are merely incidental. Yet the contention that Parnell is/was a god that died cannot avoid admitting the proximity of Nietzsche's declaration on that weary topic. The first part of the poem deals with historical succession, the cycle of tragic and comic eras, its final stanza summing up the dreadful transition from "we" as mere observers to participants in these violent acts—"we devoured his heart." The verb here aligns "we" with the hounds and wolves presented as having dragged "this quarry" down.

In the second, shorter, and final part, the verb changes and much with it. Each of the three stanzas names a living man who did not *eat* Parnell's heart, Eamon de Valera, W. T. Cosgrave, and Eoin O'Duffy, with Kevin O'Higgins (assassinated in 1927) added as an excused defaulter. These are 1916 men to varying degrees, the first two condemned to death (commuted), the second two (for balance) inactive during Easter Week but energized immediately afterward. Thus the poem emphatically all but concludes with the refusal or incapacity of modern leaders to partake in the sacrificial meal, a consumption profanely accomplished by "we" at an animalistic level. The poem was not the only occasion on which Yeats read Parnell within a Christ-typology. "When he came among his followers, his hands were full of blood, because he had torn them with his nails"—in this detail from *The Trembling of the Veil*, Yeats presents Parnell as a self-crucifying messiah of his people, imposing composure under gross provocative accusation by means that produce the stigmata.[59] Eating the dead god's heart surely derives from ancient ritual belief, but its emergence in Yeats follows a pervasive and prolonged cult of the (living) god's heart in Ireland, represented in a million domestic images, scapulars, lapel badges, and the names of schools. It is this throng, in the poet's view, who destroyed Parnell and refused the legacy. Violence and timidity in harness.

René Girard and Onora O'Neill

Enigmas began with some near antiquarian enquiries into pamphlet controversies of the Victorian age, mainly arising within the Anglican Church. These doubtless seemed to many readers dry-as-dust affairs of little contemporary relevance. Not quite so. In 1968, the New York–born, Ulster poet John Montague published *The Bread God*, a collage-sequence in which he sought to place the bilious anti-Catholicism of the Reverend Ian Paisley in a cultural and historical context essentially focused on debates about the Eucharist in the nineteenth century and after. In doing so, he delicately advised that the imminent Troubles would have religious difference at heart even if nationalist and unionist politics played louder tunes.[60] When "The Bread God: A Collage of Religious Misunderstandings" was gathered into *The Rough Field* (as section 3), it was followed (in section 5) with an epigraph taken from a reflection by a member of the IRB's Supreme Council on the events of Easter Week. Patrick McCartan, from county Tyrone (and hence an Ulsterman), recorded how he "alone opposed it" (that is, the Dublin insurrection). In Faulknerian terms, the past wasn't over in 1968, it wasn't even the past yet.[61]

Since the sixteenth-century Reformation, Catholics and Protestants have differed sharply about the sacraments, the former maintaining seven from the late medieval church, the latter retaining "two only, as generally necessary for salvation," that is baptism and Holy Communion ("the supper of the Lord"). Were it not for the intense campaign to propagate the Catholicity of the insurrection after the fact, these distinctions might not matter.[62] While Catholic doctrine declares the Real Presence of Christ's body and blood in the Mass (the wafer and wine being appearances), Protestantism generally uses the term *consubstantiation* to explain the physical presence of wine and bread with, in, under the spiritual presence of Christ's body also. Thus Protestantism leans away from the miraculous towards the commemorative view of the sacrament. T. H. Abbott, who had translated Kant's second critique and advised Meredith in his work on the third, published a sharp paper in 1890 dismissive of any sacrificial meaning in or behind Jesus's injunction, "this do in remembrance of me" (Luke 22:19), with specific reference to the verb "to do." Then aged sixty-one, and with twenty-three years to live, he began by complaining that the view he aimed to revoke "had obtained in recent times a wide acceptance on what seem to [him] entirely inadequate grounds."[63] He named no adversaries; he intended to proceed along purely philological arguments. If nothing else, the article indicates an awareness among the Dublin Kantians of a growing inclination toward interpretation of Holy Communion as a sacrificial "redoing" of Jesus's Easter passion: this hardly complied with Kant's own recommendation of "religion within the limits of reason." Dying in 1913, Abbott was spared the international crescendo of bugle calls to self-sacrifice on the battlefields of France, and the Pearsean call on the nation's children to sacrifice themselves, having also shot the wrong people. His article appeared too early to pick up even the preliminary stages of the liturgy-fication of contemporary politics—Parnell was still alive, Dreyfus an officer untouched by allegation or suspicion.

Abbott's argument in the American *Journal of Biblical Literature* was expanded for British and Irish readers as *Do This in Remembrance of Me* (1893, repr. 1894, 1895, 1898), specifically rebutting the positions of William Rathbone Supple and others. Supple came of a county Louth family, was ordained by the Church of Ireland, but after 1905 ministered in the Church of England, where his "high" opinions were more welcome. He was responsible for erecting a family tombstone in Dunshaughlin, the sculptor being James Pearse, father of Patrick and William. Abbot's *Essays, Chiefly on the Original Texts of the Old and New Testaments* (1891) also addressed the problem of Holy Communion, its commemorative or sacrificial status. The prolific and energetic Welsh, Calvinist, and Anglican W. H. Griffith Thomas applied Abbott's antisacrificial arguments in *A Sacrament of our Redemption* (1904). All of this is to illustrate how disputes about sacrifice in liturgy arose in Irish (Protestant) church circles in the 1890s and after, partly as a negative byproduct of the Catholic Revival in England but also—by way of affinity—in parallel to the growth of a French political ideology in which sacrifice was extolled.

Catholic theology, subject to a controlling oversight from Rome, gave rise to few controversies of the kind that involved Abbott and Supple. In Ireland, where the church was only emancipated from prohibitions on clerical training a century earlier and where the faithful included a small proportion of those achieving a higher education to research level, exploratory or original Catholic theology was doubly frustrated. The notable exception, George Tyrrell (1861–1909), was a Dublin-born Anglican who converted, was ordained a Jesuit, and fell foul of the papacy for his commitment to theological modernism. Excommunicated in 1908, he had openly declared that the *Pascendi* encyclical identified Catholic doctrine with scholastic theology and minimized the positive aspects of doctrinal development. A formidable intellectual, Tyrrell's fate underscored the extreme difficulty of independent philosophical reflection in Ireland—where he was quickly forgotten. By so old-fashioned a notion as nature's abhorring a vacuum, new ideas from the continent quickly appealed to serious readers and thinkers.

The Catholic Bulletin (founded 1911) quickly became a vehicle for vehement expressions of opinion. In 1916 Father T. H. Burbage (died 1966) flew the flag for sacrifice, but flew it upside-down in a series of articles on Jewish ritual murder in Russia. The following year, he was elected to Sinn Féin's executive committee along with G. N. Plunkett, Hannah Sheehy Skeffington, Eoin MacNeill, and others, none of whom appeared to have objected to his reverence's blood libel.[64]

Bergson's preeminence in this influx of foreign ideas is signaled in the articles by Maurice Bourgeois, published in the secular *Irish Review*, and followed up by Jean Malye's "Le Mouvement philosophique en France" (March 1914). Catholic Ireland, through *The Irish Monthly*, kept in touch with Bergson, but with little enthusiasm. The vehicle for sustained and, at times, even lively discussion was the Protestant (Anglican) *The Irish Church Quarterly*. The contributors belonged to a younger generation than Abbott, and most were (like him) ordained ministers of the Church of Ireland. They principally were R. T. Byrn, Maurice H. F. Collis, Charles D'Arcy, W. M. Foley, and Reginald Rogers. Of these D'Arcy (1859–1938) achieved ecclesiastical distinction as archbishop of Armagh; Rogers, his good-humored tormentor in *The Irish Church Quarterly*, died young in 1923. Collis, vicar of Antrim parish, devoted some time to commemorating the nineteenth-century Dublin Platonist William Archer Butler (1814–1848), including publication of Butler's poem about Robert Emmet, Pearse's idol in the years before 1916.

In the issue for January 1916 Foley, writing about teleology, used the well-established device of referring to Bergson as the modern Heraclitus. In the same issue, Robert Thomas Byrn, writing "Creative Limitations and Development," ventured into more disturbed waters, and cited *Creative Evolution* on several occasions to illustrate difficulties still confronting the Christian believer who sought to grasp Darwin's discoveries. For example, life seems to have succeed in penetrating matter "by dint of humility, by making itself very small and very insinuating, bending to physical and chemical forces, consenting even to go a part of the way with them, like the switch that adopts for a while the direction of the rail it is endeavouring to leave."[65] Had Byrn done more to acknowledge Bergson's fondness for up-to-the-minute comparisons, he might have reproduced the opening sentence of the chapter he quoted: evolutionary movement, Bergson explained, "proceeds rather like a shell, which suddenly bursts into fragments, which fragments, being themselves shells, burst in their turn into fragments destined to burst again." Though Byrn did not sustain his reliance on the philosopher of intuition, he notes the conclusion that "Man too in the process of creation has had to abandon something of this higher way of life. The power of intellect has asserted itself at the cost of intuition."[66]

The remainder of Byrn's article emerges as a commentary on "the war of frightful barbarity which Germany is waging throughout the world," for which Nietzsche is blamed.[67] For support the retired historian J. Neville Figgis's prewar *Gospel and Human Needs* (1909) is cited, specifically for sardonic lines by an unidentified poet, "To purge the world of Christianity, / The sacrifice of every human life / That now enjoys or nauseates the sun / Would not be too exorbitant a price!" In large measure, Bergson has been dropped from the argument, and Byrn concludes his condemnation of German warfare by quoting Saint Paul with unintended irony, "The weapons of our warfare are not carnal, but mighty through God to the pulling down of strongholds; casting down imaginations and every high thing that exalteth itself against the knowledge of God, and bringing into captivity every thought to the obedience of Christ" (2 Corinthians 10:4–5).

The notion of sacrifice as a means to the elimination of Christianity is a contorted blasphemy in that the Christian faith proclaims that Jesus took upon himself the sacrifice otherwise required of all under the Law, and so terminated the requirement. It certainly has no claim on Bergson's thought or reputation. But it does chime with a politics often said to owe debts to Bergson's intuitionism—Sorelian syndicalism. The Bergson-Sorel "affinity" has been asserted rather examined, at least by Anglophone historians.

In 1890s Sorel, an engineer by profession, began a critique of "scientistic" Marxism in which he substituted myth for economics in the self-understanding and motivation of proletarian revolt. Not revolution in the classic sense, but the general strike, was to be the pinnacle of socialist efforts toward total change. "In Bergsonian language Sorel argued that the scientific analysis of revolutionary socialism is static and misses the essential nature of historical change which must be intuited in its durational flux."[68] Charles Péguy argued to the same effect in relation to Christianity, its mindless repetition of fixed ideas, even though Péguy was (in his last years) a devout if unusual Catholic. To some limited extent, Tyrrell thought in similar terms. Sorel, however, repeatedly invoked religious history (including primitive

Christianity, Pascal, Calvin, and John Henry Newman) in his *Reflections on Violence* (1908). Irving Horowitz subtitles his chapter on Bergson and Sorel, "The Liberation of Will from Intelligence." The same chapter deals with Bergson's work in psychology, which—Horowicz argues—predated Freudian psychoanalysis, but drew on common sources, for example Charcot and Janet's work on hysteria. Sorel too is a psychologist of sorts and, like Freud later, is impressed by myth. Freud, however, remains ever the analyst, whereas Sorel moves to incorporate contemporary notions into the corpus of effective myth. Bergson stood back from these applications of his intuition-philosophy, yet his psychology "provided a foundation for Sorel's myth of the general strike, since images . . . were a human creation and not something found in the spirit of society."[69]

In this light, Plunkett's poems, especially those gathered under the "Occulta" heading, could be read as images of a broadly Sorelian kind. Their perspective on religion (that is, Catholicism) is not steady or collectively organized; on the contrary, the images are dispersed reflections of a larger *imago abscondita*, certainly religious in content, but uncertain at reception. If a compliment were in order, then "Occulta" would be a tentative exercise in Baroque literary cubism. "Now bend the cracking spars / Athwart the mast of the world—and five deep scars / From that strong Cross call you to their abode" (7). Little of the political or social world appears, or appears to intrude. Yet, in "La Pucelle," with comets, nenuphars, and scimitars whizzing through the early lines, we also encounter contemporary sounding "battle ranks . . . marching / Squadron by squadron, battalion by battalion, / Both horse and foot" (13). The pucelle is Joan of Arc with sound effects from the Battle of the Marne around her. She is couched in unspeakable archaic phrasing, while doubling for one or the other living woman Plunkett signals to in code—"the imperishable Dove," "your body's grace," and so on.

Discussion of Bergson in the *Irish Church Quarterly* took its sharpest form in several items by D'Arcy and Rogers, an exchange further enhanced by its straddling the insurrection of which Joseph Plunkett was a major sponsor. Beyond R. T. Byrn's loyal bugle calls, D'Arcy and Rogers had to contend with palpable evidence of military conflict on Irish soil, in the Irish capital. Though there is little to suggest any divergence of opinion between them on the fundamental issues at stake—the union with Great Britain, the promise or threat of Home Rule, the declaration of a republic—the younger man displayed no hesitation in citing the insurrection while arguing with the bishop. The latter was an established author; indeed the first item in the exchange was Rogers's review of D'Arcy's *God and Freedom in Human Experience*, published in London in 1915. Rogers, a Trinity don, had commenced publication with *A Short History of Ethics, Greek and Modern* (London: Macmillan, 1911). There had also been learned articles, "Berkeley and Kant" (1904) and "The Deduction of Space from Time" (1905), and a dutiful two-volume posthumous edition (1914) of George Salmon's *Treatise on the Analytical Geometry of Three Dimensions* (1862).[70]

None of these perspectives, whether derived from *The Catholic Bulletin* or *The Irish Church Quarterly*, offers much understanding of April 1916 in Dublin. Bergson and Sorel no longer ring in our ears. The underlying difficulty was formulated decades ago by Francis Mulhern when he complained about Irish historians, politicians, and some visiting critical theorists, who can only discuss nationalism in nationalist terms. However, to seek a point of leverage outside the field—as Archimedes is said to have remarked—is to miss the point. How then to search for it, with some hope of avoiding the established errors?

Although the ideology of sacrifice was central to the outlook and practice of the 1916 insurrectionists, it had existed in one form or another for many centuries, never exclusively European nor exclusively Judeo-Christian but persuasively linking both those contexts. The social anthropologists expanded our awareness of its reach through fieldwork in Africa, Asia, Australia, and the Americas, but the politicization of sacrifice was to be a western European achievement of the nineteenth century. A philosophical response became the life's work of René Girard (born 1923 in Avignon), notably in *La Violence et la sacr*é (1972; English, *Violence and the Sacred*, 1977). A prolific author, he is acknowledged as a French intellectual and a permanent presence in the Northern American academic world. His work on literature should not be discounted.[71] Close study of Dostoyevsky and a small number of other novelists led him to abandon agnosticism for Roman Catholicism. Acceptance of Real Presence theology duly follows, with the implication that the sacrifice of the mass is a fully genuine reenactment of Christ's sacrifice on the cross, miraculous in relation to time and to material appearances. Goldmann found Girard's first book, *Deceit, Desire and the Novel* (1961), useful in his own efforts toward a sociology of literature. The breadth of Girard's learning and cultural sensitivity is such that his extended meditation on sacrifice repays the attention of all, even those who do not join him at the altar. Returning to Plunkett, we should note that, while his behavior is everywhere scented with the ideology of sacrifice, his writings and recorded utterances give little evidence of the same. Girard's social anthropology is grounded in the observation that humans are imitative creatures. The capacity for mimesis is fundamental to their most complex behavior not only at the individual level but in the social and cultural spheres generally. Mimesis is a familiar term from Aristotle's *Poetics* (350 B.C.), reinforced in the twentieth century by Erich Auerbach (1892–1957), who entitled his study of "the representation of reality in western literature" *Mimesis* (1953). Girard, however, takes the term out of the (as we would now say) aesthetic realm into the dynamics of all constitutive human activity. Thus, man *is* man because s/he imitates. Moreover, humans *desire* to imitate; mimesis could be classified (in Freudian terms Girard would deplore) as a drive. A neat account of mimetic desire is provided in an essay (1997) on Dostoyevsky:

> To say that our desires are imitative or mimetic is to root them neither in their objects nor in ourselves, but in a third party, the model or mediator, whose desire we imitate in the hope of resembling him or her, in the hope that our two beings will be "fused."[72]

The position of this model is all-important in determining the outcome of the subject's drive to imitate: Girard posits two—an internally and an externally positioned model. In the latter case, sufficient distance separates the model from the subject to establish a bulwark against mere emulation and to create a dynamic field of imitation. In the case of an internal model rivalry (not achieved imitation) arises through conflictual mimesis.[73] In essence, desire is a triangular affair and, in happy cases, may produce a relationship that Philip Sidney characterized (in *Astrophil and Stella*, sonnet 41) as the "sweet enemy." Unhappy cases may result in monstrous doubles (e.g., enemy brothers) or narcissism. Plunkett's efforts with the sonnet make clear his familiarity with the Petrarchan form used by Sidney. His unposted letters to Columba O'Carroll invite a diagnosis of narcissism.

The order of chapters in *Violence and the Sacred* is mildly surprising. Only in the sixth does Girard concentrate on mimetic desire, having opened with "Sacrifice" (chap. 1) and "The Sacrificial Crisis" (chap. 2). According to these, sacrifice is a social institution (not a drive), activated or implemented when occasion demands: the scapegoat is its primary mascot. For sacrifice is, in several senses, a matter of choice. Its function is to restore order or prevent widespread disorder, often through the nomination of ritual surrogate victims. En passant, Girard expresses views about the modern juridical system, central authority, and so forth.

Despite these, and a few details drawn from the work of anthropologists, the material upon which *Violence and the Sacred* is constructed is drawn from literary or other revered texts. Homer, the Greek tragedies, and Greek mythology in more diffuse form predominate, especially the plays of Euripides. Some pages attend to Shakespeare. Toward the end of chapter 2, an unexpected aside briefly surfaces:

> If there are really such events as sacrificial crises, some sort of breaking mechanism, an automatic control that goes into effect before everything is destroyed, must be built into them. In the final stages of a sacrificial crisis the very viability of human society is put in question. Our task is to discover what these final stages involve and what makes them possible.[74]

The apparent concession or—better—hypothesis, that there might not be any such events *really*, raises a barrier to any general understanding, in a Girardian sense, of sacrificial ideology as preached and practiced by the leading Irish insurrectionists of 1916. While the appearance of concession may be a temporary mirage, generated in part through translation from the French, it is true that in the 1990s he shifted ground on the use of the term *sacrifice*. This change is discussed in his *By Whom Scandal Comes* (2014) by way of comparison with *Things Hidden since the Foundation of the World* (1978, in French). The argument is, of course fundamentally theological, arising from Girard's close reading of the Swiss Jesuit thinker Raymund Schwager. In somewhat broader terms, he sees his project "first and foremost as a means of subverting the intellectual foundations of the relativism that dominates our world."[75] This, together with the suggestion that "the modern is postsacrificial," leaves the nonconfessional historian of early twentieth-century events at a disadvantage.[76]

Nevertheless Girard's particular terms—acquisitive mimesis, conflictual mimesis, mimesis of appropriation, and so forth—can prove helpful at a secondary level, but the central question remains historical. The individual proponent of a sacrificial ideology—Plunkett is a different case from Pearse—may be gradually understood through the closer analysis of his behavior, textual and otherwise, under the headings that Girard provides. The one-sided affair with Columba O'Carroll lacked a model of sufficient distance to mitigate the ravages of internal mediation. Complex interfamily tensions, banishments, mild derangements, lift the affair out of the individual mismatch into a small collective impasse, the stalemate of trench warfare among two Irish families. The about-turn engagement to Grace Gifford lay too near his friend MacDonagh's marriage to her sister, Muriel Gifford, requiring Plunkett to invoke *the will*, not love, as the primary motive force. His honesty on this point is impressive, if also disturbing. In January 1922, Edith Balfour encountered vivid memories of the nocturnal wedding ceremony as "not at all a romantic one."[77]

In making these remarks, we should take strength from the kind of personal psychology that Girard accommodated within his theory of myth, religion, and sacrifice. In Plunkett's social origins, some of his problems may be traced. Dr. Joseph O'Carroll had some bond with (or desire for) Josephine Cranny, who, from her three suitors, chose her second cousin, George Noble Plunkett. Her eldest son, Joseph, took the Christian name of the neighboring doctor in November 1887; a few months later, the doctor's eldest son took the same Christian name. In time, both of the younger Josephs rebelled against their inheritance, Joe O'Carroll spectacularly if to little effect, Joe Plunkett clandestinely and with lasting effect. Dr. O'Carroll beat his children; Countess Plunkett beat hers, nothing wholly untypical of the bourgeois household. But Joe Plunkett psychologically beat up Columba O'Carroll, even after his early death. Is there a dispersed, multiparty primal scene behind the drapes?

Beyond relationship, the crux arises in any attempt to assess Plunkett's choice of death. Unambiguously informed by his physician—Dr. Charles MacAuley (1887–1956), who happened to be a member of the IRB—that he had only weeks to live, Plunkett adopted a course of action guaranteed to end by a violence directly or indirectly of his own choice. (Yeats could have found material for "An IRB Man Foresees His Death," had he wished.) In terms of political tactics, Plunkett could have lain low without any loss of *kudos* (a Greek term Girard likes), later to emerge as the elusive survivor, the rallying point, the Republic's once and future king. Even if he were to die within weeks or months, his brothers (loyal like no one else he dealt with) would provide continuity essential to the transmission of sovereignty. Personal courage under fire may be commended in the abstract, but his example only served to underscore the lure of self-sacrifice. With death inevitable from TB or cancer inside a few weeks, Plunkett chose an alternative end consistent with Pearse's notion of sacrifice, but hardly commensurate with that of healthy young Sean Heuston.

An accessible exposition of Girard's thought suggests that he developed the notions of pseudomasochism and pseudosadism, not just as clinical terms but as "realities . . . that are often rooted in far broader social and historical shifts." What follows, however, leads to no focal topic more specific than modernity itself, and that examined through Stendhal's novel, *Le Rouge et le noir* (1830). While Chris Fleming urges us to note Girard's "acute sensitivity to historical contingencies," the enclosing presence of novelistic form once again frustrates access to historical substance.[78] Several characteristics of the novel, translated into English as late as 1900 by Charles Tergie for the Waterford-born publisher Edmund Downey, deserve attention. First, it is the tale of a young man making his way in French society from humble provincial origins, not unlike the earlier Crannys, O'Carrolls, and Plunketts. Second, Julien Sorel's path is marked out by dichotomies of secular and religious life, the rival attractions of each and the attendant operations of power and desire. Third, Girard noted of the period treated in the novel that increased democratization and upward social mobility gave rise to heightened forms of rivalry. Specifically, he pointed to the former influence of the divine right of kings in presiding over lesser and derivative degrees of differentiation. Unlike Balzac, he passes over market competition as a social dynamic.

Much of this is germane to the study of Irish social realities in the decades leading up to 1916, the competition between churches for authority, the growth of a professional middle class drawing in talent from provincial towns, the influence of French schools and religious orders, and elimination of some fundamental and distinguishing cultural markers (especially reliance on the Gaelic language and maintenance of folk practices). But we remain within one circle only of the comparative Venn diagram: Girard pays no attention to the fiction of George Moore, Patrick Sheehan, or James Joyce (why should he?); and Irish historians pay no attention to French theory or any species of philosophical analysis (why not?).

In fairness to Girard, whose work is endlessly suggestive, one should conclude by noting the historical situation in which he worked. France was profoundly damaged and disturbed by the Great War and its successor; internally, national feeling was intensified through demands for *revanche*, reparations, and the emasculation of Germany; then, twenty years later, by capitulation, Vichy, anti-Semitism, and resistance. French thought drew mightily on the classical past for nourishment. The wartime *Antigone* of Jean Anouilh (1910–1987) is a suitably ambiguous and popular case in point, but Albert Camus's *Myth of Sisyphus* (1942) and *Caligula* (1944) have proved more durable. Beyond these literary references, the French tradition of classical studies consolidated itself in the postwar period. Girard's reliance on Euripides for much in *Violence and the Sacred* and for much of his mimetic theory is part of an extensive intellectual trajectory. An immediate postwar solidarity among some French intellectuals could be illustrated by Girard's inviting Goldmann to speak at an American conference, with the latter's early death closing off further possibilities.

Since the collapse of the Soviet Union, and the subsequent growth of international disorder, especially that involving the Islamic world, a renewed interest in the phenomenon of sacrifice has emerged among philosophers of politics and ethics. In a recent collection of essays, the editors noted (or conceded) that "one major narrative of European modernity involves . . . its systematic and increasing repudiation of sacrifice."[79] This being so, one can only wish that Girard had acknowledged the counterargument, historical though it may be, by citing Theodore Beza, John Toland, Johann von Goethe, T. W. Adorno, or others of that opinion. In an essay entitled "Sacrifice as Self-Destructive Love: Why Autonomy Should Still Matter to Feminists," Pamela S. Anderson effectively answers the Girardian view that "the celebrants do not and must not comprehend the true role of the sacrificial act."[80] In the process, she draws on a "Kantian, modal conception of principled autonomy," directing readers to Onora O'Neill's *Bounds of Justice* (2000).[81] Autonomy of the person, specifically for Anderson autonomy of the woman, brings obligation and freedom, values and attributes wholly inadmissible to that world of sacrifice propounded by Girard almost exclusively through his study of ancient myth and drama, augmented by a select body of modern prose literature. In the specific case of the 1916 insurrection, drama can contribute an instance where this relegation of individual reality is reimposed—"Ireland is greater than a wife"—in terms that desexualize all concerned in preparation for the acts of sacrifice. What remains couched in gendered terms is Ireland herself, Cathleen ní Houlihan, the Sean Bhean Bocht.

The late arrival of Onora O'Neill's name into the discussion for the first time permits the readmission of another—J. C. Meredith's—which had disappeared from the record before April 1916. Both devoted time and intelligence to the study of Immanuel Kant, though in dissimilar ways. For more than two decades Meredith was primarily though privately a translator-scholar who rarely ventured a philosophical remark in public, his own or Kant's. As a student philosopher first at Oxford and later in Harvard, O'Neill (born 1941) was (to use her own words) "not inclined to give priority to scholarship over argument."[82] Yet such were the times of Meredith's youthful maturity that he found himself an influential member of Irish Volunteer committees and, after 1920, a judge in an ascending range of Irish courts. She, on the other hand, pursued an academic career from the outset, culminating in appointment as principal of Newnham College, Cambridge. Her philosophical work can be considered under two headings; first, there is Kant; second, there is bioethics. These are linked through her particular interest in Kant's practical philosophy, that is, his writings in the area of politics and ethics. For the moment, we are concerned with O'Neill's publications under the first heading.

Published in 1975, *Acting on Principle: An Essay on Kantian Ethics* opens with a chapter entitled "Principles of Action" that leads into discussions how a particular act can relate to a philosophical principle or indeed to several. These are more technical issues than the matter of Hamlet's losing the name of action, or the loose contrast between action and thoughtful inactivity considered in *Enigmas*' earlier pages. O'Neill is not greatly interested in the history of Kant's reception, apart from some remarks (in the introduction to her second edition of *Acting on Principle*) about J. S. Mill's strictures on Kant's ability to deduce from his general precepts any of the actual duties of ethics or morality.

Constructions of Reason (1989) is indeed a defense of reason, both in relation to Kant's critical method and to politics in the Kantian enterprise. The discussion of obligations and rights, and the subfields of these, would provide a basis for conversations with that learned fellow Kantian, the late J. C. Meredith, about his decisions in the autumn of 1914 and after. The interest in action, and consistency in action, leads into a number of chapters where contemporary social problems are investigated, for example children's rights, and conduct between consenting adults. *Bounds of Justice* (2000) is divided into two parts, the first concentrating on philosophical, and the second on political, matters. Transnational issues, economic and otherwise, now occupy a good deal of space. Action, Reason, Justice—these constitute a triad of essential Kantian concerns that O'Neill has been effective in reestablishing for contemporary debate.

In the middle, or in a position less structurally prominent than the corners of the triangle, is the notion of consent. As "informed consent" it plays a major role in ethico-medical debates and acquires a legal status as well as a moral one. We encountered the simple form in the excursion to clarify Sean MacDermott's complaints of slavery in Victorian Ireland that in turn led us to Swift's observation, in the *Drapier's Letters*, that "all government without the consent of the governed is the very definition of *slavery.*" It is not entirely clear what "all" means in this sentence—does it mean "each and every instance of" or does it mean "total" (i.e., absolute, and hence absolutism)? As Swift's purpose was polemical and his field of operation political, neither clarity nor fineness was his concern. His argument, however, drew on an earlier publication, William Molyneux's *The Case of Ireland's Being Bound by Acts of Parliament in England, Stated* (1698), which did proceed through legal reasoning and the citation of precedent. Molyneux, Swift, and others after them came to be regarded as the founders of "colonial nationalism," a movement of feeling rather than political organization.[83] Much had altered between Swift's time and MacDermott's and, with it, the connotations of "consent." Since 1800 no Irish parliament existed, though Irish elected members sat in what was now called "the imperial parliament" in Westminster, where they formed of course a permanent (not united) minority. Since 1829, Catholics (British as well as Irish) were entitled to sit in the House of Commons, and with the reform acts of 1832, 1867, 1872, and 1884 the franchise throughout the kingdom was open to a much wider social constituency (still male only).

Neil Manson, discussing O'Neill's views of informed consent, illustrates a point that is helpful in the present (very different) argument. "A slave owner may be friendly and polite and may have intimate knowledge of, and even an interest in, the personal life of some of his slaves, but he—and it would typically be a 'he'—still fails to treat his slaves as persons. What is lacking in the context of slavery, we might now think, is *consent*." These interactions are not consensual.[84] Of course, we could argue that there are Uncle Toms (in Ireland, Seoneens) who believe interactions with their owner are consensual, giving rise to philosophical questions about false consciousness. O'Neill, discussing the related concept of autonomy, quotes a brilliant and perverse discussion in Iris Murdoch's *The Sovereignty of Good* (1970) in which the novelist-philosopher apostrophizes "the ideal citizen of the liberal state" with great eloquence, concluding, "his proper name is Lucifer." O'Neill prefers etymology and, for once, ancient history to account for autonomy: "The term was used in Greek political discussion . . . to characterize independence from tyranny or foreign rule: autonomous polities are those that make their own laws, and to be contrasted with those polities whose laws are given them by a mother city." Kant's contribution to the development of autonomy as a philosophical concept was to attach it, via Rousseau, to "human agents, or quite specifically, the human will rather than to polities."[85] These individuals have become "the primary locus of autonomy" for Kantians.

There is a crux here that novelists have illuminated from time to time. E. M. Forster published a much quoted essay "What I Believe" in 1938, where he declared that, if he had to choose between betraying his country and betraying his friend, he hoped to have the guts to betray his country. On the eve of the Second World War, this scandalized many. His illustration of the preference is less well known: "It would not have shocked Dante, though. Dante places Brutus and Cassius in the lowest circle of Hell because they had chosen to betray their friend Julius Caesar rather than their country Rome."[86] Betrayal riddles most narratives of the 1916 insurrection. Eoin MacNeill, as leader of the Irish Volunteers, strongly felt betrayed by Pearse, Plunkett, and his academic colleague MacDonagh. When MacNeill moved to protect his own authority, Thomas Clarke felt that he was "guilty of the blackest treachery."[87] The British government concluded that a large number of the insurgents were traitors, and executed the leaders. *The Red and the Green* (1965), Iris Murdoch's novel about the events of Easter 1916 in Dublin, appeared two years after she resigned from teaching philosophy in Oxford. Any critic with a sense of Kantian obligations to investigate the insurrection and its ideology of sacrifice could do worse than begin with Murdoch and work backward to O'Casey and Yeats.

Having considered two thinkers—Girard and O'Neill—whose work might illuminate persistent difficulties facing students of the Dublin insurrection and its notable leaders, we should specify what these difficulties are. The first is myth, more particularly the differences between people who believe that such and such is mythic (or is a myth) and other people who take it as a true statement. Many historians regard popular accounts of the insurrection as incorporating mythic elements: Girard is of limited use here for he believes one of these elements (the doctrine of sacramental sacrifice) to reflect a permanent reality. It is still possible to apply much of his method to sifting through mixed materials.

The second difficulty is built into the phrase "the insurrection and its leaders," for active rank-and-file members did not necessarily share all the views of those leaders who formulated these views in books or articles, poems or plays. Here one refers to Onora O'Neill's work. Fundamental to the Kantian enterprise is the need for autonomy in making ethical decisions. O'Neill's account of the origins of autonomy (from the Greek *nomos*, law) among ancient city-states leaves unexplained the links needed now to relate the possible autonomy of collectives (colonial populations, religious minorities, or whatever) to that of the Kantian model individual citizen. For good or ill, the world of 2016 has few entirely homogeneous population zones. Autonomy, consent, trust—each involves a different degree of relation between the collective and the individual. Consent additionally relates to more than a single issue; the citizen consents to be governed because, on balance, the issues on which s/he consents are deemed more important than those where consent is withheld, silently or otherwise. All government is mixed, likewise consent to be governed.

For the present context, O'Neill's trenchant arguments can be focused on the clear evidence of a very small Kantian "intelligentsia" among the larger body of Irish Volunteers and the even larger and more amorphous body of nationalistically inclined Irish men and women. Is it possible for a professional philosopher, using O'Neill's criteria, to "test" the Dublin Kantians of 1916—Bernard, Meredith, and O'Sullivan—for adherence to Kant's principles in ethics or politics? Or does the evidence indicate that the conditions of that time, whether military, cultural, social, or personal, inhibited any such consistency?

It is reassuring to think that questions remain: without them the case would never alter. So let two further areas of enquiry be noted. If a degree of philosophical influence (or affinity) can be ascribed to the mental world of Pearse and his followers (including Plunkett, though he was far from the most eloquent), does the Bergson-Sorel amalgam adequately illuminate the principal features of their thought? Similarly, for the numerically smaller group including Meredith and O'Sullivan (perhaps including Eoin MacNeill on the basis of the long document he confronted the conspirators with c. mid-February 1916), do the Kantian principles, of that time or as reconsidered by Professor O'Neill, adequately support their conduct, personally or politically?[88]

Under the same heading, one could raise more tentatively the contrasting figures of Thomas Clarke and James Connolly. In the latter's case, it is generally accepted that he had adopted a form of Marxist analysis to which, at the end of his life, he applied the preferred solution of Fenian insurrectionism. Clarke was no Marxist, but he shared with Connolly one powerful formative experience—residence and active employment in the United States of America. Life there differed strikingly from Dublin, Belfast, and Edinburgh. Crudely expressed, to what extent was the urgency of Clarke and Connolly's demands for an early rising driven by their rough tutelage under the Do It Now! imperatives of American business, either as model or goad? Or, too un-crudely, can one justify recourse to the philosophy of pragmatism in trying to explain their response to Irish conditions in 1907 (when Clarke returned to Ireland)? In the same year the psychologist William James published his lectures titled *Pragmatism*, and we expect to find no correlation between its arguments and Clarke's movements and subsequent decisions. James mentions Bergson only once, and Sorel not at all; their heyday had not quite dawned, though the American philosopher-psychologist will be linked to them in much subsequent discussion. (Plunkett, by the way, had James's *Principles of Psychology* on his reading list.) In this subsequent discussion, the loose coming together of ideas of intuition and spontaneity found Bergson, James, and Sorel involved in the same conversation. Thus, the *Irish Review*'s extensive treatment of Bergson, and J. M. Hone's eagerness to introduce Sorel to *Irish Times* readers, carry William James with them, though recently dead. *The Irish Church Quarterly* once again comes to the rescue of the island's reputation for saints and scholars, though the James-aware scholar James Houghton Kennedy left it to 1912 to review *Pragmatism* (1907). Once again, Kant emerges as a benchmark for Irish philosophically inclined readers. Not everyone accepted the view that James and Bergson (let alone James and Sorel) thought from the same hymn-sheet. Horace Meyer Kallen wrote "a study in contrasting theories of life" to disprove the point emphatically.[89] James made one semiphilosophical distinction early in *Pragmatism* that might be applied to tendencies and personalities active in 1916—between the tough- and the tender-minded. It is not a party matter. MacDermott and John Redmond were tough-minded though facing in opposite directions. Markiewicz was tough-, Meredith tender-minded, though the quality of mind should be taken into consideration as well as the texture. Both Pearse and Connolly possessed both kinds of outlook, though in different ways. With them, and indeed with Plunkett, the lure of sacrifice as rhetoric or tactic or ultimate goal or all three (one compromising another), complicates the Jamesian distinction. Yet the distinction might serve to break down the rigid classifications still firmly accepted in popular commemoration.

As the final question to be posed, let us choose a topic inherent in any critique of the Dublin insurrection—national or state independence as a political objective. A Girardian might argue that desire for independence involves both *removal from* a relationship and *imitation of* the (other, former, and, maybe, abusive) partner. (The Alice Stopford Green position, as encapsulated by Ciaran Brady, resembles this.) An Archimedean might argue that there can be no fixed point that is also unattached, with which to effect the transition. The Kantianism of today, as expounded by Onora O'Neill with reference to duties and obligations in a world of international assemblies, forums, courts, and other bodies, might argue that independence, like the autonomy of old, has migrated to the sphere of individuals in society from the sphere of polities. This, fundamentally, may be the greater problem.

At the outset of this chapter, a possible understanding of the insurrection in philosophical terms was raised despite the slim evidence manifesting itself. Plunkett's archive provided next to nothing, hardly surprising in so young an activist. There was, to be sure, a vocal doctrine of sacrifice without textual provenance. In another quarter, there was second-level philosophical scholarship (Kantian translations, mainly) without much original published thought of that or any other school. Now at the close of this chapter, the situation is hardly better. Girard helpfully offers limited prescriptive diagnoses (e.g., conflictual mimesis) by which one might identity a problem by naming it properly, but the systematic Girardian philosophy is too close to the sacrificial crisis (in Dublin, also on the Somme, to look no further) to provide a comprehensive understanding—close, that is, on grounds of theology. Kant at least is exempt from accusations of excessive proximity, his valorization of autonomy standing too remote from the insurgents' envy of independence. The notion of affinity came to mind as a tool for disinterring historical material that, on examination, might persuade the Girardian to relativize just a little and the Kantian to pull up the chair, move closer. More is needed if Adorno's chewing gum–as-metaphysics is not to become our amnesiac of choice.

Waiting for the End

For one who died so young, Joseph Plunkett's story runs on and on. The year 2016 brings his centenary, together with that of many others equally famous or totally unknown. It is implied modern Ireland began at that moment, but did so as the culmination of ancient Ireland's griefs and ambitions. There are other readings, generally discounted to one degree or another. For example, some Unionists see the insurrection as an assault on Britain in wartime, resulting in no benefit for anyone. Some nationalists—most recently, John Bruton, former Taoiseach (or prime minister of the Republic)—regard it as an act of sabotage directed against the Home Rule settlement agreed before war came in August 1914. More abstractly perhaps, I have proposed that the insurrection owed much to contemporary right-wing French nationalism, especially in its religious doctrine of sacrifice. There are other interpretations—1916 as the harmonization of nationalism and socialism—entertained by thinkers as different as Carl Schmitt and Desmond Greaves. Or the reconciliation of Fenian conspiracy to the Catholic Church. But there is widespread (not universal) acceptance that the insurrectionists, their religious opinions, political objectives, and inherited culture, were of a piece, somehow representative of their milieu.

Surveying dozens of political activists from the period 1890–1923, Roy Foster discovered an "enclosed, self-referencing hectic world which the revolutionaries inhabited."[90] In retrospect, the revolutionary aspect appears inflated, despite Connolly's ultimate objectives or the typhoid "frightfulness" planned by Diarmuid Lynch, Richard Mulcahy, and Jack Plunkett.[91] Foster's entirely valid observation sits oddly with the Plunketts, the "hellhole" of their family life with its domestic violence, the count's studied lack of personal focus and his wife's financial chicanery. The Plunketts lived on hyperbole, the children inducted to their sacrificial roles before reaching puberty. Plunkett domestic discipline appears to have intuited and implemented the sacrificial ideology without benefit from France.

In essence, Foster detects two distinct but complementary groups: (1) those "revolutionaries" who grew into that condition either by following in their parents' Fenian tread or by studying at the feet of ardent nationalist schoolteachers, and (2) those "revolutionaries" who escaped into the condition from homes of (generally) oppressive conformity and imaginative dimness. The Plunketts did not fit into either, though they resembled the second. An attempt was made to equip the count with a Fenian past or at least with "advanced" sympathies in youth, but he was too self-absorbed to act the part. And the young Plunketts did not escape the nest of thorns, even with the insurrection.

Part of the problem lies in the reluctance of contemporary historians to offer models for our understanding of these events, collective and individual. The now traditional view, which is no older than the events per se, would have it that Pearse was the successor to Robert Emmet (executed 1803), a view originating with Pearse himself, not proclaimed by his associates. That Pearse also venerated Wolfe Tone and Thomas Davis hardly alters the notion of tradition as repeat performance to, ideally, loud applause this time. The centenary of the United Irishmen's rebellion had been marked by much quarrelsome rivalry, but it did succeed in establishing a rhetoric of commemoration, a republican communion without Young Irelander or Fenian equal. As such it was new, future-inclined, not retrospective. The dinners and speeches of 1898, white-tie though many of them were, suggested a Do This in Remembrance of Me directive to the exiles in Boston, London, New York, or Paris. Pearse took up the messianic hint in his 1913 oration at the deist Tone's grave, "the holiest place in Ireland." It is, to borrow Roy Foster's term, a "self-referencing" tradition.

Comparative analysis is virtually unknown, by which I mean an analysis that advances our understanding of the 1916 events in Dublin by studying external events of broadly the same period. Norwegian independence, attained in 1905, is ignored perhaps because it was a peaceful process without bloody sacrifices. Hungarian independence in 1919 came as the result of the Great War's end, not from any policy of exploiting the Hapsburgs' wartime difficulties; and, as one Budapest scholar recently expressed it, "we found that independence brought little freedom." The Russian revolutions of 1917 are occasionally invoked, even though these were internal and social convulsions, not politico-military campaigns to escape "the alien usurper" (as just-rebellion theology expresses the matter). The earlier Russian attempt at revolutionary change, in 1905, was certainly noted by thoughtful Irish political figures, for example Michael Davitt at the time (he did not approve), and Patrick McCartan much later. But each and all of these comparisons is imperfect in some way, necessarily so, for without the element of difference the comparison would simply amount to duplication. On such grounds or less is comparative work scorned or ignored.

Faced now with the self-referencing of commemorative committees, one might as well advance a thoroughly unwelcome comparative opportunity. It is introduced, but left undeveloped, in Conor Cruise O'Brien's *Godland: Reflections on Religion and Nationalism* (1988). In two quite separate excursions, he notes the identification of seventeenth-century Irish Catholics with the biblical Israelites in Egypt and, almost simultaneously, the identification of English Protestant settlers in Massachusetts with the same chosen people. In response to this distraction of opposites, he observes, "a new form of typology began to emerge, taking the Old Testament as prefiguring, no longer Christ, but whichever nation happens to be talking about itself." This is our author at his glibbest, but the point is also made in a more limited and specific form: the Puritans in England and the colonies "read the Old Testament as prefiguring themselves, and the land of their sacrifices and labours."[92] The notion and, just as important, the practice of sacrifice is the pivot on which the double flail of religion and nationalism spins.

In *Glory and Agony* (2010), Yael Feldman sets out to trace the modern state of Israel's notion and rhetoric of sacrifice in its national narrative. On the one hand, he has scores of individual Israelis whose experience and opinions in profound criticism of the state cannot be gainsaid, though outsiders might say they constitute an insignificant minority when measured against the state's military and propaganda might. On the other, he draws upon an impressive line of artists and thinkers—Calasso, Euripides, Faulkner, Freud,

Girard, Goethe, Handel, Kant, Kierkegaard, Rushdie, and others—to illustrate the concept and actuality of sacrifice in relation to politics and theology. Marx, Nietzsche, and George Steiner are not called upon.

Like the English Puritans of old, the Israelis look back to Abraham as their founding father. Ordered by God to kill his son Isaac, Abraham's sacrificial filicide is averted at the last minute when God provides a surrogate nonhuman victim, a ram (see Genesis, chap. 22). Examining successive generations of Zionist writers, activists and proclaimed heroes, Feldman distinguishes the "Isaac generation, 1967–1973" as repudiating the orthodox view that the Genesis story dealt with Abraham's burden (the obligation to slay his son), and insisted on the greater burden imposed on the youth who was bound and trussed for execution.[93] Parallels between the foundation of Israel and of an independent Ireland are inevitably discontinuous, blurred, and scarcely legible at times. But the powerful common denominator is the presumption that nationality is identified with a specific religious orthodoxy. In the first case it is simply Judaism, though the simplicity is complicated by the modern divisions into Liberal, Reform, Orthodox, and ultra-Orthodox groups, not to forget those Jews (including some ultra-Orthodox) who reject territorial Zionism. In the second, the identification is practical rather than formal or articulate. And insofar as the events of Easter Week can claim to be foundational, the orthodoxy is Catholic Christian. During the decades following the establishment of an Irish Free State (in 1922), the distinction between church and state in practice became blurred, especially in matters involving sex. Divorce, contraception, and abortion were prohibited; illegitimacy was policed through a series of "homes" run by Catholic religious orders and funded by the state. The regime in some of these might, without recourse to metaphor, be regarded as slavery. Society and government alike were suffused with Catholic notions and requirements.

The Isaac generation voiced a revolt against founding fathers. In Ireland, the insurrectionists had been strikingly fatherless. Of the principal figures executed or otherwise dying, the following were the children of progenitors dead by 1916—Roger Casement, Eamon Ceannt, Thomas Clarke, Con Colbert, James Connolly, Edward Daly, Eamon de Valera (death sentence commuted), Sean Heuston (effectively fatherless, but not actually), Thomas Kent, John MacBride, Sean Mac Diarmada, Thomas McDonagh, Constance Markiewicz (death sentenced commuted), M. J. O'Rahilly, Patrick and

William Pearse. Thus of the seven signatories to the Proclamation, only Plunkett still had a living father, the count, who soon encashed an unexpected political legacy. Of the seven-man secret Military Council, Plunkett is again the solitary exception. Finally, of the fourteen leaders executed in Dublin after the Rising, Plunkett is close to being the solitary exception. It is certain that eleven—Ceannt, Clarke, Colbert, Connolly, Daly, MacBride, MacDiarmada, MacDonagh, O'Hanrahan, and the Pearse brothers—had been predeceased by their fathers. Plunkett unquestionably was survived by both his parents. A modified terminology is required in the two remaining cases. John Mallin, whose son Michael was a leading member of the Irish Citizen Army, was working in Liverpool, and only heard about the Easter insurrection through censored newspaper reports. On the eve of his execution, Mallin wrote an affectionate letter to both his parents.[94] There are good grounds for concluding that Heuston Senior's absence in London had been longer-term, commencing when the boy was ten or less.[95] If these two absent-but-alive fathers are discounted, then proportions of eleven to one represent the fatherless.

In a discussion principally focused on Joseph Plunkett, it would seem natural to proceed with an account of the father as successor in politics and military subversion to the son. Indeed some such note will be unavoidable. But, with the emphasis on the collective condition of the insurrectionists, a more general conclusion is possible. In Yael Feldman's terms, we should not conclude that the great majority of the leaders in 1916 were Isaacs whose Abrahams had died, thus presaging an enlightened, nonsacrificing Irish "Isaac Generation." They—old Tom Clarke and young Sean Heuston alike—were Abrahams of the new style, many of them childless as well as fatherless. Patrick Pearse's general but intense anxiety on the issue of generation failure spread like a stain from Abraham's liberated knife.

The argument has been made that, insofar as the figures and events were revolutionary, they constituted a local variant on the continental model of a conservative revolution.[96] After the Great War ended (November 1918), the Irish "troubles" commenced (January 1919). Then a civil war (1922–1923). Authoritarianism certainly emerged as elsewhere in Europe. But the Irish model located its oppressive and reactionary engine within the Catholic Church rather than in a powerful state. The state complied, especially in legislation dealing with *generation*—that is, divorce, birth control, abortion, and the discussion of these topics in print or other media. Religion pervaded every aspect of policy—education, public ceremony, local government, diplomacy, broadcasting and the press, medical provision, even external relations with the United Kingdom through the "unresolved problem" of Northern Ireland. Feldman's Israel certainly had a foundational problem, Palestine and the Palestinians: militant northern Irish aspirants to national unity (more like territorial unity, plus authoritarianism *redivivus*) took up the Palestinian cause, leaving northern Protestant activists reverting to a seventeenth-century identification with historic Israel. In the first decade of the present century, rival Middle Eastern flags marked out tribal boundaries inside county Armagh.

The cultural results of this postrevolutionary situation are well known, the flight of writers and thinkers from the country (Beckett, Bernal, Clarke, Dodds, Joyce, Murdoch, Kate O'Brien, O'Casey, J. O. Wisdom, and dozens more), censorship of the most comprehensive and ignorant kind, conformity in public debate, even assaults on the racier side of traditional Gaelic lore. Feldman quotes a disillusioned nineteenth-century Russian progressive, Alexander Herzen, in words that are hardly excessive:

> The submission of the individual to society, to the people, to humanity, to the Idea, is merely a continuation of human sacrifice, of the immolation of the lamb to pacify God, of the crucifixion of the innocent for the sake of the guilty. All religions have based morality on obedience, that is to say, on voluntary slavery.[97]

Nor was Herzen wholly ignorant of Irish history, having the male voice in his dialogue "Consolatio" declare, "There is, I imagine, proportionately a greater amount of suffering amongst the slaves in Russia and of starvation amongst the Irish than amongst all the beasts and all the animals of the world." There were no slaves in Russia at the time, but the particular was not Herzen's focus. Instead he inveighed against the folly of saving the world by violence, by memories (that is, recitals of tradition) or by "*réchauffé* religion," all three remedies familiar in Irish political discourse of the nineteenth century and after.[98] Plunkett, as conservative revolutionary, was an adept of reheated mysticism beyond any of his comrades in life.

So what of the surviving Abrahams of 1916—John Heuston, John Mallin, and G. N. Plunkett? Little can be said of the first and second; indeed, in a study of Joseph Plunkett, little need be said. I think it likely that Heuston Senior remained in England after his son's execution. Mallin poses a different challenge; though both men evidently emigrated to find employment, Mallin Senior was the better qualified and the more experienced. The accepted account of his employment—in Jacob's Liverpool biscuit factory—does not sound wholly convincing, in a man with skills including boat-building on a small scale. Was he in any way engaged in "war work," a commitment unmentionable after his son's "martyrdom"?

As for Plunkett *père*, we are informed by D. R. O'Connor Lysaght that, in his cradle, the future count was visited by "two drummers from the republican army at Vinegar Hill [County Wexford] in 1798." That would have been in December 1851 at the earliest, some fifty-two years after the rebels' defeat.[99] One wonders what had happened to the Third Wise Man. Other instances of political pedigree construction are traceable, though none quite so harmonic to the messianic theme. While Joseph Plunkett and his younger brothers were preparing bombs and forgeries at Kimmage in the spring of 1916, the count was employed as a director of the nascent national museum in Dublin. In April, the month of the insurrection, the son inducted the father into the IRB, to qualify him as an emissary to the Vatican, bearing news of the planned rebellion for papal approval. This mission, of which there appears to be no more evidence than of the Two Wise Drummers, constituted the sum of Count Plunkett's involvement in the national movement before his eldest son's execution and the sentencing of his other two sons to death.

Amid the general lockup of republican prisoners, the count and countess were banished to Oxford where he spent much of his time in the Bodleian Library. Early in 1917, a by-election took place in Roscommon South, with Count Plunkett standing as an unofficial Sinn Féin candidate. Though unknown in the constituency, he won by a margin of almost a thousand votes. General elections in 1921, 1922, and 1923 saw him reelected under fluctuating republican auspices. But in June 1927, when a constitutionalist republican party (Fianna Fáil, led by Eamon de Valera) contested the elections, Plunkett failed to win a seat and thereafter existed in the political wilderness, well supplied with private milk and honey. Having briefly been minister for foreign affairs in 1919–1920, he served even more briefly as minister for the arts but never rose above the position of dignified figurehead. He did, however, stick to his republican principles, and was interned by the authorities.

In December 1938, he and six others transferred a sovereignty they believed to be vested in them (as veterans of the Second Dáil) to the Irish Republican Army's (IRA) Army Council. This gesture indemnified him in relation to bombings conducted in Coventry and London the following year, but did so by transferring his authority as a former elected representative to the (pro-Nazi) IRA.

Never a significantly active figure in the republican movement, yet embodying the legacy of Easter Monday 1916, Plunkett stands in complete contrast to Roddy Connolly (1901–1980), only son of the ICA leader and by 1917 a communist attaching himself to Leninist orthodoxy. Plunkett was not son-less; the sentences of death passed on George and Jack were commuted, and they became active in the War of Independence and Civil War. If the analogy retains any power, Abraham had two surviving sons. Their careers were welded to the intransigent republican cause; they opposed the treaty in 1922–1923, rejected de Valera's constitutional turn in 1926, scorned the leftward turn of Republican Congress in 1934, and stuck with the pro-Nazi leadership throughout the Second World War. George and Jack were both interned or jailed after war broke out; both went on hunger strike. When Jack was finally released, "ill and depressed, he found that [his mother] had taken over his bedroom and thrown out his stuff as if he were already dead." George, who wanted to become a cattle farmer, was forced to ask the countess for a weekly allowance to support his wife and children. He died in a farm accident in 1944. Jack, who survived till 1960, was socially handicapped by melancholia, "constant since his hunger-strike," preventing him from managing his portion of the family wealth.

These rigors within the primary relationship of parent and child, imposed when the children were in their forties, are no less powerful than the more tangible sufferings inflicted on them by jailers and prison guards intermittently from 1916 onward. The victims were not all soldiers or gunmen; the Plunkett daughters suffered also. Mimi died aged forty in 1926, severely tubercular and much bullied; in spring 1916, she had brought insurrectionist messages to New York. Moya died at the age of thirty-nine in Port Said, worn out by many years spent in badly planned family schemes for her future as a nun, or a midwife, or whatever might do—her last will was burned by the countess. Fiona, who had been emotionally involved with Rory O'Connor—and, later, with at least two others—never married but acted as an unpaid home help in her parents' house. She suffered from prolonged mental illness after 1940, but lived until 1976.

Somewhat approximately, one could date the more extreme of these phenomena to the years following Count Plunkett's transfer of sovereignty to the IRA's army council in December 1938. In doing so, the evidence of genetic damage arising from the marriage of second cousins should not be discounted, nor the impact of the countess's physical and emotional violence. The focus helpfully turns to the head of family if we consider an incident reported by his daughter Geraldine. She had come upon Jack, perhaps in some unidentified Plunkett property, "at the beginning of the war, before he was interned, trying to transmit to Germany." She asked him "why on earth he was doing it and he said he had orders and was terrified that he would be killed if he did not carry them out."[100] These orders perhaps came from some relatively low-ranking IRA officer. Directly or indirectly, however, they came from the council to whom Count Plunkett had ceded his portion of Irish sovereignty a year or less earlier, a council on which his elder son, George, sat. One may regard the count's claim to possess this vestige of 1922 sovereignty as a mirage, a figment of the republican imagination. But it had the appearance at least of establishing continuity between an elected democratic assembly (the Second Dáil) and the military council of 1938 onward. Jack is placed between family dignitaries—his dead brother, Joseph, beside whom he had fought (aged eighteen) in April 1916, and his ninety-year-old father. Joseph shed glory, George Noble cast shadows. These were what one encyclopedic intransigent has called the IRA's "twilight years."[101] In 1939 the IRA's chief of staff was Sean Russell, who died the next year on board a German U-boat while heading home with Nazi support. Yes, mother wielded the stick but in circumstances permitted or tolerated by her husband.

In this political murk, Yael Feldman's Abrahamic reading of nationalist trauma shines all the brighter. Jack Plunkett had good reason to fear for his life, despite his family connections. Sean O'Casey had summarized the priorities in his tragic-comic play about Easter 1916, *The Plough and the Stars* (1926). In response to the declaration, "the time is rotten ripe for revolution," a member of the ICA answers, "Ireland is greater than a mother," and another adds, "Ireland is greater than a wife."[102] The political and familial are strictly ranked, and so it was among the higher echelons of the IRA in 1939. It was evidently little comfort to Jack Plunkett or his sister that their brother sat at this higher table or that their father had graced it with the authority by which it proclaimed itself a legitimate government. The confusion of democratically elected assembly and national government can be traced back to the 1916 Proclamation. It promised elections, not for any assembly, not for any oppositional minority representation, but simply and (apparently) solely on that one (unlikely) occasion of victory, elections for a government. If this was democratic, it fell into the category of plebiscite endorsement much favored by French right-wing nationalist *ligues*. By such means, the people may become their own messiah, but just once and therefore just for a day.

Jack looks up from his signaling pad, takes off his headphones. His sister repeats her question, "why on earth?" Hearing nothing from above, no count, no brother of the martyr, no God of Abraham, they nod mutely. There was to be no Isaac Generation in Ireland, then or since. Within a few weeks, he was on hunger strike in jail. There was to be no intervention. When the count finally died in 1948, his coffin was draped in the Irish tricolor; on it were laid his sword, hat, and cloak, insignia of the Knights of the Holy Sepulchre. He had outlived all but three of his seven children, none of the three undamaged. Translations of a pagan Greek poem, itself translated by Goethe, earn their disinterment:

> From the house, so silent now, are driven
> All the gods who reign'd supreme of yore;
> One Invisible now rules in heaven,
> On the cross a Saviour they adore.
> Victims slay they here,
> Neither lamb nor steer,
> But the altars reek with human gore.[103]

EPILOGUE

Two Items Preserved among the Papers of George Noble Plunkett

The disruption of their household that the Plunkett family experienced in the years after 1916, and lasting well into the 1920s, inevitably led to some disordering of papers relating to Joseph's politico-military activities and writings. The distribution of books and papers after his father's death in 1948 added a further hazard to orderly preservation. It is therefore gratifying that G. N. Plunkett's archive in the NLI should disclose a small amount of material generated by his eldest son. Mss. 12,009–10 contain two notebooks, the first labeled Philosophy and dating from 1908 to 1909, the second containing literary matter from the following year. Ms. 12,009 is principally made up of brief notes of reading in (principally) Scholastic philosophy, with frequent reference to a textbook by Father John Rickaby, SJ. It shows little evidence of academic distinction or personal originality.

Of greater interest is the literary notebook, despite the many blank leaves. The principal item, dated to October 1909, is a short essay on his favorite author, G. K. Chesterton.

> I am, perhaps, pre-eminently qualified to write about Mr Chesterton, as I have such knowledge of him as is given to very few. I know him as a Poet,

as a Person, as a Mystic and as a Mountain, and it is mainly as a Mountain that I propose to speak of him here.

I choose this aspect of Mr Chesterton not because it is the aspect that first impresses one, but because it is from this point of view that he is in most danger of being overlooked. As he would put it himself, he is so big that he bids fair to be invisible. His literal bodily, intellectual and mystical size is so great as to make him to escape observation as the firmament escapes it. He entangles the stars in his hair, his feet tread the floor of the world, he bulges out of Space and out of Time, but he also bulges out of our vision. But he is not merely huge, he has this also in common with the mountains his brothers, he is wide, as wide as Croagh Patrick and as lasting, which is an additional reason for his enduring unremarked.

On my meeting with Mr Chesterton I did not at once discover his size. On the contrary I saw him as a small object on the horizon and I saw him through a haze—one of those early morning hazes that make for heat. I travelled slowly through the scorching day, and when I came up to him it was dusk and cool. I rested, then set out to walk round him. I failed. Everyone (save One) who has ever tried to walk round him, or fly round him has failed, and all who ever try will fail. Life is too short, so is Time. Immortality and Eternity would be too short, for he is a Symbol of both, and as such, outside them.

Then I tried to climb him. {One after another} I started up several paths one after another and got a little way on each. Criticism, Poetry, Philosophy I went up each side, but it was not until I essayed the mystical side that I reached anywhere near the summit. Then I had my reward, for {I saw the dawning of the second day [long break in the original] I saw the white clouds and the green grass alike stained with the crimson flush with which the mountain from whose heart it seemed to arise, was suffused}

That was how I got to know Mr Chesterton, and that was the beginning of my learning from him; but of the things he taught me I have only space to mention one. He it was who first showed me that the grass was green. Understand, I do not mean that until then I was under the impression that the grass was black or gold. Nothing of the kind. When people spoke to me of the greeness [*sic*] of the grass I never thought of correcting them. I always spoke, myself, of "the green grass." But the form of words meant nothing to me *I [*sic*] even though I knew the psychological of [*sic*] explanation of the sensation "greeness" [*sic*] (which is no explanation at all) and the physical explanation of the nature of ether waves which impinging on the sensitive retina of the eye (the physiological explanation of which, being quite as useless I also knew) give rise to this sensation (which is much worse than no explanation at all.)* Mr Chesterton showed me that the grass really was and is and shall be green and showed it in a manner that left no room for doubt or misapprehension. He stripped the platitude of its cloak of obviousness (a platitude really being the expression of some truth one is destined to find out for one's self) and left it clad in its own gleaming beauty, the mystical explanation of green, which is the only explanation of any value whatever.

Being thus provided with a pair of green spectacles with which to view the world (and I can affirm that they give the most helpful outlook), I {commenced} began to see things in a new light, and not the least changed was Mr Chesterton. For one thing, he looked green—green with the green fire of perpetual Spring, green with the green ocean of ever-swelling Hope, green with the green earth of all-fulfilling promise and green with the green winds of everlasting memory.

I do not always wear these green glasses (for indulgence in Chestertonics must be in moderation) so that I frequently see him from other points of view, but he always resembles a mountain. For instance, I have seen him as the Pyramids of Egypt—the burial place of those accounted great; standing strong, sublime, solid, huge, lasting and symbolic. He also contains sarcophagi; he who has mummified Mr McCabe, wrapped and coffined Rudyard Kipling, and embalmed and bandaged Bernard Shaw. Sometimes I have an unquiet vision of someone, at a date very far distant

---

*The passage between asterisks is canceled by a diagonal line, rather than the usual practice of crossing through. In the left margin, however, it is also marked Stet. It would appear that the manuscript was intended as a near fair copy—a typescript is also preserved. If this is accepted, it is difficult to explain away its bizarre tone and content by declaring it appropriate in an essentially oral performance—say, a student debate in which bumptious humor might be welcome. In any case by October 1909, Plunkett had left Stonyhurst where—to pick at straws—his reference to Croagh Patrick (a mountain in the west of Ireland visited annually by pilgrims) would fall flat. Further annotation—the "green spectacles" derives from Goldsmith's *Vicar of Wakefield* and the "man-mountain" phrase from Swift's *Gulliver's Travels* (book 1)—scarcely mitigates the pressing need for a deeper or more comprehensive response.

> in the future, some searcher with more zeal than discretion, when engaged on the exploration of G. K. Chesterton discovering some of these remains and, if they have not altogether decayed, giving them to the world for its museums.
>
> I have also seen him as Dante's Mount of Purgatory and around him the nine circles through which the heretic must climb before he can become orthodox. I could enumerate these nine circles, but refrain for their very names are harrowing to the hearing of heretics.
>
> The chief, however, and the most important vision that I have had has been Mr Chesterton as the symbol of Good. It, like the others, is reassuring but it recurs oftener and with more vividness than any other of the visions. Briefly it is his size, and especially his stoutness—Hugeness is a symbol of Good. If Lucifer was not thin before his fall he must have since become so. Though his horns reach to the floor of Heaven while his cloven foot rests on the hard hot pavement of Hell, he cannot be huge. Hugeness requires wideness, and the Devil must be thin. Slender as Satan should be a byeword [*sic*]. Thinness is essential to evil. The Scholastics recognised this and wrote "All evil is a privation." Thinness is the symbol of privation and therefore a proper emblem for evil. But great size is the anthithesis [*sic*] of tenuity, especially that extension which is most aptly described as "tallness sideways" and it is perfectly meet that it should be the outward and visible sign of Good.
>
> This then is the mystical explanation of the man-mountain, he who bulges out of Space and out of Time. "But" it may be enquired "What is the cause of the bulge?" The answer is extremely simple. {The cause presents an analogical similarity to that of the bulge of the bear who met Algy.} The bulge {in this case} is Mr Chesterton's opponents.

Plunkett never met Chesterton or, at least, no evidence that they did meet has come to light. Thus the essay is an elaborate digression away from what appears to be a false but unimportant claim. It is true that he wrote (most deferentially) to Mrs Chesterton when his favorite author was ill, and true also that he referred early in his "German diary" of March 1915 to Chesterton as a friend. In the same diary paragraph, he described a light French novel as "good fooling," a phrase that might be applied (generously) to the essay above. But Plunkett advances a case for his hero as a thinker well above—sublimely above—good fooling. His problem is that he cannot convey this quality except through digressions into greenness and metaphoric sarcophagi containing the free-thinker John (or Joseph) McCabe, the critical imperialist Kipling and Shaw the Fabian socialist. All three opponents are given a genial drubbing in Chesterton's *Heretics* (1905) of which Plunkett's essay is a shy review. Chesterton as mountain is a crude metaphor, Chesterton as funereal Pyramid an absurd one.

However, Chesterton as Mount Purgatory (though absurd and marginally blasphemous) has the merit of employing what is already a sublime metaphor, accessible through the text of Dante's imaginative vision in the *Divine Comedy*. Plunkett is not exact in his casual description of the poem—there are circles in the *Inferno*, terraces in the *Purgatorio* (seven of them), and spheres in the *Paradiso*. However, the general allusion introduces the topic of sin and (eventual) redemption, on which matters the Scholastics (none named however) dwelt. Between Chesterton and Plunkett, one may now make a simple if incomplete comparison—Chesterton is fat and a symbol of Good; the tubercular Plunkett is thin (like Lucifer), painfully so in his own self-image. The profound self-analysis that might have been expected is avoided by another swerve into good fooling: Plunkett's canceled reference to a bear and someone named Algy requires recuperation of an anonymous (and probably American) ditty:

> Algy met a bear.
> The bear met Algy.
> The bear was bulgy.
> The bulge was Algy.

Instead of self-analysis, the reader (if one was intended) gets digression. "Mr Chesterton" appears eight times, with two further variants of the surname. God is never mentioned unless "Everyone (save One)" is such an allusion.

◆ ◆ ◆

Following the essay comes a much shorter prose piece headed and (perhaps) entitled "The seventeenth day of October in the year nineteen hundred and ten." Whatever personal significance the date may have had, what follows reads:

> God drew aside the veil that hangs within the windows of my soul. I saw you as you were, as you are, and as you shall be. I see you now but with my bodily eyes—the eyes of my soul are again veiled. Yet the bare memory is overpowering. You are young, there are seven veils yet between your real eyes and the things of this world, but at the moment of my vision my soul was bare and luminous with the lamp of God. Some-thing you saw, I know not what, nor do I know the force of your young memory. I cannot tell when I shall see you again but I pray God it may be soon, for though I have but to see you as you are, you must look upon the original work of God, you must see me as I could be.

A loose-leaf penciled draft adds at the bottom—"(cf Ezech XLIII 5)," a verse that reads, "And the spirit lifted me up and brought me into the inner court: and behold the house was filled with the glory of the Lord" (Douay translation). The relevance of the biblical quotation to the preceding text awaits further elucidation.

It could be argued that this item is an undelivered (and undeliverable) letter comparable to those Plunkett wrote in New York. They, however, dealt in circumstantial matters, however vague—what had happened recently, the question of returning, and so on. The present text is initiatory in two senses: it marks the beginning of something vitally important; it initiates another person into that something. What is described as already having happened possesses something of the "primal scene," the occasion (in the Freudian usage) where the child witnesses his or her parents copulating, that is, witnesses the same action by which he or she is conceived and brought to life. Yeats dramatized such a scene in "Purgatory" (1938)—"while those two lie upon the mattress / begetting me."

The Plunkettian scene cannot be so primary, though it too emits the aura of privileged transgression. His reference to seven veils indicates some debt to Oscar Wilde's *Salome*, the first English publication (with illustrations by Aubrey Beardsley) occurring in 1894, rather than the short biblical account. The religious character of the piece is urged by the occurrence of "God" four times. But a different characterization emerges if we note the pervasive occurrence of words associated with sight—"windows" (and, negatively, "veils"), "eyes," "vision," "lamp," "luminous," also the verbs "to see" and "to look." By contrast, in the Chesterton essay the verb "to see" arrives in reduced circumstances—"as a small object . . . through a haze." The green spectacles that aid the seeing of grass as green are Chesterton's influence or philosophy, metaphors for metaphor, with a dubious reference back to Goldsmith's trickster. The "Ezechiel" item (148 words) uses "you" or "your" fourteen times. It is a concentrated exercise in seeing the unnamed young addressee. Even writing is a form of seeing. Given the evidence of the undelivered New York letters, and the embarrassed admissions of his family, it would be difficult to consider anyone but Columba O'Carroll in this role.

Between the two items reprinted above, the significant word occurring in each is "bodily." There is a distinction between bodily eyes and "eyes of my soul," common enough in the Old Testament prophetic books. Dichotomies arise and sink amid the seven sentences. The verbs of sight are distinguished—the speaker constantly *sees*, his addressee "*must look*." The second to the last sentence—"Some-thing you saw, I know not what, nor do I know the force of your young memory"—appears incomplete, or depends on a reversal of verb and accusative that postpones or frustrates an immediate understanding of the sentence. What she saw, and his not knowing what, is him; anxiety attaches to the issue of what she remembers. *Force* of memory can only imply resistance to the initiator. In reductive and crude terms, the item might be read as a Peeping Tom episode gone wrong, even if the episode never acquired the name of action, remained an imaginary one. He saw her, by design or accident. Whereas he simply has "but to see you as you are," she "must look upon the original work of God," that is (I suggest) prefallen man, or at least the man released from sin through the sacraments. These alterations of both the see-er and the seen require a future—"you must see me as I could be."

At this point in considering the second text, we should recall Plunkett's reference in the first to the Scholastic idea that "all evil is privation" of good. A source is readily to hand, the third book of Augustine's *Confessions*, in E. B. Pusey's translation of 1838, where, in the twelfth paragraph, we read:

> As yet I knew not that evil was nothing but a privation of good, until at last a thing ceases altogether to be; which how should I see, the sight of whose eyes reached only to bodies, and of my mind to a phantasm? And I knew not God to be a Spirit, not one who hath parts extended in length and breadth, or whose being was bulk; for every bulk is less in a part than

> in the whole: and if it be infinite, it must be less in such part as is defined by a certain space, than in its infinitude; and so is not wholly every where, as Spirit, as God.

Here, central features of both essays are found together—evil as privation of good, eyes whose sight reaches only to bodies, the notion of bulk. But Augustine's strictures against length and breadth as any sign of God stand in absolute contrast to Plunkett's dogged pursuit of a metaphor.

Toward the end of his essay, Plunkett mixed rhetorical registers when he said of "tallness sideways" that "it is perfectly meet that it should be the outward and visible sign of Good." The "outward and visible sign" can be traced back to Augustine's definition of a sacrament: it endures in the Catholic and Anglican catechisms of today. It is an awkward joke to propose Chesterton's great girth as a sacrament of good—presumably other men-mountains (Henry VIII, Stout Cortez, Count Fosco, and perhaps even Count Plunkett) were not so graced. More seriously, it is also an earnest of Plunkett's underlying and inarticulate intentions. The awkwardness stems from the conceit of Chesterton's opponents being bodily absorbed in the Mount of Purgatory (or pyramid) and transformed into the bulge, for the substratum of the conceit is ingestion, the kind of sanctified and sublimated cannibalism that aggressive anti-Catholic rhetoric finds in the doctrine of transubstantiation.

Thus the two prose items share a religious preoccupation, incompletely disclosed. In the first case, the concern with sin, and with thinness as an emblem of evil (cf. Shakespeare, *Julius Caesar*, "Yond Cassius has a lean and hungry look, / He thinks too much; such men are dangerous") is masked by good fooling about Chesterton, who, incidentally, was not yet a Catholic in 1905 or even in 1910. Caesar's imminent assassination is apprehended in the victim's theory of the lean man as dangerous to the state, as indeed Joe Plunkett demonstrated in 1916. In the second case, the wordily stated date at the head of the text should scarcely be taken to indicate when the event or primal scene occurred, but instead compared with prophetic utterances, for example, in Isaiah 6:1—"In the year that king Ozias died, I saw the Lord sitting upon a throne high and elevated: and his train filled the temple" (Douay). It may be a date of composition but may also be an imitation of initiating conventions employed in the prophetic tradition. The book of Ezekiel is predominantly concerned with the wicked condition of Israel and the wrath to come. It is this imitation of religious writing that, in Plunkett's piece of October 1910, masks the interplay of see-er and look-er, anxious on his part, incomplete on hers—she had just turned seventeen the previous month—and implicitly erotic. Masking is yet another instance of manipulated sight, as veiling and unveiling is.

Some, of course, may challenge an identification of the addressee as female, let alone the naming of her as Columba. The seven veils reference, without any biblical authority, should be conclusive, not only through the proximity of Wilde's *Salome* but the wider currency gained through Beardsley's drawings and Richard Strauss's opera. The biblical Salome was a quite different character, a woman who stood with Mary Magdalen and others, watching the crucifixion from a distance and visiting Jesus's tomb (Mark 15 and 16). The dancer before Herod is not named. Salome in relation to Herod and Herodias is named in Flavius Josephus's *Jewish War*, available in many translations, including that of 1851 commenced by Robert Traill, J. M. Synge's grandfather.

The interplay of see-er and look-er also turns on a crucial difference of power relations between the two—the speaker sees but also insists that the addressee *must* look at him, *must* see him as he could be. If his regeneration to be (again?) "the original work of God" depends on the addressee's response, the latter is unquestionably placed in the subordinate role of obliging respondent. A note of pleading, even of pathos, may be heard, yet the structure of male dominance remains in place. To insist on the indeterminacy of gender or sexual identity is, in effect to raise the possibility of a male addressee. Only Edith Balfour reports an opinion—secondhand evidence—to lend any support to that interpretation of Plunkett as (in the language of the day) "a degenerate"—a pejorative term applied also to Casement in the same document.

In this connection, one might prefer the idiom of "sexual inversion" adopted by Freud in *Three Essays on the Theory of Sexuality* (1905). The letters that Plunkett wrote in New York were—before any reference to sexuality—inverted in the fundamental sense that they were written, if not *to* the self, then certainly *for* the self. Beardsley's frontispiece to Wilde's *Salome*, generally referred to as *The Woman in the Moon*—but occasionally as *The Man in the Moon*—shows a face consisting of an inverted triangle of two triangular eyes and (below) a triangular mouth. Plunkett's doodles of eyes and geometric forms in notebooks to some extent resemble this alleged caricature of Wilde; the principal space of the image is given over to a pair of slender figures, the naked one emaciated and with a diminished penis, the clothed one behind him indeterminate in appearance as to sex.

Much has been written about *Salome* as a study of the femme fatale or even a new dominatrix, drawing on attendant theories of sexuality including Freud's. In the first of his *Three Essays*, Freud dealt with what he termed "the sexual aberrations" in the course of which he distinguished clearly between so-called degeneracy and inversion, and found also against the view that homosexuality was always innate. Experiences in early life can give rise to alterations of sexual focus or direction. It is hardly necessary to conclude that, in the dysfunctional and at times violent Plunkett household—the violence generally conducted by the dominant mother—such experiences were not impossible, for example in the countess's attempted surgery on her eldest son's neck glands. Her husband, opinion has long held, played a remote and passive role in the governance of his household.

The one-sided dialogue of "The seventeenth day of October in the year nineteen hundred and ten" provides through intensity what it withholds in terms of length. So too the Wilde-Beardsley *Salome* employs looking, seeing, longing, and verbal summaries of these with a minimization of action on stage. The family that provides the central dramatis personae is radically fractured—Herodias is Herod's second wife, Salome is Herodias's daughter, not Herod's. The doubling name Herod/ias suggests the illicit closeness of these relations. For the theater manager Plunkett, looking at the illustrated play and authoring "The seventeenth day of October" (Wilde was born on 16 October), Columba is the daughter the countess did not have by her suitor, Dr. Joseph O'Carroll, preferring instead her own cousin. Within this tight *haut-bourgeois* emotional society, Columba is the sister-nonsister the author of "The seventeenth day" sees, thanks to God's unveiling a window, a euphemism for unveiling Columba. The titular date of the little item is certainly not primal as an encounter, for the O'Carroll and Plunkett children knew each other virtually from birth, had almost grown up together. Does this intimacy of attraction and prohibition signal transgressive or invert or digressive responses in the youth?

Worked out at greater length to include—say—the outlawed Wild Joe O'Carroll, and the entrapped wireless-operating Jack Plunkett, might the mise-en-scène point toward a homology of roughly the kind proposed by Lucien Goldmann in *Towards a Sociology of the Novel* and *The Hidden God*? In the latter, Goldmann dealt with Jansenist theology and its "worldview" and with the writings of Pascal and Racine. Ahead of all this strode the once-brilliant pillar of Marxist fire—Lukácsian totality. How could anything comparable be discovered amid the drab opulence of Dublin's Merrion Square and Upper Fitzwilliam Street, among the Catholic nouveaux riches and the self-publishing *Irish Review* editors? What offers some hope is the evidence of fracture—for example in the poet Plunkett's dispersed imaging of the Sacred Heart, as if devotion in his circumstances could not be assembled. A different sample for analysis might be the contrarian superstructure emblazoned in the antagonist but mutually supportive political inclinations of two households, the one (O'Carroll) loyal to the empire's army, the other (Plunkett) contemptuous of democracy for the populace. Certainly, the ideology of sacrifice informs both these positions, while the economics of accumulation keeps their refined businesses in business.

Even a scaled-down homology of Goldmann's kind may prove elusive, yet the effort to conceptualize it, to choose likely zones for excavation, can assist in releasing us from the rituals of commemoration according to the rites of nationalism. The influence of French right-radical ideology (literary as well as political), the presence of Kantian ideas among at least a few thoughtful Volunteers, the perspectives offered by latter-day thinkers such as René Girard, Lucien Goldmann, and Onora O'Neill—there are others—offers a variety of approaches.

APPENDIX 1

Two Book Lists (1909 and circa 1915)

Bibliography Notebook

The Plunkett Papers in the NLI contain a red softback Stonyhurst notebook: cover inscribed "Bibliography Joseph M. Plunkett." Internally this can be dated to 1909 (or possibly 1910 for the later-entered items), by which point Plunkett had left Stonyhurst. A transcript of the page-by-page contents appears in O Brolchain's book *16 Lives: Joseph Plunkett* (2012, 410–13), omitting doodles and casual nonbibliographical notes, and consolidating some entries. Part I below attempts an alphabetical-by-author relisting of almost all the books noted, together with some brief bibliographical description, without any claim to full identification of all items.

Most of the material is entered on the verso side of pages, with extensive brief classifications added on the opposing recto pages for much but not all of the material. The system used is a mix of English letters or contractions (M for magic; Sc for science etc.) or occasional Greek letters (e.g., Φ for philosophy). The English *O* stands either for Obtained or, possibly Ordered. The letter *E* appears frequently, signifying Egypt. The total number of books listed is about two hundred, depending on how book parts and multivolume works are tallied). Egypt accounts for fifty. It is only among these one finds marginal notes indicating Plunkett's response as reader—Steevens's *Egypt in 1898* is declared "rotten," whereas Ebers's *Egypt* is "v good & readable." In describing his father's near-namesake, George Tindall Plunkett's, *Walks in Cairo* as "useful," Joseph here provides rare evidence confirming that he did, on at least one occasion, visit Egypt, unbeknownst (it seems) to his parental family.

The books marked *Sc* are numerous and, among them, are essentially medical texts designed for student use. Here is support for the hope that he might have taken up the profession, could he but matriculate. His scientific interests are broad, ranging from physics to psychology, but veering decidedly into the area of applied science—possibility of flight, use of radium, radiotechnology, etc. Alongside this "progressive science," as the publishers liked to style their merchandise, one finds as much material dealing with magic and spiritualism, with hypnotism perhaps serving as a bridge. Freud nowhere surfaces, nor anything "like that." Plunkett had pet authors—Chesterton the best-known instance—and the American C. G. Leland (1824–1903) is represented by ten items listed. We know he read at least two of these, but he passes over the legend-rewriting author's posthumously published *The Alternate Sex; or, The Female Intellect in Man and the Masculine in Woman* (London: Welby, 1904).

Given his involvement in political (then, instead, military) affairs, it is striking how few titles in the main list relate to this area. The near total absence of specifically Irish material may be explained by his reliance on books bought by others in the household. Of non-Irish politically attuned authors we find only three—W. H. Mallock, Herbert Spencer, and Gustave Le Bon. The first strongly condemned socialism while celebrating Olde England, and publicly satirized Walter Pater's homosexuality. The third won fame for *The Crowd* (1896 in English), but Plunkett listed a different title of Le Bon's. With the second, more philosopher than political man, matters become more challenging. Spencer's name has the distinction of being displayed across the page of Plunkett's notebook with a substantial listing given below. It is worth examining in itself:

Herbert Spencer

- His Autobiography 28/- net (later 12/6)
- System of Synthetic Philosophy 10 vols
- First Principles 7/6

- First Principles of Biology 36/-
- First Principles Psychology 36/-
- Sociology 55/-
- Ethics 27/6
- Total £8: 1: 0.

Also Descriptive Sociology 8 numbers & others forthcoming.
H. Spencer (continued)

1. English 18/-
2. Ancient American Races 16/-
3. Forest Races, Negritto, Polynesians 18/-
4. African 16/-
5. Asiatic 18/-
6. American 18/-
7. Hebrews & Phoenicians 21/-
8. French Civilisation 30/-

Also

- An Epitome of The Synthetic Philosophy 21/-
- All the above Williams & Norgate

Though Plunkett's Egyptological interests were focused mainly on the work of two authors, Flinders Petrie and E. Wallace Budge, even these prolific figures scarcely rival Spencer in his planned investments in books. In practice, the only title marked with O for obtained is *The Principles of Biology*, an enlarged edition of which had appeared in 1898. Spencer's *Descriptive Sociology* is more intriguing. Subtitled "groups of sociological facts, classified and arranged," it first appeared in 1873, and was subsequently reissued in parts, each dealing with a particular culture (ancient, extinct, or modern) such as African, French, Hebrew, Hellenic, etc. The prominence given Spencer in the notebook raises questions to which no obvious answers emerge. Was Plunkett's a short-lived enthusiasm? Why was it unsupported by reference to other late-Victorian and Edwardian thinkers—for example, L. T. Hobhouse, John Hobson, or the Webbs? Or was he more concerned with Spencer's cultural comparativism than his philosophical accounts of the sciences?

The seed of an answer might be found what appears the least important feature of the notebook—its listing of book prices. These, it seems reasonable to assume, were culled from publishers' catalogs or from the extensive advertisements bound in at the back of books. The frequency with which Williams & Norgate crop up as publishers further underscores the commercial resources from which Plunkett set out, sellers of contemporary publications—no Bagehot, no Carlyle, no J. S. Mill. Taking all this into consideration, the list indicates an eager mind with broad (essentially British) horizons.

◆ ◆ ◆

Amherst, Lady. *A Sketch of Egyptian History from the Earliest Times to the Present Day*. London: Methuen, 1904.

Apuleius. *Works of.* London: Bohn, 1853–.

Aristotle. *History of Animals*. London: Bell, 1862. [Reissued 1902.]

Aristotle. *Treatise on Rhetoric* [and] *the Poetics* [trans. Theodore Buckley]. London: Bell, 1883. [Reissued 1888, 1914.]

Arrhenius, Svante. *Worlds in the Making: The Evolution of the Universe.* London: Harper Bros, 1908.

Avebury, J. L. *Prehistoric Times, as Illustrated by the Ancient Remains and the Manners and Customs of Modern Savages*. London: Williams & Norgate, 1913. [7th ed.]

Barden, Hugh. "The Storm." [Unpublished play?]

Barnett, L. D. *Religions Ancient and Modern*. London: Constable, 1905–. [Booklet series.]

Belloc, Hilaire [Novels of].

Belloc, Hilaire. *On Nothing and Kindred Subjects*. London: Methuen, 1908.

Betham, William. *Etruria Celtica.* Dublin: Hardy, 1842.

Blavatsky, Helena. *The Secret Doctrine*. Point Loma [CA]: Aryan Theosophical Press, 1909. 2 vols. [1st pub. 1888.]

Borrow, George. [Borrow's books, no details.]

Brugsch, Heinrich. *Grammaire demotique, contentant les principes* généraux de la langue et de l'écriture populaires des anciens egyptiens. Berlin: Dümmler, 1855.

Brugsch, Heinrich. *Histoire d'Egypte dès les premiers temps*. Leipzig: Hinrichs, 1869.

Brunsen, C. C. J. *Egypt's Place in Universal History . . . in Five Books.* London: Longmans, 1867.
Burgin, G. B. [Novels of].
Butler, Alfred J. *Ancient Coptic Churches of Egypt*. Oxford: Clarendon Press, 1884.
Buttles, Janet R. *The Queens of Egypt*. London: Constable, 1908.
Chabas, François [trans.]. *Le Papyrus magique Harris*. Chalon-su-Saône: Dejussieu, 1860.
Chatley, Herbert. *The Problem of Flight: A Textbook of Aerial Engineering.* London: Griffin, 1907.
Chesterton, G. K. [Various books, including novels, no further details given.]
Confucius. *Sayings*. London: Murray, 1907.
Crook, Herbert Evelyn. *High Frequency Currents, Their Production, Physical Properties, Physiological Effects and Therapeutic Uses*. London: Balliere, 1906.
Crooks, William. *Researches into the Phenomena of Spiritualism*. London: Burns, 1874. [Cheap ed. 1903.]
Despaux, A. *Explication mechanique des proprieties de la matière—cohésion, affinité, gravitation.* Paris: Alcan, 1908.
The Dhammapada: A Collection of Verses Being One of the Canonical Books of the Buddhists [trans. Max Muller]. Oxford: Clarendon Press, 1898. [2nd ed.]
Ebers, Georg [Novels of].
Ebers, Georg. *Egypt, Descriptive, Historical and Picturesque* [trans. Clara Bell]. London: Cassell, 1883.
Ennemoser, Joseph. *The History of Magic* [trans. Wm. Howitt]. London: Bell, 1893. 2 vols.
Erman, Adolf. *Egyptian Grammar* [trans. J. H. Breasted]. London: Williams & Norgate, 1894.
Erskine-Murray, James. *A Handbook of Wireless Telegraphy*. London: Cosby Lockwood, 1909. [2nd ed.]
Eucken, Rudolf. Philosophical Works. [No titles specified.]
Fleming, J. A. *An Elementary Manual of Radiotelegraphy and Radiotelephony for Students and Operators*. London: Longmans, 1908.
Fleming, J. A. *The Principles of Electric Wave Telegraphy*. London: Longmans, 1906.

Flint, Robert. *Agnosticism*. Edinburgh: Blackwood, 1903.
Flint, Robert. *Anti-Theistic Theories*. Edinburgh: Blackwood, 1879. [And later editions.]
Foster, Matthew. *Textbook of Physiology*. London: Macmillan, 1884.
Frazer, J. G. *Adonis, Attis, Osiris: Studies in the History of Oriental Religion* [i.e., *The Golden Bough*, Part 4]. London: Macmillan, 1907. 2nd ed. rev and enlarged.
Frazer, J. G. *Questions on the Customs, Beliefs and Languages of Savages*. Cambridge: Cambridge University Press, 1907.
Frazer, J. G. *Totemism*. Edinburgh: A. & C. Black, 1887.
Griffith, F. L. and K. B. *Egyptian Literature*. New York, 1897.
Guerville, A. B. De. *New Egypt*. London: Heinemann, 1905.
Gurney, Edmund, et al. *Phantasms of the Living*. London: Trubner for the Society for Psychical Research, 1886.
Haechel, Ernst. *The Riddle of the Universe*. London: Rationalist Press, 1900.
Hall, H. Fielding. *The Inward Light*. London: Macmillan, 1908.
Hardy, R. Spence [trans.]. *Manual of Budhism [sic] in its Modern Development*. London: Williams and Norgate, 1880.
Heine, Heinrich. *The Works* [trans. C. G. Leland]. London: Heinemann, 1891–1905. 12 vols.
Hewlett, Maurice [Novels of].
Hopf, Ludwig. *The Human Species Considered from the Standpoints of Comparative Anatomy, Physiology, Pathology and Bacteriology*. London: Longmans, 1909.
Hutton, Mary [trans.]. *Tain Bo Cuailgne: An Irish Epic Told in English Verse*. Dublin: Maunsel, 1907.
James, William. *Principles of Psychology*. London: Macmillan, 1890.
James, William. *Textbook of Psychology*. London: Macmillan, 1892.
Kant, Immanuel. *Critique of Pure Reason* [trans. Max Mueller, with a historical introduction by Ludwig Noiré]. London: Macmillan, 1881. 2 vols.
Keane, A. H. *The World's Peoples: A Popular Account of Their Bodily and Mental Characters, Beliefs, Traditions, Political and Social Institutions* [with photographs]. London: Hutchinson, 1908.
Kulpe, Oswald. *Outlines of Psychology*. London: Swan Sonneschein, 1895. [Reissued 1909.]

Lack, L. A. H. *Introduction to Physiology*. Edinburgh, London: William Green, 1905.
Ladd, C. T. *Elements of Physiological Psychology*. London: Longmans, 1889.
Lanchester, F. W. *Aerodynamics*. London: Constable, 1909.
Lane, Edward William. *An Account of the Manners and Customs of the Modern Egyptians*. London: Everyman Library, 1908. [1st pub. 1836.]
Le Bon, Gustave. *The Evolution of Forces*. London: Kegan Paul, 1908.
Leland, C. G. *The Algonquin Legends of New England*. London: Sampson Low, 1884.
Leland, C. G. *English Gypsies and their Language*. London: Trubner, 1893. [4th ed.]
Leland, C. G. *Etruscan Roman Remains*. London: Unwin, 1892.
Leland, C. G. *The Gypsies*. London: Trubner, 1882.
Leland, C. G. *Gypsy Sorcery and Fortune Telling*. London: 1891.
Leland, C. G. *Hans Breitmann's Ballads*. London: Hotten, 1869. [Many editions under various titles.]
Leland, C. G. *Have You a Strong Will; or, How to Develope* [*sic*] *Will-power . . . by the East Process of Self-Hypnotism*. London: Redway, 1899.
Leland, C. G. *Legends of Florence, Collected from the People and Retold*. London: Nutt, 1896.
Leland, C. G. *Unpublished Legends of Virgil*. London: Elliot Stock, 1899.
Lettsom, W. N. [trans.]. *The Nibelungenlied* [*sic*]*: The Fall of the Nibelungers*. London: Williams & Norgate, 1873. [2nd ed.]
Lilly, William. *An Introduction to Astrology* [ed. Zadkiel, pseud.]. London: Bell, 1852. [Reissued 1881.]
Lodge, Oliver. *The Ether of Space*. London: Harper, [1909].
Lodge, Oliver. *Modern Views of Electricity*. London: Macmillan, 1907. [3rd ed.]
Lucretius. *On the Nature of Things* [trans. Watson]. London: Bell, 1898.
Maartens, Maarten [Novels of].
Macleod, Fiona [Novels and Poems of].
MacNamara, N. C. *Human Speech: A Study in the Purposive Action of Living Matter*. London: Kegan Paul, 1900.
Mahaffy, J. P. *The Flinders Petrie Papyri*. Dublin: Royal Irish Academy 1905. 3 vols. [Also published in London by Williams and Norgate.]
Mahony, Francis. *The Reliques of Father Prout*. London: Bell, 1875.

Makower, Walter. *The Radioactive Substances, Their Properties and Behaviour*. London: Kegan Paul, 1908.
Mallock, W. H. *A Critical Examination of Socialism*. London: Murray, 1907.
Mariette-Bey, Auguste. *The Monuments of Upper Egypt* [trans. Alphonse Mariette]. Alexandria, Cairo: Mourès; London: Trubner, 1877. [A revised ed. appeared in Boston, MA in 1890.]
Mariette Bey, Auguste. *Outlines of Ancient Egyptian History*. London: Murray, 1890.
Maspero, G. C. C. *Manual of Egyptian Archaeology . . . for the Use of Students and Travellers*. London: Grevel, 1895. [4th ed.]
Maxim, H. S. *Artificial and Natural Flight*. London: Whittaker, 1908.
Mead, G. R. S. [trans.]. *Thrice Great Hermes*. London: Theosophical Publications Society, 1906. 3 vols.
Mirville, Jules Eudes de. *Pneumatologie: Des Esprits et leurs Manifestations Fluidiques*. Paris, 1853. [Expanded to 6 vols. after 2nd ed.]
Moll, Albert. *Hypnotism*. London: Walter Scott, 1890.
Mortimer, F. J., and S. L. Coulthurst. *The Oil and Bromoil Process*. London: Hazell, Watston, 1909.
Moylan, Thomas King. "Paid in His Own Coin" [Unpublished play?]
Murray, D. Christie [Novels of].
Myers, C. S. *A Textbook of Experimental Psychology*. London: Arnold, 1909.
Newman, John Henry. *Works* [no titles specified]. London: Longmans.
Oldenberg, Hermann. *Buddha, His Life, His Doctrine, His Order* [trans. Wm. Hoey]. London: Williams and Norgate, 1882.
Pennell, E. R. and J. *Life of James McNeill Whistler*. London: Heinemann, 1908.
Petrie, Flinders. *Egyptian Decorative Art*. London: Methuen, 1895.
Petrie, Flinders. *Egyptian Tales Translated from the Papyri*. London: Methuen, 1895.
Petrie, Flinders. *History of Egypt*. London: Methuen, 1894–1905. 6 vols.
Petrie, Flinders. *Methods and Aims in Archaeology*. London: Macmillan, 1904.
Petrie, Flinders. *Personal Religion in Egypt before Christianity*. London: Harper's Library, 1909.
Petrie, Flinders. *The Pyramids and Temples of Gizeh*. London: Field and Tuer, 1883. [Also subsequent editions.]

Petrie, Flinders. *Religion and Conscience in Ancient Egypt*. London: Methuen, 1898.
Petrie, Flinders. *Syria and Egypt from Tell El Amarna Tablets*. London: Methuen, 1898.
Pierret, P. *Dictionnaire d'Archaeologie Egyptienne*. Paris: Imprimerie nationale, 1875.
Plato, *Works*. 6 vols. London: Bell, 1854–.
Plunkett, G. T. *Walks in Cairo: A Guide to the Most Picturesque Streets and Buildings in the Capital of Egypt*. London: Richardson, 1889.
Podmore, Frank. *Modern Spiritualism: A History and a Critique*. London: Methuen, 1902. 2 vols.
Pring, J. N. *Some Electrochemical Centres: A Report to the Electors of the Gartside Scholarships*. Manchester: Manchester University Press, 1908.
Przibram, Hans. *Experimental Zoology. Part I, Embryology: An Account of the Laws Governing the Development of the Animal Egg*. Cambridge: Cambridge University Press, 1908.
Rawnsley, H. D. *Notes for the Nile; Together with a Metrical Rendering of the Hymns of Ancient Egypt, and of the Precepts of Ptah-hotep (the Oldest Book in the World)*. Leipzig, London: Heinemann and Balestier, 1892.
Ray, P. C. *A History of Hindu Chemistry from the Earliest Times to the Middle of the Sixteenth Century AD*. London: Williams and Norgate, 1907.
Renouf, Peter. *On the Religion of Ancient Egypt*. London: Williams and Norgate, 1880.
Réville, Albert. *On Native Religions of Mexico and Peru*. London: Williams and Norgate, 1884.
Rhys, John. *Lectures on the Origin and Growth of Religion as Illustrated by Celtic Heathendom*. London: Williams and Norgate, 1892. [2nd ed.]
Rhys Davids, T. W. *Buddhist Suttas*. Oxford: Clarendon Press, 1881.
Rhys Davids, T. W. *Lectures on Indian Buddhism*. London: Williams and Norgate. 1881. [4th ed. 1906.]
Rhys Davids, T. W. *The Questions of King Milinda*. Oxford: Clarendon Press, 1890. [And subsequent parts.]
Robins, Elizabeth [Novels of].
Rockhill, W. W. [trans.]. *The Life of the Buddha and the Early History of His Order Derived from Tibetan Works*. London: Kegan Paul, 1907.

Rougé, Jacques de. *Chrestomathie egyptienne; ou, Choix de texts transcrits . . . fasc 3 and 4*. Paris, 1867–1876.

Rougé, Jacques de. *Inscriptions et notices recueillies a Edfu (Haute Egypte)*. Paris: Leroux, 1880.

Sayce, A. H. *Lectures on the Origin and Growth of Religion as Illustrated by the Religion of the Ancient Babylonians*. London: Williams and Norgate, 1897. [4th ed.]

Schäfer, E. A. *Essentials of Histology: Descriptive and Practical for the Use of Students*. London: Longmans, 1892. [3rd ed.]

Schlegel, Friedrich von. *The Philosophy of Life and the Philosophy of Language in a Course of Lectures* [trans. A. J. W. Morrison]. London: Bell, 1913. [Earlier editions also.]

Schopenhauer, Arthur. *Works* 2 vols. [i.e.? *Selected Essays* (ed. E. B. Bax) and *On the Fourfold Root of the Principle of Sufficient Reason* (trans. Hillebrand)] London: Bell, 1910–1912.

Shaw, G. B. [Novels of].

Skeat, W. W. *Malay Magic*. London: Macmillan, 1900.

Soddy, Frederick. *The Interpretation of Radium*. London: Murray, 1909. Progressive Science Series.

Spencer, Herbert. *Autobiography*. London: Williams and Norgate, 1904. 2 vols.

Spencer, Herbert. *Descriptive Sociology; or, Groups of Sociological Facts Classified and Arranged*. London: William and Norgate, 1873–, in parts [nos. 1–8 listed].

Spencer, Herbert. *An Epitome of the Synthetic Philosophy*. London: Williams and Norgate, 1901. [5th ed., "the philosophy completed and in part revised."]

Spencer, Herbert. *System of Synthetic Philosophy*. London: Williams and Norgate. 10 vols.

Spinoza, Benedict. *Chief Works* [ed. R. H. M. Elwes]. London: Bell, 1905.

Steevens, G. W. *Egypt in 1898*. Edinburgh: Blackwood, 1898.

Sutta-nitpata: A Collection of Discourses [trans. V. Fausboll]. Oxford: Clarendon Press, 1898. [2nd ed.]

Symons, Arthur. *William Blake*. London: Constable, 1907.

Talbot Kelly, Robert. *Egypt Painted and Described*. London: A and C Black, 1903.

Tattam, Henry. *A Compendious Grammar of the Egyptian Language as Contained in the Coptic, Sahidic, and Bashmuric Dialects*. London: Williams and Norgate, 1863.
Taylor, Isaac. *Leaves from an Egyptian Notebook*. London: Kegan Paul, 1888.
Toynbee, Paget. *Dante Alighieri: His Life and Work*. London: Methuen, 1910. [4th ed.]
Toynbee, Paget. *Dante Studies and Researches*. London: Macmillan, 1902.
Thompson, J. A. *Heredity*. London: Murray, 1912. [2nd ed.]
Thompson, J. J. *The Discharge of Electricity Through Gases*. Edinburgh: Constable, 1900
Thompson, S. P. *Light Visible and Invisible: A Series of Lectures*. London: Macmillan, 1897. [Reissued 1910.]
Trenckner, V. [trans.]. *Pali Miscellany*. London: Williams & Norgate, 1879.
Turpain, Albert. *La Télègraphie sans fil*. Paris: Gunthier Villars, 1908. [2nd ed.]
Wallis Budge, E. A. *The Book of the Dead* [translated]. London: Longmans, 1894.
Wallis Budge, E. A. *The Book of the Kings of Egypt*. London: Kegan Paul, 1908.
Wallis Budge, E. A. *The Decrees of Memphis and Canopus*. London: Kegan Paul, 1904.
Wallis Budge, E. A. *The Gods of the Egyptians; or Studies in Egyptian Mythology*. London: Methuen, 1904.
Wallis Budge, E. A. *Cook's Handbook for Egypt and the Sudan*. London: Thomas Cook, 1905. [3rd ed. 1911.]
Wallis Budge, E. A. *The Earliest Known Coptic Psalter*. London: Kegan Paul, 1898.
Wallis Budge, E. A. *Egyptian Magic*. London: Kegan Paul, 1899.
Wallis Budge, E. A. *An Egyptian Reading Book for Beginners*. London: Kegan Paul, 1896.
Wallis Budge, E. A. *The Mummy: Chapters on Funereal Archaeology*. Cambridge: Cambridge University Press, 1893.
Wallis Budge, E. A. *The Nile: Notes for Travellers in Egypt*. London: Cook, 1907. [10th ed.]
Wallis Budge, E. A. [trans.]. *The Paradise or Garden of the Holy Fathers* [in ancient Christian Egypt]. London: Chatto & Windus, 1907.

Wallis Budge, E. A. *Some Account of the Collection of Egyptian Antiquities in the Possession of Lady Meux*. London: Harrison, 1896.
Ward, John. *Our Sudan: Its Pyramids and Progress*. London: Murray, 1905.
Westermarck, Edward. *History of Human Marriage*. London: Macmillan, 1891. [3rd ed. 1901.]
Westermarck, Edward. *The Origin and Development of the Moral Ideas*. London: Macmillan, 1906–8. 2 vols.
Wilkinson, J. G. *Handbook for Travellers in Egypt*. London: Murray, 1907. [11th ed.]
Wilkinson, J. G. *Manners and Customs of the Ancient Egyptians*. London: Murray, 1837. 3 vols. [Also subsequent eds.]
Wilkinson, J. G. *A Popular Account of the Ancient Egyptians*. London: Murray, 1854.
Wright, A. E. *Studies in Immunisation and the Application to the Diagnosis and Treatment of Bacterial Infections*. London: Constable, 1909.
Wundt, Wilhelm Max. *Outlines of Psychology*. London: Williams and Norgate, 1897. [2nd ed. 1902.]
Wundt, Wilhelm Max. *Principles of Physiological Psychology* [trans. E. B. Titchener]. London: Swan Sonneschein, 1904.

Books on Military Tactics, Firearms, Explosives, etc.

Elsewhere in the NLI is preserved a single, folded sheet of lined paper, similar in appearance, size, and quality to pages of the Stonyhurst notebook. This paper carries a list of thirty-five books and pamphlets on topics such as military tactics, the use of firearms, and explosives. The following is a transcript of this list, with a few details added in square brackets.

- *Royal Engineers Field Service Pocket Book* 3/6
- *Knowledge for War*. Capt Lake 2/6 Harrison.
- X *Field Service Pocket Book* 1/- W[ar] O[ffice]
- *Scout-sniping*. "Periscope." 3/6 Gale & Polden
- *Engineer Training*. 6d. W. O.
- X *Manual of Field Engineering* 9d. W. O.

- X *Manual of Map Reading & Field Sketching* 1/- W. O.
- *Tactical Notes*. Kinsman. 5/- Ponsonby.
- X *Hotchkiss Portable Machine Gun Handbook* 1/- Cliffe [?]
- *Handbook for the .303" Vickers Machine Gun* 6d W. O.
- *Instruction on the Lewis Automatic Machine Gun*. Simplex 2/6.
- Foster, Groom
- X *Machine Gunners Handbook* (Vickers & Lewis) Lieut. Botall [?]
- 3/- Smith
- X *Machine Gun Manual*. Capt. Douglas. 1/- [?] Harrison.
- *Handbook for the .303" Maxim Machine Gun*. 9d. W. O.
- X *The Complete Lewis Gunner*. An Instructor 2/- Gale & Polden
- *.303" Machine Guns & Small Arms*. 6d. W. O.
- *Complete Guide to the Hotchkiss Machine Gun*. An Instructor.
- 2/6. Gale & Polden
- X *Lewis Gun Mechanism Made Easy* 1/6. Gale & Polden.
- *.303" Vickers Machine Gun* [Instruction Card] 3d. Gale & Polden.
- *Lewis Gun Stoppages* [Reference Card.] 3 d. Gale & Polden
- *Machine Gunner's Handy Reference Card*. 2d. Gale & Polden
- Instructions *for Armourers (Small Arms etc)*. 2/6 W. O.
- *Military Engineering*: - W. O.
- *Part IIIa. Military Bridging. Principles & Materials* 1/-
- Part *IIIb. Military Bridging. Bridges* 1/3
- X *Part IV Mining & Demolitions* 1/- Withheld
- X *Range Finder Handbooks*: -
- *Infantry No. 2* 6d. W. O.
- *Signalling. Imperial Army Series*. Capt Solano [?] 1/6 Murray.
- X *Text Book of Small Arms*. 2/6 W. O.
- *The Modern Pistol & How to Shoot It*. Winans [?] 12/6 Putnam
- X *The Automatic Pistol*. Noel. 1/6 Foster Groom
- *How to Shoot with a Revolver*. Noel. 1/6 Foster Groom.
- X *Hand Grenades*. Capt. Ainslie. 6/- John Wylie
- *The Service Revolver & How to Use It*. Capt Tracey. 3/- Harrison.
- *Muskretry Regulations Parts I & II*. 10d. W. O.
- X *Elements of Military Education*. Brockington[?]. 4/6 Longmans.
- *Treatise on Service Ordnance*. 1908. 7/6 2 vols. W. O.

- *Handbook of Artillery Instruments.* 1/6. W. O.
- Chapman & Hall
- Eisner *The Modern High Explosives* 17s net
- Wearly[?] [illegible] *Military Explosives* 12/6 net

APPENDIX 2

Contents of *The Irish Review* (1911–1914)

Volume 1, number 1: March 1911

- [Editorial] 1–6
- George Moore: "A Flood" [fiction], 7–19
- James Stephens: "In the Poppy Fields" [poem], 20
- John Eglinton: "Irish Books," 21–29
- Lord Dunsany: "Alone the Immortals" [fiction], 30–31
- George W. Russell: "The Problem of Rural Life," 32–36
- Padraic Colum: "The Parrot and the Falcon," 37
- Thomas MacDonagh: "Catullus to Himself" [poem], 38
- Mary G. Maguire: "John Synge," 39–43
- P. H. Pearse: "Sliocht Duanaire Gaedhilge—Specimens from an Irish Anthology" [bilingual texts, Gaelic and English], 44–47
- Unsigned reviews, 48–51

Volume 1, number 2: April 1911

- Frontispiece by Jack Yeats: "A Night at Ballycastle."

- Editorial: 53–56
- Grenville A. J. Cole: "The Gate of Ireland," 57–61
- Lord Dunsany: "The Man with the Golden Ear-Rings" [fiction], 62
- An Ulster Protestant, "Nationalism and Imperialism," 63–71
- James Stephens: "Bessie Bobtail" [poem], 72
- George W. Russell: "The Problem of Rural Life II," 73–79
- Dermot Freyer: "Love Virginal" [poem], 80
- Padraic Colum: "The Old Man Angry" [poem], 81–83
- Thomas MacDonagh: "Ancient Irish Poetry," 84–87
- P. H. Pearse: "Sliocht . . . Anthology" continued, 88–91
- James Stephens: "Mary: A Story" [fiction], 92–99
- Unsigned reviews: 100–104

Volume 1, number 3: May 1911

- Frontispiece by Norman Morrow: "South Holland Types"
- Editorial: 105–8
- M: "The Financial Relations of Ireland and Great Britain," 109–16
- George W. Russell: "The Problem of Rural Life III," 117–23
- George Moore: "La Réponse de Georges Moore à son Cousine Germaine, une Carmélite Depuis 23 ans quit lui a demand de Brûler ses Livres," 124–27
- Oscar Grünwald: "A Line from Rabelais" [poem], 128–29
- Frederick Ryan: "The Prospects of Democracy in Ireland," 130–34
- Seumas O'Sullivan: "Philip Sharon" [fiction], 135–37
- P. H. Pearse: "Sliocht . . . Anthology" continued, 138–41
- James Stephens: "Mary: A Story" continued, 142–49
- Thomas Bodkin: "The Royal Irish Academy," 150–51
- Reviews, one signed by F. Sheehy Skeffington, 152–56

Volume 1, number 4: June 1911

- Frontispiece by John B. Yeats: "Standish O'Grady"
- Editorial: 157–60

- Standish O'Grady: An Event of World History," 161–64
- George W. Russell: "The Problem of Rural Life IV," 165–72
- T. Coulson: "The Revival in Letters," 173–76
- Thomas MacDonagh: "The Man Upright" [poem], 177–78
- Joseph M. Plunkett: "White Dove of the Wild Dark Eyes" [poem], 178
- Padraic Colum: "Catherine Mulamphy and the Man from the North" [fiction], 179–86
- Ella Young: "The Rose-Queen" [fiction], 187–89
- P. H. Pearse: "Sliocht . . . Anthology" continued, 190–93
- Mary McCrossan: "The Operation" [fiction], 194–96
- James Stephens: "Mary: A Story" continued, 197–204
- Reviews, one signed by Frederick Ryan, 205–8

Volume 1, number 5: July 1911

- Frontispiece by Grace Gifford: "Abbey Players"
- Gerard McCarthy: "Emigration, Climate and Race," 209–14
- Gael: "A Note on Standish O'Grady," 215–16
- Emily Lawless: "A Munster Skirmish (circa 1581)" [poem], 217–18
- George W. Russell: "The Problem of Rural Life V," 219–29
- Sorcha: "Some Nursery Songs from the Bengali, with Notes" [poems], 230–33
- R. J. Kelly: "Dr Johnson and Ireland," 234–42
- E. A. Aston: "Irish National Insurance: An Open Letter," 243–47
- James Stephens: "Mary: A Story" continued, 248–56
- Review, signed Maud Joynt, 257–60

Volume 1, number 6: August 1911

- Frontispiece by Gerard Festus Kelly: "The Golden Parasol"
- John Eglinton: "Thomas Moore as Theologian," 261–68
- Arthur Griffith: "True and False Imperialism," 269–72
- Maurice Bourgeois: "A Great Modern French Thinker: Henri-Louis Bergson," 273–78

- Thomas MacDonagh: "Grange House Lodge" [poem], 279–80
- Padraic Colum, "The Beggar's Child" [poem], 280
- Frederick Ryan: "The Persian Struggle," 281–86
- K. F. Purdon: Christina Divelly" [fiction], 287–95
- P. H. Pearse: "Sliocht . . . Anthology" continued, 296–99
- James Stephens: "Mary: A Story" continued, 300–8
- Reviews, one signed by Elizabeth Bloxham, 309–12

Volume 1, number 7: September 1911

- Frontispiece by AE: "The Dark Place in the Wood"
- Standish O'Grady: "The Silent Race" [on the ancient Dorians], 313–21
- Grenville A. J. Cole: "The Lost City" [poems], 322–24
- Walter Mennloch: "Dramatic Values," 325–29
- Maurice Bourgeois: "A Great Modern French Thinker: Henri-Louis Bergson" continued, 330–34
- Padraic Colum: "Song from an Unpublished Peasant Play" [poem], 335
- Lord Dunsany: "King Argimēnēs and the Unknown Warrior" [play], 336–51
- James Stephens: "Mary: A Story" continued, 352–60
- Unsigned reviews, 361–64

Volume 1, number 8: October 1911

- Frontispiece by Jack B. Yeats: "The Tinker's Curse"
- George W. Russell: "The Problem of Rural Life" [VI], 365–72
- T. M. Kettle: "A Church Crisis in Germany," 373–76
- Maurice Bourgeois: "A Great Modern French Thinker: Henri-Louis Bergson" concluded, 377–82
- An Ulster Protestant: "True and False Imperialism," 383–89
- Susan L. Mitchell: "Leaguers and Peels; or, the Apple Cart" [play], 390–406
- James Stephens: "Mary: A Story" continued, 407–14
- Review of George Moore, signed Mary C. Maguire, 415–16

Volume 1, number 9: November 1911

- Frontispiece by Dermot O'Brien: "Sheep Shearing"
- Arthur Burrowes: "Fleshpots and Freedom," 417–21
- Edmund Curtis: "Gael and Norman in Irish History," 422–29
- AE: "Children of the King" [poem], 430
- Thomas MacDonagh: "An Bunan Buídhe" [poem], 431
- Rutherford Mayne: "The Freeholder" [fiction], 432–34
- Florence M. Wilson: "A Dreamer" [poem], 435
- P. H. Pearse: "Sliocht . . . Anthology" continued, 436–39
- M. C. Maguire: "The Artist," 440–48
- Edward Martyn: "The Gaelic League and Irish Music," 449–51
- Thomas Bodkin: "An Exhibition of Paintings at St Stephens Green," 452–53
- James Stephens: "Mary: A Story" continued, 454–65
- Reviews, one initialed F. S. S., 466–68

Volume 1, number 10: December 1911

- Frontispiece by William Orpen: "Portrait of the Artist"
- George A. Birmingham: "Politics in the Nude," 469–76
- W. B. Yeats: "On those who Dislike the Playboy" [poem], 476
- St John Whitty: "Murtagh the Goldseeker" [fiction], 477–82
- Maud Gonne: "Responsibility' 483–85
- Lord Dunsany: "The Gods of the Mountain" [play], 486–504
- James Stephens: "Mary: A Story" continued, 505–17
- Unsigned reviews, 518–20

Volume 1, number 11: January 1912

- Frontispiece by Nathaniel Hone: "The Wave"
- Frederick Ryan: "The Latest Crusade," 521–26
- James Stephens: "Mac Dhoul" [poem], 527–28
- Forrest Reid: "The Early Work of Mr W. B. Yeats," 529–36

- Moireen Fox: "Finvarra to the Mountain Ben Bulben" [poem], 536
- W. M. Letts: "The Companies of Saints and of Angels" [fiction], 537–44
- Piaras Beaslaí: "Daithi O Bruadair," 545–49
- Padraic Colum: "A Country Marriage" [fiction], 550–56
- Thomas MacDonagh: "The Art and the Craft," 557–59 (rev. of J. M. Plunkett)
- James Stephens: "Mary: A Story" continued, 560–68
- Reviews, one signed by Bryan Cooper, 569–71

Volume 1, number 12: February 1912

- Frontispiece by E. A. Morrow: "The Beggars"
- F. Cruise O'Brien: "Home Rule and After," 573–78
- Selwyn Merle: "To His Friend the Apothecary Poet" [poem], 579–80
- Seumas O'Sullivan: "On Madame St Julien" [poem], 580
- P. J. Sheridan: "The Renaissance of Alsace-Lorraine," 581–84
- Thomas MacDonagh: "Metempsychosis: or A Mad World" [play], 585–99
- P. H. Pearse: "Fornocht do chonnac thú . . ." [poem in Gaelic], 600
- Padraic Colum: "A Meeting on the Road" [fiction], 601–5
- G. Hamilton Gunning: "The Decline of Abbey Theatre Drama," 606–9
- James Stephens: "Mary: A Story" continued, 610–17
- Review, signed by R. A. S. Macalister, 618–20

Volume 2, number 13: March 1912

- An Ulster Imperialist: "An Appreciation of the Situation," 1–11
- [Anon.:] "The Need of Medical Inspection of School Children in Ireland," 12–19 (with folded inset of plates)
- J. H. Orwell: "A Note on Cucumbers: From the Notebooks of the late J. H. Orwell," 20–22
- Seosamh Mac Cathmhaoil: "Irishry" [poems], 23–24
- D. Corkery: "No Miracle" [poem], 25

- Padraic Ó Conaire: "Le Grad [*sic*] Dá Mhaoi" [fiction in Gaelic], 26–28
- Miriam Alexander: "The Sin of Conn Mòr," 29–44
- Constantine Curran: "Cardinal Newman in Ireland, 45–50
- Reviews, one initialed F. S. S., 51–56

Volume 2, number 14: April 1912

- Frontispiece by Gerald Festus Kelly: "A Burmese Girl"
- Standish O'Grady: "Paganism—Greek and Irish," 57–67
- Seosamh Mac Cathmhaoil: "Irishry" [poem], 68–69
- Ruth Duffin: "Aill and Etain" [poem], 70–71
- Peter McBrien: "Meredith" [poem], 71
- Susanne R. Day: "The Crime Called Out-door Relief," 72–80
- Padraic Ó Conaire: "Le Grádh Dá Mhaoi," 81–86
- W. M. Letts: "The Challenge" [fiction], 87–96
- W. A. Sinclair: "The Hibernian Academy, 1912," 97–99
- James Stephens: "The Wisdom of the West," 100–102
- Justin Phillips: "Government Departments, An Opportunity," 103–8
- Reviews, one signed Seamus Na [*sic*] Casaide, 109–12

Volume 2 number 15: May 1912

- Frontispiece by Beatrice Elvery: "The Members of the Arts Club"
- Arthur Griffith: "Home Rule and the Unionists," 113–18
- An Ulster Protestant: "Light on Ulsteria," 119–23
- Walter Mennloch: "The Empress: A Monologue," 124–29
- I. M. [translator]: "The Monks" [poems], 130–34
- Pádraic Ó Conaire: "Le Grádh Dá Mhnaoi," 135–39
- Dermot O'Byrne: "Hunger" [fiction], 140–51
- Daniel Corkery: "In Memoriam" [poem], 152–53
- Anon.: "Press Cuttings 1914," 154–63
- Ellen Duncan: "Modern French Pictures at the United Arts Club," 164–66
- Unsigned reviews, 167–68

Volume 2, number 16: June 1912

- Frontispiece by Casimir Markievitz: "A. E. (George W. Russell)"
- Susanne R. Day: "The Workhouse Child" [fiction], 169–79
- W. A. Sinclair: "Painting: A Prelude," 180–85
- M. C. Maguire: "New Irish Poetry," 186–90
- James Stephens: "An Adventure of Seumas Beg" [poem], 191
- Seomamh Mac Cathmhaoil: "Irishry" [poems], 192–93
- Joseph Plunkett: "Sonnet," 194
- Daniel Corkery: "Alibi or Home?" [fiction], 195–202
- Arthur Colet: "Heat" [fiction], 203–8
- D. J. O'Donoghue: "Swift as an Irishman," 209–14
- Seán Mac Giolla-an-Átha: Láimhscríbhinní Airt Mhic Uidhir" [Gaelic texts and English translations], 215–19
- Another Irish Protestant: "Another Light on Ulsteria," 220–21
- Reviews, 222–24

Volume 2, number 17: July 1912

- Frontispiece by Richard Long: "Reflections"
- Hanna Sheehy Skeffington, "The Women's Movement—Ireland," 225–27
- An Ulster Scot: "The Denial of North-East Ulster," 228–34
- Hannah Berman: "Nothing—and Nothing" [fiction], 235–42
- Padraic Colum: "Two Poems," 243–44
- Seosamh Mac Cathmhaoil: "Irishry" [poems], 245
- Susan L. Mitchell: "Light of Lights" [poem], 246–47
- Thomas MacDonagh: "Dublin Tramcars" [poem], 247
- Anon.: "The Hosting of Death" [Gaelic text and English translation], 248–51
- Francis Bickley: "Deirdre" [essay], 252–54
- D. J. O'Donoghue: "Swift as an Irishman" continued, 256–63
- R. Arnold: "The Old Folks" [fiction], 264–71
- Seumas O'Kelly: "The Ballad of the Twelve Marys" [poem], 272–75
- Reviews: 276–80
- Anon.: "Irish in Phonetic Script," 280

Volume 2, number 18: August 1912

- Frontispiece by George W. Russell: "A Donegal Courtship"
- James Creed Meredith: "Proportional Representation," 281–86
- Bligh Talbot Crosbie; "Jimmy Beg: A Munster Peasant's Story" [poem], 287–95
- James Stephens: "How the Husband of the Thin Woman Lost His Brother" [fiction], 296–303
- Seán Mac Giolla An Átha (ed.): "Raghaille an Chúil Bháin" [Gaelic text], 304
- D. J. O'Donoghue: "Swift as an Irishman" (concluded), 305–11
- "Bricriu," "Dublin-Night of July 18th 1912" [poem], 312
- Ella Young: "An Ancient Doctrine" [on W. T. Evans Wentz], 313–16
- Joseph Campbell: "The Turn-Out" [play], 317–35
- Review, 336

Volume 2, number 19 September 1912

- Frontispiece by Jack B. Yeats, "Romance"
- An Ulster Imperialist: "On History Repeating Itself," 337–42
- Batha MacCrainn: "Ireland and the German Menace," 343–45
- Frederick Ryan: "The Suffrage Tangle," 346–51
- Seosamh MacCathmhaoil: "Irishry" [poem], 352–53
- L. T. N.: "The Winged Victory of Samothrace" [poem], 353
- Roger Casement: "In the Streets of Catania" [poem], 354
- Conal O'Riordan: "His Majesty's Pleasure" [play], 355–69
- Lord Dunsany: "Beyond the Fields We Know" [fiction], 370–77
- Osborn Bergin (ed.): "The Brown Cloak" [Gaelic text and English translation], 378–79
- Laurence Keeran: "Language and Liberty," 380–83
- James Stephens: "The Irish Year" [on Padraic Colum], 384–87
- Reviews: 388–92

Volume 2, number 20 October 1912

- Frontispiece by Casimir Markievitz: "The Fencing Master"
- Hanna Sheehy Skeffington: "Irish Secondary Teachers," 393–98
- F. C. Ormsby: "Irish Unionism," 399–402
- Thomas Bodkin: "Modern French Poetry," 403–8
- Seosamh Mac Cathmhaoil: "Irishry" [poem], 409
- B. Brinsley MacNamara: "The Crude Rhyme of the Tinker's Wife" [poem], 410–11
- Daniel Corkery: "The Peasant" [poem], 411
- Joseph Plunkett: "Signs and Wonders" [poem], 412–13
- E. Fortesque Moresby: "An Aviation Meeting" [poem], 413
- Seaghán O Murthuile (ed.): "Dán ar Bhás Shéarlais Mhic Dhomhnail Chille nEoin" [Gaelic text]: 414–16
- Miriam Alexander: "Sciath na Rith" [fiction in English], 417–24
- Lord Dunsany: "Beyond the Fields We Know" continued [fiction], 425–30
- Conal O'Riordan; "His Majesty's Pleasure" continued [play], 431–43
- Walter Mennloch: "The Art of Gordon Craig," 444–45
- Reviews, 446–48
- Roger Casement: "In the Streets of Catania" [poem reprinted with corrections], 448

Volume 2, number 21: November 1912

- Frontispiece by Augustus John: "Professor Kuno Meyer"
- Kuno Meyer: "Learning in Ancient Ireland," 449–59
- AE, i.e., George W. Russell: "Krishna" [poem], 460
- E. Bloxham: "Northeast Ulster," 461–70
- Osborn Bergin (ed.): "Courtier and Rebel" [Gaelic text and English translation], 471–73
- Lord Dunsany: "Beyond the Fields We Know," continued [fiction], 474–80
- Conal O'Riordan: "His Majesty's Pleasure" concluded [play], 481–93

- Stephen B. Walsh: "Food and the Hungry School Children," 494–501
- Reviews, 502–4

Volume 2, number 22: December 1912

- Frontispiece by Power O'Malley: "The Fisherman's Daughter"
- W. B. Yeats: "At the Abbey Theatre" [poem], 505
- John Eglinton: "Reafforestation," 506–11
- P. J. Sheridan: "'Home Rule' in the German Parliament," 512–16
- Osborn Bergin (ed.): "A Hot Friend Cooling" [Gaelic text and English translation], 517–18
- Dermot O'Byrne: "The Call of the Road" [fiction], 519–33
- Con O'Leary: "The Fugitive" [poem], 534
- Lord Dunsany; "Beyond the Fields We Know" continued [fiction], 535–40
- E. T. Culverwell: "The Montessori Method of Home and School Education," 541–44
- E. F. Phibbs: "A Western Sanctuary" 545–49
- D. O'B.: "The Crock of Gold" [about James Stephens], 550–52
- Moireen Fox: "Some Aspects of the Celtic Movement," 553–56
- Reviews: 557–60

Volume 2, number 23: January 1913

- Frontispiece by Mary Duncan: "Portrait of Seumas O'Sullivan"
- An Craoibhin [*sic*] Aoibhinn [i.e., Douglas Hyde]: "An Answer to Mr Yeats' [*sic*] Poem, 'In the Abbey Theatre'" [poem], 561
- J. R. White: "Protestantism and Home Rule," 562–65
- Crawford Neil: "Hendrik Conscience: A Centenary Impression," 566–73
- James Stephens: "The Daisies" [poem], 574
- Darrell Figgis: "Bogach Bán" [poem], 575–76
- Daniel Corkery; "The Callous One" [poem], 576

- Edmund Curtis: "The Wars of Turlogh," 577–86
- Lord Dunsany: "Beyond the Fields We Know" concluded [fiction], 587–93
- Osborn Bergin (ed.): "The Empty School" [Gaelic text and English translation], 594–96
- A[nthony] T. M[ahaffy]: "The Seven Soldiers of the Northern World," 597–604
- Hannah Berman: "Little Abram" [fiction translated from Yiddish], 605–7
- The Editor: "An Irish Educationalist—Mr H. P. [*sic*] Pearse," 608–9
- Reviews, including contributions by Edward Martyn and Frank Sheehy Skeffington: 610–15
- "Sechilienne": "Correspondence," 615–16

Volume 3, number 24: February 1913

- Frontispiece by Wilhelmina M. Geddes: "Usher's Well"
- P. H. Pearse: "The Education Problem in the Home Rule Parliament," 617–20
- Thomas MacDonagh: "The Night Hunt" [poem], 621–22
- Osborn Bergin (ed.): "A Letter to London" [Gaelic text and
- English translation], 623–27
- Ernest A. Boyd: "The Abbey Theatre," 628–34
- Justin Phillips; "The New Peasant Ireland—1. Land Purchase," 635–40
- Thomas Markham: "[The New Peasant Ireland—] 2. The Decay of Irish Geniality and Hospitality," 641–43
- Edmund Curtis: "The Wars of Turlogh" continued, 644–47
- Dermot O'Byrne: "On the Hill" [play], 648–63
- Lord Dunsany: "Of Roon, the God of Going and the Thousand Home Gods" [fiction], 664–66
- Reviews: 667–71
- R. D.: Correspondence, 672

Volume 3, number: 25 March 1913

- Frontispiece by George W. Russell: "The Plough and the Earth Spirit"
- E. Creagh Kittson: "Irish Schools: An Exhortation," 1–7
- Justin Phillips: "The Land Purchase Deadlock," 8–12
- Osborn Bergin (ed.): "Two Poems on the Shannon" [Gaelic texts and English translations], 13–17
- Daniel Corkery: "The Spancelled" [fiction], 18–23
- Bligh Talbot-Crosbie: "The Story of James Fitzstephen Mayor of Galway" [poem], 24–33
- Edmund Curtis: "The Wars of Turlogh," concluded, 34–41
- Miriam Alexander: "Irish History in English Magazines," 42–51
- Reviews, including T. B. Rudmose-Brown on Thomas MacDonagh: 52–56

Volume 3, number 26: April 1913

- Frontispiece by John Lavery: "Portrait of Dr Sigerson"
- Ernest A. Boyd: "The Jingoism of the Gael," 57–62
- J. R. White: "A Ride in Andalusia," 63–67
- Dermot O'Byrne: "Exile" [poem], 68
- Darrell Figgis: "Inishgallun" [poem], 69
- M. A. Rathkyle: "The Cuckoo Lamb" [fiction], 70–81
- Osborn Bergin (ed.): "Who Will Buy a Poem" [Gaelic text and English translation], 82–83
- Thomas Bodkin: "A Note on the Royal Hibernian Academy," 84–87
- Mary Maguire Colum: "Strindberg in Dublin—1. The Dramatist," 88–90
- Bryan Cooper: "[Strindberg in Dublin—] 2. "There are Crimes and Crimes,"' 91–92
- James C Meredith: "The List System of Proportional Representation," 93–98
- Miriam Alexander: "Irish History in English Magazines," 99–103
- Reviews: 104–12

Volume 3, number 27: May 1913

- [Index to volume 2, March 1912–February 1913, 4 pp. unnumbered]
- F. Sheehy Skeffington: "Frederick Ryan," 113–19
- Justin Phillips: "Irish Land Purchase Finance," 120–24
- Lord Dunsany: "The Eye in the Waste" [fiction], 125–26
- Bligh Talbot Crosbie: "The Allmuirigh" [poem], 127–28
- James Stephens: "The Reason" [poem], 129
- St John Whitty: "The Bog Singer" [fiction], 130–35
- Osborn Bergin (ed.): "The Downfall of the O'Donnell's [*sic*]" [Gaelic text and English translation], 136–39
- Bryan Cooper: "The Drama in Ireland," 140–43
- Ernest A. Boyd: "Feminism and Woman Suffrage," 144–49
- "Sechilienne": "[A Letter to the Editor on] Art and Life," 150–53
- P. C.: [Review of] "A Celtic Miscellany," 154–57
- Eleanor Farjeon: "The Soul of Kol Nikon" [fiction], 158–66
- Reviews: 167–68

Volume 3, number 28: June 1913

- Simon Ridgard: "Our Mandarins," 169–74
- J. A. L. F.: "The Oratory of Daniel O'Connell," 175–78
- Lord Dunsany: "Two Tales" [fiction], 179–80
- Daniel Corkery: "Mother and Son" [poem], 181
- L. T. N.: "The Venus de Milo" [poem], 182
- Albanach: "Dhá Phighinn" [fiction in Gaelic], 183–86
- Sechilienne: "Art and Life, II," 187–90
- Madeleine Reynier: "La Mentalité Féminine Française," 191–94
- MacLIAG: "Chronicle" [refs. to Malye], 195–99
- Eleanor Farjeon: "The Soul of Kol Nikon" [fiction], 200–212
- Reviews: 213–16

Volume 3, number 29: July 1913

- Frontispiece by Harry Clarke: "The Silver Apples of the Moon, the Golden Apples of the Sun"
- Shan Van Vocht: "Ireland, Germany and the Next War," 217–27
- AE: "The City" [poem], 228–29
- James H. Cousins: "Three Poems," 230–32
- An Ulster Imperialist: "Half Time: A Survey of the Political Situation," 233–37
- Lord Dunsany: "The Demagogue and the Demimondaine" [prose poem], 238
- Ernest A. Boyd: "Dogmatism in Irish Life," 239–44
- Sean Mac Giollanatha: "Raftery's "Song of the Whiteboys" [Gaelic text and commentary in English], 245–47
- Jean Malye: "Maurice Barrès, La Colline Inspiré," 248–53
- Eleanor Farjeon: "The Soul of Kol Nikon" [fiction], 254–69
- Notes: 270–72

Volume 3, number 30: August 1913

- Frontispiece by Jack Morrow: "The Seaweed Gatherers"
- Thomas MacDonagh: "The Beginning of the Book of Images" [poems], 273–81
- Mary Hayden: "Women in the Middle Ages," 282–95
- James Stephens: "Jealousy" [poem], 295
- Justin Phillips: "The Transit Problem," 296–99
- P. H. Pearse (ed.): "Songs of the Irish Rebels" [Gaelic texts and English translations], 300–305
- Katharine Tynan: "Lullaby" [poem], 306–7
- Nesta de Robeck: "Walther von der Vogelweide," 308–15
- Eleanor Farjeon: "The Soul of Kol Nikon" [fiction], 316–25
- Reviews: 326–28

Volume 3, number 31: September 1913

- Frontispiece by Dermod O'Brien: "Summer Sketch"
- Joseph Plunkett: "Lux in Tenebris" [poem], 329–35
- James Stephens: "The Threepenny Piece" [fiction], 334–42
- Peter McBrien: "The Poet" [poem], 343
- Mary Hayden: "Women in the Middle Ages, conclusion," 344–58
- Thomas MacDonagh: "Druimfhionn Donn Dilis, translated from the Irish" [poem], 359
- P. H. Pearse: "Songs of the Irish Rebels" continued, 360–67
- Patrick J. Little: "Irish History and Dogma," 368–74
- Eleanor Farjeon: "The Soul of Kol Nikon" [fiction], 375–84

Volume 3, number 32: October 1913

- Frontispiece by Freda Perrott: "On the Canal"
- James Connolly: "Labour in Dublin," 385–91
- James Bertram: "Liberty Under Capitalism," 392–96
- Thomas MacDonagh: "The Song of Joy" [poem], 397–402
- William Dunlop: "Peter McCrea" [fiction], 403–20
- Joseph Plunkett: "My Lady Has the Grace of Death" [poem], 421
- P. H. Pearse: "Songs of the Rebels" continued, 423–27
- Eleanon Farjeon: "The Soul of Kol Nikon" [fiction], 428–38
- Two reviews, signed F. Cruise O'Brien and Susan L. Mitchell: 439–40

Volume 3, number 33: November 1913

- Frontispiece by Jack Morrow: "September Sunshine"
- T. M. Kettle: "The Agony of Dublin," 441–49
- Justin Phillips: "The Irish Land Bill," 450–57
- Seumas O'Sullivan: "from The Praise of Angus" [poem], 458–59
- Peter McBrien: "The Quiet Eyes of God" [poem], 460
- Edward Lysaght: "The River Meadow" [poem], 461
- Standish O'Grady: "An Irish Sunrise," 462–69

- P. H. Pearse: "Songs of the Irish Rebels" continued, 470–77
- Joseph Plunkett: "Your Songs" [poem], 478
- Arthur E. Clery: "The Religious Aspect of Women's Suffrage," 479–84
- Eleanor Farjeon: "The Soul of Kol Nikon" [fiction], 485–95
- Signed review by Thomas Bodkin: 496

Volume 3, number 34: December 1913

- Frontispiece by Gabriel Gifford: "Portrait Study"
- An Ulster Imperialist: "The Problem," 497–99
- Thomas MacDonagh: "Marching Song of the Irish Volunteers," 500–502
- Anon.: Manifesto of the Irish Volunteers, 503–5
- Justin Phillips: "The New Land Bill and Compulsory Purchase," 506–11
- J. Justin Dempsey: "The Revolt of the Middle Classes," 512–15
- P. H. Pearse: "Songs of the Irish Rebels" continued, 516–21
- Eoin MacNeill: The Re-Discovery of the Celts," 522–32
- Peter McBrien: "Alcaics, adapted from Horace" [poem], 533
- Joseph Plunkett: "The Vigil of Love" [poem], 534
- Edward Martyn: "Wagner's Parsifal, Or the Cult of Liturgical Aestheticism," 535–40
- Eleanor Farjeon: "The Soul of Kol Nikon" [poetry and fiction], 541–51
- Anon., "Note" [on Gabriel Gifford], on unnumbered advertising page

◆ ◆ ◆

In 1914, the title changed to *The Irish Review: A Monthly Magazine of Irish Politics, Literature and Art.*

Volume 3, number 35: January 1914

- Frontispiece by John Butler Yeats: "Isaac Butt"
- Ita O'Shea: "The Messiah: A Vision," 533–55
- E. Creagh Kittson: "A Norte on the Teaching of History," 556–60
- Bligh Talbot-Crosbie: "Buile Suibhne," 561–72

- James H. Cousins: "Three Poems," 573–74
- Joseph Plunkett: "Invocation" [poem], 575
- P. H. Pearse: "Songs of the Irish Rebels" continued, 576–81
- St. John Whitty: "The Vanity of the Widow O'Toole" [fiction], 582–89
- Jean Malye: "Chronique de France," 590–93
- Eleanor Farjeon: "The Soul of Kol Nikon" [fiction, concluded], 594–606
- Unsigned reviews: 607–8

Volume 3, number 36: February 1914

- Frontispiece by Sarah Purser: "A Kinsale Fisherwoman"
- An Irish American: "From 'Coffin Ship' to 'Atlantic Greyhound,'" 609–13
- Justin Phillips: "Taxation of Land Values: The Irish Standpoint," 614–20
- Liam de Róiste: "Some Thoughts on the Irish Question," 621–24
- Joseph Plunkett: "The White Feather" [poem], 627
- Joseph Plunkett: "Obscurity and Poetry," 628–33
- P. H. Pearse: "Songs of the Irish Rebels" continued, 634–41
- Harry Reginald King: "A Word for the Police" [poem], 642–43
- The Author of "Farewell to Garrymore": "Bryan Dillon's Busy Day," 644–59
- Edward Martyn: "The Recent Performance of Ibsen's *Rosmersholm*," 660–61
- B. T-C: "A Note on Buile Suibhne," 662–63
- Two unsigned reviews: 664

Volume 4, number 37: March 1914

- Frontispiece by Estelle Solomons: "Jack Morrow"
- An Irish American: "From 'Coffin Ship' to 'Atlantic Greyhound'" II, 1–11
- P. J. Sheridan: "At the Irish Junction," 12–15

- Justin Phillips: "Afforestation," 16–23
- Roger Casement: "Two Sonnets," 24–25
- Joseph Plunkett; "The Dark Way" [poem], 26–27
- Thomas MacDonagh: "Within the Temple [poem], 28
- Thomas MacDonagh: "Antigone and Lir," 29–32
- Peter McBrien: "Le Pouvoir de la beauté d'une plaisante dame (adapted from Henri Estienne)" [poem], 35
- Maurice Moore: "George Henry Moore," 34–45
- Jean Malye: "Le Mouvement philosophique en France" 46–51
- Lily Fogarty: "A New Poet [i.e., Francis Ledwidge]," 52–54
- Two unsigned reviews: 55–56

Volume 4, number 38: April 1914

- Frontispiece by Jack Morrow: "North Strand"
- An Irish American: "From 'Coffin Ship' to 'Atlantic Greyhound' III," 57–67
- Justin Phillips: "The Policy of 'The Department,'" 68–74
- James Stephens: "Four Poems," 75–78
- Edward Martyn: "A Plea for the Revival of the Irish Literary Theatre," 79–84
- Thomas MacDonagh: "Two Poems," 85–86
- Joseph Plunkett: "Two Poems," 87–88
- M. A. Rathkyle: "The Tree of the Field is Man's Life," 89–92
- Maurice Moore: "George Henry Moore, II," 93–103
- Arthur Colet: "An Odd Volume" [fiction], 104–12

Volume 4, number 39: May 1914

- Frontispiece by Ellen Duncan: "Corn"
- Alec Wilson, Alice Stopford Greem, H. Barbour, and Douglas Hyde: "The Connemara Islands," 113–27
- Justin Phillips: "The Department Again," 128–33
- Joseph Plunkett: "The Living Wire" [poem], 134

- Thomas MacDonagh: "May Day" [poem], 135
- Thomas MacDonagh: "Criticism and Irish Poetry," 136–42
- W. M. Letts: "The Man Who Burnt His Crucifix" [fiction], 143–67
- Two unsigned reviews: 168

Volume 4, number 40: June 1914

- Frontispiece by Dermod O'Brien: "From a Painting by . . ."
- Eoin MacNeill, L. J. Kettle (Secs): "Manifesto of the Irish Volunteers," 169–70
- P. H. Pearse: "An Ideal in Education," 171–73
- Geraldine Plunkett: "June" [poem], 174
- Joseph Plunkett: "O Lovely Heart" [poem], 175
- Thomas MacDonagh: "Language and Literature in Ireland," 176–82
- Eimar O'Duffy: "The Walls of Athens: A Comedy in Allegory," 183–216
- Padraic Colum: "Lord Dunsany's Plays," 217–22
- Unsigned review: 223–24

Volume 4, number 41: July–August 1914

- Index [to volume 3, 3 pp. unnumbered]
- Frontispiece by Casimir Dunin Markiewitz: "From a Painting . . ."
- Thomas MacDonagh: "Clontarf 1914" ["Supplement to the Irish Review July–August 1914," 4 pp. unnumbered]
- Anon.: "Manifesto of the Irish Volunteers," 225
- Harry Reginald King: "Some Thoughts on the Industrial Question," 226–30
- W. M. Letts: "The Doctor" [poem], 231–36
- Justin Phillips: "The Post Office Savings Bank," 237–42
- Daniel Corkery: "Storm-Struck" [fiction], 243–47
- P. H. Pearse: "The Wood" [bilingual prose fiction], 248–55
- Proinnsias Airmeas: "The Ideal of the State in Irish Education," 256–61
- R. B. Anderson: "Youth at the Cross-Roads" [fiction], 262–66

- Jane G. Mitchell: "The Devout Murderer" [fiction], 267–70
- Jean Malye: "Le Home Rule et La France," 271–73
- Peter MacBrien: "Boxing Literature," 274–77
- Thomas MacDonagh, "The New Anthology," 278–80

Volume 4, number 41 [*sic, recte* 42]: September–November 1914

- Frontispiece by Grace Gifford: "Cupid and Psyche"
- Eoin MacNeill (and 19 others): "Manifesto of the Irish Volunteers," 281–84
- Anon.: "Twenty Plain Facts for Irishmen," 285–86
- Thomas MacDonagh: "The Best Living Irish Poet" [i.e., Alice Milligan], 287–93
- Geraldine Plunkett: "To Saint Francis" [poem], 294
- M. Holmes: "Futurist Poetry," 295–300
- E. Creagh Kittson: "Ideals in Education: A Counterblast," 301–5
- P. H. Pearse: "The Wood, II" [bilingual prose fiction], 306–7
- Lord Dunsany: "A Story of Land and Sea," 318–36
- [Editorial note]: "Guarantee to the Reader," 336
- Joseph Plunkett: "Notes," 337–39
- Unsigned review, 340

APPENDIX 3

The Forged Dublin Castle Document 1916

The "Secret Orders issued to Military Officers" survives in only a small number of copies, largely because its original purpose—rapidly to sway the minds of relatively few public figures—required only a short print run, of perhaps no more than a few hundred copies.[1] Additionally, the paper used was fragile, not intended for mass circulation, and so likely to be casually damaged.

From this meager evidence, puzzles arise. Even within the surviving copies, it is possible to distinguish between two settings of the type and (less certainly) to propose an order in which these were printed. I will refer to them as the three-dot version and the five-dot version.

The twelfth line of the purported transcript of the Dublin Castle's document (fourteenth line of text) ends with a number of dots (an ellipsis), three in one version and five in the other. This is the most obvious difference between the two settings. A close examination of the text will reveal no verbal difference, though three to seven variants or "accidentals" will indicate that the settings differ in ways reaching beyond the line just specified.

In order to investigate the significance of these, a fuller description of the two versions is needed.

Five-Dot Version	**Three-Dot Version**
Title: "r" of "Secret" faintly printed, right serif invisible	Title: "r" of "Secret" faintly printed, right serif invisible
"t" in the word "document" over "u" in the word "measures"	"t" in the word "document" over first "s" in the word "measures"
Text depth 15.0 cm	Text depth 15.5 cm
Text 37 lines	Text 38 lines
Accidentals	***Accidentals***
Line 26: No	Line 14: A2 (no space)
Line 28: 4 I	Line 18: Iremain
Line 33 PREMISES (with first "s" upside down)	Line 19: permit·
Line 26: No (lacks full stop)	Line 20: all (with third letter raised)
line 37: Endas	Line 30: city (first two letters offline)

Why do these variants exist within so brief document, and why does no one accidental appear in both versions? Three incidents occurred during typesetting (or printing, perhaps) that may throw light on the uneven performance. (1) It is known that a portion of type was dropped during setting, though it is not known whether it amounted to more than a single stick. (2) A more substantive incident occurred when the typesetters queried their copy text's reference to Ara Coeli (as the archbishop of Dublin's residence): Jack Plunkett was sent across the city to Joe's sickbed for directions on this point. (3) Colm Ó Lochlainn left the operation, though it is impossible to say whether this occurred before typesetting was completed, before printing began, or during the printing process. It is equally impossible to determine his motive—had he other business (e.g., to meet his mother), or had he become suspicious of his sponsors' bona fides, or had he lost patience with the amateurish performance of his coworkers? A sworn member of the IRB and a Volunteer, Ó Lochlainn remained loyal to Eoin MacNeill, and did not "rise" on Easter Monday. Ó Lochlainn is the author of the late evidence (1947 and 1954) considered below.

In general terms, the typographical faults (including poor inking here and there) resulted from the inexperience of most participants. Joe Plunkett, who had acquired some skill using the press that he owned, was on the far side of Dublin, in Mrs. Quinn's Nursing Home, Mountjoy Square, East. This circumstance adds to the pathos of the endeavor, and may have been contrived for that purpose. George Plunkett had no doubt some familiarity with his brother's printing jobs (his own poetry, for the most part), but the assistance of Ó Lochlainn was deemed necessary, despite the risk to security of involving a relative stranger. Rory O'Connor was no stranger, and he was a professional engineer, busy making bombs in the Plunketts' Kimmage stronghold. My own view is that O'Connor's role was political rather than technical.

A quick perusal of the accidentals tabulated above indicates that all (in both the three-dot and the five-dot versions) occur from line 14 onward. However, if one studies lines 11–12 in both versions, the word "Volunteers" is split by a hyphen in the five-dot version, and appears complete as the first word of line 12 in the three-dot version. Similarly, from line 12 in both versions, it is clear that the word "Committee" is included at the end of the line in the five-dot version, whereas it appears as the first word of line 13 in the three-dot version. Even from this limited comparison, it is clear that type was certainly reset for the text from line 11 to the end, and probably from the beginning of the first paragraph, starting "The following." Whether the greater number of accidentals occurring in the three-dot Version argues for its being the earlier setting (improved on in the second attempt), or for its being the second (and rushed) setting, remains an open question for the moment.

The paper used in all the examples examined appears to come from the same stock, buff-yellow sheets, of a size used for personal correspondence. It tells us nothing about the printing history of the document. However, a few variants in size and page layout provide a little extra information. Of the four examples available in Dublin libraries, all in good condition, the following variants of overall size are noted:

TCD: Samuels 3/27	(three-dot version)	19.0 × 13.0 cm
TCD: 159 a 59 no. 4	(three-dot version)	19.4 × 12.4 cm
NLI: Ir 94109 p 29 (1	(five-dot version)	18.9 × 12.7 cm
TCD: Samuels 3/45	(five-dot version)	18.9 × 12.7 cm

In addition there are statistics for the margins of blank paper to the left and right of the text:

TCD: Samuels 3/27	(three-dot version)	left 1.0 cm : right 1.0 cm
TCD: 159 a 59 no. 4	(three-dot version)	left 1.3 cm : right 1.1 cm
NLI: Ir 94109 p 29 (1)	(five-dot version)	left 1.0 cm : right 1.6 cm
TCD: Samuels 3/45	(five-dot version)	left 1.2 cm : right 1.4 cm

Before trying to squeeze ink from these pebbles, let it be admitted that the variants, though measurable, are quite slight. Moreover, the tables relate to distinct stages or exercises within the printing process. The first gives evidence of the paper as cut, probably with a small guillotine. The second gives evidence of how the paper was placed in relation to the type.

For the five-dot examples, the size of the paper is identical in both cases. In contrast, a variant of 0.4 cm in length, and of 0.6 cm in width, is observable between the three-dot examples. It might be permissible to conclude that two paper cutters were at work successively, the tidier being responsible for the paper used with the five-dot version of the text. An alternative explanation could be based on haste in executing the three-dot version, without any change of personnel.

However, the margins have yet to speak. Here is less consistency. Two of the copies have a left margin of 1.0 cm, one copy is three-dot, the other five-dot. Though the other five-dot example has a left margin of 1.2 cm, this variant is noted between examples that share an identical overall width. Again, to contrast the three-dot copies, we find a left margin variant of 0.3 cm and a striking variant of 0.8 in the right margins. These differences were effected by the person who placed the sheet of paper in position for the imposition of inked type.

Is it possible to propose even provisional substantive findings from these measurements and comparisons? In advance of any rash statement, it should be emphasized that the number of copies examined is numerically small (although it may amount to 4–5 percent of the original print run). Access to a further example of each version would give additional weight to any conclusion, provided the new examples fell within the parameters observed above.

The identical size of the two five-dot version examples, together with the greater tidiness of their imposition, would suggest that these were produced when the team was performing to the best of its ability. In additional support to this argument, one can add the fact that the number of accidentals in the five-dot version is only three, whereas the three-dot includes seven. Of the latter, the printing of Saint Enda's College (Patrick Pearse's school, and a center of Gaelic revival activity) without the apostrophe in Enda's was the most regrettable. In noting this detail, one is of course reverting to the politics of the "Secret Orders," as well as examining its technical defects.

The questioning of Ara Coeli in the copy-text constitutes another moment of that kind. The dropping of type does not. The third incident that occurred during the printing process at Kimmage that April day in 1916 was Colm Ó Lochlainn's departure. I suggest that the five-dot version was set up and a good quantity of paper cut while he was present, and that the three-dot version was worked out after he left. This proposed sequence of the two versions does not answer all the questions. Why was type being carried around after printing had begun? Or did the type fall before either of the two known and surviving versions were fully set? These questions underline the sense of a decidedly amateurish project, directed remotely by Joe Plunkett.

There are two basic sources of information on this prelude to the Easter Rising. One is Plunkett family tradition, as disclosed through Geraldine Plunkett's *All in the Blood* (2006), a lengthy memoir edited by Honor O Brolchain, and in O Brolchain's biography of her famous kinsman, *16 Lives: Joseph Plunkett* (2012). The other is a three-page note by Colm Ó Lochlainn, published in *The Irish Book Lover* in 1954, though based on a paper read to the Bibliographical Society of Ireland in November 1947.[2] This last item confirms the proposal that Ó Lochlainn somehow was central to the existence of two versions of the typesetting, though it contradicts the supposition that only a small print-run was required.

Only a small portion of the short article deals with the printing of "Secret Orders," though it provides details of Thomas MacDonagh's selling a small handpress to J. M. Plunkett early in 1915, and Plunkett's subsequent acquisition of a second and larger press with additional type. According to *All in the Blood*, Plunkett's earliest experiments were aided by a professional printer called Latchford, who set the type (the difficult part) and left Plunkett to pull the lever (the easy part).[3] There is no account of how, when, or why the quite bulky equipment was moved from No. 17 Marlborough Road, Ranelagh, to the family stronghold at Larkfield, Kimmage, where "Secret Orders" was printed. (Ó Lochlainn, we might note in passing, gives the document's title as "Secret Instructions to Military Officers.") All that he records of the enterprise itself is that George Plunkett and he "printed the first five hundred copies." By implication, further copies were printed by another team, and this is consistent with the Plunkett family report that Ó Lochlainn left before the entire project was completed. It does not follow that the second team (probably including George Plunkett, perhaps unaided) printed an equal number, but it does follow that 500 was not deemed sufficient (if Ó Lochlainn's memory for figures can be relied on).

Desmond Ryan, in *The Rising: The Complete Story of Easter Week* (Dublin: Golden Eagle, 1949), devoted a chapter (pp. 64–75) to what he termed "a most opportune document." Conceding in practice that it was fabricated by Plunkett, he characterized the forger as follows: "romantic as is the haze which screens his memory, and courageous as was his bearing when, a half-dying man, he went into insurrection, his contemporaries very often regarded him as an adult Tom Sawyer trimming a revolution with conceits borrowed from romances."

Notes

A Long Prologue: Crisis and Criticism

1. W. B. Yeats, *Autobiographies*, ed. W. H. O'Donnell and Douglas N. Archibald (New York: Scribner, 1999), 115.

2. Ibid., 276.

3. See E. R. Fairweather, ed., *The Oxford Movement* (New York: Oxford University Press, 1964), 3–4.

4. Max Weber, *The Protestant Ethic and the Spirit of Capitalism*, trans. Talcott Parsons (London: Allen and Unwin, 1976), 224. Fredric Jameson, "The Vanishing Mediator; or, Max Weber as Storyteller," in *The Ideologies of Theory, Essays 1971–1986*, vol. 2, *Syntax of History* (London: Routledge, 1988), 21, 23.

5. See George Dangefield, *The Damnable Question: A Study in Anglo-Irish Relations* (London: Constable, 1977), 143.

6. See H. G. Von Treitschke, *History of Germany in the Nineteenth Century*, 7 vols. (London: Jarrold, 1915–1919) and *Germany, France, Russia and Islam* (London: Jarrold with Allen and Unwin, 1915).

7. Review by M. C. of Treitschke, *Germany, France, Russia and Islam* and H. W. C. Davis, *The Political Thought of Heinrich von Treitschke* (London: Constable), *Studies* 4, no. 13 (March 1915): 143.

8. J. M. Synge, *Collected Works*, vol. 4: *Plays, Book II*, ed. Ann Saddlemyer (London: Oxford University Press, 1968), 3–4nn.

9. W. J. Mc Cormack, "Notes from the Borderland," in *Playboys of the Western World*, ed. Adrian Frazier (Dublin: Carysfort Press, 2004), 144–60.

10. See Fairweather, *The Oxford Movement*, 11.

11. E. A. Stopford, *The Bread of Life: A Sermon Preached before the Irish Teachers of the Kingscourt District, in the Parish Church of Kingscourt, on All Saints' Day 1845, with an Appendix* (Dublin: Grant and Bolton, 1846).

12. Irene Whelan, *The Bible War in Ireland: The "Second Reformation" and the Polarization of Protestant-Catholic Relations, 1800–1840* (Dublin: Lilliput, 2005), 172–76.

13. E. A. Stopford, *The Altar which We Have Considered in Relation to the Sacrifice of Christian Worship* (Dublin: Hodges Smith, 1866), 11. See also A. A. Dawson, *The Christian Sacrifice* (Dublin: Hodges Smith, 1866).

14. For the full text, see Alan O'Day and John Stevenson, eds., *Irish Historical Documents since 1900* (Dublin: Gill and Macmillan, 1992), 76–77.

15. E. A. Stopford, *The Keystone of the Sacerdotal System; or, the Real Presence of Christ in the Lord's Supper in the Souls of the Faithful only, According to the Book of Common Prayer and English Divines* (Dublin: Hodges, Foster, 1870), 1.

16. *Irish Times*, 31 May 1870, 5.

17. *Irish Times*, 12 October 1870, 5.

18. Richard Chenevix Trench, *Letters and Memorials* (London: Kegan Paul, 1888), 2:128.

19. See W. J. Mc Cormack, *Dublin 1916: The French Connection* (Dublin: Gill and Macmillan, 2012).

20. Donal Nevin, *James Connolly: A Full Life* (Dublin: Gill and Macmillan, 2005), 33. On Meillet in Britain, see also Austen Morgan, *James Connolly: A Political Biography* (Manchester: Manchester University Press, 1988). For a jaundiced view, Yves Fremion, *The Orgasms of History: 3000 Years of Spontaneous Insurrection*, trans. Paul Sharkey (Edinburgh: AK Press, 2002).

21. *Forward*, 12 July 1913.

22. *Forward*, 7 February 1914.

23. Michael J. Lennon, "The Easter Rising from the Inside—II," *Irish Times*, 4 April 1949, 4. Lennon quotes extensively from MacNeill and others in the course of six rambling articles. The remark quoted here is assigned to 8 July 1944.

24. Søren Kierkegaard, *Fear and Trembling* and *The Sickness unto Death*, trans. Walter Lowrie (Princeton, NJ: Princeton University Press, 1954), 27 et seq.

25. Cesare Pavese, *This Business of Living*, trans. Alma E. Murch (London: Consul, 1964), 103.

26. T. S. Eliot, *Collected Poems, 1909–1962* (London: Faber, 1965), 80.

27. J. G. Frazer, *The Golden Bough* (New York: Macmillan, 1922), 460–81.

28. *Weekly Irish Times*, 24 December 1898, 1.

29. Albert Edward Johnson, "The Laying on of Hands," *Irish Church Quarterly* 4, no. 16 (October 1911): 312.

30. *Studies* 12, no. 46 (June 1923): 314.

31. C. C. Martindale, "The Fruits of the Golden Bough," *Dublin Review* 155 (July–October 1914): 33.

32. *Irish Church Quarterly* 9, no. 35 (July 1916): 247.

33. Paul Ricoeur, *The Rule of Metaphor*, trans. Robert Czerny et al. (London: Routledge, 2003), 8.
34. Ibid., 93.
35. Ibid., 92.
36. J. M. Plunkett, *Poems* (Dublin: Talbot Press, 1916), 50.
37. The term was introduced by Gilbert Ryle in the first chapter of his *Concept of Mind* (1949).
38. Padraic Pearse, "The Coming Revolution," in *Political Writings and Speeches* (Dublin: Phoenix, 1924), 98–99.
39. John Mitchel, *Jail Journal* (Dublin: University Press of Ireland, 1982), 4.
40. In his highly informative *Vivid Faces* (2014), Roy Foster notes en passant numerous other users of *slavery*, including Patrick McCartan, Geraldine Plunkett, and (probably, yet improbably) Frank Sheehy Skeffington, referring to Cumann na mBan as "slave women." The term "abyss of slavery," used by a young Volunteer, may disclose a parallel hyperbolic rhetoric used in revivalist preaching and exhortation—the slavery of sin, etc.—a parallel that further underlines the religious dimension to Irish nationalism of the period. See R. F. Foster, *Vivid Faces: The Revolutionary Generation in Ireland, 1890–1923* (London: Allan Lane, 2014), 23.
41. James Connolly, "Wood Quay Ward Election Address" *Workers' Republic* December 1901; "Some Irish Slaves and Slavishness"; *Labour in Ireland*, vol. 1: *Labour in Irish History*, vol. 2: *The Re-conquest of Ireland* (Dublin: At the Sign of the Three Candles, [n.d.]), 223. In fact, Connolly's use of the term *slavery* is frequent, e.g., "To The Linen Slaves of Belfast" (1913).
42. See entry on slavery in Tom Bottimore et al., eds., *A Dictionary of Marxist Thought* (Cambridge, MA: Harvard University Press, 1983), 440.
43. J.-J. Rousseau, *The Social Contract & Discourses*, trans. G. D. H. Cole (London: Dent, 1913). Swift, in one of his most comprehensive satirical poems, refers with emphasis to "a slave in power" ("Verses on the Death of Dr Swift," line 346); see *Jonathan Swift*, ed. Angus Ross and David Woolley (Oxford: Oxford University Press, 1984), 524.
44. G. D. H. Cole, "Introduction," in Rousseau, *Social Contract.*
45. *Jonathan Swift*, 442. See also Anne Kline Kelly, "Swift's Explorations of Slavery in Houyhnhnmland and Ireland," *PMLA* 91, no. 5 (October 1976): 846–55.
46. James Joyce, *A Portrait of the Artist as a Young Man* (New York: Everyman's Library, 1991), 131.
47. Ibid., 226.
48. James Joyce, *Ulysses*, ed. Hans Walter Gabler (London: Bodley Head, 1986), 17.
49. Patrick Pearse, "Ghosts," in *Political Writings and Speeches*, 226, 245.
50. W. B. Yeats, "Man and the Echo," in *The Poems*, ed. Daniel Albright (London: Everyman's Library, 1992), 392.
51. W. B. Yeats, *The Plays*, ed. David R. Clark and Rosalind E. Clark (New York: Scribners, 2001), 90.

Chapter 1. Naming the Parts of a Life

1. Moira Laffan, *Count Plunkett and His Times* (Dublin: Foxrock Local History Society, 1992), 11.
2. National Library of Ireland (hereafter NLI) Ms. 12,015.

3. Sometime in 1896, Michael Davitt referred slightingly to "a count Plunkett" who might stand in an election as a "liquor" candidate possibly with clerical support. See TCD Ms. 9521/6004.

4. The signature occurs on the flyleaf of an English-language (Rheims version) pocket-sized New Testament, published in London sometime in the nineteenth century, now preserved in the Librarian's Office, NLI. "Oliverius" (further exoticized with Gaelic spelling) is an unnecessary Latinism for Oliver Plunkett, (1625–1681).

5. G. N. P. (Plunkett), "Our Child Angel," *Irish Monthly* 4 (April 1876): 270, appeared eight years before the Plunkett-Cranny wedding, and so should not be taken as referring to the death of an offspring. It may relate to the death (from tuberculosis at about age sixteen) of Maria Eliza Cranny, sister of the future Countess Plunkett, though that death is assigned to c. 1869 (see Geraldine Plunkett Dillon, *All in the Blood: A Memoir of the Plunkett Family, the 1916 Rising and the War of Independence*, ed. Honor O Brolchain [Dublin: Farmar, 2006], xiv). Other poems on similar themes followed much later—"A Baby Sonnet" (*Irish Monthly* 17 [January 1889]: 21); "To the Children" (*Irish Monthly* 18 [December 1890]: 639–40); "My Baby Boy" (*Irish Monthly* 23 [November 1895]: 573).

6. National Army Archives Bureau of Military History (hereafter NAA BMH) Witness Statement 358 (Mrs. Geraldine Plunkett Dillon), 5.

7. Plunkett Dillon, *All in the Blood*, 52.

8. Laffan, *Count Plunkett*.

9. The scrupulous researcher Father Paul Walsh avoids any reference to these Plunketts in his account of "The Plunket Family" in *Blessed Oliver Plunket* [*sic*]*: Historical Studies* (Dublin: Gill, for the League of Prayer for the Canonisation of Blessed Oliver Plunkett, 1937), 21–25.

10. See D. O'Connor Lysaght's entry on G. N. Plunkett in *Dictionary of Irish Biography* (Dublin: Royal Irish Academy, 2009), 8: 178–79.

11. Muckross was sold to the Dominican order of nuns in 1901 for £4,000—see Dublin Registry of Deeds: 1901: 11:175. In the memorial there is a scribal error resulting in a reference to Joseph Mary Plunkett as a party to the sale: his mother, Josephine Mary Plunkett, is intended throughout.

12. See *Daily Herald* (Dublin), 27 October 1913; also Padraig Yeates, *Lockout, Dublin 1913* (Dublin: Gill and Macmillan, 2000), 109.

13. Belvedere College Register. I am grateful to Oliver Murphy, archivist and mathematics teacher, for his assistance in this matter.

14. Jack Plunkett, in a statement recorded in 1951, makes a curious reference to friends of the family named Gurrin, who ran a translating agency in London. "Old Tom Gurrin was the best authority in England on handwriting. Not so long ago we had occasion to consult the firm about an obscure clause in my mother's will." See NAA BMH Witness Statement 488, 7.

15. NLI Ms. 11,389. Among the notes that frame this account of the Dutch Protestant's commercial duplicity, one finds Plunkett also taking into account the use of false place-names for the protection of the Douai Bible (that is, the English translation used by Catholics). False imprints were commonplace deceptions practiced during the centuries of religious intolerance.

16. *Irish Times*, 14 December 1907, 9. The letter purported to come from the United Irish Land League, an otherwise unknown organization, and may have been circulated to discredit the United Irish League.

17. Neither James Greenan (age sixty-three) nor his son, John (age thirty), declared themselves speakers of Irish in the 1911 census.

18. George Noble Plunkett, "A Personal Note on Joseph Mary Plunkett," *Ireland American Review* no. 1 (1938): 103–4. Italics added for clarity's sake.

19. Geraldine Plunkett, "Joseph Plunkett: Origins and Background," *University Review* 1 (1957), no. 11: 40.

20. Bodkin's account is re-reprinted in Richard Ellmann, *James Joyce* (New York: Oxford University Press, 1959), 49.

21. NLI Ms. 12,011.

22. G. N. Reddin, "Joseph Mary Plunkett: I, The Man," *Belvederian* 4, no. 3 (1917): 1–2.

23. Austin Clarke, "Joseph Mary Plunkett: II, The Poet," *Belvederian* 4, no. 3 (1917): 5.

24. NLI Ms. 10,999 (iii), JMP to Countess Josephine Plunkett, 11 December 1904.

25. Plunkett Dillon, *All in the Blood*, 70.

26. For a full account of this category, see H. J. A. Sire, *Gentlemen Philosophers: Catholic Higher Studies at Liège and Stonyhurst College, 1774–1916* (Worthing, West Sussex: Churchman, 1988).

27. I am grateful to the Stonyhurst archivist, David Knight, for details of Plunkett's years at the college. Geraldine Plunkett Dillon suggests that her brother "was put in the Philosophers' class: ordinary school would have been too hard for him." It is not clear whether the rigors alluded to were those of the Jesuit curriculum (which he had not completed at Belvedere) or the playing field.

28. Peter Daybell, *With a Smile and a Wave: The Life of Captain John Aidan Liddell, VC MC* (Barnsley: Pen & Sword, 2005), 57. (Liddell was a contemporary of Plunkett's at Stonyhurst.)

29. NLI Ms. 10,999 (iii), JMP to Philomena Plunkett, 12 October 1906.

30. TCD Ms. 10,076/19/7.

31. NLI Ms. 5021, ff. 76–78.

32. NLI Ms. 12,009, f. 22.

33. Curly brackets have been used throughout the book to indicate canceled phrases in the original sources.

34. Other titles by Flint include *The Philosophy of History in Europe* (1874), *Theism* (1877), *Vico* (1884), *Historical Philosophy in France* (1894), and *Philosophy as Scientia Scientarum* (1904). Flint's interests included sociology.

35. Sire, *Gentlemen Philosophers*, 62–63.

36. David Knight to the present writer, 23 March 2006. For an example of the legend, see Oliver Murphy, ed. *The Cruel Clouds of War* (Dublin: Belvedere Museum, 2003), 83.

37. Daybell, *With a Smile*, 62–63.

38. A. R. Waller, ed., *Steps to the Temple* (Cambridge: Cambridge University Press, 1904). Preserved in NLI.

39. Geraldine Plunkett, "Joseph Plunkett," 40. See also Plunkett Dillon, *All in the Blood*, 102–5 where Joe's stay with the Raffertys is said to have been a year in duration.

40. NLI Ms. 10,999 (v). The poem survives as a fair copy and may predate in composition the circumstances of its preservation with "The New Judas" dated 24 October 1913.

41. Plunkett Dillon, *All in the Blood*, 114.

42. Ibid., 39.

43. See John Mitchel, *Jail Journal* (Dublin: University Press of Ireland, 1982), esp. chapter 5 (74–93).

44. Bertie may be Bernard Sheridan (born c. 1890), brother of Sylvia Sheridan, in whom Joe Plunkett took a romantic interest; Bernard Sheridan was a medical student at TCD.

45. For Moloney's account of Joyce and Skeffington, see Andrée Sheehy Skeffington, *Skeff: A Life of Owen Sheehy Skeffington, 1909–1970* (Dublin: Lilliput, 1991), 10.

46. Plunkett Dillon, *All in the Blood*, 145.

47. Johann Norstedt, *Thomas MacDonagh: A Critical Biography* (Charlottesville: University Press of Virginia, 1980), 46–51.

48. Karl Marx, "The 18th Brumaire of Louis Bonaparte," in Marx, *Surveys from Exile*, ed. David Fernbach (London: Allan Lane, 1973), 147.

49. W. J. Mc Cormack, *Blood Kindred: W. B. Yeats, the Life, the Death, the Politics* (London: Pimlico, 2005), 153.

50. NLI Ms. 10,999 (iv) notebook. Sylvia Mabel Sheridan (born 1889) was the daughter of Francis Sheridan, chief clerk at the Estates Branch of the Congested Districts Board. The family lived on Pembroke Road.

51. NLI Ms. 10,999 (iii) from Falcarragh, county Donegal, JMP to Countess Josephine Plunkett ("a mathair dilis," or Dear Mother); the text throughout is in English.

52. Plunkett Dillon, *All in the Blood*, 117.

53. Geraldine Plunkett, foreword, *The Poems of Joseph Mary Plunkett*, ed. Geraldine Plunkett (Dublin: Talbot Press, 1916), viii.

54. NLI Ms. 10,999 (iii), JMP to Countess Josephine Plunkett, 29 October 1911.

55. Two sets of proofs are preserved in NLI Ms. 10,999 (viii) together with letters from George Roberts in which it is noted that the proofs were to be sent to No. 63, Fitzwilliam Street. This could be an error of Roberts's—he was prone to error.

56. NLI Ms. 10,999 (iii), JMP to "A chara" (friend, the addressee is obviously Thomas MacDonagh, dated "Samhain" (November) 1911.

57. Plunkett Dillon, *All in the Blood*, 118.

58. Marie O'Neill, *Grace Gifford and Irish Freedom: Tragic Bride of 1916* (Dublin: Irish Academic Press, 2000), 12.

59. See Donal Nevin, *James Connolly: "A Full Life"* (Dublin: Gill and Macmillan, 2005), 397, 403–4.

60. National Archives (Kew) HO 45/10665/216252.

61. Plunkett Dillon, *All in the Blood*, 125.

62. Ibid., 125–27.

63. Ibid., 80, 143, 83, 166.

64. Ibid., 61 (caption), 316–17.

65. Geraldine Plunkett Dillon indicates that, at the commencement of Joe's printing operations, texts were set up in linotype by "the printer, Mr Latchford" and the printed sheets pulled by Joe; see Plunkett Dillon, *All in the Blood*, 136.

66. Charles Townshend, *Easter 1916: The Irish Rebellion* (London: Allan Lane, 2005), 413 (where Plunkett is also credited with graduating from UCD in 1909). In 1908 Moloney certainly encountered a couple named Plunkett at a nursing home that they ran on the edge of the western desert; see NLI Ms. 21,629. Honor O Brolchain (23 January 2015) suggests that this may relate to the family of Patrick Plunkett, half-brother of the count.

67. When inspected in September 2006, both of these items were preserved in NLI at LO 1,554 (though one was officially missing).

68. Plunkett Dillon, *All in the Blood*, 84.

69. NLI Ms. 10,999 (xi).

70. Patricia Boylan, *All Cultivated People: A History of the United Arts Club, Dublin* (Gerrards Cross: Smythe, 1988), 42–44; see also *Irish Freedom*, issue for May 1911.

71. Ellen Duncan, "Modern French Pictures at the United Arts Club," *Irish Review* 2, no. 15 (May 1912): 166.

72. See the political articles by Péguy collected by Denise Mayer, *La République . . . notre royaume de France* (Paris: Gallimard, 1946), 319.

73. Plunkett Dillon, *All in the Blood*, 132.

74. G. K. Chesterton, *The Man Who Was Thursday: A Nightmare* (New York: Modern Library, 2001), 74.

75. Ibid., 79.

76. Ibid., 45, 21.

77. Plunkett Dillon, *All in the Blood*, 195.

78. Martin Gardner in G. K. Chesterton, *The Napoleon of Notting Hill* (Mineola: Dover, 1991), xviii.

79. Chesterton, *Napoleon of Notting Hill*, 24.

80. Ibid., 78, 95.

81. For comment on some Irish unionist interests, see Jeremy Smith, *The Tories and Ireland, 1910–1914: Conservative Party Politics and the Home Rule Crisis* (Dublin: Irish Academic Press, 2000), 85.

82. A. N. Wilson, *Hilaire Belloc* (Harmondsworth: Penguin, 1986), 184.

83. British Library (hereafter BL) Add Ms. 73454.

84. H. G. Wells, *Little Wars* (London: Palmer, 1913).

85. Plunkett Dillon, *All in the Blood*, 132.

86. Ibid., 166–67. One wonders if Mrs. Dillon's memory may have inadvertently confused two visits by Asquith; in July 1912, the new prime minister was pursued by English suffragettes who had traveled over to extend their campaign to Ireland. This would have provided a more apt context

for Little Snowdrop's message, though, by that date, the actual messenger would have been seventeen or eighteen years old.

87. Chesterton, *Man Who Was Thursday*, 161.

88. Plunkett Dillon, *All in the Blood*, 157.

89. For a succinct account of the spiders' web, see Patrick Maume, *The Long Gestation: Irish Nationalist Life, 1891–1916* (Dublin: Gill and Macmillan, 1999), 63–65.

90. Honor O Brolchain, *16 Lives: Joseph Plunkett* (Dublin: O'Brien Press, 2012), 217.

91. In addition, the committee issued a printed appeal to Dublin citizens seeking support for a truce in the dispute; the document was signed by Kettle, Dillon. and Plunkett (see NLI EPH B522).

92. *Irish Times*, 1 November 1913, 12.

93. See Yeates, *Lockout Dublin 1913*, 379–84.

94. Plunkett Dillon, *All in the Blood* 148.

95. NLI Ms. 10,999 (iii).

96. Robert Gittings, ed., *Letters of John Keats* (Oxford: Oxford University Press, 1970), 271.

97. NLI Ms. 10,999 (xi).

98. See O'Carroll material in the T. P. C. Kirkpatrick files, Royal College of Physicians in Ireland. The honor was Commander of the Most Excellent Order of the British Empire.

99. Nuala O'Carroll married Captain Alan Nihil, and later became Lady Nihil.

100. For a short autobiographical essay by Charles Plunkett, see Paul Avrich, ed., *Anarchist Voices: An Oral History of Anarchism in America* (Oakland, CA: AK, 2005), 214–19. In summary, Charles Robert Plunkett (1892–unknown), wrote "Dynamite!" and other pieces for Emma Goldman. See *Anarchy!: An Anthology of Emma Goldman's Mother Earth*, ed. Peter Glassgold (Berkeley, CA: Counterpoint, 2012). These circles and their journals brought together many leading writers, including Eugene O'Neill, Katherine Anne Porter, and even Padraic Colum. C. R. Plunkett married Helen Rebecca (Becky) Edelsohn, and they had a son, Robert Plunkett (1919–unknown), who became an engineer. C. R. Plunkett was a professor of biology in New York University.

101. J. F. O'Carroll to T. P. C. Kirkpatrick, 18 September 1915. Royal College of Physicians.

102. Communication from Honor O Brolchain, January 2015.

103. Paul Avrich, *The Modern School Movement: Anarchism and Education in the United States* (Oakland, CA: AK, 2006), 190–91.

104. For a series of letters addressed to Joseph O'Carroll, see "Some Letters of George Sterling," *California Historical Society Quarterly*, ed. John R. Dunbar, 40, no. 2 (June 1961): 137–55. In 1925, Blanaid O'Carroll married Herbert Alen-Buckley, of Cultra House, county Down. The officiant was her father's brother, Reverend C. W. O'Carroll.

105. NLI Ms. 10,999 (iii), JMP to Countess Josephine Plunkett, 24 September 1909; the practice of indicating an aspirated consonant by placing a dot over it, current in Plunkett's day, has now been replaced by use of the letter *h* after the consonant in question. Here, and throughout the present work, the latter-day usage is silently imposed. Reference to the "modh direch" probably relates to a textbook by John P. Henry for children learning Irish, *An Modh Direach chun na Gaedhilge d'Fhoghluim* (Dublin: Gill, 1905 and subsequent editions).

106. Plunkett Dillon, *All in the Blood*, 110.

107. Plunkett Dillon, *All in the Blood*, 139–41.

108. See the excellent article in Theo Snoddy, *Dictionary of Irish Artists: 20th Century*, 2nd ed. (Dublin: Merlin, 2002), 188–90. In the 1911 census, both parents of the Gifford girls are listed in their Palmerstown Road residence; no sign of the sons. One of these, Claude, had already married and set up his own home nearby.

109. Plunkett Dillon, *All in the Blood*, 196.

110. NAA BMH Witness Statement 358 (Mrs. Geraldine Plunkett Dillon), 6.

111. If we assume that the note on the brown envelope was written by a member of the Plunkett family, summarizing its long-held view of the three documents, then we are more or less obliged to accept the interpretation that Plunkett never sent them to Columba O'Carroll and (less absolutely) that he never intended to send them. The diary for 1911 makes clear that he and she did correspond at that time, but no letters on either side have come to notice.

112. Upper Fitzwilliam Street and Merrion Square are not far apart. While the two families (also the children) knew each other prior to the meeting of Joe and Columba in the west of Ireland, the emotional drama that Plunkett's poetry creates requires a late-adolescent first encounter or some other traumatic occurrence. This is closer to Paolo and Francesca than Romeo and Juliet.

113. NLI Ms. 10,999 (ii), draft letter dated 7 September 1915.

114. In the possession of Honor O Brolchain.

115. The lines come from the second section of Patmore's "Aetna and the Moon," which is canto 7, book 1 of *The Angel in the House*.

116. NLI Ms. 10,999 (ii), draft letter dated "a week before your 22nd Birthday."

117. NLI Ms. 10,999 (ii), draft letter beginning, "He said something like this." Most of these names are unproblematic as to referents; "Apothecary Theory" may echo an "old saying" recorded or invented by Plunkett—"They say the toad sold her soul to the Apothecary for a crimson cloth." (See NLI Ms. 10,999 (iv).

118. Robert Cortes Holliday, *Joyce Kilmer* (London: Hodder & Stoughton, 1917), 1:55, 77.

119. NLI Ms. 10,999 (xi).

120. NAA BMH Witness Statement 257 (Mrs. Grace Plunkett).

121. William J. Feeney, *Drama in Hardwicke Street: A History of the Irish Theatre Company* (Rutherford, NJ: Fairleigh Dickinson University Press, 1984), 185, 237, 260–61.

122. Guest published material on the botany of Iraq, on which he was something of an expert. Less professionally, he advised Lady Ethel Stephana Drower (1879–unknown) on botanical matters related to her book, *Peacock Angel: Being Some Account of the Secret Cults and Their Sanctuaries* (London: Murray, 1941). After service in the Middle East, he took up a post at Kew Gardens, c. 1958.

123. Dr. Tarif Khalidi, of the American University in Beirut, has very helpfully commented in the following terms: "As a preliminary observation, these gradations of love were quite common in pre-modern Arabic treatises on love. Because of the spelling, it looks as if Plunkett plucked them out of a French orientalist work. Conceivably, given the date, this could have been the edition of a very famous treatise on love by Ibn Hazm 994–1064 AD) by the orientalist D. K. Petrov (1872–1925), with an introduction in French, published in Leiden in 1914. In addition to Petrov

and Ibn Hazm, these gradations of love were also quite common in classical Arabic dictionaries of synonyms unlikely to have been the source of Plunkett's list." Email to the author, 9 February 2015.

124. The sexual element is found in Plunkett's deliberate reference to Yeats's childlessness, not use of the term "queer."

125. Until the issue is resolved in some other way, I assume that this work is essentially Plunkett's own composition and not a translation. An Arab poet of the name Ahmed Bey Chawky is described as contemporary in a Project Gutenberg online anthology.

126. I have placed the stress mark invariably over a vowel, though in some cases (six, five, are examples) the mark is clearly placed over a neighboring consonant.

127. Bertram D, Lewin, *The Psycho-analysis of Elation* (London: Hogarth Press, 1951), 166.

128. Plunkett to Aidan MacCabe, 22 August 1913; this correspondence is quoted by kind permission of Honor O Brolchain, in whose possession it is preserved.

129. Plunkett to MacCabe, 27 August 1913.

130. Plunkett to MacCabe, 16 October 1913.

131. O Brolchain, *16 Lives*, 253.

132. Terence Denman, *A Lonely Grave* (Dublin: Irish Academic Press, 1995), 123.

133. James Creed Meredith, *Proportional Representation in Ireland* (Dublin: Ponsonby; London: Simpkin, Marshall, 1913). On d'Hondt, see 38. The book was noticed in *The Irish Review* by Frank Cruise O'Brien with little warmth (3, no. 32 [October 1913]: 439–40).

134. Immanuel Kant, *Critique of Practical Reason and Other Works on the Theory of Ethics*, trans. T. K Abbott, 6th ed. (London: Longmans, 1909), 38.

135. Kant, *Critique of Practical Reason*, 26.

136. Marnie Hay, *Bulmer Hobson and the Nationalist Movement in Twentieth-Century Ireland* (Manchester: Manchester University Press, 2009), 141, 152.

137. *Mind* (new series) 21, no. 84 (October 1912).

138. T. K. Abbott, *Sight and Touch: An Attempt to Disprove the Received (or Berkeleian) Theory of Vision* (London: Longman, 1864).

139. J. P. Mahaffy, "Kant and His Fortunes in England," *Princeton Review* no. 2 (1878): 204–38, 230.

140. Immanuel Kant, *The Critique of Aesthetic Judgment*, trans. J. C. Meredith with additional material (Oxford: Clarendon Press, 1911), 263.

141. *Journal of Philosophy* 20, no. 26 (20 December 1922): 718.

142. See Bulmer Hobson, *Ireland, Yesterday and Tomorrow* (Tralee: Anvil Books, 1968), 66–67. The *Memoirs of Brigadier-General Gordon Shephard* were posthumously and privately printed in 1924, by another chameleon figure of Anglo-Irish gentry involvement in the conflicts of 1912–1922, Shane Leslie.

143. See Hilary Pyle, *Cesca's Diary, 1913–1916: Where Art and Nationalism Meet* (Dublin: Woodfield Press, 2005).

144. See *Irish Press*, 1 February 1938.

145. Anon., *Forgotten History: The Kilcoole Gunrunning 2nd August 1914* (Greystones: Ross Print, 2014). Peter Murtagh, "Stealthy Operation off Coast of Wicklow," *Irish Times*, 19 July 2014.

146. I am grateful to Professor Brady for giving me this pithy synopsis; on Conan Doyle, see Brian Inglis, *Roger Casement* (London: Penguin, 2002), 240.

147. C. Desmond Greaves, *Liam Mellows and the Irish Revolution*, 2nd ed. (London: Lawrence & Wishart, 1971), 68.

148. NAA BMH Witness Statement 130 (Sean Fitzgibbon).

149. Kant, *Critique of Practical Reason*, 33–49.

150. J. C. Meredith, "Perpetual Peace and the Doctrine of Neutrality," *International Journal of Ethics* 25, no. 4 (July 1915): 436, citing Kant's *Rechtslehre* #60. For the latter see passages from the "Metaphysics of Morals" included in Immanuel Kant, *Toward Perpetual Peace and Other Writings on Politics, Peace and History*, ed. Pauline Kleingeld (New Haven: Yale University Press, 2006), esp. 144.

151. For two articles on the issue of conscription first appearing in *The Workers' Republic*, see James Connolly, *Political Writings, 1893–1916*, ed. Donal Nevin (Dublin: SIPTU, 2011), 583–84, 587–90.

152. *Dictionary of Irish Biography*, 5: 911–14; see 913 for quoted matter.

153. Ivan Strenski, *Contesting Sacrifice: Religion, Nationalism, and Social Thought in France* (Chicago: University of Chicago Press, 2002), 2–3.

154. Reinhart Koselleck, *Critique and Crisis: Enlightenment and the Pathogenesis of Modern Society* (Cambridge, MA: MIT Press, 1988), 81–82.

155. William Alexander, "Joseph de Maistre," *Dublin University Magazine* 54 (December 1859): 678. Alexander (1824–1911) was successively bishop of Derry, and archbishop of Armagh (primate of All Ireland). For his references to Edmund Burke and de Maistre see pp. 657, 658, 662, 667.

156. The de Maistres were not without an Irish presence. Stephanie de Maistre, a writer of fiction, contributed to the *Catholic Bulletin* in 1917. A Gaelic translation of Xavier de Maistre's *La jeune Sibérienne* appeared in 1958.

157. I am grateful once again to David Knight, archivist at the school, for his comments on the absence of any traceable reception of de Maistre at Stonyhurst via, for example, the library. Father T. B. Scannell responded to publication of the biography with a short article in *The Irish Ecclesiastical Record*, March–April 1894.

158. Cf. de Maistre "En un mot, on dirait que le sang est l'engrais de cette plante qu'on appelle *genie*." Quoted in Jesse Goldhammer, *The Headless Republic: Sacrificial Violence in Modern French Thought* (Ithaca, NY: Cornell University Press, 2005), 91.

159. Alexander, "Joseph de Maistre," 665.

160. Sean O'Casey, *Collected Plays*, vol. 1 (London: Macmillan, 1949), 201, 258–59. All ellipses in the original.

161. Goldhammer, *The Headless Republic*, 107, 105. I have altered the use of italic in Goldhammer's quotation.

162. Samuel Beckett, *Watt*, in *Novels*, vol. 1 (New York; Grove Press, 2006), 172.

163. I owe this point to Dr. Christopher Woods.

164. See a note in *Irish Book Lover* 1, no. 1 (August 1909): 10.

165. The popular song by Ethna Carbery (1866–1911) was loosely based on an older ballad, for which see Georges Denis Zimmermann, *Songs of Irish Rebellion: Irish Political Street Ballads and Rebel Songs, 1780–1900* (Dublin: Four Courts Press, 2002), 158–59.

166. The Statute of Westminster is hardly regarded now as a landmark in a progressive separation of Ireland from British control, though, at the time, Yeats treated it as such; see Bernard G. Krimm, *W. B. Yeats and the Emergence of the Irish Free State, 1918–1939: Living in the Explosion* (Troy, NY: Whiston, 1981).

167. See Christopher Murray, *Sean O'Casey: Writer at Work* (Dublin: Gill and Macmillan, 2004), 104–5.

168. Padraic H. Pearse, *Political Writings and Speeches* (Dublin: Phoenix, 1924), 134.

169. For a discussion of Ibsen's *Ghosts* and its influence in Ireland, see W. J. Mc Cormack, *Fool of the Family: A Life of J. M. Synge* (London: Weidenfeld, 2000), 160–71.

170. Pearse, *Political Writings and Speeches*, 224.

171. Ibid., 224, 230.

172. James Stephens, *The Insurrection in Dublin* (Gerrards Cross, UK: Smythe, 1992), 76.

173. For a brief discussion of Lawrence's brushes with the law at this time, and his attitude toward the war, see Adam Parkes, *Modernism and the Theater of Censorship* (New York: Oxford University Press, 1996), 21–64.

174. Pearse, *Political Writings and Speeches*, 255.

175. See Hilary Pyle, *Cesca's Diary, 1913–1916* (Dublin: Woodfield Press, 2005), 66.

176. For an extensive treatment of Yeats's politics in these particular regards, see McCormack, *Blood Kindred*.

177. This is not the place to develop the comparison, but a few salient points can be noted. (1) The United Irishmen's insurrection occurred in three of the four provinces, and was conducted over a period of several months. (2) In Wexford and the West, it was supported by a large body of previously unpoliticized tenants, and thus deserved something of the character of a "popular uprising." The leadership was mixed in religious background, including notable Protestants and a good number of well-to-do Catholics; in Ulster, (though not elsewhere) the rebel forces included large numbers of Protestants. (4) Foreign support succeeded in landing and, for a time, appeared decisive. (5) The organization of the rebellion, necessarily secret, was conducted by a Society that originally had been open. (6) Informers and spies had penetrated the organization to a damaging degree.

178. Goldhammer, *The Headless Republic*, 115.

179. NLI Ms. 21,155 (5). Dated by Plunkett.

180. NLI Ms. 21,155 (5). The date appears to have been added by a hand other than Plunkett's, and not necessarily Gifford's.

181. NLI Ms. 21,155, dated 4 December 1915 by a hand other than Plunkett's. The letter does not name Grace as the addressee, nor does Plunkett sign it with his own name or any affectionate nickname.

182. NLI Ms. 21,155 (5) on paper with the printed address, 26 Upper Fitzwilliam Street, dated by Plunkett.

183. These copies of *The Circle and the Sword* are preserved in the Aidan Heavey Collection, Westmeath County Library, Athlone. For the Latin, see Horace, *Epistles*, book 1, no. 6.

184. W. B. Yeats, "September 1913," in *The Poems*, ed. Daniel Albright (London: Everyman's Library, 1992), 159–60.

185. Frances Nesbitt Oppel, *Mask and Tragedy: Yeats and Nietzsche, 1902–10* (Charlottesville: University Press of Virginia, 1987).

186. On the question of Nietzsche's familiarity, see Elio Gianturco, *Joseph de Maistre and Giambattista Vico* (New York: Columbia University Press, 1937), 114–15.

187. See Robert Vallery-Radot, *Sources d'une doctrine nationale de Joseph de Maistre à Charles Péguy* (Paris: Sequana, 1942). At the time of publication, the author's sons (to whom the book was dedicated) were prisoners of war in Germany. For an assessment of Péguy's appropriation by extreme right-wing opinion, see David Carroll, *French Literary Fascism: Nationalism, Anti-Semitism and the Ideology of Culture* (Princeton, NJ: Princeton University Press, 1994), 42–70 and 267 n. 4. At the latter reference, the role of Péguy's son in transforming his father into a prophet of National Socialism is noted. Cross-generational tensions occurred in France as in Ireland.

188. Koselleck, *Critique and Crisis*, 70–74. For the most part, Koselleck is concerned with eighteenth-century France and Germany, not Britain; but see 74–75.

189. Goldhammer, *The Headless Republic*, 115.

190. See *The New Age*, 9 November 1911.

191. These were reconstructed by Herbert Read under the title "The Philosophy of Intensive Manifolds"; see T. E. Hulme, *Speculations*, ed. H. Read (1924; London: Routledge, 1960), 171–213.

192. Thomas Kettle, *The Open Secret of Ireland* (Dublin: University College Dublin Press, 2007), 17.

193. Desmond FitzGerald, *Desmond's Rising: Memoirs 1913 to Easter 1916* (Dublin: Liberties Press, 2006), 9, 31, 34.

194. Suzanne Guerlac, *Thinking in Time: An Introduction to Henri Bergson* (Ithaca, NY: Cornell University Press, 2006), 26–28.

195. Bertrand Russell, *History of Western Philosophy and Its Connection with Political and Social Circumstances from the Earliest Times to the Present Day*, new ed. (London: Allen & Unwin, 1961), 756. Russell was unfair toward Bergson (to put it mildly) in this political characterization; during the German occupation of France, Bergson officially registered himself as a Jew, although he had been assimilated many years earlier—see Guerlac, *Thinking in Time*, 10.

196. Russell, *History of Western Philosophy*, 759–60.

197. In Gaelic literary tradition, Ireland is figured as a woman, especially in *aisling* (vision) poetry. In some regards, this is related to the classic trope of characterizing the homeland as female/feminine—Roma, Britannia, Germania, etc. Though, to place the *aisling* genre in its historic context, one should further investigate its relation to Jacobitism and, hence, to political Catholicism.

198. Quoted in Russell, *History of Western Philosophy*, 761.

199. See Georges Sorel, *Reflections on Violence*, trans. T. E. Hulme, rev. ed. (Cambridge: Cambridge University Press, 1999), 178–82. Citing Paul Allard's recent study of the early Christians in Rome (*Dix leçons sur le martyre*, 1905), and the classic authority of Ernest Renan and Adolf von Harnack, Sorel coolly assesses the strategic and entirely relativistic importance of persecution and martyrdom for the underground church. The growth of what Liam Kennedy has wittily called MOPE (Most Oppressed People Ever) as a rhetorical "argument" to establish the exemplary suffering of the historic Irish nation might usefully be traced to this model.

200. See William A. Johnsen, *Violence and Modernism: Ibsen, Joyce, and Wolf* (Gainesville: University Press of Florida, 2003), esp. chap. 5, "To Live, Not Die for His Country: Stephen D(a)edalus and Ireland's Future," 84–107.

201. A. A. Luce, *Bergson's Doctrine of Intuition: The Donnellan Lectures for 1921* (London: Society for Promoting Christian Knowledge, 1922). Luce became a world-renowned scholar and exponent of Berkeleyan immaterialism. I am grateful to Jean-Paul Pittion for drawing my attention to this publication.

Chapter 2. Actions of This Kind or That

1. Oscar Wilde, *Complete Works*, ed. Merlin Holland (London: HarperCollins, 1999), 302–50.

2. See Margreta de Grazia, *Shakespeare Verbatim: The Reproduction of Authenticity and the Apparatus of 1790* (Oxford: Clarendon Press, 1991), 224–25.

3. A. C. Bradley, *Oxford Lectures on Poetry*, 2nd ed. (London: Macmillan, 1909), 71. In the second edition, Bradley added a note acknowledging his debt to Dowden.

4. W. J. Monypenny, *The Two Irish Nations: An Essay on Home Rule* (London: Murray, 1913), 3.

5. John Norstedt, *Thomas MacDonagh: A Critical Biography* (Charlottesville: University Press of Virginia, 1980), 65.

6. See Tom Clyde, *Irish Literary Magazines: An Outline History and Descriptive Bibliography* (Dublin: Irish Academic Press, 2003), 161–63.

7. Norstedt, *Thomas MacDonagh*, 98–99.

8. O Brolchain, *16 Lives*, 137.

9. In the United States, Boyd published studies of Maupassant and H. L. Mencken, among other works of criticism. His wife published as a translator. Some of their correspondence can be traced in major American archives—e.g., the Beinecke Library, Harvard University Library, and Princeton University Library.

10. See NLI Ms. 13,267 (3), where numerous postcards from Bourgeois are preserved in Holloway's correspondence.

11. NLI Ms. 13,267 (3), M. Bourgeois to J. Holloway, 12 July 1911, from London.

12. *Irish Review* 1, no. 6 (August 1911): 276–77.

13. *Irish Review* 1, no. 7 (September 1911): 331–32.

14. *Irish Review* 1, no. 8 (October 1911): 381.

15. O Brolchain, *16 Lives*, 138.

16. Brian Inglis, *Roger Casement* (London: Penguin, 2002), 205.

17. NAA BMH Witness Statement 358 (Mrs. Geraldine Plunkett Dillon), 2.

18. O Brolchain, *16 Lives*, 139.

19. Ibid., 241, 155.

20. *Irish Review* (second series) 1, no. 4 (9 December 1922): 42–43.

21. William J. Feeney, *Drama in Hardwicke Street: A History of the Irish Theatre Company* (Rutherford, NJ: Fairleigh Dickinson University Press, 1984), 37.

22. Ibid., 39.

23. Copies of three plays are preserved at NLI: Ms. 5021.

24. Quoted by Feeney, *Drama in Hardwicke Street*, 46. Holloway's vast diaries are preserved in the National Library of Ireland.

25. O Brolchain, *16 Lives*, 106–7.

26. See *University Review* 1, no. 11 (Winter 1956): 32–48.

27. Quoted in Michael J. Lennon, "The Easter Rising from the Inside—I," *Irish Times*, 18 April 1949, 4.

28. *The Monitor: Catholic Organ for Great Britain*, 11 August 1899, 13. Other names appearing in the same list are George Gavan Duffy (Roger Casement's defense solicitor in 1916) and Vivian Holland (Oscar Wilde's younger son).

29. Seamas O Síocháin, *Roger Casement: Imperialist, Rebel, Revolutionary* (Dublin: Lilliput, 2008), 603 n. 97.

30. Miguel de Unamuno, *The Tragic Sense of Life*, trans. J. E. Crawford Flitch ([n.p.]: Fontana, 1962), 257.

31. The clearest evidence that Joseph Mary Plunkett had not matriculated for admission to UCD is the application form dated simply 1914 on which he applied to attend classes in psychology and metaphysics. The portion relating to matriculation and other qualifications is left blank, the form itself never returned to the college.

32. NLI Ms. 10,999 (xi) 3.

33. NLI Ms. 10,999 (v).

34. See a debate in *Seanad Eireann* during "the Emergency," vol. 28, 24 November 1943, when the events of 1912 were recalled; the speaker was urging a transfer to the North Wall of Dublin's cattle market then located in Prussia Street. Plunkett wrote a comic ballad about the 1912 outbreak; see Colm Ó Lochlainn, *Irish Street Ballads* (Dublin: Three Candles, 1967), 206.

35. The article is included in a little-known anthology, *A Socialist and War, 1914–1916*, ed. P. J. Musgrove (London: Lawrence and Wishart, 1941), 115–19.

36. For an account of these differences, see Emmet O'Connor, *James Larkin* (Cork: Cork University Press, 2002), 36–38.

37. For a good selection of such work see I. F. Clarke, ed., *The Great War with Germany, 1890–1914* (Liverpool: Liverpool University Press, 1997).

38. "Two years after the publication of *The Great War of 189-*, the tales of future warfare became a regular feature in the popular press . . . there was a marked decline in the quality of the writing and a sharp rise in the authors' ignorance of military affairs"—ibid., 72.

39. See Luke Netterville [pseud.], *The Queen of the World; or, Under the Tyranny* (London: Lawrence & Bullen, 1900).

40. Austin Harrison, "Strindberg's Plays," *English Review* no. 13 (December 1912): 80–97.

41. See Mary Maguire, "Strindberg in Dublin," *Irish Review* 3, no. 26 (April 1913): 88.

42. See Edward Martyn, "The Recent Performance of Ibsen's Rosmersholm," *Irish Review* 3, no. 36 (February 1914): 660–61.

43. Jerry Nolan, *Six Essays on Edward Martyn, 1859–1923, Irish Cultural Revivalist* (Lampeter, UK: Mellen, 2004).

44. Padraic H. Pearse, *Political Writings and Speeches* (Dublin: Phoenix, 1924), 221.

45. See Padraic H. Pearse, *Political Writings*, 219–55.

46. Toril Moi, *Henrik Ibsen and the Birth of Modernism: Art, Theater, Philosophy* (Oxford: Oxford University Press, 2006), 191–92.

47. Geraldine Plunkett, foreword to *The Poems of Joseph Mary Plunkett*, ed. Geraldine Plunkett (Dublin: Talbot Press, 1916), xi.

48. Most of Gifford's surviving correspondence with Holloway is undated, though the folder containing the items employed here has been labeled 1913–1916 by the cataloger; the note referring to her presence in Hardwick Street is dated 4 March 1916, and another (undated) refers to her imminent marriage. See NLI Ms. 13,267 (8).

49. O Brolchain, *16 Lives*, 132–33.

50. See the second essay in Erich Heller, *The Divided Mind* (Harmondsworth: Penguin, 1961), 33–55.

51. I draw on D. G. Kirby, *The Baltic World, 1772–1993* (London: Longman, 1995).

52. George Noble Plunkett, "Sursum Corda," *Catholic Bulletin* 6, no. 3 (March 1916): 152.

53. See Jérôme aan de Wiel, "Monsignor O'Riordan, Bishop O'Dwyer, and the Shaping of New Relations between Nationalist Ireland and the Vatican during World War One," *Archivium Hibernicum* 53 (1999): 95–106.

54. www.vatican.va/holy_father/Benedict_XV.

55. Reuters, quoted in the *Weekly Irish Times*, 17 June 1933, 8.

56. O Brolchain, *16 Lives*, 360–61. This point about the blessing was reiterated by a Vatican spokesman in 1933, who remarked that "the Apostolic Benediction which Count Plunkett said was conferred on him by the Pope was obviously meant for those obeying the constitutional authorities. It is a fundamental tenet of the Roman Catholic Church (concludes the message) that Catholics must be loyal to any constituted Government," *Sunday Despatch*, 28 May 1933.

57. Charles Townshend, *Easter 1916: The Irish Rebellion* (London: Allan Lane, 2005), 123.

58. *Irish Press*, 26 May 1933, 1.

59. *Irish Times*, 27 May 1933, 10. *Mr* is a demeaning term in relation to Professor or Dr. MacNeill, as is the use of his English Christian name, John.

60. *Irish Times*, 23 April, 1949, 8 (emphasis added).

61. Jérôme aan de Wiel, *The Catholic Church in Ireland, 1914–1918: War and Politics* (Dublin: Irish Academic Press, 2003), 85–86.
62. Reinhard R. Doerries, *Prelude to the Easter Rising: Sir Roger Casement in Imperial Germany* (London: Frank Cass, 2000), 206–9.
63. For the numbered list, see NLI Ms. 10,999 (v).
64. Peter Charleton, *Lies in a Mirror: An Essay on Evil and Deceit* (Dublin: Blackhall, 2006), 7.
65. Padraic Pearse, "Ghosts," in *Political Writings and Speeches*, 245.
66. W. B. Yeats, "A Prayer for My Daughter," *The Poems*, ed. Daniel Albright (London: Everyman's Library, 1992), 236–38.
67. See Richard Barrett, *Twice Condemned: Irish Views of the Dreyfus Affair* (Dublin: Original Writing, 2010), 47.
68. See Norman Cohn, *Warrant for Genocide: The Myth of the Jewish World Conspiracy and the Protocols of the Elders of Zion* (London: Serif, 2005), 176–80.
69. O Brolchain, *16 Lives*, 354–65.
70. Sheila Caden, *The Alderman: Alderman Tom Kelly (1868–1942) and Dublin Corporation* (Dublin: Dublin City Council, 2007), 99.
71. Bernard Shaw to H. W. Massingham, 30 April 1916. *Collected Letters 1911–1925*, ed. Dan H. Laurence (London: Max Reinhardt, 1985), 397–98.
72. T. S. Eliot, *Selected Prose*, ed. Frank Kermode (London: Faber, 1975), 40–41.
73. Past Masters, *Letters of W. B. Yeats* (Charlottesville: Intelex, 1992), Accession No. 2935.
74. NAA BMH Witness Statement 81 (Bulmer Hobson), 6.
75. Quoted in Fearghal McGarry, *The Rising. Ireland: Easter 1916* (New York: Oxford University Press, 2010), 99, emphasis added.
76. M. J. Kelly, *The Fenian Ideal and Irish Nationalism, 1882–1916* (Woodbridge: Boydell & Brewer, 2006), 60, 240, 61.
77. Austen Morgan, *James Connolly: A Political Biography* (Manchester: Manchester University Press, 1988), 169.
78. Donal Nevin, *James Connolly: "A Full Life"* (Dublin: Gill and Macmillan, 2005), 626–31.
79. Ryan made up for the deficiency in *The Rising* (Dublin: Golden Eagle, 1949), where a chapter (47–63) is devoted to the incident.
80. Desmond Ryan, *James Connolly* (Dublin: Talbot Press, 1924), 84.
81. Marnie Hay, *Bulmer Hobson and the Nationalist Movement in Twentieth-Century Ireland* (Manchester: Manchester University Press, 2009), 186, 193–94.
82. *Joseph Holloway's Abbey Theatre: A Selection from His Unpublished Journal* (Carbondale: Southern Illinois University Press, 1967), 178.
83. Quoted in O Brolchain, *16 Lives*, 381.
84. NLI Ms. 4,700, f. 53.

85. Desmond FitzGerald, *Desmond's Rising; Memoirs 1913 to Easter 1916*, 2nd ed. (Dublin: Liberties Press, 2006), 139–44, 150.

86. National Archives (Kew) WO 71/349. The proceedings are available in Brian Barton, ed., *The Secret Court Martial Records of the Easter Rising* (Stroud: History Press, 2010).

87. NLI Ms. 11,399.

88. NLI Ms. 11,399. From a statement made many years later, it is clear that Josephine Plunkett heard this account of her son's last minutes when she met Father Albert (Order of Friars Minor) in a nursing home or private hospital on Appian Way, Donnybrook, Dublin. The occasion was a crisis in the illness of Mrs. Kathleen Clarke (see www.bbc.co.uk/history/war/easterrising). A rather less tidy image of events, preserved in a memoir in the Capuchin house in Church Street, suggests an element of haste in administering the sacrament to Plunkett as he was led from his cell; while the military authorities bear responsibility for the timing of all this, the priests (it seems) had arrived ill-equipped for their spiritual task.

89. Richard J. Loftus, *Nationalism in Modern Anglo-Irish Poetry* (Madison: University of Wisconsin Press, 1964), 150.

90. NAA BMH Witness Statement 29 (Mrs. Geraldine Plunkett Dillon).

91. Peter McBrien, "Poets of the Insurrection III, Joseph Plunkett," *Studies* 5, no. 20 (December 1916): 540.

92. See D. D. Balfour (i.e., Edith Sophy Balfour), "Some Notes about Ireland . . . 1922," Church College, Cambridge, Archives: CHAN 1/6/4.

Chapter 3. Affinity and Mimesis

1. See H. H. Gerth and C Wright Mills, eds., *From Max Weber* (London: Routledge, 1991), 62–63; R. H. Lowe, "Max Weber's Elective Affinities: Sociology within the Bounds of Pure Reason," *American Journal of Sociology* 84, no. 2 (September 1978): 366–85.

2. See Lowe, "Max Weber's Elective Affinities," 366.

3. Howard Caygill, *A Kant Dictionary* (Oxford: Blackwell, 1995), 60.

4. T. S. Eliot, *Selected Prose*, ed. Frank Kermode (London: Faber, 1973), 40.

5. T. M. Kettle, "The Agony of Dublin," *Irish Review* 3, no. 33 (November 1913): 441.

6. For economy's sake, a long extract from MacDonagh's book is omitted.

7. Geraldine Plunkett, foreword to *The Poems of Joseph Mary Plunkett*, ed. Geraldine Plunkett (Dublin: Talbot Press, 1916), xiii.

8. Originally published in the *Irish Times*; reprinted in Pádraig Yeates, *Lockout Dublin 1913* (Dublin: Gill and Macmillan 2000), 218–19.

9. Quoted in Johann Norstedt, *Thomas MacDonagh: A Critical Biography* (Charlottesville: University Press of Virginia, 1980), 84.

10. NLI Ms. 22,934. MacDonagh to Dominick Hackett, 19 May 1915.

11. NLI Ms. 10,999 (xi). The note passages appear as quasi-footnotes on Plunkett's first sheet of paper. I have standardized the symbols used to indicate the second of these.

12. H. G. Wells, *Modern Utopia* (London: Chapman and Hall, 1905), 17.

13. H. G. Wells, *First and Last Things* (London: Constable, 1908).

14. Henri Bergson, "Aristotle's Concept of Place," trans. John K. Ryan, *Studies in Philosophy and the History of Philosophy* 5 (1970): 64.

15. Henri Bergson, *Creative Evolution*, trans. Arthur Mitchell (London: Macmillan, 1911), 284. Bergson's *La Pensée et le mouvant* appeared almost two decades after Plunkett's death: reference to Heraclitus is minimal, in one footnote culminating in a significant question, "Encore une fois, nous n'écartons nullement par là la *substance*. Nous affirmons au contraire la persistence des existences. Et nous croyons en avoir facilité la représentation. Comment a-t-on pu comparer cette doctrine à celle de Heraclite?" (Paris: Presses Universitaires, 2009), 211.

16. T. E. Hulme, *Speculations*, ed. Herbert Read (1924; London: Routledge, 1960), 147. Among other notices, that by Dublin-born Father George Tyrrell SJ in *The Hibbert Journal* (January 1908) might have come to Plunkett's attention.

17. See the source available through the *Stanford Encyclopedia of Philosophy* site.

18. *Poems of Joseph Mary Plunkett*, 1.

19. G. T. W. Patrick, *The Fragments of the Work of Heraclitus of Ephesus on Nature* (Baltimore: Murray, 1889), no. 130.

20. Cf. ethnography (1834), ethnology (1843), ethnopsychology (1886).

21. On Dante and C.-L. Philippe, see Gyorgy Lukács, *Soul and Form*, trans. Anna Bostock (London: Merlin Press, 1974), 91, 98, 104.

22. George Berkeley, *Works*, vol. 2, ed. T. E. Jessop (Edinburgh: Nelson, 1949), 62. The text quoted is *Principles of Human Knowledge.*

23. Marx to Engels, 10 December 1869, in Karl Marx and Frederick Engels, *Ireland and the Irish Question* (Moscow: Progress, 1971), 284.

24. Engels, from "The English Elections" (1874), Karl Marx and Frederick Engels, *Ireland and the Irish Question* (Moscow: Progress, 1971), 311.

25. W. J. Mc Cormack, *"We Irish" in Europe: Yeats, Berkeley, and Joseph Hone* (Dublin: UCD Press, 2010), 69–90.

26. Kant, *Critique of Judgment*, xii.

27. Douglas Hyde, *A Literary History of Ireland*, 2nd ed. (London: Benn, 1967), 79, my emphasis.

28. Patrick, *Fragments of the Work of Heraclitus*, #67.

29. W. B. Yeats, *Letters*, ed. Allan Wade (London: Hart Davis, 1954), 918.

30. Scott Edgar, "Hermann Cohen," *The Stanford Encyclopedia of Philosophy* (Winter 2012 edition), ed. Edward N. Zalta, http://plato.stanford.edu/archives/win2012/entries/cohen/.

31. Lucien Goldmann, *Immanuel Kant* (London: New Left Books, 1971), 112.

32. Ibid., 114.

33. Ibid., 186, 117, 121.

34. See Kōjin Karantani, *Transcritique: On Kant and Marx* (Cambridge, MA: MIT Press, 2003); and Richard J Bernstein, *Radical Evil: A Philosophical Interrogation* (Cambridge, UK: Polity Press, 2002).

35. Mitchell Cohen, *The Wager of Lucien Goldmann: Tragedy, Dialectics and a Hidden God* (Princeton, NJ: Princeton University Press, 1994).

36. G. W. Cunningham, *Philosophical Review* 19, no. 3 (May 1910): 338.

37. *Irish Monthly* 42, no. 487 (January 1914): 54. The book in question was Thomas J. Gerrard, *Henri Bergson: An Exposition and Criticism from the Point of View of St Thomas Aquinas* (London: Sands, 1913).

38. For a longer discussion of this point, see W. J. Mc Cormack, *Dublin 1916: The French Connection* (Dublin: Gill and Macmillan, 2012), 97–121.

39. James Joyce, *Stephen Hero: Part of the First Draft of "A Portrait of the Artist as a Young Man,"* ed. Theodore Spencer, rev. ed. (London: Four Square, 1966), 64. *Stephen Hero* is the only work by Joyce to have been banned in his home country.

40. Bulmer Hobson, *Defensive Warfare: A Handbook for Irish Nationalists* (Belfast: West Belfast Branch of Sinn Féin, 1909), 13.

41. Ibid., 19.

42. Ibid., 19, 26.

43. G. W. F. Hegel, *Phenomenology of the Spirit*, trans. A. V. Miller (Oxford: Oxford University Press, 1977), 520.

44. Jonathan Githens-Mazer, *Myths and Memories of the Easter Rising: Cultural and Political Nationalism in Ireland* (Dublin: Irish Academic Press, 2006), 2, 35, 83, 96.

45. Ernst Kantorowicz, *The King's Two Bodies: A Study in Mediaeval Political Theology* (Princeton, NJ: Princeton University Press, 1995), 195–96.

46. Ibid., 196–97.

47. See *Banquet des Travailleurs Socialistes* (Paris: Chez Pages, 1849) for the original French.

48. For Plunkett's translation, see NLI Ms. 10,999/16/5.

49. W. J. Mc Cormack, *Fool of the Family: A Life of J. M. Synge* (London: Weidenfeld and Nicolson, 2000).

50. Kantorowicz, *The King's Two Bodies*, 64–65.

51. See Phil Kilroy, *The Society of the Sacred Heart in France, 1800–1865* (Cork: Cork University Press, 2012).

52. There is evidence of a folk-art assimilation of the Sacred Heart, both in the Gaelic language and in material culture. See Tadhg O Shuilleabhain, "Duan Chroidhe Iosa," in *The Pious Miscellany*, ed. John O'Daly (1802; Dublin: O'Daly, 1868), 60–61. A painted wooden panel with the central iconography hangs in the 1848 "warhouse" at Ballingarry, county Tipperary.

53. *Catholic Book Bulletin* (later *Catholic Bulletin*) 1, no. 1 (January 1911): 18.

54. For a discussion of Dante and Justinian relevant to the present argument, see G. P. Raffa, *Divine Dialectic: Dante's Incarnational Poetry* (Toronto: University of Toronto Press, 2000), 113, 221 nn. 76–77.

55. For the full text of the proclamation issued by Emmet's provisional government, see Patrick M. Geoghegan, *Robert Emmet: A Life* (Dublin: Gill and Macmillan, 2002), 288–96.

56. TCD Ms. 9555/240–41. I am grateful to Carla King for this reference, and much else.

57. W. B. Yeats, "Parnell's Funeral and Other Poems," from "A Full Moon in March": *Manuscript Materials*, ed. David R. Clark (Ithaca, NY: Cornell University Press, 2002), 5, 9, 13, 15.

58. For more on the Taylor-Yeats relationship, see Mc Cormack, *Blood Kindred: W. B. Yeats, the Life, the Death, the Politics* (London: Weidenfeld and Nicolson, 2005), 351–53.

59. W. B. Yeats, *Autobiographies*, ed. W. H. O'Donnell and D N. Archibald (New York: Scribner, 1999), 191.

60. John Montague, *The Bread God* (Dublin: Dolmen Press, 1968).

61. John Montague, *The Rough Field*, 2nd ed. (Dublin: Dolmen Press, 1974), 43.

62. On this campaign, see Mc Cormack, *Dublin 1916*.

63. T. K. Abbott, "Has ΠΟΙΕΙΝ in the New Testament a Sacrificial Meaning?" *Journal of Biblical Literature* 9th Year (1890), Part II. See the edition published by ISHA, 2.

64. See *Irish Times*, 30 October 1917. Burbage sent a letter of support to a Sinn Féin meeting chaired by Kevin O'Higgins, in which he complained about "the blight" of Redmondism, "this pernicious Unionist faction" (*Irish Times*, 24 November 1917, 1). Under the Free State government, he objected to the development of a county library system assisted by the millionaire Andrew Carnegie, specifically referring to "publications of Mr Lennox Robinson and Mr Yeats to which he took strong exception" (*Irish Times*, 27 December 1914).

65. Henri Bergson, *Creative Evolution*, trans. Arthur Mitchell (London: Macmillan, 1911), 103–4.

66. R. T. Byrn, "Creative Limitations and Development," *Irish Church Quarterly* 9, no. 33 (January 1916): 54, where *Creative Evolution* (278 ff.) is given for source.

67. Ibid., 57.

68. Stephen Kern, *The Culture of Time and Space 1880–1918*, 2nd ed. (Cambridge, MA: Harvard University Press, 2003), 26.

69. Irvine Louis Horowitz, *Radicalism and the Revolt against Reason: The Social Theories of Georges Sorel* (Carbondale: Southern Illinois University Press, 1968), 39, 46, 52.

70. The exchange of articles runs as follows:

    1. Rogers: "Idealism and Realism" (i.e., review of D'Arcy's *God and Freedom*), *The Irish Church Quarterly* 9, no. 34 (April 1916): 97–107.

    2. D'Arcy: "Idealism and Realism: A Reply," *The Irish Church Quarterly* 9, no. 35: 169–79.

    3. Rogers: "Idealism and Realism Again," *The Irish Church Quarterly* 9, no. 36: 308–14.

    4. D'Arcy: "Realism and Reality," *The Irish Church Quarterly* 10, no. 37: 15–24.

    5. Rogers: "The Bishop of Down [i.e., D'Arcy] on Realism," *The Irish Church Quarterly* 10, no. 38: 146–48.

71. For Girard's literary criticism in English translation, see especially *Desire, Deceit and the Novel*, trans. Yvonne Freccero (Baltimore: Johns Hopkins University Press, 1966); and *Mimesis and Theory: Essays on Literature and Criticism, 1953–2005*, ed. Robert Doran (Stanford: Stanford University Press, 2008).

72. René Girard, "Mimetic Desire in the Underground," in Girard, *Mimesis and Theory*, 246.

73. See Chris Fleming, *René Girard: Violence and Mimesis* (Cambridge, UK: Polity Press, 2004), 16–23.

74. René Girard, *Violence and the Sacred*, trans. Patrick Gregory (London: Continuum, 2005), 70.

75. René Girard, *The One by Whom Scandal Comes*, trans. M. B. DeBevoise (East Lansing: Michigan State University Press, 2014), 34.

76. I am grateful to Professor W. A. Johnsen for his comments on this portion of *Enigmas*, while taking responsibility for my own surviving faults.

77. See D. D. Balfour, "Some Notes about Ireland . . . 1922," Churchill College Archives, Cambridge, CHAN.

78. Fleming, *René Girard*, 28–30.

79. Julia Meszaros and Johannes Zachhuber, eds., *Sacrifice and Modern Thought* (Oxford: Oxford University Press, 2013), 1.

80. Girard, *Violence and the Sacred*, 7.

81. Meszaros and Zachhuber, *Sacrifice and Modern Thought*, 29.

82. Onora O'Neill, *Acting on Principle: An Essay in Kantian Ethics*, 2nd ed. (Cambridge: Cambridge University Press, 2013), 6.

83. For an introduction, see J. G. Simms, *Colonial Nationalism, 1698–1776* (Dublin: Mercier Press, 1976).

84. Neil Manson, "Informed Consent and Referential Opacity," in *Reading Onora O'Neill*, ed. David Archard et al. (London: Routledge, 2013), 80.

85. Onora O'Neill, *Bounds of Justice* (Cambridge: Cambridge University Press, 2000), 40.

86. E. M. Forster, *Two Cheers for Democracy* (London: Arnold, 1951).

87. George Dangerfield, *The Damnable Question: A Study in Anglo-Irish Relations* (Boston: Little, Brown, 1976), 173.

88. For O'Neill's memorandum of February 1916, see the first item reprinted in "Eoin MacNeill on the 1916 Rising," ed. F. X. Martin, *Irish Historical Studies* 12, no. 47 (March 1961): 226–71.

89. See H. M. Kallen, *William James and Henry Bergson: A Study in Contrasting Theories of Life* (Chicago: University of Chicago Press, 1914).

90. R. F. Foster, *Vivid Faces: The Revolutionary Generation in Ireland, 1890–1923* (London: Allan Lane, 2014), 23.

91. This was a plot to introduce typhus into the water supply at Portobello Barracks, a first (or nearly) in chemical warfare if it had been successful.

92. Conor Cruise O'Brien, *Godland: Reflection on Religion and Nationalism* (Cambridge, MA: Harvard University Press, 1988), 26–27.

93. Yael S. Feldman, *Glory and Agony: Isaac's Sacrifice and National Narrative* (Stanford, CA: Stanford University Press, 2010), 215–63.

94. See Brian Hughes, *Michael Mallin* (Dublin: O'Brien Press, 2013), appendix 1.

95. The *Dictionary of Irish Biography* entry on Mallin provides very little information on his background; in the case of Heuston, the 1901 census has him living with his mother and siblings in the home (at No. 34 Jervis St., Dublin) of his mother's unmarried sister; ten years later, the mother is living alone in Dominick St. In both censuses she lists herself as married, not widowed.

96. See Mc Cormack, *Dublin 1916*, 146, 152.

97. Alexander Herzen, *From the Other Shore* and *The Russian People and Socialism* (London: Weidenfeld and Nicolson, 2011), 134–35.

98. Ibid., 108, 152.

99. *Dictionary of Irish Biography*, 8:178–79.

100. Plunkett Dillon, *All in the Blood*, 315–18.

101. Uinseann Mac Eoin, *The IRA in the Twilight Years, 1923–1948* (Dublin: Argenta Publications, 1997). See page 415 for an account of Jack Plunkett's arrest on 29 December 1939.

102. Sean O'Casey, *Collected Plays*, vol. 1 (London: Macmillan, 1949), 213.

103. *The Poems of Goethe Translated in the Original Metres* by E. A. Bowring (London, 1853) (stanza 9 of "The Bride of Corinth").

Appendix 3. The Forged Dublin Castle Document 1916

1. Late evidence in this connection will be considered in due course.

2. See Colm [Ó Lochlainn], "Joseph Mary Plunkett, Printer," *Irish Book Lover* 32, no. 5 (March 1954): 57–59.

3. See Geraldine Plunkett, *All in the Blood: A Memoir* (Dublin: A. and A. Farmar, 2006), 136–37. The printer-compositor was Richard A Latchford or his son, Hector George Latchford, natives of County Limerick, and members of the Church of Ireland. The family lived in Anna Villa Lower, close to Marlborough Road where Joseph and Geraldine Plunkett were living in 1915.

Select Bibliography of Primary Sources

Manuscripts

British Library

Add Ms. 73454 (Chesterton Papers)

Add Ms. 73484 (Chesterton Papers)

National Archives (Kew)

CO 904/193–216 Dublin Castle Special Branch (1899–1921)

HO: 45/10665/216252 George Noble Plunkett (1912)

WO: 71/349 Court Martial Records (1916)

Churchill College, Cambridge, Archives

Chandos Papers

Dublin Diocesan Archives

Archbishop William Walsh Papers

National Archives (Dublin)

Hoey & Dennison Parcel 42 Josephine Plunkett

Department of the Taoiseach: "Women in 20th Century Ireland"—Selected Files

National Army Archives (Cathal Brugha Barracks, Dublin)

Bureau of Military History Witness Statements

Nos. 29, 358, 424 (Geraldine Plunkett)

Nos. 257, 488, 865 (Grace Gifford)

No. 865 (John Plunkett)

National Library of Ireland

The files listed below include more than material specific to Joseph Plunkett.

Ms. 4165	George Noble Plunkett (Songs etc.)
Ms. 4700	General Post Office, Dublin, Easter 1916
Ms. 5019	Drama
Ms. 5459	Letters to Roger Casement
Ms. 8121	Paul O'Farrell Collection
Ms. 8320 (2)	George Roberts Papers (Pos. Micro-F. 8406)
Mss. 9955–57	Newspaper Cuttings, etc. re. George Noble Plunkett
Ms. 9690	Childhood (1896) signature of Joseph Plunkett
Ms. 10,999 (i–xvi)	Joseph Plunkett Collection
Ms. 11,374	Letters to George Noble Plunkett (1871–1939)
Mss. 11,375–81	George Noble Plunkett Collection
Mss. 11,375–76	Correspondence between Count and Countess Plunkett (1877–1940)
Ms. 11,377	Jack Plunkett's letters to his parents (1916–1940)
Ms. 11,379	Letters between family members re. politics (1916–1923)
Ms. 11,380	Two letters from Countess Josephine to George Noble Plunkett, 1903 and 1918
Ms. 11,381	*Irish Review*
Ms. 11,389	George Noble Plunkett's notes on early printing in Europe
Ms. 11,397	Jack Plunkett
Ms. 11,400	Documents relating to the "Castle Document"
Ms. 11,401	Jack Plunkett

Ms. 11,408	Copies of letters to Herbert Asquith and others June 1916
Ms. 11,410	Documents re. military engineering
Ms. 11,981	Jack Plunkett
Mss. 12,009–10	Theology Notebook
Mss. 12, 011–12	George Plunkett Collection
Ms. 12,013	Notebook of George Noble Plunkett (1876)
Ms. 12,015	Notebook of an Eccentric Philosopher (1868)
Mss. 12,016–21	Civil War notebooks
Mss. 13,073–92	Roger Casement Papers
Ms. 13,099	The Irish Theater, 1914
Ms. 13,267	Joseph Holloway Correspondence
Ms. 15,003	Thomas MacDonagh Papers
Ms. 15,413	Correspondence, Thomas MacDonagh to Joseph Plunkett
Ms. 17,034	Roger Casement to Plunkett
Ms. 17,301	Theater of Ireland Agreement
Ms. 17,484	Joseph McGarrity Papers
Ms. 18,099	John Devoy Papers
Ms. 21,155	James O'Donovan Papers
Ms. 21,174	George Noble Plunkett (1936)
Mss. 21,590–99	Grace (Gifford) Plunkett Papers
Ms. 22,114	J. J. O'Connell Memoir
Mss. 33,605, 33,627	Hanna Sheehy Skeffington Papers
Mss. 33,731, 33,993	Geraldine Plunkett Dillon Papers
Microfilm no. 5992/p. 6547 (George Plunkett, 1916)	

National Museum of Ireland

Joseph Plunkett's Despatch Book

University College, Cork

Ms. U./48 George Noble Plunkett

University College Dublin, Archives

Ernest Blythe Papers

George Noble Plunkett Papers

Royal College of Physicians in Ireland

Joseph Francis O'Carroll Cuttings etc. (in T. P. C. Kirkpatrick Files)

Westmeath County Library (Athlone)

Draft Agreement between Thomas MacDonagh, Joseph Plunkett and Edward Martyn, 1 July 1914

Printed Sources by J. M. Plunkett

Poems in Periodicals etc.

"The Gull," *Weekly Freeman*, January 1909

"Francis Thompson Villanelle," *Irish Monthly*, December 1909

"Distant Thunder," *Bean n h-Eireann*, December 1910

"The Saxons," *Bean na h-Eireann*, January 1911

"As Ye Have Sown," *Sinn Féin*, June 1911

"Sonnet to Ireland," *National Student*, January 1911

"White dove . . . ," *Irish Review* 1, no. 4 (June 1911): 178

"The Task" (later "Your Pride"), *Academy*, 1 July 1911

"Sonnet" (Leila!), *Irish Review* 2, no, 15 (June 1912): 194

"I Sought Him," *Studies* 1, no. 2 (June 1912): 363–64

"Sonnet" ("The Seven Stars"), Columba Press, May 1912

"When Satan Laughs," Columba Press, May 1912

"Signs and Wonders," *Irish Review* 2, no. 19 (October 1912): 412–13

"Sonnet" ("I Saw the Sun"), *Dublin Review*, July 1913

"Lux in tenebris" ("Heaven and Hell"), *Irish Review* 3, no. 31 (September 1913): 329–33

"The Grace of Death," *Irish Review* 3, no. 32 (October 1913): 421

"Sonnet" ("Your Songs"), *Irish Review* 3, no. 33 (November 1913): 478

"Sea Wraith" (signed Israfel), *National Student*, November 1913, 22

"Sonnet" ("The Vigil of Love"), *Irish Review* 3, no. 34 (December 1913): 534

"Invocation," *Irish Review* 3, no. 35 (January 1914): 575

"The White Feather," *Irish Review* 3, no. 36 (February 1914): 627

"Our Heritage," *Irish Volunteer*, 7 February 1914, 7

"The Dark Way," *Irish Review* 4, no. 37 (March 1914): 26–27

"Two Poems" ["Her Hair's the Canopy" and "I Do Not Know How You Can Shun"], *Irish Review* 4, no. 38 (April 1914): 87–88

"The Living Wire," *Irish Review* 4, no. 39 (May 1914): 134

"O Lovely Heart," *Irish Review* 4, no. 40 (June 1914): 175

"The Pattern Maid" (signed An Gam Eile), *National Student*, June 1914, 138

"Ath Cliath" (signed An Gam Eile), *National Student*, November 1914, 19–20

"Two Unpublished Poems" ["On an Irish Mountain: Slievemore" and "To G. K. Chesterton"], *Ireland American Review* 1, no. 1 [c. August 1938]: 101–2

"Thou Shalt Renew the Face of the Earth," *Ireland American Review*, book 5 [no date, not later than 1943], 55

"Some Unpublished Poems" ["Testimony from Temples of the Holy Spirit," "The Distant Princess of the Spirit," "The Seagull," "The Dancer," and "Love is Boundless"], *Ireland American Review*, book 5 [no date, not later than 1943], 59–61

"Some Unpublished Poems" ["Pulse of the World," "The Devil of Indecisions," and "God's Love Conquers All"], *Oriel Review* 1 (n.d., c. 1943): 68–69

"I See His Blood upon the Rose," "The Stars Sang," "White Waves on the Water," "Irish Lament," [by JMP translated into Gaelic, by Torna, i.e., Tadhg Ó Donnchadha] *The Capuchin Annual* (1943), 384–85

Prose Contributions to Journals

"Obscurity and Poetry" [review of Thomas MacDonagh and George W. Russell], *Irish Review* 3, no. 36 (February 1914): 628–33

"Civilised Nationhood," *Irish Volunteer*, 7 February 1914, 4

"A Marconi Operator" [anon.], *Irish Volunteer*, 7 February 1914, 11

"Notes" [on the Irish Theater], *Irish Review* 4 (September–November 1914): 337–38

"The Irish Review" [its financial difficulties], *Irish Review* 4 (September–November 1914): 338–39

Separate Publications

The Circle and the Sword. Dublin: Maunsel, 1911.

"The Rann" (single small sheet, dated 1913, a flier for *The Rann*, a proposed series of verse publications by the Columba Press)

"The Donnybrook News" (single small sheet, dated 3 March 1913, with the imprint of the Columba Press)

Sonnets to Columba. Donnybrook: Columba Press, 1913. (13 copies printed.)

"Secret Orders Issued to Military Officers." [Anonymous. Larkfield: Columba Press, 1916] A single sheet.

The Poems of Joseph Mary Plunkett. Edited with a foreword by Geraldine Plunkett. Dublin: Talbot Press; London: Fisher Unwin; New York: Frederick Stokes, 1916. (Talbot Press edition reissued 1919.)

Index

N